DUTCH STUDIES IN RUSSIAN LINGUISTICS

STUDIES IN SLAVIC AND GENERAL LINGUISTICS

VOLUME 8

edited by

A.A. Barentsen
B.M. Groen
R. Sprenger

Rodopi

1986

DUTCH STUDIES IN RUSSIAN LINGUISTICS

edited by

A.A. Barentsen
B.M. Groen
R. Sprenger

Editorial address : Vakgroep voor Slavische taal- en letterkunde
Rijksuniversiteit
Postbus 9575
2300 RA LEIDEN

Subscriptions : Editions Rodopi B.V.,
Keizersgracht 302-304
1016 EX AMSTERDAM
The Netherlands

CIP-GEGEVENS KONINKLIJKE BIBLIOTHEEK, DEN HAAG

Dutch

Dutch studies in Russian linguistics / ed. by A.A.
Barentsen, B.M. Groen, R. Sprenger. — Amsterdam : Rodopi.
— (Studies in Slavic and general linguistics, ISSN
0169-0124 ; vol. 8)
ISBN 90-6203-988-X geb.
SISO russ 833 UDC 808.2 NUGI 941
Trefw.: Russische taal.
©Editions Rodopi B.V., Amsterdam 1987
Printed in The Netherlands

PREFACE

The eighth volume of *Studies in Slavic and General Linguistics* is entirely devoted to Russian Linguistics. The eighteen contributors to this volume are all active members of the Dutch Slavic community. The scope of the articles presented here clearly reflects the scope of interests and activities of this community in the field of Russian linguistics: the reader will find papers on phonetics/phonology (both historical and synchronic, including intonation), morphology (including accent), syntax (including aspect), semantics, and text-linguistics.

The editors should like to draw the reader's attention especially to the fact that Odijk's contribution "*Blagodarja*: A reply" is a reaction to Houtzager's "On Russian prepositional *blagodarja*". Both articles are published in this volume.

We should like to thank the contributors, who took responsibility for providing fair copies of their articles. This appears the only way in which a series like SSGL can be produced.

We hope the reader will enjoy reading this volume.

The editors.

CONTENTS

THE USE OF THE PARTICLE *БЫЛО* IN MODERN RUSSIAN*

A.A. BARENTSEN

1. *INTRODUCTION*

(1) Настена шагнула было к двери, но он остановил:
   - Куда ты? (Распутин)

Constructions in which the particle *било* is used constitute an interesting feature of modern Russian.[1] Such constructions are by no means uncommon[2]; nevertheless, translators of Russian literary texts vary considerably in their treatment of them, which suggests the absence of a consistent understanding of their function. For an interesting discussion, see Nilsson, 1967.

Few text-books of Russian grammar include an adequate discussion of *било*-constructions[3]; some omit the topic altogether[4]. An over-literal interpretation of definitions given in the standard dictionaries can lead to confusion: the following dictionary extracts all suggest that the action in question was not completed, whereas, in example (1) above, it seems clear that Nastena's action - taking a step - actually <u>was</u> completed.

Ušakov: "действие началось, было предположено, начато, но не совершилось."[5]

MAS: "действие началось или предполагалось, но не было закончено в силу каких-то причин."

BAS:[6] "начатое, но не оконченное или не имевшее результата действие."

A recent study of the translation of Russian verbal categories into French (Kunert 1984) contains a brief discussion of the *било*-

phenomenon. This discussion highlights some of the problems arising
from definitions like the ones just quoted. Kunert uses a definition that is essentially identical with the above-mentioned ones:
according to him, the combination 'perfective preterite + было'
indicates an action that has begun, but has not been completed
("eine begonnene, aber nicht vollendete Handlung").[7] His only
example is the following sentence from Dostoevskij's 'Prestuplenie
i nakazanie':

(2) - Умирать-то не след! - крикнула Катерина Ивановна и уже
    бросилась было растворить дверь ... но столкнулась в дверях
    с самою госпожой Липпе-Вехзель... (Kunert 1984: 153)

The two translations into French that are mentioned by Kunert
differ in the choice of the verbal form to render the phrase
бросилась было растворить дверь. While one of the translators
(Guertik) uses the 'imparfait': '/elle/ se précipitait /.../ pour
ouvrir la porte', the other one (Ergaz) uses the 'passé défini':
'se précipita'. Kunert seems to prefer Guertik's solution because
he assumes that 'se précipiter pour ouvrir la porte' is treated
here as a single action, viewed as uncompleted. According to
Kunert, this is just what the Russian author intended. In Ergaz's
translation, the action 'se précipiter' is separated from 'ouvrir
la porte', and therefore it can be presented as completed even when
the door is not opened.[8] Clearly, examples like (2), in which the
preterite form is combined with an infinitive, present a special
problem, because the definition does not specify what must be taken
as the action to which the notion of '(non)completion' must be
applied: the 'rushing' indicated by the preterite form *бросилась* or
the 'opening' indicated by the infinitive *растворить*.[9] However, the
final part of (2) mentions the collision of *Катерина Ивановна* with
госпожа Липпе-Вехзель at the very door, which indicates that the
"rushing" did in fact take place; whereas the act of "opening the
door", denoted by the infinitive, remains as a possible non-completed action. This seems to suggest that where the finite verb
form is combined with an infinitive, the notion of (non)completion
has to be applied essentially to the action denoted by the infinitive. Because of the difficulty of applying the notion of '(non)-
completion' to verbs like *хотеть*, this view seems to be supported

by examples of the following type:

(3) Катя <u>хотела</u> <u>было</u> <u>растворить</u> дверь, но Маша ее позвала
 обратно. (ИНФ)[10]

We might conclude that the definition used by Kunert could easily
be adjusted to account for cases like (2) and (3). However, it is
certainly not immediately clear how it could be applied to the far
more frequent examples which do not contain an infinitive[11], such
as the examples (1) and (4):

(4) Катя <u>бросилась</u> <u>было</u> к двери, но столкнулась на полпути с
 Машей. (*idem*)

If we assume that the non-completed action must be that denoted by
the *было*-verb, then here it must be the one denoted by *бросилась*.
However, it is difficult to see this action as different from that
denoted by *бросилась* in example (2) above. As Kunert with regard to
(2) does not seem to reject an interpretation according to which
the (part of the) action denoted by *бросилась* is completed, sentences like (4) really must present him with a problem.

 In view of the difficulties mentioned above, a closer examination of the use of the particle *было* seems appropriate. This
article presents a study of the various ways in which *было* is used,
based on more than 500 examples. Approximately half the examples
were found in the grammatical and lexicographical literature, the
rest were located by searching various texts.[12] All 149[13] occurrences of *было* in the works of Puškin were easily located in the
"Bol'šoe akademičeskoe izdanie"[14], with the aid of the information
provided in the *Словарь языка Пушкина* (SJaP). The *Словарь автобио-
графической трилогии М. Горького* (SATG) provided all instances from
the three autobiographical novels (appr. 600 pages - but only 3
examples). About a hundred examples were added during an examination of approximately 2500 pages of other texts, mainly written in
the 20-th century.[15]

 We may now proceed to a survey of the various morphological
forms used in conjunction with *было*. This will be followed by an
examination of the meaning of the particle.[16]

2.   *Было IN CONJUNCTION WITH FINITE PRETERITE FORMS*

It is usually stated in the literature that *было* is used with preterite forms. Guidance is not always given regarding the choice of aspect, although the examples usually contain perfective forms. Garde (1980: 402) names the perfective preterite as the only possibility. The authors who mention the occurrence of imperfective forms usually state that the perfective aspect is predominant. (Cf. Isačenko: "die Partikel *было* die sich mit der Form des (meist perfektiven) Präteritums zu einer Einheit verbindet" (1968/62: 292); Borras/Christian: "This particle is used almost exclusively with the perfective past" (1971/59: 139); Forsyth: "in the case of a single action the verb is invariably perfective (except for the occasional occurrence of *хотел* and *собирался* /.../" (1970: 105) (emphasis mine - A.A.B.))

In the examples collected for the purposes of the present study the perfective aspect predominates (377 out of 480 finite preterite forms are perfective, i.e. 79 percent); however, the use of imperfective preterite forms is less infrequent than either Borras and Christian or Forsyth suggest. In view of the important distinction between constructions which contain an infinitive and those which do not, they will be discussed separately.

The construction consisting of *было* and a single perfective preterite is exemplified in (1) and (4) above. Many more such examples will be given elsewhere in this article. The small number of examples that contain a negation[17] all belong to this group. The following extracts contain instances of negative *было*-constructions:

(5) Вот видишь ли, аристократами /.../ называются те писатели, которые с нами не знаются, полагая вероятно, что наше общество не завидное. Мы было того и не заметили, но уже с год как спохватились, и с тех пор ругаем их наповал...
    (П: Ж₁ 137.23)
(6) - А я его не узнал было, старика-то, - говорит солдат на уборке тел, за плечи поднимая перебитый в груди труп /.../
    (Л. Толст.)

A minority (about 28 procent) of the examples which contain a finite perfective preterite form, also contain an infinitive, as in (2). Such combinations exhibit considerable variation in type, as can be seen from the following:

(7) Мы вышли было пройтись, но дождь заставил нас вернуться. (Гвоздев 1952: 143)

(8) Мы остановились -было смотреть на учение; но он просил нас идти к Василисе Егоровне /.../. (П: КД 297.8)

(9) - доста-а-нєм!
С испугу Настена кинулась было грести во весь дух, но тут же опустила весла. Куда? Зачем? (Расп.)

(10) Только один /.../ принялся было ковырять землю, но на него сейчас же зашипели: - Стыдно, Петя, перестаньте сию же минуту. (А. Толст.)

(11) Совпадение варианта *b* с текстом письма показывает, что Пушкин начал было перерабатывать этот вариант, но после двух не удовлетворительных его попыток снова вернулся к нему. (Note of the editor in Полн. собр. соч. Пушкина, т. 13: 362)

(12) Я стал было его бранить. Савельич за него заступился /.../. Савельич был прав. Делать было нечего. (П: КД 287.33)

(13) Одно время она решила было поехать к отцу в Самару, но подумала, что полторы тысячи верст не спасут от искушения, и махнула рукой. (А. Толст.)

(14) Я попытался было объяснить, но черта с два! Меркулов уже несся прыжками по лестнице. (Незн.)

Where the imperfective aspect occurs, the situation is reversed: examples in which an infinitive is used are in the majority and only 11 percent of the *было*-sentences contain only a single imperfective finite form. The following are examples of this latter (minority) group[18]:

(15) /.../ в утешение нашел я ваши письма и Марфу. И прочел ее два раза духом. Ура! - я было, признаюсь, боялся, чтоб первое впечатление не ослабело потом: но нет - я все-таки при том же мнении: Марфа имеет европейское, высокое достоинство. (П: Пс 542.5 (letter to Pogodin))

(16) Он <u>было</u> и ее <u>выписывал</u>, да матушкины родные ее не пустили, написали, что больна. (Островский; **Mazon** 1914: 180, also cited by Karcevski 1927: 143, and Bogusławski/Karolak 1973/70: 369)

Within the <u>imperfective</u> <u>preterite + infinitive</u> group, examples like (3), containing the verb *хотеть*; are very frequent (85 percent of the group). The following instances are typical:

(17) Бопре в смятении <u>хотел</u> <u>было</u> <u>привстать</u>, и не мог: несчастный француз был мертво пьян. (П: КД 280.31)

(18) Солдаты вернулись и <u>хотели</u> <u>было</u> уже <u>отвечать</u>, но увидев зайца, крепко выругались по его адресу. (Степ.)

(19) Я <u>было</u> совсем <u>отчаявался</u> <u>получить</u> Записки, столь нетерпеливо мною ожидаемые. Слава богу, что теперь попал на след. (П: Пс 1120.10)

(20) Волин <u>пытался</u> <u>было</u> <u>втиснуться</u> в это хлебное дело, но его оттерли - раньше надо было родиться. (Незн.)

(21) /Проскуряков/ вызвал машину и <u>собирался</u> <u>было</u> <u>уезжать</u> домой, когда дверь кабинета неслышно отворилась и вошел Пименов. (Сем.)

3. *OTHER TYPES OF било-CONSTRUCTION*

Other constructions containing *било* are seldom mentioned in the literature. However, Černov (1970) pays special attention to such cases: he presents an almost complete survey of *било*-constructions, omitting only those containing an infinitive.

Amongst these 'other constructions', the type which occurs most frequently is the one which contains a <u>past participle</u>. Some authors make no explicit mention of this possibility, although they may provide one or more examples, usually of a perfective active past participle, in a *било*-construction: see Boyer/Spéranski 1921/05: 253; Karcevski (1927: 142) (Boyer/Spéranski and Karcevski use the example from AS, as does MAS). These authors apparently consider that the category of 'preterite forms' normally includes such participles. However, there are other writers who do not subsume participial expressions under the heading 'preterite

forms', but accord them a separate mention. Vinogradov (1972/47:
463) only discusses the active perfective participle: "в сравни-
тельно редких случаях частица *было* сочетается с формой причастия
действительного совершенного вида".[19] The examples given by him are
the same as Boyer/Spéranski's. Other authors (AS; Unbegaun 1951:
254; Ferrell 1953: 114; Švedova 1960: 112; Isačenko 1940: 195 and
1968/62: 606; Nilsson 1967: 41 – footnote; Černov 1970: 260; RG
1980, I: 727; II, 102) do not exclude the passive participle,
although AS, Ferrell, Švedova and Isačenko do not give examples of
its use.

The following extracts illustrate the use of *было* in conjunction with participles of each type:

Past participle active[19]

(22) Чиж, <u>выглянувший</u> <u>было</u> из каземата, быстро юркнул назад.
      (Степ.)
(23) <u>Спавший</u> <u>было</u> днем мороз к вечеру заметно усилился /.../.
      (Степ.)
(24) Появились <u>попрятавшиеся</u> <u>было</u> ротные командиры, и понемногу
      части стали отходить к своим эшелонам. (А. Толст.)

Perfective passive participle

(25) <u>Застигнутые</u> <u>было</u> врасплох в самом селе, гитлеровцы оправились;
      на улицах и огородах завязался неравный бой.
      (М. Алексеев; Černov 1970: 260)
(26) Показали гнездо аиста, улетевшего отсюда, <u>напуганного</u> <u>было</u>
      грохотом стройки. (газ.; RG 1980, II: 101)

In view of the equivalence of participial constructions and attributive clauses, sentences like (22) – (26) can, in principle, be
transformed into sentences using the conjunction *который* and a
finite form of the verb. Some sentences of this type were found in
the course of collecting material for the study, although they are
even less frequent than sentences containing a participial construction. The next few examples illustrate the use of *было* in this
type of attributive clause:

(27) Послушайте, как пишет он (Ломоносов) этому самому Шувалову,
      Предстателю Муз, высокому своему патрону, который <u>вздумал</u>
      <u>было</u> над ним пошутить /.../. (П: Ж$_1$ 254.28)

(28) Он проворно вскочил в седло, не дождавшись казаков, которые хотели <u>было</u> <u>подсадить</u> его. (П: 335.2)

(29) /Наталья/ явилась к дедушке, упала ему в ноги и просила /.../ забыть ту дурь, которая на нее <u>нашла</u> <u>было</u> и которая, она клялась, уже больше не возвратится. (Л. Толст.)

Perfective gerunds

The occurrence of *было* in conjunction with perfective gerunds is even less frequent than with participles[20], and is mentioned only by Unbegaun (1951: 254), Černov (1970: 260) and RG (1980, I: 727). The following are examples of such occurrences:

(30) Сам съешь есть ныне главная пружина нашей журнальной полемики. Является колкое стихотворение, в коем сказано, что Феб, <u>усадив</u> <u>было</u> такого-то, велел его после вывести лакею, за дурной тон и заносчивость, нестерпимую в хорошем обществе – и тотчас в ответ явилась эпиграмма, где то же самое пересказано немного похуже, с надписью: сам съешь. (П: Ж$_1$ 151.21)

(31) - Слушай, Валя, - сказал Серпилин, <u>принявшись</u> <u>было</u> за чай, но отодвинув от себя стакан. - Знаешь, что я хотел тебе сказать? (Симонов; Чернов 1970: 260)

(32) Максим одеревенел и, <u>сделав</u> <u>было</u> до этого несколько шагов от порога, опять потянулся рукой к полушубку. (Сартаков; *ib.*)

The adjective *готовый*

The occurrence of *было* in conjunction with this adjective is mentioned only by Černov, who emphasises the exceptional nature of the construction ("совершенно исключительные случаи" 1970: 260). In view of its rarity, all his three examples are reproduced here:

(33) Ныне байкальские волны размывают уже совсем <u>было</u> <u>готовый</u> котлован. (Лит. газета)

(34) Саша Казанцев рассказывает, как "споткнулись" об этот гриф представители крупного завода, уже совсем <u>было</u> <u>готовые</u> заключить с "Факелом" соглашение... (Лит. газета)

(35) Это необычайое зрелище так поразило Свету, что зонт, уже <u>готовый</u> <u>было</u> <u>раскрыться</u> в ее руках, так и остался закрытым. (Б. Привалов)

This use of *готовый* rests on the fact that it denotes a state similar to states which can be expressed by certain verbs. When used without an infinitive, as in (33), the state indicated by *готовый* can sometimes be equated with the state that results from the action denoted by a verb like *закончить*. This resultant state can be presented as an attribute of an individual by the use of the passive past participle. For this reason, *готовый* in (33) might be replaced by *законченный*, resulting in the slightly more common construction exemplified in (25) and (26). In conjunction with an infinitive, *готовый* has the somewhat different meaning of 'intention' or 'readiness'. In the case of an animate being, the existence of intention can be expressed by the use of an imperfective verb like *намереваться*, or by a perfective verb like *собраться* (in the latter case, the coming into existence of this state is emphasised). For this reason, *готовые* in (34) can be directly replaced by *намеревавшиеся* or *собравшиеся*. In this sentence, the participial construction might in principle be transformed into a subordinate clause, using the short form of the adjective: *которые уже совсем было готовы были заключить соглашение* although this sounds rather awkward because two almost identical forms are used in close succession. Replacement of *готовы были* by the finite verb forms *намеревались* or *собрались* results in a more acceptable sentence with practically identical meaning (cf. examples (27) – (29) above).

Although the construction in (35) is of the same type as that in (34), the replacement of *готовый* by a verbal form is not possible here, for lexical reasons: apparently there is no Russian verb that can express the variant of 'readiness' intended in (35), i.e. a kind of 'tendency', characteristically ascribed only to inanimate entities.

Present tense forms

While it is true to say that *было* has a special connection with past events, this does not mean that it can never be used with present tense forms, since there are situations where these forms can perfectly well be used to refer to past events. Nevertheless, examples of present tense forms used in conjunction with *было* are extremely rare, and mentioned only by three authors: Potebnja,

Švedova and Černov. All their examples are quoted here.

The most obvious category contains sentences with an imperfective present form used as *praesens historicum*. Here are two
examples:

(36) - Мне бы хотелось пригласить вас в воскресенье на прогулку
      в горы, /.../ ну как?
    - Я с удовольствием, - говорит Адриен.
    - А ты, Мартин?
    - Да, - <u>начинаю было</u> я, - тут...
    - *Also, Verabredet! Jawohl*, все прекрасно.
    ('т Харт; translated from the Dutch by V. Belousov)
(37) Золушкин <u>берется было</u> за револьвер, помышляя о
     самоубийстве, но тут /.../ потянуло к родным краям.
     (Лит. газета; Чернов 1970: 261)

(Note the presence of a preterite form in the immediate context,
in (37)!)

The following example, also given by Černov, is somewhat different:

(38) Фадеев <u>откидывает</u> мяч назад <u>было</u>, но Хурцилава не
     успевает. (радиорепортаж)

I assume that this sentence was produced by someone reporting on a
football match. This use of present tense forms closely resembles
the so-called 'actual present'; but where events take place in
rapid succession, each one has already become part of the past
before it can be reported. Apparently, for the speaker in (37),
this awareness of the shift to the past is strong enough to permit
the use of *било*.

Stage directions form a special category where tenses are
concerned, although not all grammarians distinguish the use of
imperfective present in these cases - the *praesens scenicum* - from
praesens historicum. Whereas with the *praesens historicum* the
association with the past is quite clear, and the switching from
present to preterite forms in the same context is permissible (cf.
(37)), in modern Russian stage directions are normally given in the
imperfective present. One might argue that this is only natural, as
the events expressed by these forms are intended to be reproduced

every time the play is performed. On the other hand, when a play is considered as just one way of telling a story (which is easy when the play is read), its difference from novels and other narrative texts diminishes, and reference to a previous time is suggested. The only example to hand of the use of было in this type of text is one quoted by Švedova (1960: 111). It is taken from Tolstoj's 'Плоды просвещения':

(39) Федор Иваныч садится было за газету.

As is well-known, the use of <u>perfective present</u> verb forms to describe habitual actions in the past is common in modern Russian. The particle бивало can be added to emphasise both habitual occurrence and past reference. Most commonly, the events referred to are elements of a 'chain of events'. The notion of 'habitual nature' has to be applied to the whole chain. When the relations between the elements of the chain are such that the use of было would have been justified in the description of one single chain of this type (normally with perfective preterite forms), it seems permissible to use было in conjunction with perfective present forms which express the habitual nature of the chain in the past. In such circumstances one gains the impression that the particle бивало is 'replaced' by было. Было partly takes over the function of бивало (emphasizing past habitual nature of the action), but adds its own meaning (to be discussed below). A sentence that can be seen as an example of this use of было is quoted by Potebnja (1888/74: 268):

(40) Пойдет, было, и вернется.

A more recent example is given by Černov, who states that it clearly refers to the past ("Здесь четко выражено отнесение действия к прошлому") (1970: 263):

(41) Он (критик) соберет, было, рекомендации у известных
     писателей, изловчится, да и ударит по приемной комиссии.
     А его возьмут да и отшибут. (Лит. Россия)

Habitual past events can be expressed by <u>imperfective</u> present tense forms too.[21] Instances of the use of было in this setting appear to be still more infrequent than the types mentioned above. The only example to hand is the following sentence, taken from Potebnja.

Here there is some special reason to oppose the imperfective verb
to the following perfective:

(42) Говорит, <u>было</u>, говорит, и ничего не скажет (1888/74: 286)

<u>'Elliptical'</u> <u>sentences</u>

When the nature of the event that has to be reported is sufficiently clear from the accompanying adverbial expressions, the verb
form is sometimes omitted. Even in these circumstances, *было* can
still be used. According to Černov (1970: 261), this is a recent
development[22]. No instances are to be found in Puškin, but Švedova
(1960: 112) gives an example from Gogol':

(43) Акакий Акакиевич еще <u>было</u> <u>насчет</u> <u>починки</u>, но Петрович не
    дослышал...

In the Academy grammar, the following sentence is given as an
example of this use of *было*:

(44) Она <u>было</u> <u>в</u> <u>слезы</u>. (RG 1980, I: 101)

In the few examples of this type located during the present study,
the event is usually an utterance or a movement. The following
examples, taken from other authors, may supplement the picture:

(45) Я <u>было</u> <u>то</u> <u>да</u> <u>се</u>, а он чуть было не закричал на меня...
    (Достоевский; Шведова 1960: 112)
(46) Он <u>было</u> и <u>наутек</u>, да в прихожей, сказывают, задержали.
    (Салтыков-Щедрин; *ibid.*)
(47) Все-таки несколько слов Эдик сказал. Галя пошла, он <u>было</u>
    <u>за</u> <u>ней</u>. (В. Шугаев; Чернов 1970: 261)
(48) Я ему рупь за работу, он два требует. Я <u>было</u> <u>горлом</u>
    <u>на</u> <u>него</u>, а он костыль половчее берет... (А. Иванов; *ibid.*)

<u>Infinitives</u>

Examples of combinations of the particle *было* with an infinitive are very rare, and the meaning of some of them is doubtful.
The only example known to me in which *было* undoubtedly has the same
meaning as in the examples presented above is given by van Holk in
his article on the 'actor-infinitive construction'. He uses it to

emphasise the quality of past reference of the construction that is
labelled by him 'historical infinitive' (1951: 140):

(49) Те (мачеха и дочери) было прятаться, но куда ни
      бросятся - глаза за ними так и глядят. (Афанасьев)

This example closely resembles the 'elliptical' sentences quoted
above. Here again, the reference to an action in the past is very
clear.

      In the section on было in Švedova (1960) quite a different
example is given:

(50) /Скотинин/ Все меня одного оставили. Пойти было
      прогуляться на скотный двор. (Фонвизин)

According to Švedova this can be viewed as a special use of было:
"особое значение неуверенного, с оттенком сомнения утверждения,
предположения" (1960: 113). The other examples which she gives in
this connection contain a preterite verb form, and are thus closer
to the 'normal' uses of было:

(51) - Надо дырочками вниз ставить.
      - Я было так и ставила. (Из разг. речи)
(52) - Ты ее пересолила.
      - Да я было чуть-чуть посолила. (Из разг. речи)

Native speakers of Russian, when asked to comment on example (50),
regarded it as quite abnormal, at least from the standpoint of
modern usage. They suggested the replacement of было by что ли. The
difficulty is, that it seems impossible to interpret (50) as referring to a past event. In view of the absence of similar examples it
seems preferable to regard the occurrence of было in example (50)
as outside the scope of this study.[23]

      The survey of было-constructions given above shows that they
are more diverse than is generally thought. Nevertheless, all examples share one important feature: they refer to past events. The
new Academy grammar offers this formulation: "Эта частица сочетается с глаголом в форме прош. вр. или вводится в предложение с
общим значением прошедшего" (RG 1980, I: 727; emphasis mine -
A.A.B). As I hope to demonstrate below this naturally follows from
the meaning of было. It will be argued below that this feature -

reference to past events - proceeds naturally from the meaning of
било. A survey of various definitions located in the literature
will be followed by a discussion of how best to formulate the meaning of the word.

4.   *SURVEY OF DEFINITIONS OF било*

The definitions of the meaning of *било* which are to be found
in the literature can be divided into two groups, according to
whether they concentrate on the non-completion of the action (type
A) or whether they admit - explicitly or implicitly - that the
action may be completed, while at the same time suggesting that its
results are unsatisfactory or cancelled (type B).[25]

TYPE A. NON-COMPLETION OR INTERRUPTION OF ACTION

1. To this group belong the <u>dictionary definitions</u>, and <u>Kunert</u>'s
definition, quoted in section 1.
2. A.X. <u>Vostokov</u> (quoted by Švedova 1960: 109), draws a distinction
between the functioning of *било* "в окончательном виде" and "в начи-
нательном виде". According to Vostokov, in the second group (examples: *Стал било читать. Стал било говорить*), *било* indicates "что
начавшееся действие не имело продолжения". This seems to correspond
to the notion of 'interruption'. *Прочел било* and *Сказал било* are
given as examples of the first group. According to Vostokov, in
these cases, *било* is used "для показания, /.../ что действие не до-
шло до исполнения".
3. <u>Buslaev</u> (1959/1881: 286): "для означения несовершенного
действия".
4. <u>Mazon</u> (1914: 217): "exprime une action considérée dans son
accomplissement intégral, mais non réalisée".
5. <u>Pedersen</u> (1916: 163): "*било* udtrykker, at noget var lige ved
at ske, men så blev opgivet eller forhindret" ('*било* expresses
that something was just going to happen but was given up or
prevented').
6. <u>Šaxmatov</u> (1941/25-27: 405): "действие не достигло результата,
не выполнено".[26]

7. <u>Gvozdev</u> (1952: 143): "Особый оттенок прерванности действия".

8. <u>Kuznecov</u> (1959: 231): "/выражение/ действия в прошлом, прерванного другим действием".

9. <u>GRJa</u> (1960/52, I: 472): "оттенок неосуществленного действия"; (646): "действие началось, но не было закончено в силу каких-то причин, непредвиденных условий, помешавших осуществиться этому действию".[27]

10. <u>Galkina-Fedoruk/Gorškova/Šanskij</u> (1958; cited by Nilsson 1967: 40): "действие, которое могло совершиться, но не совершилось, или действие начавшееся, но прерванное другим действием".

11. <u>Tauscher/Kirschbaum</u> (1967/58: 421): "/*было* drückt aus/, dass eine Handlung beabsichtigt oder auch begonnen wurde, aber nicht zur Ausführung bzw. zur vollen Ausführung gelangte".

12. <u>Isačenko</u> (1968/62: 292)[28]: "Vorgänge, die in der Vergangenheit zwar einsetzten, aber durch andere Vorgänge unterbrochen wurden"; (606): "Modalität einer unterbrochenen Handlung".

13. <u>Nikitevič</u> (1963: 202): "не полностью осуществившееся или прерванное действие".

14. <u>Tagamlickaja</u> (1964: 188): "/характеристика действия/ начавшегося, но чем-то прерванного", "сложное и своеобразное значение - начинательное незавершенное".

15. <u>Forsyth</u> (1970: 105): "/*было*/ expresses the fact that the action of the verb it accompanies was contemplated or even begun, but that the performer then changed his mind or was prevented from carrying the action to its conclusion".[29]

16. <u>Černov</u> (1970: 260): "действие не достигает своего конечного предела"; (261): "/общее значение/ начатого или задуманного, но не осуществленного действия".

17. <u>Rozental'</u> (red.) (1971: 378): "значение невозможности завершить действие вследствие каких-либо причин".

18. <u>Kiselev</u> (in Astaf'eva et al.) (1971: 17): "действие /.../ начало осуществляться, но было прервано".

19. <u>Demidenko/Naumovič</u> (1972: 64): "действие, которое могло совершиться, но не совершилось, или начатое, но прерванное действие".

20. <u>Garde</u> (1980: 402): "action commencée et interrompue ou une action projetée mais non réalisée".[30]

21. <u>Crome</u> (in Eckert et al.) (1983: 172): "die Bedeutung einer beinahe zustande gekommenen, dann aber nicht ausgeführten Handlung".

TYPE B. ACTION COMPLETED, RESULTS UNSATISFACTORY OR CANCELLED

1. I.I. <u>Davydov</u> (cited by Švedova 1960: 109): "для означения неудачи".
2. K.S. <u>Aksakov</u> (cited by Vinogradov (1970/47: 463; footnote) and Švedova (1960: 119)): "действие /.../ уже началось и встретило препятствие, или совершилось и было уничтожено".[31]
3. A. <u>Potebnja</u> (1888/74: 266)[32] "оттенок действия, недошедшего до надлежащего исполнения, лишенного своих прямых последствий".
4. <u>Boyer/Spéranski</u> (1921/05: 252): "une action verbale commencée n'a pas été achevée, - ou /.../ cette action, même achevée, n'a pas produit l'effet qu'on en pouvait légitimement attendre, ou enfin /.../ cette action a été simplement projetée, mais non mise à exécution".
5. <u>Peškovskij</u> (1920: 87): "/особый оттенок/ неудачности, без-результативности".
6. <u>Karcevski</u> (1927: 142): "acte annulé en fonction de son résultat".
7. <u>Vinogradov</u> (1970/47: 463) uses the formulation "прерванность осуществления действия". In a footnote on the same page, this is equated with "значение аннулированного результата". Later in his book, the following definition appears: для обозначения действия с неосуществленным или аннулированным результатом" (1970/47: 573) (an identical statement can be found in 1975/50: 79).
8. <u>Unbegaun</u> (1951: 253): "/Le mot *било*/ indique l'acte abandonné, à quelque stade que ce soit, que cet acte ait eut lieu, ou fût seulement projeté: l'essentiel est que cet acte n'ait pas mené au résultat attendue ou escompté".
9. <u>Borras/Christian</u> ((1971/59: 139): "expresses the fact that the <u>result</u> which might naturally have been expected from a completed perfective action was <u>frustrated</u>. The action may actually have been begun or simply projected" (emphasis mine - A.A.B.)
10. <u>GSRLJa</u> (1970: 578): "значение действия начатого, но прерванного или не давшего желаемых результатов".[33]

11. RG (1980, I: 727): "значение действия осуществившегося, но или прерванного, не доведенного до конца, или не приведшего к желаемому результату, не достигшего цели".[34]

12. Pennington (1980: 283): "to indicate incomplete or unsuccesful actions".

As these definitions show, the various authors differ to a surprising extent in their formulations of the meaning of било. This variety might be accounted for at least in part by the ambiguity of the expressions used in the definitions. Owing to the ambiguity of terms like 'result' or 'action', and to the fact that it is often not clear to which 'actions' some of the notions must be applied (cf. section 1.), it is possible that some of the authors whose definitions are classed here under group A in fact hold a view which is closer to that of the writers whose definitions are placed in group B.[35] For the purposes of the classification, I have taken the definitions quite literally. Of course, the authors illustrate their definitions with one or more examples, and in practice, some well-chosen examples can often exclude undesirable interpretations. Still, the possibility of confusing the reader remains, especially when the number of examples is limited. Group A definitions are the most difficult. This point has already been illustrated in section 1., with reference to Kunert's definition, and since this kind of definition seems to be favoured by the majority, it will be elaborated in the next section.

5.   *THE PROBLEM OF IDENTIFYING 'THE ACTION'*

All definitions of type A refer to a characteristic of 'the action'. However, as already stated in section 1, when one tries to apply such a definition to the expressions containing било, it is often not immediately clear to what the term 'action' in fact refers. To illustrate this point, let us turn to Garde's definition (A20): it is a recent formulation, fairly representative of the definitions of type A, and Garde's examples have some interesting features.

Accoring to Garde, *било* indicates an action that was begun
and interrupted, or intended but not realised. He gives the following two examples, taken from literary texts:

(53) Он <u>было</u> <u>бросился</u> на шею к дяде, но тот ... держал его в
некоторм расстоянии от себя. (Гончаров)

(54) <u>Поехали</u> <u>было</u> в Париж, но там нам показалось холодно, и мы
вернулись в Италию. (Чехов)

Unless it is otherwise stated, one naturally assumes that the word
'action' is being used in the same way as in accounts of the verbal
aspects: for example, in discussions of the perfective aspect, the
'action' is 'that which is presented as a single whole'. Such a
conception of 'totality' presupposes a certain 'critical point', a
terminus (henceforth: 'Term.') that must be reached. There are
considerable differences between verbs, and between different uses
of the same verb, with respect to the relation between the situations preceding and following this 'Term.': with some verbs, e.g.
написать, the situation[36] immediately preceding the 'Term.' is
conceived as an 'activity' (writing), leading up to a 'result' (the
situation immediately following the 'Term.'). In the case of other
verbs, like *заговорить*, the situation immediately following the
'Term.' (the talking) would normally be thought of not so much as a
'result', but rather as an 'activity'. This 'activity' must not,
however, be confused with the essential 'action' denoted by the
verb *заговорить*: the <u>start</u> of the talking. It is clear that the
notion of 'totality' associated with the perfective aspect must be
applied here to the <u>start</u> of the talking and not to the talking
itself. A considerable number of verbs in Russian have a similar
meaning, i.e. they place the main emphasis upon the 'postterminal'
situation. At the centre of this group are the so-called 'ingressive' verbs ('ingressive Aktionsart', 'начинательный способ действия'). The essential 'action' denoted by these verbs is in fact
the start of something else.

It is interesting to note that the verbs in both of Garde's
examples are of an 'ingressive' nature. The verb *поехать* is in fact
generally considered to be of the 'ingressive Aktionsart'. This
verb - like others formed by adding the prefix *no-* to a 'determinate verb of motion' (*пойти*, *побежать* etc.) - denotes the 'action'

of transition from a resting state to a state of a movement in a
certain direction. A similar meaning can be expressed by the verb
броситься, although this verb is not considered to be a member of
the 'ingressive Aktionsart'. In the sentences in the present sample
the verb *броситься* can always be interpreted as referring to an
energetic start - a transition into a <u>fast</u> movement. The following
are all the other examples at the autor's disposal (see also (2),
(4) and the example in note 11):

(55) Ибрагим, узнав Петра, в радости к нему <u>было</u> <u>бросился</u>, но
почтительно остановился. (П: АП 10.21)

(56) - Ах ты, я доберусь до тебя... - <u>бросился</u> <u>было</u> солдат к
поручику, но тут же был сбит с ног ударом кулака. (Степ.)

(57) Я <u>бросился</u> <u>было</u> к нему на помощь: несколько дюжих казаков
схватили меня и связали кушаками /.../ . (П: КД 324.15)

(58) Он <u>бросился</u> <u>было</u> на помощь Юрасевскому, но поняв, в чем
дело, кинулся к Малееву. (Степ.)

(59) Мятежники <u>бросились</u> <u>было</u> на них, но были рассеяны пушечными
выстрелами с противного берега. (П: ИП 59.11)

(60) Я <u>бросился</u> <u>было</u> за ним, но на левой руке моей повисла
тяжесть. Эта была она /.../. (Л. Толстой; Бондарко 1983: 141)

(61) "А где же Екимовна? Позвать ее сюда". Несколько слуг
<u>бросились</u> <u>было</u> в разные стороны, но в ту же минуту старая
женщина (i.e. Екимовна - А.А.Б) /.../ вошла припевая и
подплясывая. (П: АП 20.19)

(62) Я <u>бросилась</u> <u>было</u> <u>бежать</u>, но он схватил меня за руку.
(Тургенев; Nilsson 1967: 46)

(63) Встречаясь с генералом Раевским и боясь его шуток, он, дабы
их предупредить, <u>бросился</u> <u>было</u> его <u>обнимать</u>; Раевский
отступил и сказал ему с улыбкою /.../. (П: Ж$_2$ 166.13)

(64) Шурка исподлобья посмотрела на отца, а затем <u>бросилась</u> <u>было</u>
<u>очищать</u> его от грязи. - Не трожь, дура! Как есть - до
командира пойду /.../ (Степ.)

(65) Сказал волк и пустился к деревне; увидал свинью с
поросятами и <u>бросился</u> <u>было</u> <u>схватить</u> поросенка, а свинья не
дает. (Афанасьев; Mazon 1914: 217)

The 'ingressive' nature of such events is important when they occur
in combination with *было*. The usual definitions of *было* run into

trouble over ingressive-type verbs, because it would have to follow
from them that the <u>start</u> of the action has not been fully realised,
i.e. the <u>start</u> was begun but interrupted, or intended but not realised. In either case, the activity itself, the 'post-terminal'
activity, never happened at all. It seems unnecessary to interpret
in this way any of the examples in this section (including Garde's
examples, (53) and (54)). Several of them make sense only when it
is assumed that the 'post-terminal' activity did actually come into
existence. Sentence (55), in which the subsequent action is denoted
by a verb of opposite meaning, is an especially clear case. The
same applies to the following examples, which illustrate the use of
verbs generally acknowledged to be 'ingressive': the *поехать*-type,
and the *заговорить*-type:

(66) Помощник <u>было</u> <u>пошел</u>, но приостановился и крикнул /.../
     (Серафимович ГРЯ 1960/52, II, 1: 392)

(67) Я <u>поехал</u> <u>было</u> за Нижегородским полком, но лошадь моя
     хромала. Я отстал. (П: ПА 471.21)

(68) В вагоне рослые мужики тащили с полок чемоданы, выкидывали
     их через окошки. Человек в пенсне <u>полез</u> <u>было</u> на откос к
     вагону: - Господа, господа, там у меня физические приборы,
     ради бога, осторожнее, это хрупкое...
     На него зашипели, схватив сзади за непромокаемый плащ,
     втащили в толпу пассажиров. (А. Толст.)

(69) Схватка была коротка, четверо казаков осталось лежать на
     бугре, двое, спешенных, <u>побежали</u> <u>было</u> и упали под выстрелами.
     (А. Толст.)

(70) Мы <u>заговорили</u> <u>было</u> о деле, но нас отвлекли.
     (Гвоздев 1952: 143)

(71) С Потугиным он <u>заговорил</u> <u>было</u>, но тот неохотно отвечал ему.
     (Тургенев; Nilsson 1967: 44)

(72) Я <u>было</u> <u>заговорил</u> о чем-то постороннем, но старик только
     рукой махнул. (Достоевский; Шведова 1960: 112)

(73) Собаки <u>было</u> <u>залаяли</u>, но узнав Антона, умолкли и замахали
     косматыми хвостами. (П: Д 175.25)

(74) - А знаете ли, господа, отчего мы сегодня сидим повесив
     носы? - сказал Злов, который <u>запел</u> <u>было</u> "*mihi est
     propositum*" и остановился, видя, что никто ему не подтяги-
     вает. (Жихарева; Прокопович 1982: 112)

(75) Он (Волин) <u>было загрустил</u>, но оттаял, потому что как раз в
     это время именно там, в Скатертном переулке, познакомился
     со своими благодетелями - Володей Казаковым и Юрой
     Леоновичем. (Незн.)

In sentences like these, the notions of 'interruption' or 'non-realisation' in Garde's definition can hardly apply to the action
directly denoted by the verb (the start of a another activity or
the inception of a state (cf. (75)), but seem to make sense only
when applied to the activity or state resulting from the transition[37] Note the fact that sometimes the verb used in conjunction
with *было* is followed by a more or less direct antonym (cf. (66),
(73) and (74)). With verbs of the *заговорить-* or *поехать*-type, the
nature of this activity or state is wholly defined by the meaning
of the corresponding non-prefixed imperfective verb. The meaning of
броситься can come very close to the meaning of *побежать* (cf. (4),
(55)-(62) and the example in note 11). However, when combined with
an infinitive other than *бежать* (as in (2) and (63) - (65)), the
movement suggested by *броситься* often merges with the initial phase
of the action denoted by the infinitive. In these cases, it is
feasible that the movement leading up to that action is actually
completed, but that the notion of 'interruption' or 'non-realisation' has to be applied to the latter action (cf. the discussion in
section 1).

     We may conclude that definitions of type A have a serious
shortcoming: they do not make it clear that the 'action' of which
they speak may be only indirectly related to the 'action' denoted
by the *было*-verb. The examples discussed in this section show that
in some cases, what is really meant is, activities or states resulting from the *было*-event. It might be that the distinction between
'beginning' - 'interruption' on the one hand, and 'intention' -
'non-realisation' on the other (a distinction that is made by Garde
and some other authors, most notably Vostokov) reflects the authors' awareness of the problem. The question is, to what extent
uses of *было* with verbs that are more or less distinctly 'ingressive' must be distinguished from its uses with other verbs, e.g.
'resultative' verbs. However, before we move on to this question,
more examples will be given of ingressive constructions.

6. FURTHER EXAMPLES OF THE USE OF было IN INGRESSIVE CONSTRUCTIONS

The idea of 'ingressiveness' can be conveyed by constructions in which a finite verb form expresses the start of an activity specified by a following imperfective infinitive. We have already come across the construction *бросился бежать* in the preceding section. Similar examples can be found containing verbs like *кинуться* (cf. (9)), *пуститься* and *пойти*:[38]

(76) Тут он <u>пустился</u> <u>было</u> <u>бежать</u>, но Саша догнал его, толкнул в спину, и мальчишка упал со всех ног /.../. (П: Д 216.21)

(77) А то А. <u>пошел</u> <u>было</u> <u>ставить</u> чай... (Из разговора)

As well as sentences like these, where the meaning of the finite verb form more or less clearly exceeds the notion of ingressiveness, the present sample contains a relatively large number of sentences with verbs which specialise in expressing ingression: *стать*, *начать* and *приняться*. These verbs are not confined to the inception of motions but cover a much wider field. Their use is illustrated in (10)-(12) and in the following examples:

(78) Со вздохом выпрямилась она, <u>принялась</u> <u>было</u> <u>шить</u>, уронила иголку, оперла лицо на руку и, легонько покусывая кончики ногтей, задумалась /.../. (Тургенев; Nilsson 1967: 48)

(79) Обольщенный моею славою, он <u>стал</u> <u>было</u> <u>искать</u> моего дружества; но я принял его холодно, и он без всякого сожаленья от меня удалился. (П: В 69.18)

(80) Эта мысль успокоила его немного: он <u>стал</u> <u>было</u> <u>засыпать</u>. "Ну, что ежели вдруг ночью возьмут Севастополь, и французы ворвутся сюда? Чем я буду защищаться?" Он опять встал и походил по комнате. (Л. Толст.)

(81) <u>Стал</u> <u>было</u> он (француз) своим словам <u>учить</u> меня, да мать запретила. (Горьк.)

(82) Пишу тебе у Рейна /.../. <u>Начал</u> он тебе <u>было</u> <u>диктовать</u> письмо в своем роде - но заблагорассудил изорвать его. (П: Пс 28.38)

(83) Г. Федоров, в журнале, который <u>начал</u> <u>было</u> <u>издавать</u>, разбирая довольно благосклонно 4 и 5-ую главу, заметил однако ж мне, что /.../ (П: Ж₁ 149.18)

(84) Граф приблизился ко мне с видом открытым и дружелюбным; я старался ободриться и начал было себя рекомендовать, но он предупредил меня. (П: В 71.37)

(85) /.../ князь начал было рассказывать о своих похождениях на берегу, но лейтенант его перебил вопросом /.../. (Степ.)

(86) Саша Пискунов начал было хлебать громко, как всегда, и вдруг осекся. (Дудинцев; Чернов 1970: 259)

(87) Я начал было извиняться за поздний приход, но мой так называемый отчим замахал руками и потащил меня в столовую. (Незв.)

(88) - Расследованием, произведенным стажером Турецким, было установлено - начал было я фиглярничать, но увидел, что этот номер сегодня не проходит /.../. (Незн.)

The last example is interesting because it is close to a use of *начал было* without infinitive that occurs relatively frequently in the literature, - in the writing of dialogue: "It indicates that the speaker is interrupted or does not bother to complete the speech that was begun" (Nilsson 1967: 44). Nilsson gives a number of examples from Turgenev that are of the same type as the following examples taken from more recent literary works:[39]

(89) - Наш флот настолько слабее японского... - начал было Агатеев, но грохот взрыва не дал ему закончить. (Степ.)

(90) - По положению о морских собраниях, не полагается... - начал было один из офицеров.
- Ну вас к черту с вашими положениями, - оборвал его князь. (Степ.)

(91) - Ну, как работается? Как Меркулов, не обижает? /.../
- Да какой начальник не обижает... - начал было я с приторной шутливостью в тоне. Но Пархоменко не намерен был уходить от серьезной темы /.../. (Незн.)

(92) - По-моему, они говорят о тебе, - начал было Грикспоор, но тут громко закричала Мария, и все затихли. (Вестд.)[40]

All of the above examples, with one possible exception, allow the interpretation that the 'terminus' of the 'action' denoted by the *было*-verb is reached. The doubtful case is (84): in view of the meaning of the verb *предупредить*, it might be argued that the subject of the sentence did not actually start the act denoted by the verb *рекомендовать*, being pre-empted by the action of the count. However, in some of the other sentences, it is clear that the activity of which the *било*-verb marks the beginning has already been in progress for some time, cf. (76), (79), (82), (83), (85) and (89)-(92).

The points made in this section and the preceding one lead to the conclusion that where *било* is used with ingressive-type verbs, its meaning must be defined in relation to the state of affairs resulting from the action denoted by the *било*-verb, and not that action itself. The state of affairs comes into being, but does not progress as might have been expected.

7.   *SENTENCES CONTAINING 'RESULTATIVE' VERBS*

We may now turn to an examination of the functioning of *било* in combination with other kinds of verb. As already stated in section 5, there is a notable diference between 'ingressive' and 'resultative' verbs with respect to the temporal location of the main activity - whether it starts or ends at the 'Term.' of the action that is directly denoted by the verb. One might expect, therefore, that when *било* is used with a resultative verb, it would operate on the state of affairs preceding the 'Term.', i.e. on the action itself. It might be thought that the second part of Garde's definition ("action /.../ intended but not realised") applies especially to the 'resultative' cases. However, this is not borne out by the uses of *било* in the present sample.

This point is best illustrated with the aid of examples containing the verb *написать*: it is an excellent example of the group of 'resultative' verbs because it is a verb with an object, denoting something that comes into existence as a result of the action. Alle eight instances in the present sample are reproduced here:

(93) Я <u>было</u> <u>написал</u> письмо, да опять изорвал.
  (К.С. Аксаков, cited by Švedova)

(94) Не разжимая зубов, Катя мотнуло головой. <u>Написала</u> <u>было</u> Даше коротенькое письмо, но сейчас же порвала. (А. Толст.) (Cf. GRJa (1960/52, II, 1: 392) and Borras/Christian (1971/59: 139).)

(95) Я из Пскова <u>написал</u> тебе <u>было</u> уморительное письмо - да сжег.
(П: Пс 223.39)

(96) Он (Ганибал) <u>написал</u> <u>было</u> свои записки на французском языке,
но в припадке панического страха, коему был подвержен, велел
их при себе сжечь вместе с другими драгоценными бумагами.
(П: Ж$_2$ 313.9)

(97) Милый мой ангел! Я <u>было</u> <u>написал</u> тебе письмо на 4 страницах,
но оно вышло такое горькое и мрачное, что я его тебе не
послал, а пишу другое. (П: Пс 950.2)

(98) Я <u>было</u> <u>написал</u> на него ругательскую Антикритику, слогом
Галатей - взяв в эпиграф *Павлуша медный лоб приличное*
названье! собирался ему послать, не знаю куда дел.
(П: Пс 439.17)

(99) - Вы хотели просить меня, чтоб я написал Александру /.../.
- Да, напишите... напишите что хотите... А вот это... -
она торопливо пошарила у себя в кармане и достала
небольшую тетрадку. - Это я <u>было</u> для него <u>написала</u>...
перед его бегством... Но ведь он поверил... поверил тому!
(Тургенев)

(100) Кстати: Лиза <u>написала</u> <u>было</u> мне письмо в роде духовной:
croyez à la tendresse de celle qui vous aimera même au
delà du tombeau и проч., да и замолкла; я спокойно себе
думаю, что она умерла. Что же узнаю? Элиза влюбилась в
вояжера *Mornau* да с ним кокетничает! Каково? *O femme,*
femme! créature faible et décevante... (П: Пс 654.36)

In all this sentences, *било* is clearly not being used to show that
the action 'to write something' has not reached its 'Term.'. The
context suggests that something has been written and that it has
existed at least for a short moment. The use of *било* seems to indicate that something has disturbed the subsequent course of events.
In (93)-(96) the document is destroyed[41], apparently because the
subject was dissatisfied with what he had written ((93)-(95)) or
became afraid that it might cause trouble (96). In (97) the subject's dissatisfaction prevents him from posting the letter. In
(98), the document was lost and could not be posted for that
reason. In (99) it probably did not reach the addressee (because
he had fled).[42] In all these examples, there appears to have been

some disturbance of the 'normal' course of events: a letter is
usually dispatched by the writer, and received and read by the
addressee; memoirs are written for future generations to read, and
are published for that purpose, etc. However, as example (100)
illustrates, the use of *было* is still possible even when all the
events that normally follow the writing of a letter actually take
place: the letter has been written, has been psoetd, is received by
the addressee, and is read by him. What, then, is the function of
было here? The context shows that there is a certain inconsistency
between the message that the writer sent, and her subsequent behaviour. The content of the letter led the recipient to believe that
the writer was in love with him, and close to dying, but afterwards
it comes to his knowledge that she is very much alive, and flirting
with someone else.

An examination of examples (93)-(100) shows that even with
such typical 'resultative' verbs as *написать*, it is perfectly normal for the action to reach its 'Term.'. The same applies to most
of the other sentences containing more or less 'resultative' verbs.
A number of examples are given below:

The following four sentences describe a change of position
that was wholly or partly cancelled by the action denoted by a
following verb:

(101) Базаров, который встал было навстреу Павлу Петровичу,
      присел на край стола и скрестил руки. (Тургенев)
(102) Дампфер сел было, но сразу же встал снова и отыскал взглядом
      Максимова. (Аксенов; Forsyth 1970: 105)⁴³
(103) Демин лег было, а теперь опять поднялся на локте...
      (А. Рыбаков; Švedova 1960: 111)
(104) Барабан умолк; гарнизон бросил ружья; меня сшибли было
      с ног, но я встал и вместе с мятежниками вошел в крепость.
      (П: КД 324.13)

In the next four sentences the verb following the *было*-verb is
not its direct opposite, but again it is quite clear that the
result of the action of the *было*-verb has existed for at least a
short period before being 'annulled' by the following action:

(105) Воротился старик ко старушке,/ Рассказал ей великое чудо./
      "Я сегодня поймал было рыбку,/ Золотую рыбку, не

простую / /.../ Не посмел я взять с нее выкуп;/
Так пустил ее в синее море". (П: РР 30)

(106) Послание к Давыдову - прелесть! Наш боец чернокудрявый
окрасил было свою седину, замазав и свой белый локон, но
после Ваших стихов опять его вымыл - и прав.
(П: Пс 1175.22)

(107) Здесь Перовский его (Брюлова) было заполонил; перевез к
себе, запер под ключ и заставил работать. Брюлов насилу от
него удрал. (П: Пс 1188.17)

(108) Один из солдат вскинул было винтовку, но другой толкнул
его в плечо, и тот не выстрелил. (А. Толст.)

In the next set of examples, the *было*-verb implies that some
other person was persuaded to act according to the wish of the
subject of this verb. However, the context indicates that this
other person apparently changed his mind afterwards:

(109) Отдавая ему (отцу) имение, я было выговорил для тебя
независимые доходы с половины Кистенева. Но видно отец
переменил свои мысли. (П: Пс 1205)

(110) Он было спас и офицеров полка Прусского короля, уговорив
мятежников содержать несчастных под арестом; но после
его отъезда убийства совершились. (П: Ж$_2$ 200.28)

In the next example, the result did come about - the book has
been opened -, but the reader did not find the solace she had hoped
for:

(111) Даша усаживалась в большом кресле то боком, то поджав ноги,
раскрыла было книгу - отчет за три месяца "деятельности
Городского союза", - столбцы цифр и совершенно непонятных
слов, - но в книжке не нашла утешения. (А. Толст.)[44]

The last example in this section was noticed in the ordinary
speech of a Russian, in the following situation: the telephone had
rung once only. She went to the telephone and dialled the number of
her friend (В.). On finding out that this number was occupied she
commented:

(112) Б. разговаривает. Она было мой номер набрала по ошибке.
Сразу опустила трубку.

The preceding examples show that there are no essential differences between 'resultative' and 'ingressive' constructions, with
respect to the interpretation that the action reached its 'Term.'.
било seems to act upon situation(s) following the 'Term.'.[45] This
does not necessarily mean that it affects our perception of the two
kinds of situation in the same way. Whereas with 'ingressive' verbs
the notion of 'interruption' normally seems quite adequate to
describe our idea of what happens with the 'postterminal' activity,
this notion often seems inapplicable to 'resultative' verbs.
However, a closer look at the examples shows that even this difference is not a major one. Garde's second example (example (54) in
section 5 of this article) is instructive in this respect. Although
this example contains a typical 'ingressive' verb (*поехать*), the
'postterminal' activity - the movement towards Paris - is clearly
not interrupted at all: as the immediate context shows, the subject
actually arrived in Paris (where the next action - *нам показалось
холодно* - is located). Here, as in examples (93)-(112) above, the
only reason for the use of *било* appears to be that there is something disturbing in the ultimate development of things. In this
case, the subject had apparently planned to stay for some time in
Paris but owing to bad weather the travellers changed their plans.

The above observations, and a study of examples like (54) and
(100) lead us to the conlusion that the assumption that there is no
essential difference between the meaning of *било* as used in conjunction with 'ingressive' verbs, and as used in conjunction with
'resultative' verbs. With both kinds of verb, *било* does not preclude the completion of the action denoted by the verb, i.e. the
attainment of the 'Term.'. *Било* can be used in conjunction with
both kinds of verb to suggest a disturbance in or annulment of the
situation immediately following the 'Term.'. Alternatively it can
apply to subsequent developments - the occurrence of unexpected
events only indirectly connected with the *било*-event. Clearly,
definitions of *било* should account for such uses, since they are
commonplace enough. It is argued above that group A definitions are
not satisfying because they imply that the action of the *било*-verb
does not reach its critical point.[46] Group B definitions are supe-
rior in this respect, although some of them are unfortunately vague
(cf. B1, B5), and others contain elements which unduly restrict the

applicability of the definition. The term 'result', often used in
the Group B definitions, gives rise to difficulties similar to
those which we encountered in connection with the term 'action' in
group A definitions. The plural form 'results' (B10), or the term
'effect' (B4), are preferable because they can be taken to include
the more indirect effects of the action. Other elements, like
'annulment of the result' or 'non-attainment of the desired result'
cannot adequately explain some of the more extreme cases like (54)
and (100). Nevertheless, some of the definitions contain certain
elements that point the way to a more generally applicable definition; for example, Borras/Christian's notion of 'frustration' (B9)
(which is less specific than 'annulment'); the notion of 'expectation' in Boyer/Spéranski (B4) and in Unbegaun (B8); and the notion
of 'consequences' ('*последствия*') in Potebnja (B3).

However, before attempting to formulate an alternative definition, we must consider at least the following questions:
a) Is non-attainment of the critical point a possible interpretation at all, and if so, what factors are important here?
b) What is the relation between *било* and *чуть* (*било*) *не*?
c) How does *било* function in negative sentences like (5) and (6)?
d) How does *било* function with imperfective verbs?

8. *PRETERMINAL INTERRUPTION*

Some definitions of *било* suggest that its use precludes the
reaching of the 'Term.', the 'critical point', which is such an
important element in the meaning of perfective verbs. We have
decided that this is not the case. We will now consider whether the
use of *било* <u>can</u> preclude the reaching of the 'critical point'. Of
the examples quoted up to this point, practically only (84) could
really be interpreted in this way, and even so, it could be argued
that here the 'Term.' of the interrupting action does not in fact
precede the 'Term.' of the *било*-verb, but practically coincides
with it. In the present sample there is no real instance where the
context compels us to locate the 'Term.' of the interrupting event,
if any, before the 'Term.' of the *било*-verb, or otherwise makes it
clear that the 'Term.' is not reached. Even in the cases where the

expected post-terminal situation clearly did not come about it is
possible that the 'critical points' of the *было*-event and of the
interrupting event coincide. The following example is a clear case
of such a coincidence: the phrase '*в дверях*' indicates that the
subject halted at the very 'border' that has to be crossed to leave
the room:

(113) Тут он <u>было</u> <u>вышел</u>, но остановился в дверях, оглянулся
      на простреленную мною картину, выстрелил в нее почти не
      целясь и скрылся. (П: В 74.31)

The following example, a note written by Puškin to accompany a
text sent to his brother - is one of the few cases that probably
could be interpreted as an instance of non-attainment of the
'Term.':

(114) Я <u>было</u> <u>послал</u> это в Сын Отечества, да кажется журнал сей
      противу меня восстанет, судя по сухому объявлению Пчелы.
      В таком случае мне не годится там явиться, как даннику
      атамана Греча и эсаула Булгарина. Дарю отрывки тебе: печатай
      где хочешь. (П: Пс 141.1)

It seems possible here to assume that the manuscript was never
actually sent off to the journal. Nevertheless, it could be argued
that some might already have been made for its despatch. A consulted native-speaker suggested the possibility that the text had
already been handed over to a servant, but was afterwards taken
back.
      The following example is taken from Isačenko (1968/62: 293):

(115) Он уже <u>миновал</u> <u>было</u> заборик Журбиных, когда над головами
      собравшихся ... ударил гулкий выстрел.

According to Isačenko's interpretation the subject had not yet
passed the fence: 'Er hatte den Zaun der Schurbins <u>beinahe schon</u>
hinter sich, als ...' (emphasis mine - A.A.B.). My Russian advisers
preferred the interpretation that at the moment when the sound was
heard, the subject was already at the very edge of the fence or
even slightly further.
      In the following two examples, 2 interpretations are possible:
1) the critical points of the two verbs coincide; 2) the critical

point of the *было*-verb is anticipated by that of the second verb.
Both are acceptable.

(116) Сережа <u>вошел</u> уже <u>было</u> в ворота, но вдруг заметил возле урны с
мусором папиросную коробку. (Шварц)

(117) /Меркулов/ занялся осмотром, рукава моей нейлоновой куртки.
Я <u>было</u> <u>сунул</u> руку в карман за синим пакетом, но Меркулов
сказал: - Ш-ш-ш... (Незн.)

(It was dangerous to show the packet. It is not clear whether the
hand was actually slipped into the pocket, but of course the packet
was left there:)

The next example is the only one where the second part of the
sentence makes it clear that the action was interrupted before the
critical point:

(118) Он <u>упал</u> <u>было</u>, да удержался за перила. (Pedersen 1916: 163)

However, it is interesting to note that Boyer/Spéranski give an
example where the same verb is used, but the second part of the
sentence means just opposite:

(119) Он <u>упал</u> <u>было</u>, но сейчас же поднялся (1921/05: 253)

We may conclude that interruption of the action before the
terminus is reached is in principle possible, although there seems
to be a strong tendency to locate the interrupting event farther
'to the right', i.e. at the very point when the 'Term.' is reached,
or after it. One gains the impression that the presence of the
particle *было* often causes the situation around the critical point
to become faint or blurred. The help of the context is needed to be
able to determine whether the 'Term.' of the *было*-event was actually reached or not. However, the notion of pre-empting or non-
attainment of the 'Term.' seems to be more marked: when the context
does not provide information that points to the contrary, the
interpretation of attainment of the terminus seems preferable.

According to some grammarians, the presence of the adverb
совсем would tend to encourage the view that the action is
pre-empted before its critical point is reached. The next section
contains a brief discussion of the functioning of this adverb.

9. *THE ADVERB* совсем

Boyer/Spéranski seem to assume that the presence of *совсем* indicates preterminal interruption: "Parfois *было* s'accompagne de l'adverbe *совсем*; c'est alors l'action verbale n'a pas même reçu un commencement d'execution" (1921/05: 253). They contrast example (119) with the following example:

(120) Он совсем <u>было</u> <u>упал</u>.

example (119) is translated as follows: "il est tombé, mais s'est relevé aussitôt". It is followed by this comment: "- et l'auxiliaire *было* indique que cette chute n'a point eu les suites fâcheuses qu'on pouvait craindre". In the case of (120) they state "il était sur le point de tomber, il a failli tomber, mais il n'est réellement pas tombé".

The same assumption is made by Borras/Christian: "To express clearly that the action in the main clause was not even begun, the expression *совсем было* may be used" (1971/59: 140). They provide the following example:

(121) Он тоже взялся за ложку и уже совсем <u>было</u> <u>погрузил</u> в суп,
      но сейчас же он опять положил на стол. (Щедрин)

which they translate as follows:
'He also took hold of the spoon and was about to dip it in the soup, but straight away put it back on the table'.

My Russian advisers agree on the possibility that the spoon has not yet touched the soup, but do not wholly exclude the possibility that it was in fact dipped in the soup. Amongst the sentences in the sample which contain *совсем* it is difficult to find instances in which the attainment of the 'Term.' appears to be entirely excluded. The following example is possibly one case:

(122) Ласковой улыбкой и обещанием "прокатить" Павел Антоныч
      заманил ее в сани и повез. Дорогой Танька совсем <u>было</u> <u>ушла</u>.
      Павел Антоныч успел подхватить ее под мышки и опять начал
      уговаривать. (Бунин)

It seems clear here that Tan'ka did not succeed in escaping from the sleigh. In the next example, however, the function of *совсем*

cannot be explained as indicating the failure: the subject has
actually been quite near to the other person mentioned:

(123) Я было совсем пододвинулся к нему; но при этом последнем
     слове невольно вскочил на ноги. (Тургенев; Nilsson 1970: 47)

One of my Russian acquaintances said that in this example, the
presence of *совсем* suggests a certain progression: the subject had
been moving towards the other person for some time and had already
got very close.

   With regard to the next example, it was said that the subject
had already made up her mind to walk to the door, but that it was
not very clear whether she was already actually walking:

(124) - Простились, и она совсем уже было к двери пошла, вдруг
     оборачивается и спрашивает... (Полевой; Švedova 1967: 113)

When asked about the effect of the substitution of *она совсем уже
было к двери пошла* by *она пошла было к двери*, a native-informant
stated that in the *совсем*-variant, the subject had to be closer to
the starting-point than to the door, whereas the 'normal' variant
is neutral in this respect.

   The following example is a translation of a letter written in
French by Anna Vul'f. (Letter Nr. 233 in the *Полное собрание* of the
works of Puškin - cf. note 14):

(125) Я поэтому совсем было успокоилась на твой счет, как вдруг
     твое письмо так неприятно меня разочаровало.

Russian native-informants commented that the subject had already
stopped worrying. When *совсем было успокоилась* was compared with
почти уже успокомлась, it was felt that in the first sentence, the
subject was more at ease than in the sentence with *почти* (which
word clearly indicates that the 'Term.' has not been attained).
(The French original - *je commençais donc à devenir tranquille* -
seems to be more close to the Russian *я уже начала было успокаи-
ваться*.)

   These observations and comments suggest that the influence of
совсем on *было*-sentences is less straightforward than the authors
cited above would lead us to believe. The presence of this adverb
does not exclude the attainment of the 'Term.', but seems to con-

centrate our attention on this 'critical point'; this may cause a certain <u>shift to the left</u> of the location of an interrupting event with respect to the corresponding *било*-sentences without *совсем*. In some cases, this apparently favours the idea of a preterminal interruption. Another (accompanying?) effect of *совсем* seems to be 'indication of intensity'. It is not entirely clear to the present writer whether the location of *совсем* in relation to *било*, and the presence or absence of *уже*, play a part here. In order to elucidate this point, a special investigation would be needed, using a larger sample.

We may conclude this section with some more examples of sentences featuring *совсем*. These will help the reader to arrive at a better understanding of its use (see also (33) and (34)):

(126) Друзья совсем <u>было</u> <u>собрались</u> во дворец, когда явился курьер герцога курляндского. (Лажечников; OIG 1964: 245)

(127) - Постой, постой! - закричал вдруг Максим Максимыч, ухватясь за дверцу коляски, - совсем <u>было</u> <u>забыл</u>... у меня остались ваши бумаги, Григорий Александрович... (Лерм.)

(128) Милый мой, еще просьба: съезди к St *Florent* (т.е. к его преемнику) и расплатись с ним за меня. Я, помнится, должен ему около 1,000 руб. Извини меня перед ним - я <u>было</u> совсем о нем <u>забыл</u>. (П: Пс 572.29)

(129) Он уже совсем <u>было</u> <u>решил</u> <u>поворачивать</u> назад, но вспомнил о недавнем столкновении с Давыдовым и изменил решение. (Шолохов; Астафьева et al. 1971: 17)

(130) В суде адвокат совсем уже <u>было</u> его <u>оправдал</u> - нет улик, да и только, как вдруг тот слушал-слушал, да вдруг встал и прервал адвоката. (Достоевский; OIG 1964: 17)

(131) /Гордей Карпыч/... Спасибо, что на ум наставили, а то <u>было</u> <u>свихнулся</u> совсем. (Островский; Шведова 1960: 113)

(132) Он был уже старым прокурором, отказавшимся от некоторых перемещений, ожидая более желательного места, когда неожиданно случилось одно неприятное обстоятельство, совсем <u>было</u> <u>нарушившее</u> его спокойствие жизни. (Л. Толстой; Nilsson 1967: 41)

10. THE RELATIONSHIP BETWEEN *чуть не* AND *было*

As is shown in the following sentences, *было* can be combined with *чуть не*:

(133) /.../ княгиня завезла меня во Французский театр, где я чуть <u>было</u> не <u>заснул</u> от скуки и усталости. (П: Пс 769.19)

(134) Ришелье за нею волочился, и бабушка уверяет, что он чуть <u>было</u> не <u>застрелился</u> от ее жестокости. (П: ПД 228.11)

(135) - Андрей, что ты?! Что ты?! Что с тобой?! - испугалась она. Он чуть <u>было</u> не <u>всхлипнул,</u> но удержался. (Расп.)

(136) Грикспоор еще больше высунулся, так, что чуть <u>было</u> не <u>вылетел</u> из беседки вместе со стулом. (Вестд.)

(137) Дно то поднималось, то опускалось, и раза два Юрий чуть <u>было</u> не <u>сорвался</u> в какие-то ямы. (Арцыбашев; Sémon 1979: 95)

(138) Идя к вам я чуть-чуть <u>было</u> не <u>поссорился</u> с отцом; скажи да скажи, куда я иду. (Pedersen 1916: 161)

Presumably all such sentences indicate that the 'Term.' has been closely approached, but not reached. However, the same interpretation seems to apply to sentences containing *чуть не* without *было*, as in the following examples:[47]

(139) Бумага чуть не выпала из моих рук. (П: КД 365.6)

(140) Прочитав это письмо, я чуть с ума не сошел. (П: КД 342.13)

(141) Выслушав сей разговор, Корсаков хотел выдти из кругу, но зашатался и чуть не упал к неописанному удовольствию государя и все веселой компании. (П: АП 18.3)

(142) Кохен /.../ побрел дальше /.../ и чуть не столкнулся с голландским эсэсовцем, который сказал ему "пардон", на что Кохен ответил "*Verzeihung*" /.../. (Вестд.)

(143) /.../ долго они за ним гонялись, особенно один раза два чуть-чуть не накинул ему на шею аркана /.../. (Лерм.)

The difference in meaning between sentences of the first type (with *было*) and sentences of the second type (without *было*) is often slight. In many sentences of the second type, *было* can be inserted without changing the meaning.[48] However, it is important to note that the combination of *чуть не* with *было* appears to be restricted to sentences containing perfective preterite forms (including particles; cf. Saenkova 1971: 301). Without *было*, *чуть не* has a much greater range of applicability: it can be combined with imperfective forms, present tense forms and adjectives, cf.:

(144) Он рассказывал мне армейские анекдоты, от которых я со
     смеху чуть не валялся /.../. (П: КД 283.15)

(145) /.../ я предвидел договременное заключение в стенах
     оренбургских, и чуть не плакал от досады. (П: КД 341)

(146) /.../ Вслед/ Она глядит и чуть не плачет. (П: ГН 92)

(147) - Эти деньги чуть не краденые.
     (А. Островский; Saenkova 1971: 301)

(148) Подумай обо всем, и увидишь, что я перед тобой не только
     прав, но чуть не свят. (П: Пс 977.5)

In sentences like these, the meaning of 'approximation' associated with *чуть не* seems to operate in an other dimension: not on a scale of temporal proximity, but on a scale of similarity. Some sentences with perfective preterite can be interpreted thus as well, and this explains why some of the combinations have virtually become set idiomatic expressions. Such expressions typically indicate a high degree of confusion (cf. (140)) or grief, as in the following example:

(149) - А уж как она его любила, чуть не умерла с горя.
     (А. Островский; Saenkova 1971: 303)

In such cases, the inclusion of *было* is less probable because it would suggest that a real change of situation, as indicated by the perfective verb, had somehow been expected.

    On the basis of these observations, it seems plausible to regard *чуть было не* as a combination in which each of the two components (*чуть не*[49] and *было*) restricts and/or modifies the applicability of the other. In conjunction with *было*, the meaning of 'approximation' associated with *чуть не* is restricted to the temporal scale and can be paraphrased as 'close approach but non-attainment of the 'Term.' of an action'. On the other hand, the meaning of *было* is modified in such a way that the non-attainment of the 'Term.', which, as we have seen above, in sentences without *чуть не* is quite exceptional, becomes the only possible interpreta-

tion. Naturally, this view of the meaning of *чуть било не* has some
implications for the meaning of *било* as well. It supposes that the
meaning of *било* must be formulated in such a way that the possibility of a shift of attention from the situation(s) following the
Term. to the preterminal situation is at least not excluded.

Even if one regards the meaning of *чуть било не* in the way
described above, i.e. as analysable into its component parts, it is
clear that there is a marked difference between the meaning of
sentences featuring this combination, and sentences in which *било*
is not combined with *чуть не*. This fact seems not to have received
sufficient attention in many accounts of *било*. Sometimes, examples
of *чуть било не* are presented alongside with 'normal' uses of *било*
without any special comment on the effect of the element *чуть не*
(cf. BAS, MAS, Dal', Šaxmatov 1941/25-27: 485, Karcevski 1927: 143
("D'autres variétés de la même modalité"), Nilsson 1967: 56,
Prokopovič 1982: 112 etc.). In Demidenko/Naumovič (1972: 64), the
only example given to illustrate *било* appears to be an example of
чуть било не!

On the other hand, one can hardly regard *чуть било не* as
having little connection with other uses of *било*. Nevertheless,
some writers do seem to take this view, e.g. Saenkova 1971, and in
RG 1980,I: 727). Consider the following statement of Saenkova: "В
компоненте *било* в составе сложной частицы *чуть било не* /.../
стирается значение частицы *било*, употребляющейся в аналитической
форме "глагол + *било*"" (1971: 302). However, Saenkova presents a
formulation of the difference between *чуть не* and *чуть било не* that
demonstrates that she is aware of the more verb-like character of
the latter particle. Whereas *чуть не* is compared with *почти*, *чуть
било не* is equated to "*бил близок к тому, чтоби*" (1971: 300). The
presence of the finite form in the latter formulation can be interpreted as an indication of the temporal dimension.

The differences between *било, совсем било, чуть било не* and
чуть не can sometimes be very subtle. This is best seen in sentences
containing the verb *забить*, cf.:

(150) Офицер воротился. - Я <u>было</u> <u>забыл</u> самое важное. Дайте мне честное слово, что все это останется между нами - честное ваше слово. (П: Д 201.23)

(151) Осман-Паша /.../ просил графа Паскевича за безопасность харема /.../. В первые дни об нем <u>было</u> <u>забыли</u>. Однажды за обедом /.../ граф вспомнил о хареме Османа-Паши и приказал г. Абрамовичу съездить в дом паши /.../. (П: ПА 480.1)

(152) Тогда Гаврик почувствовал ухо, о котором <u>было</u> <u>забыл</u>. (Катаев; Ferrell 1953: 113)

(153) /Дарья/ Ах, сударыня! я <u>было</u> и <u>забыла</u> совсем, Иван-то Петрович приказывал... (Островский; Шведова 1960: 111)

(See also (127) and (128) for other examples with *совсем*.)

(154) - Ах, да! чуть <u>было</u> не <u>забыл</u>... Пожалуйста два рубля! (Чехов; Саенкова 1971: 301)

(155) Да..., чуть <u>было</u> не <u>забыл</u> тебе <u>сказать</u>... Велите завтра наших лошадей к Федоту выслать на подставку. (Тургенев; *ibid.*)

(156) Ах! боже мой, чуть не забыл! вот тебе задача /.../. (П: Пс 115.40)

As can be seen from examples (127), (150), (153)-(156), all types can be used to convey something the speaker just remembered. However, *чуть (было) не* presents this as something that was in danger of being forgotten, whereas *(совсем) было* presents it as something that was already forgotten, but (just now) recalled. In example (150) the choice of *было* seems to be more natural than *чуть было не*: it is quite obvious that the speaker actually forgot to tell what he had to say, and only remembered after he had already left.

In the remaining examples - (151) and (152) - it would be quite unnatural to choose *чуть (было) не*, because the context clearly indicates that the thought or the feeling has been forgotten for some time.

11. *Было* IN NEGATIVE SENTENCES

Negative sentences containing *было* in which the negation of the verb is not preceded by *чуть* or *едва* are relatively rare (about 2 percent of the cases with a finite perfective preterite form). They are, nevertheless, important, because a proper definition of the meaning of *было* should be able to account for the less usual *было*-constructions as well as the more central ones.

The following instances are the only ones in the current sample, except for examples (5) and (6), given in section 2:

(157) Ваню я сперва было и не заметил. (Тургенев; Boyer/Speranski 1921/05: 253; also cited by Vinogradov 1972/47: 463 and GRJa 1960/52, I: 646)

(158) И свет совсем не тот. Мы было не заметили, да Фаластов пришел, смеется. (Сологуб)

(159) Через час я выехал, оставив Касьяну немного денег, которые он сперва было не принял, но потом, подумав и подержав их на ладони, положил за пазуху. (Тургенев; Nilsson 1967: 50)

(160) Б. Согласен.
А. Русские журналисты не заслуживали такого унизительного сравнения!
Б. А так извини: я с тобой не согласен.
А. Как так?
Б. Я было тебя не понял. Мне казалось, что ты находишь обиженными демократических писателей XVIII столетия /.../
(П: $Ж_1$ 170.29)

A little further on in the same text the same combination occurs:

(161) Б. Извини, брат. Опять было тебя не понял. Этого в газете не сказано. (П: $Ж_1$ 171.13)

All these cases can probably be seen as indicating a change that initially failed to occur. It is significant that the adverb *сперва* is present in two of the seven cases. According to a Russian colleague this adverb (or its synonym *сначала*) could be inserted in the other sentences as well.[50]

Cases like these are difficult to explain on the basis of the traditional definitions, which suggest just the opposite: something positive is intended or brought about, but somehow prevented or

cancelled by the following course of events. However, a permanent
feature of both positive and negative *било*-sentences appears to be
the idea of a <u>contrast</u> between the state of affairs directly
denoted by the *било*-verb, and a subsequent state of affairs. In
both types, the presence of *било* apparently evokes the idea of a
<u>subsequent change</u>, but in order to account for the negative cases,
the definition of the meaning of *било* should not specify whether
the subsequent change is of a negative, 'cancelled' nature (as in
the non-negated sentences) or has a positive character (as in the
negated sentences).

The suggestion of a subsequent change, which the use of *било*
apparently always conveys, presupposes a comparison between two
situations. In general, the use of a negated perfective form
suggests a situation where certain features, normally resulting
from the action denoted by the perfective verb are absent. The
choice of the perfective aspect in negative sentences usually
suggests that this change was likely to occur and could somehow
have been expected on the basis of the preceding state of
affairs.[51] It is interesting that amongst the negative *било*-sen-
tences, there is only one – example (159) – where the negation of
the perfective form is clearly accompanied by this notion of
expectation on the basis of the preceding situation: the money was
left for Kas'jan, so it would have been quite normal for him to
accept it. The sentence *он /их/ не принял* tells us that this
expected action did not follow, and Kas'jan, contrary to our
previous expectations, did not dispose of the money. However, the
presence of *било* tells us that things changed. The presence of the
adverb *сперва* reinforces the contrast.

The sentences containing *не заметил(и)*, *не узнал* and *не понял*
apparently involve a different use of the negated perfective
preterite form. In such sentences the idea of expectation on the
basis of the preceding state of affairs seems to be less prominent
or completely absent. Instead of a special relationship with a
preceding situation, we see a special relationship with a following
one, typically the speech-situation.[52] This accounts for the strong
air of <u>retrospection</u> which these sentences have. One gains the
impression of backward reasoning: the speaker points to the fact
that the subject (usually himself or including himself) has become

aware of something that he had previously <u>not yet</u> noticed. The
initial situation is negated primarily by comparison with the more
recent knowledge of the subject/speaker.

The idea of retrospection, which is a prominent feature of
such sentences, appears also relevant to all other uses of *было*.
Looking forwards in time from the situation denoted by the
было-verb, the second state of affairs is not yet real, merely
possible or expected. However, at the time of speaking, it is the
second situation which is <u>more real</u>, <u>more recent</u>. The speaker's use
of the particle *было* indicates that on the basis of his present
knowledge, he is able to state that things developed differently
from what might have been expected at the time when the state of
affairs denoted by the *было*-verb prevailed. The use of *было* presupposes knowledge which was obtained at two different points in time,
one more recent than the other. This explains why *было* can be used
only with respect to events occurring in the past.

12. *SINGLE IMPERFECTIVE PRETERITE FORMS*

As already pointed out in section 2, *было*-sentences containing
an imperfective preterite form <u>not</u> combined with an infinitive are
relatively rare. All the examples available to the author are given
below (except for examples (15), (16) and (51) already quoted in
sections 2 and 3):

(162) Каждый раз он <u>садился</u> <u>было</u>, но сразу же вставал снова.
(Forsyth 1970: 105)

(163) Также рассказывал Антон много о своей госпоже, Глафире
Петровне /.../ как некоторый господин, молодой сосед,
<u>подделывался</u> <u>было</u> к ним, часто стал наезжать, и как они для
него изволили даже надевать свой праздничный чепец, с лентами
цвету массака и желтое платье из трю-трю-левантина; но как
потом, разгневавшись на господина соседа за неприличный
вопрос: "Что, мол, должон быть у вас, сударыня, капитал?"
приказали ему от дому отказать. (Тургенев; Nilsson 1967: 47)

(164) Дело <u>решалось</u> <u>было</u> тем, что если земляки мои подпишутся,
что я точно такой-то из кизлярских пленных, то буду
отпущен. (Даль; BAS, in the article on *решаться*)

(165) <u>Ходил было</u>, да не достиг своей цели.
    (И.И. Давыдов, cited in Švedova 1960: 109 - footnote)
(166) - Catherine, значит, была у вас?
    - Была, и <u>просила было</u> ...[53]
    - И что же?
    - Разумеется, ничего. (Писемский; Švedova 1960: 113)
(167) Надобно вам знать, что я <u>готовился было</u> не в учителя, а
    в кандиторы - но мне сказали, что в вашей земле звание
    учительское не в пример выгоднее ... (П: Д 200.38)
(168) <u>Говорили было</u>, что приедут артисты, а их все нет.
    (GSRLJa 1970: 578; RG 1980, II: 101)
(169) "Слава богу!" - вскричал он, увидя меня, - Я <u>было думал</u>,
    что злодеи опять тебя подхватили. (П: КД 328.40)
(170) - Как самочувствие его высочества?
    - Сейчас он спит. Сперва <u>было</u> немного <u>нервничал</u>, но затем
    выдул бутылку коньяку и успокоился. (Степ.)

It is well known that one of the main functions of the Russian imperfective forms is to express repeated events. In such cases the imperfective form itself does not usually reflect the aspectual properties of each individual occurrence of the event. This means that in such cases, the imperfective aspect is compatible with contextual elements suggesting attainment of the 'Term.'. As we have seen, this notion of 'attainment' plays an important part in most of the *было*-constructions: practically all the examples with a perfective preterite form allowed an interpretation according to which the critical point was reached. The frequency of these cases leads to a strong association between *было* and the 'post-terminal' situation. One might have expected, therefore, that a substantial number of *было*-sentences containing an imperfective would be concerned with recurring complete events. Interestingly, this assumption is not confirmed by the facts: sentence (162) is the only example of this type. It is interesting to note that it is not found in an original Russian text, but was apparently especially constructed by Forsyth on the basis of example (102), to demonstrate the compatibility of elements like *было*, *едва не* and *чуть не* with the imperfective aspect "when a multiple action is concerned" (Forsyth 1970: 105). As my informants confirm the acceptability of this sentence, we must conclude that the system allows the possibility, although the preference for indicating non-repeated events must clearly be regarded as a very characteristic feature of the *било*-construction.[54] It seems that this cannot be adequately explained by the usual definitions of the meaning of *било*, which concentrate on the properties of the event itself. The previous discussion has shown that the use of *било* implies a comparison of the *било*-situation with a subsequent situation known to the speaker, i.e. the meaning of *било* is essentially relational. The relationship between the two situations may be so specific that it is unlikely that the whole configuration will be repeated.

In examples (163), (164) and (16), we see another important function of imperfective aspect, viz. the presentation of the action in the course of its development. This use of the imperfective preterite can have a more or less strong 'conative' or 'tendential' connotation. Examples (16) and (163) are clear examples of 'conation': a paraphrase with *питался* plus the corresponding perfective infinitive is possible here.[55] In such cases, where the aspect-opposition is strongly associated with the contrast 'attempt' - 'success' (cf. Maslov 1984/48: 59), apparently emphasises the unsuccessfulness of the action. At the very moment of naming the action, it is already indicated that the subject has not succeeded in bringing about the change of situation that he intended. In (163), the choice of the single imperfective form (*поддельвался*) may be motivated at least in part by the fact that the following expression (*часто стал наезжать*) gives more details of the same action. When there is no such reason to concentrate on the way in which the subject tries to attain his objective, a more specialised way of expressing the notion of unsuccessful attempt is normally preferred, viz. a combination of *било* with the finite form of (*по*)*питаться* or (*по*)*пробовать*, followed by the (usually perfective) infinitive[56], see (14), (20) and the following examples:

(171) Возвратясь, я <u>попытался</u> <u>было</u> <u>завести</u> речь с моим ямщиком, но он как будто избегая порядочного разговора, на вопросы мои отвечал одними: "не можем знать, Ваше Благородие, а бог знает, а не что..." (П: МЧ 405.1)

(172) Дальше Ростова, в глубь Дона и Кубани, немцы не пошли. Они
попытались было замирить Батайск /.../. Но несмотря на
ураганный огонь и кровопролитные атаки, взять его так и не
могли. (А. Толст.)

(173) Он попытался было жаловаться на то Дефоржу, но знания его
фо французском языке были слишком ограничены для столь
сложного объяснения - француз его не понял, и Антон
Пафнутьич принужден был оставить свои жалобы. (П. Д 198.19)

(174) Андрюша пытался было подойти к нему, но по дороге
споткнулся, упал, /.../ и от боли потерял сознание.
(А. Толст.)

(175) Некоторые пытались было ему подражать и выдти из пределов
должного повиновения, но Кирила Петрович так их пугнул, что
навсегда отбил у них охоту к таковым покушениям /.../.
(П: Д 162.33)

(176) Одно затрудняло ее: она попробовало было пройти по двору
босая, но дерн колол ее нежные ноги, а песок и камушки
показались ей нестерпимые. (П: БК 113.25)

(177) Уля попробовала было заговорить о посторонних делах, мать
неловко поддержала ее, но так фальшиво это прозвучало, что
обе замолкли. (Фадеев; Чернов 1970: 259)

(178) Шаповаленко пробовал было возражать... (Куприн)

When the change of situation that normally results from a given
action is not desirable, or if the action is not performed by an
animate agent, the concept of 'tendency' is more appropriate than
that of 'conation'. Example (164) could be regarded as expressing a
'tendency'. The verb *решалось* indicates a certain development: in
the given situation, all things pointed to a certain outcome - the
liberation of the hero after the fulfilment of certain conditions.
Although the further context of this example is not to hand, it
seems plausible to assume that *било* is being used to indicate that
the expected outcome was not realised, that things developed otherwise. It is interesting to note that the idea of expectation is
very prominent here: the development expressed is primarily a
projection of the things to come, based on an evaluation of the
available information.

Examples (165) and (166) bear a certain resemblance to the
'conative' cases ((163) and (16)), as they too have strong connotations of unsuccessfulness. The main difference is that the verbs
ходить and *просить* in (165) and (166) lack the strong 'terminativity' of verbs like *выписывать* and *подделываться* . The 'aim' of
the action is therefore less clearly defined in the verb itself.

In examples (167) - (169) and (15), the *было*-verbs are not
primarily associated with an 'activity', but point to something
that goes on in the mind of the subject - 'intention' (167), the
'expression of thought' (168), 'thought' (169) or 'thought accompanied by worry' (15). With the exception of (169), all these
examples contain the image of a subsequent event: 'the subject will
become a confectioner' (167); 'some artists will arrive' (168);
'the impression will weaken' (15). The use of *было* in these cases
is probably motivated by the speaker's wish to emphasise that up to
the moment of speaking, events have not taken the expected direction: the intention was not fulfilled, the artists have not yet
arrived and the impression is not weakened.[57] A similar effect can
be found in example (169). Here, again, the speaker emphasises that
the state of affairs, associated with the *было*-verb, does not coincide with the knowledge that has become available to him by the
time he makes the utterance. The only difference between (169) and
the other examples is that in (169), the event that is associated
with the *было*-situation is not a subsequent event but a preceding
one. As the following sentences demonstrate, this is not a fundamental difference, but a consequence of the fact that a verb like
думать lacks an 'inherent temporal perspective' (cf. Daneš 1975):

(179) a. А, ты здесь! А я было думал, что ты уехал! (ИНФ)
      b.   "   "   что тебя нет! (ИНФ)
      c.   "   "   что ты не придешь! (ИНФ)

There is some resemblance between the *думать*-examples and the
examples containing *не заметил(и)*, *не узнал* and *не понял* (discussed in section 11). All these examples contain the idea of
correcting one's view of the world in the light of information that
has more recently become available to the subject (typically, the
speaker).[58]

46

The fact that there is only one example of the combination of
думал + *было* in the present sample apparently relates to the
aspecto-temporal behaviour of verbs that denote thoughts and
feelings. When used in dialogues etc, i.e. in a situation where the
question of the present relevance of the actions is central the use
of imperfective preterite verb forms usually suggests that the
thought or feeling that is indicated by the verb no longer exists
at the moment of speaking; whereas the corresponding perfective
form (which often has an ingressive meaning) is normally taken to
indicate that a feeling or thought is still present. Cf. *Она мне
нравилась* vs. *Она мне понравилась*, *Мне казалось* vs. *Мне показалось*.
Думал does not, in fact, need *было* to express the change of mind:
in sentence (169), it is practically redundant, and the replacement
of *я было думал* by *А я-то думал* has hardly any effect on the
meaning. The Academic edition of Puškin's work gives some interesting variants of *Мне казалось, что ты находишь* ... at the end of
example (160): *Я думал, что ты...* and *Мне показалось было, что ты*
.... The distinctions between these variants are probably not
entirely arbitrary, but reflect the fact that with a form such as
показалось the change of mind must be explicitly indicated, and
было offers the simplest way of doing this; whereas, where *казалось*
or *думал* is used, this change is practically self-evident.

The notion of 'correcting one's view of the world', mentioned
above in connection with verbs like *думать* seems also to play a
part in the other *было*-sentences. This could be the clue to the
explanation of the use of *было* in Švedova's examples of the
'special meaning of uncertain assumption' - (51) and (52). We may
take it that in these cases, as in (167)-(169) and (15), *было* is
used primarily to emphasise the contrast between the assumptions of
the speaker, and the presentation of the real state of affairs with
which his interlocutor confronts him. The element of doubt, emphasised by Švedova, might result from the fact that it is difficult
for the speaker to accept that he apparently misjudged his own
actions. As a comparison of the two examples will show, both
aspects can occur in such cases. The choice of aspect seems to
depend on the same factors as in the case of dialogue. In (51), the
main emphasis is on the way in which the action was supposed to be
performed. This is an obvious point in favour of the choice of the

imperfective aspect. It is reinforced by factors such as doubt, and
the idea that the way in which the action was performed is open to
criticism.

Example (170), the last example to be discussed in this section, differs from the other examples containing an imperfective
preterite form. The verb *нервничать* does not evoke the idea of a
result that is to be achieved (as with *подделываться* etc.), and it
does not have a special connection with our view of the world (as
with *думать* etc.). The reason for the use of *било* with such a verb
is far from obvious, because there does not seem to be a notion of
a subsequent development that takes an unexpected turn. The only
development that can be meant here is, the continuation of the
state denoted by *нервничал*. The following part of the sentence
shows that this state came to an end. The end probably came as
something of a surprise or a relieve for the speaker, who apparently wants to emphasise the contrast between the preceding state
of nervousness and the subsequent state of tranquillity by using
the adverb *сперва*. The use of *било* in the sentence seem possible
largely on account of the presence of this adverb, which introduces
an element of comparison, contrast and development which is totally
absent from the verb itself. In a sentence like this, the particle
било seems to add very little to the total meaning of the sentence.
Its main function seems to be the strengthening of the contrast
already suggested by *сперва*.

13. *CONSTRUCTIONS CONTAINING A DEPENDENT INFINITIVE*

As stated in section 2, constructions in which *било* is used
with an imperfective preterite verb form usually contain an
infinitive. Among imperfective *било*-verbs combined with a dependent
infinitive, the verb *хотеть* undoubtedly occurs most frequently (85
percent of cases in the present sample).[59] Although the perfective
aspect predominates in *било*-sentences, the most frequently
encountered individual verb is *хотеть* (15 percent of sentences in
the sample). This seems to suggest a natural association between
хотеть and *било*; perhaps owing to the relationship between the

meaning of *хотеть* and the thought of future events: the meaning of *хотеть* is orientated towards the future.

Usually, the infinitive is in the perfective aspect. Sentences containing *хотел было* + a perfective infinitive are common enough; a few examples will suffice (see also (17), (18) and (28)):

(180) Привыкнув не церемониться с хорошенькими поселянками, он было хотел обнять ее; но Лиза отпрыгнула от него и приняла на себя такой строгий /.../ вид, что /.../   П:(БК 114.32)

(181) Я было хотел его успокоить; он мне сказал: Vous ne connaissez pas ces gens-là /.../. (П: ПА 461.1)

(182) Хотели уже было выпустить пару снарядов прямо в море, /.../ когда несколько легких японских крейсеров приблизились к Артуру. (Степ.)

(183) Я хотел было заикнуться о понятых, но Меркулов /.../ уже быстро шел, почти бежал к оранжерее /.../. (Незн.)

(184) Лев Иванович хотел было прочитать Ленькино сочинение, но завуч Мария Васильевна взяла его первой. (Сем.)

(185) Хотел было я прислать вам отрывок из моего Кавказского Пленника, да лень переписывать. (П: Пс 26.21)

(186) Что моя трагедия? отстойте ее, храбрые друзья! не дайте ее на съедение псам журналистам. Я хотел ее посвятить Жуковскому со следующими словами: я хотел было посвятить мою трагедию Карамзину, но так как нет уже его, то посвящаю ее Жуковскому. Дочери Карамзина сказали мне, чтоб я посвятил любимый труд памяти отца. /Which Puškin actually did!/ (П: Пс 528.19)[60]

It is interesting to note that in most cases, *хотел* has an 'active' meaning: it denotes the preliminaries of a 'controlled' action in which the subject will take an active part.[61] It is often clear that this activity has already started (see (180) and (181)). In such cases, the meaning conveyed by the construction comes very close to that conveyed by *было*-sentences having a single imperfective form from with 'conative' meaning (see (16) and (163)), or sentences with *(по)пытаться* ets. ('unsuccesful attempt') (see (171)-(178)). As in exampeles (171)-(178), the perfective infinitive denotes the change in situation at which the subject is aiming. The speaker's use of *было* immediately makes it clear that aim has

not been achieved. This type of было-construction may bear a special responsibility for the popularity of the definitions based on
the notion of non-completion.[62]

The meaning of было typically includes the idea of comparing/
contrasting two views of a set of circumstances, dating from
different points in time: one located in the past and directed
towards the future and the other located in the present and directed towards the past. The first view indicates one's expectations
regarding subsequent developments starting with the было-event;
this view is based on knowledge of the situation in which this
event takes place plus general experience of how things tend to
develop. The second view indicates the way things actually turned
out, which became apparent to the speaker before or at the moment
of speech. This knowledge of the real course of events enables the
speaker to evaluate the expectations previously connected with the
было-event. The use of было signals or emphasises the existence of
a certain contrast between the expected and the actual course of
events. The relative weight given to each view seems to differ in
different instances. In sections 11 and 12, we saw a number of
cases where the 'retrospective' view is more important. The sentences with хотел было can be roughly divided into two groups
according to whether the main emphasis lies on the view taken at
the moment of speech, or that taken at the time of the было-event.
Examples (180)-(183) rather fall within the latter group: in these
cases, the meaning of хотел было is often something like 'to be on
the point of'.[63] In examples (185)-(186) (and possibly (184)), the
view taken at the moment of speech seems to be more important: here
the meaning of хотел было is closer to '(I) had meant to' or '(I)
had intended to' (cf. Borras/Christian 1971/59: 140).[64]

Although the perfective infinitive is most common after хотел
было, the imperfective does occur as well. Contrary to Černov's
assertion (1970: 260), this is not limited to unprefixed verbs of
motion. The following are all the examples currently to hand (see
also (18):

(187) - Работать надо, факт! - резко ответил Давыдов и хотел было
        идти, но Лушка, чуть смутившись, его удержала.
        (Шолохов; Černov 1970: 260)

(188) Она раскрыла зонтик и <u>хотела</u> <u>было</u> <u>итти</u> домой, как вдруг из-за
угла избушки выехал, на низеньких беговых дрожках, человек
лет тридцати... (Тургенев; Ferrell 1953: 113)

(189) Мятежники <u>хотели</u> <u>было</u> <u>ехать</u> к Аракчееву в Грузино, чтоб
убить его, а дом разграбить. 30 троек были уже готовы.
Жандармский офицер, взявший над ними власть, успел
уговорить их оставить это намерение. (П: Ж$_2$ 200.25)

(190) Дедушка <u>хотел</u> <u>было</u> Ванюшу-то в полицию <u>нести</u>, да я
отговорила: возьмем, мол, себе... (Горьк.)

(191) Татьяна <u>хотела</u> <u>было</u> сперва <u>отвечать</u>, что нет , но,
одумавшись, сказала: "Да, немножко". (Тургенев; Nilsson
1967: 44)

(192) Выбор гимназии состоялся не сразу. Меня <u>хотели</u> <u>было</u>
<u>отдавать</u> в кадеты. (Боборыкин; Borras/Christian (1971/59: 140)

(193) Я <u>хотел</u> <u>было</u> <u>продолжать</u>, как начал, и объяснить мою связь
с Марьей Ивановной так же искренно, как и все прочее. Но
вдруг почувствовал непреодолимое отвращение. (П: КД 368.11)

(194) Я <u>хотел</u> <u>было</u> <u>противиться</u>, хотел было протестовать, чтобы он
выстрелил в меня; но он подошел ко мне и протянул мне
руку. (Тургенев; Nilsson 1967: 56)

(195) Исправник понизил голос и <u>хотел</u> <u>было</u> их <u>уговаривать</u>. - Да что
на него смотреть, - закричали дворовые, - ребята! долой их! -
и вся толпа двинулась. (П. Д 181.21)

With regard to (192), Borras/Christian suggest that "The imperfective infinitive here gives the sense of uncertainty and discussion". The choice of the imperfective aspect after *хотеть* (in
positive sentences) usually tends to emphasise the action itself,
or the start of the action ("приступ к действию"). This same effect
seems to be a feature of *было*-sentences.

In conjunction with an infinitive, the verbs *намереваться* and
собираться are fairly close synonyms of *хотеть*. It is, therefore,
not surprising that these verbs also occur in *было*-sentences. The
following are examples of such occurrences:

(196) Я сам хучь и не пробовал так сеять, но в этом году уж <u>было</u>
<u>намеревался</u> <u>спытать</u>. (Шолохов; Чернов 1970: 259)

(197) Дельвиг <u>собирался было написать</u> вам вместе со мною длинное
письмо, чтобы просить вас быть осмотрительным! (Translation
from the French, page 558 of volume XIII of the Poln. sobr.
soč. Puškina)

Regarding *собирался*, Borras/Christian state that this verb "is used
almost exclusively with reference to long journeys (1971/59: 140).
They give the following example:

(198) Я <u>собирался было поехать</u> этим летом на море, но
обстоятельства помешали.

However, this meaning does not predominate amongst the limited
number of instances in the sample. See (21), (197) and the
following:

(199) Соня <u>собиралась было пойти</u>, но читательская конференция
совпала с днем рождения отца. (Эренбург; Forsyth 1970: 105)
(200) На следующее утро матушка /.../ <u>собиралась было послать</u> к
нему нарочного, как он сам опять появился перед нею.
(Тургенев; Nilsson 1967: 45 and 49)
(201) Я все шел и уже <u>собирался было прилечь</u> где-нибудь до утра,
как вдруг очутился над страшной бездной. (Тургенев;
Nilsson 1967: 45)

It is interesting to note that in the present sample, the
perfective construction *собрался* + *было* + infinitive occurs three
times as often as the same construction with *собираться*. This
perfective verb has an 'ingressive' meaning: it denotes the
emergence of the intention, the existence of which is denoted by
собираться.[65] Consider the following examples:

(202) Он <u>собрался было вызвать</u> такси, но именно в эту минуту —
трах! — постучалась Старая Лошадь. (В. Каверин)
(203) Мимо Красавина прошла последняя сотня. Он <u>собрался было
идти</u>, как вдруг в темноте послышался конский топот.
(Листовский; Белошапкова 1961: 42, 43)
(204) Он (Схюлтс) уже <u>было собрался</u> по привычке <u>начать</u>
отгадывать, откуда родом каждый из них, когда его тронули
за плечо и повели в другую комнату. (Вестд.)

(205) Он /.../ уже совсем <u>было</u> <u>собрался</u> <u>отправиться</u> восвояси, да
как-то разговорился и остался. (Тургенев; OIG 1964: 244)

(206) "/.../ перенести могилку надо. Потому что то место, где она
находится, уйдет под воду. Там, - говорит, - будет
водохранилище". Кондрат <u>было</u> <u>собрался</u> <u>переносить</u>, а я
сказала, что на это не согласная. Пусть наш хлопчик лежит,
как лежал. (Пауст.)

(207) Дирке Бовенкамп /.../ отогнала наседок и только <u>было</u>
<u>собралась</u> <u>пойти</u> <u>взглянуть</u> на ведра для молока /.../, - как
на гумне появилась /.../ Марья. (Вестд.)

(208) Я пришел сюда. Ее мать /.../ <u>собралась</u> <u>было</u> <u>уходить</u>, чтоб
нас одних оставить: Надя ее к этому приучила. "Останься,
мама, - Надя ей тогда сказала, - посиди с нами /.../". (Сем.)

As these examples show, the meaning of the sentences containing
собрался было comes close to that of sentences with *собирался было*
or *хотел было*, in spite of the different aspect. The presence of
the intention can be indicated equally clearly by *собрался* or
собирался, although the former gives a slightly more dynamic
character to the sentence, which makes it preferable in sentences
like (207) (with the adverb *только*), or (208), where a connection
with the preceding action is of some importance.[65]

14. *CONCLUSION*

The argument presented in this article can be summarised as
follows:

<u>The use of the particle *было* signals or emphasises a disturb-
ance of the natural flow of the events which started with the
было-event.</u>
<u>This disturbance has become apparent before, or at, the moment
of speech.</u>

This definition should, of course, be supplemented by examples of
actual use, to illustrate the range of interpretational variants.

it should also be accompanied by a fuller explanation of some
elements in the definition. They have been discussed in detail
in the main body of the article. The following are the most
important:[66]

a)   The *било*-event is the event directly indicated by the predicative centre of the *било*-phrase (in the case of an elliptical
sentence, the picture of this event is reconstructed on the basis
of the object and/or adverbial modifier(s)). Usually, the *било*-
event is expressed by a finite verb. For other forms to convey the
било-event, see section 3.
b)   The idea of 'the natural flow of events'[67] is central to the
definition. It is based on the idea that the subjects of the speech
act have experiential knowledge of the usual relations between
events, which determines their expectations regarding a plausible
continuation of a given course of events. The existence of these
expectations is especially apparent in those cases where we need to
indicate that they have not been fulfilled, for instance, in certain sentences with adversative meaning (when a clause, introduced
by *но*, indicates a subsequent event). The same applies to the *било*-
construction: the narrative up to (and including) the *било*-event
provides a basis for regarding various possible continuations as
more or less probable.
      Since the perfective aspect presents an event as part of a
certain whole, this is the typical form for the presentation of the
flow of events. The importance of this notion for the *било*-con-
struction explains its frequent association with the perfective
aspect.
      The notion of the 'natural flow of events' must be taken as
broadly as possible: it does not only apply to 'material' events,
but also to the development of our view of the world.
c)   The term 'disturbance' must also be taken very broadly. In
this definition, it only means that at the moment of speaking
things appeared to be different from what might have been expected
at the time of the *било*-event. This implies a certain element of
contrast, which explains why *било*-clauses are very frequently
followed by adversative conjunctions like *но*, *да* and *а*.[68]

d)   In the definition, the *было*-event is presented as the starting-point of the flow of events that is disturbed. This indicates that the disturbance normally occurs only after the part of the event that is denoted by the given aspectual form, i.e. with a perfective form, the critical point ('Term.') is normally reached.[6.9]

e)   The second part of the definition indicates that the future developments expected at the time of the *было*-event are contrasted with the actual course of events known at the moment of speech. This implies that the *было*-event is located in the past, which explains why past tenses are normally used in this construction.

University of Amsterdam

NOTES

*   I would like to thank my colleagues C.E. Keijsper and R. Sprenger for their comments on earlier versions of parts of this article. I am extremely grateful to Anne Thomas who did a wonderful job correcting and editing my English.
        When referring to books or articles that were first published in an earlier edition than the one I used, I indicate both dates if known to me, e.g. 1968/62 means: first published in 1962; edition used here published in 1968.

[1]   It is generally assumed now that the *было*-construction evolved from a younger variant of the Old-Russian pluperfect: the combination of the *л*-participle with the perfect form of the auxiliary *быти*. The following example of this construction is cited by Potebnja (1888/74: 266): *Ты мя еси, сыну, самъ позывалъ Киеву, а язъ есмь былъ цѣловалъ хрестъ къ брату своему Дюргеви* (Ipat'ev chronicle; emphasis mine - A.A.B.). The present tense auxiliary (*есмь, еси* etc.) of the perfect could be omitted from an early stage and around the beginning of the 17th century, the neuter form *было* gradually began to replace the element *былъ, была* (etc.), i.e. the latter element lost its agreement in number and gender with the *л*-participle of the verb, and became an uninflected form - a particle. The meaning of the contemporary *было*-construction has apparently evolved from one of the variants of meaning of the preceding construction, relating to the use of the pluperfect in compound sentences with adversative meaning.

        Information on the history of the relevant forms can be found in the following sources: Potebnja (1888/74: 265-268), Sobolevskij (1907[4]: 164, 239-243), Isačenko (1940: 194-195), Nikiforov (1952: 163-165), Černyx (1953: 346-347), Kuznecov (1959: 231-232), Cocron (1962: 236-238), Kiparsky (1967: 229-230), Veyrenc (1970: 83), Sumnikova (in RJa 1979: 211), Pennington (1980: 283-284), Eckert et al. (1983: 172).

        Judging from the limited number of early examples of the use of the *было*-construction in the 17th century found in the above sources, the meaning of the construction at that time cannot be fully equated with its meaning in modern Russian, as discussed in this article. This point does not seem to be sufficiently appreciated in the grammatical literature: the 17th century construction and the modern construction are often defined in the same way. In this article I confine myself to modern Russian. The earliest examples to be discussed are from Puškin. My Russian contacts feel that there is no significant difference in meaning between *было* in contemporary Russian and as used in the early 19th century. For this reason, I feel free to take examples from the whole period of modern Russian.

For ease of reference, I shall underline the elements of the *было*-construction in all the examples.

[2] Authors differ considerably in the extent to which they use *было*. This seems to be primarily a matter of individual style (cf. Nilsson 1967: 42). The following figures show frequency of use of *было* in a comparable amount of text taken from two authors from each of three different periods:

	Number of pages:	Number of examples:	
Early 19th century:			
Puškin:	156	33	
Lermontov:	160	10	
First half of 20th century:			
A. Tolstoj:	525	20	(cf.: Stepanov: 383 - 37!)
Gor'kij:	600	3	
Contemporary writers:			
Neznanskij:	330	17	
Semenov:	340	6	

(The Puškin texts used for this comparison are: *Капитанская дочка* and *Повести Белкина* (without *Барышня-Крестянка*). The other texts used here are indicated in note 15.)

[3] In my opinion, the relevant sections of Unbegaun's grammar (1951: 253-254), the textbooks of Borras/Christian (1971/59: 139-140), and the much older Boyer/ Spéranski (1921/05: 252-253), offer the best descriptions in the non-specialist literature.

[4] For instance, in prestigious works such as: *Kurs sovremennogo russkogo jazyka* by Bolla, Pall and Papp (Budapest, 1970), *Die russische Sprache der Gegenwart. 2. Morphologie* by Mulisch et al. (Leipzig, 1975) and *Russkaja grammatika 1* by Barnetová et al. (Prague, 1979). Even in a special textbook on particles, (A.N. Vasilyeva: *Particles in colloquial Russian*, Progress Publishers - Moscow) no mention is made of *было*.

[5] Cf. AC: "/означение/ действия начатого или только предположенного, но не совершившегося."

The definitions in Ožegov and SATG are essentially identical with Ušakov's:
Ожегов: "действие началось или было предположено, но не совершилось."
САТГ: "действие началось, предполагалось, но не совершилось."

[6] In this dictionary, *было* does not have an entry of its own. It is discussed within the article on *быть*.

[7] Kunert opposes the meaning of this construction to the meaning of the imperfective aspect, which, according to him, does not make any statement about the completion of the action, and can therefore be used to indicate a) actions stopped before their completion, b) completed actions viewed before their completion or without emphasising their 'completed' nature.

[8] 'Man könnte vielleicht sagen, dass E. Guertik "se précipiter pour ouvrir la porte" als eine einzige Handlung betrachtet, die sie wie der Autor des russischen Textes als nicht zu ende geführt ansieht, während Ergaz die Handlung "se précipiter" von "ouvrir la porte" trennt und so die Handlung "se précipiter" als vollständig realisiert bezeichnen kann, auch wenn die Tür nicht geöffnet worden ist." (Kunert 1984: 153).

[9] Even if we accept Kunert's suggestion and take the whole combination as denoting one complex action, the decisive moment must be the (non)completion of the component denoted by the infinitive.

[10] The abbreviation (ИНФ) indicates that an example was constructed for the purpose of this article, and accepted by a native speaker of Russian.

[11] Examples containing an infinitive can also present problems. If the idea of non-completion applies to the action denoted by the infinitive, perhaps it follows that we know what the completed action would have looked like, and that it should, therefore, be indicated by a 'terminative' verb. The close relation-ship between 'terminativity' and the perfective aspect could explain the frequent use of the perfective infinitive in such constructions (see (2) and (3)). However examples like the following sentence from Puskin's 'Dubrovskij' seem to contradict this view:

Увидя его, они бросились было бежать. Дубровский со своим кучером поймал из них двоих и привел их связанных к себе на двор. (П: Д 165.8)

[12] Some examples were kindly provided by colleagues and students of mine. I am especially indebted to Ms. M. Dekker for the example using *начинаю* (36) and to my colleague H. Proeme for the example using *решалось* (164).

[13] In this article, except when stated otherwise, occurrences of *было* with *чуть не* are not considered. (The *чуть (было) не*-construction is discussed in section 10 of this article.)

In SJaP, 151 instances are given. Volume Ж₁ contains three cases where *было* is part of a fragment of test that can be found on two different pages (in identical or very slightly modified form) (151.21=169.21; 151.28=169.28; 224.14=244.35). I count these instances once only. This leaves 148 examples, to which can be added one example that does not occur in the main text, but is mentioned as a variant (*мне показалось было* as a variant of *мне казалось* on page 170 of the same volume).

In this article, examples from Puškin will be indicated by the letter П, followed by the SJaP code to indicate its exact place location (cf. the example in the previous note).

[14] А.С. Пушкин, *Полное собрание сочинений,* тт. 1-16. М.: Изд. АН СССР. 1937-1949.

[15] The following texts were searched for occurrences of *было*. Sometimes only part of a book has been used. The figures after the texts indicate the number of pages searched followed by the number of examples found there. The abbreviations given after these figures are used in the main body of the article to refer to these texts:

19th century:
М.Ю Лермонтов: *Герой нашего времени* and *Вадим*.   (160 - 10); Лерм.
Л.Н. Толстой: *Севастопольские рассказы*.   (130 - 5); Л. Толст.

20th century:
М. Горький: *Детство, В людях* and *Мои университеты*. (600 - 3); Горьк.
Ф. Незнанский: *Ярмарка в Сокольниках*.   (330 - 17); Незн.

К. Паустовский:	*Рождение моря.*	(150 – 1); Пауст.
В. Распутин:	*Живи и помни.*	(180 – 4); Расп.
Ю. Семенов:	*Петровка, 38* and *Огарева, 6.*	(340 – 6); Сем.
А. Степанов:	*Порт-Артур. Книга первая.*	(383 – 37); Степ.
А.Н. Толстой:	*Хождение по мукам.*	(525 – 20); А. Толст.

Alongside these original Russian texts, the following translation of a
contemporary Dutch novel is included:
С. Вестдейк: *Пастораль сорок третьего года.* (Translation by I. Volevič and
Šečkova)   (332 – 10); Вестд.

[16]   The question of the position of *было* in the sentence will not be treated in
this article. Some comments and information can be found in Švedova (1960: 111,
112) and Nilsson (1967: 42). Garde classifies *было* (together with *бы*) as an
enclitic that can occupy either of the two typical positions: after the word it
depends on (*я забыл было*), or after the first word of the sentence (*я было
забыл*) (1980: 119). It seems to me that these rules have to be refined to
account for all uses represented in the present sample. Some of the problematic
examples are cited in this article, cf. (99), (107), (113) and (151).

[17]   N.B. *чуть было не* constructions are treated here as a different (though
related) construction (cf. section 10). They are excluded from the various
counts.

[18]   The only example of imperfective preterite + *было* that indicates a repeated
event will be discussed in section 12.

[19]   All 25 participial constructions in the sample, with the exception of one
example given by Švedova (1960: 112) contain a perfective participle. Švedova's
example of an <u>imperfective</u> preterite participle is: *хотевший было*. Unfortunately, this example is given with no context or indication of the source.
Although the *было*-construction with an imperfective preterite participle is
certainly very rare, there seems to be no reason in principle for excluding the
possibility. A native Russian speaker accepted the replacement of *которые хотели
было подсадить его* in example (28) by *хотевших было подсадить его*, and the
replacement of *готовые* in (34) by *намеревавшиеся*.

[20]   Amongst the 149 examples from Puškin there is only 1 perfective gerund (but
no participles at all). Amongst the other 387 examples in the sample there are
27 active participles, 5 passive participles and only 4 gerunds. In approximately 2500 pages of text examined (see note 15), no passive participles and
gerunds were found, and only 7 active participles.

[21]   The most obvious form for expressing habitual past events is, of course,
the imperfective preterite. A *было*-sentence of this type will be discussed in
section 12.

[22]   According to Černov, the same applies to the use of present tense forms,
discussed in the preceding part of this section: "В наши дни модальную
конструкцию с частицей *было* образуют и формы настоящего времени" (Černov 1970:
261).

[23]   The same applies to this sentence cited by Potebnja (1888:74: 268): *быть,
было, ненастью, да дождь помешал.* Apparently this sentence is of the same type
as the following sentence from Kotošixin: *прибыль которой было быть в котором
году.* The latter sentence is discussed by Pennington (1980: 284). According to
this author, in sentences like this (characterised by a 'subject' in the dative
case), *было* has only a temporal significance, and lacks the modal sense of the

typical *было* construction (which also occurs twice in Kotošixin's work).

Another example of *было* + infinitive which apparently cannot be interpreted as an instance of the *было*-construction as studied in this article is the following sentence from the dictionary of Dal': *взяться было за ум вовремя*.

[24] Unfortunately I have not been able to consult the dissertations of Saenkova and Novgorodova (or their *авторефераты*):
Н.А. Саенкова: *Модально-приглагольные частицы было и бывало и конструкции, образуемые при их участии в современном русском языке*. АКД. Москва, 1968.
Р.Т. Новгородова: *Значение и употребление частицы "было" в современном русском литературном языке*. АКД. Новосибирск, 1971.

[25] A rather different view of the meaning of *было* has been presented by Ferrell, according to whom the main function of *было* has much in common with the English pluperfect. Ferrell emphasizes that *было* restricts the use of the preterite form in conjunction with which it occurs to describing "an action with reference to time prior to the moment of utterance"; and that it additionally marks this time as "asynchronic with the time of discourse" (1953: 113). This asynchronism can arise from one of two possible circumstances: a) "the action denoted may have been realized prior to the time of discourse" - "In this function, as Professor Roman Jakobson has pointed out, the use of the non-present with *было* closely approximates to that of the English pluperfect" - and b) "The non-present with *было* can on occasion be used to describe an uneventuated action with reference to time prior to the moment of utterance". Only the latter variant falls within one of the groups of definitions discussed in section 4 of this article (group A), as it means, that "the action is not carried out in its entirety". Ferrell cites Šaxmatov's example *Мальчик упал было*, in which sentence, according to Ferrell, "the verb can mean 'all but fell', or 'nearly fell'; i.e. the sentence means the same as *Мальчик чуть было не упал*. However, at this point Ferrell notes that his "younger informants apparently all feel that *было* is now used only to form a pluperfect" (114), i.e. variant a). As this variant seems to admit the possibility of completion of the action, it might be thought that it falls within our second group of definitions, i.e. the definitions that suggest that the results of the action are unsatisfactory or cancelled. However, no statement to this effect is made by Ferrell, and so far as I know, this is at best a marginal feature of the English pluperfect.

[26] In §555 (page 485) of his book Šaxmatov presents constructions with *было* as instances of a special mood: "недействительное наклонение". This mood is described as follows: "Говорящий, устанавливая связь субъекта с предикатом, посредством этого наклонения выражает, что связь эта не осуществилась, хотя и могла осуществиться.". Belošapkova states that in sentences where the conjunction *как вдруг* is used, the particle *было* is the formal expression of the meaning of "прерванность, недействительность"" (1961: 42; emphasis mine - A.A.B.). This apparently refers To Šaxmatov's notion of "недействительное наклонение".

[27] On page 392 of part II (Syntax) of this grammar, a different formulation can be found: "/выражение/ действия, которое было начато, но прервано или не дало желаемого результата". Because of the presence of the attribute "желаемый", this definition might be considered as belonging to group B.

[28] Cf. Kiparsky (1967: 230): "die heutige Konstruktion было + *l*-Partizip /.../, die einen Vorgang bezeichnet, der in der Vergangenheit zwar einsetzt, aber aus irgendeinem Grunde unterbrochen wird und auf Deutsch am besten durch "beinahe schon", auf Französisch durch 'a failli de' auf Finnisch durch den sog.

V. Infinitiv (*oli -maisillaan*) wiedergegeben wird."

In an article published in 1940, Isačenko discusses the predecessor of this construction - the pluperfect with finite form of the verb *быти* that agrees with the grammatical subject. According to Išačenko, these complex forms "gradually acquired a secondary meaning. They indicated an <u>action which was interrupted and rendered ineffective by some other action</u>" (1940: 195; emphasis mine - A.A.B.). Apparently Isačenko assumes that the modern *было*-construction has approximately the same meaning.

In the same article Išačenko points to the fact that the particle *было*, which replaced the inflected auxiliary, can now be used with participles as well. The example he gives is practically identical with the example in his later published grammar: *он/я разбудил заснувшего было товарища*. It is interesting to note that the translations he provides reflect a considerable difference in the interpretation of this sentence, cf.: "he woke the comrade who had been sleeping for a little while" (1940: 195) and "ich weckte den Kameraden, der beinahe schon eingeschlafen war" (1968/62: 606).

[29] This formulation seems to suggest that the *было*-action has to be 'controlled', or at least ascribed to an 'animate' subject. Although that type of *было*-sentences (i.e. with human 'agents' and 'controlled actions') is indeed the most frequently encountered, instances of other types of action and/or subject (or even impersonal sentences) are not at all uncommon. Some examples have already been given in the preceding sections ((23), (34) and (35)). Some additional examples are presented here:

(I) *Возник было пожар, но тотчас был потушен.* (Степ.)
(II) *Мелькнули было в памяти яркие обрывки дня, /.../. Но воспоминания вонзались в мозг так болезненно, /.../, что Иван Ильич замычал: скорее, скорее о чем-нибудь другом....* (А. Толст.)
(III) *Эта схоластическая величавость полу-славенская, полу-латинская, сделалась-было необходимостью: к счастию Карамзин освободил язык от чуждого ига и возвратил ему свободу /.../.* (П: Ж₁ 249.13)
(IV) *Начало было моросить, но потом посветлело.* (GSRLJa 1970: 578; also cited in RG 1980, II: 101).

[30] On page 119 of Garde's book, the formulation "action manquée" is used. This could be viewed as belonging to group B.

[31] A little earlier in the fragment cited by Švedova, Aksakov criticises Buslaev's definition (A3 above) and lays strong emphasis upon the completion the action: "-*я было пошел, я было сделал*; это совсем не то, что "несовершенное действие"; напротив: действие о котором говорится, совершено, но должно быть опять или прекращено (напр. : *я было стал читать...* да печать очень мелка), или уничтожено (напр. *я было заснул*, да меня разбудили), или обращено назад, т.е. тоже уничтожено (напр.: *я было воротился с прогулки...* да вас увидел в саду и пошел к вам)." (emphasis mine - A.A.B.) If taken literally, the first option seems contradictory: "совершено /.../ но /... прекращено". The contradiction can perhaps be resolved by applying the first characterisation to the 'action' denoted by the finite form (*стал*), and the second one to the action by the infinitive (*читать*).

[32] In this passage, Potebnja does not in fact describe the 'modern' use of *было*, but one of the variants of meaning of an earlier construction from which the *было*-construction originates: the pluperfect with the preterite of the auxiliary *быти* (cf. note 1).

[33] The same definition is given by Švedova in the article on particles (*частицы*) in RJa 1979: 390.

[34] In part II of this grammar, a different formulation is used: "предикативный признак проявился, но /.../ он или был прерван, или не дал ожидаемого результата" (RG 1980, II: 102).

[35] The opposite is also possible: owing to the vagueness of Davydov's definition (B1), it is difficult to decide whether it falls within group A or group B.

[36] The term 'situation' is used here as a blanket term to cover all temporal features; differences between 'actions', 'states' etc. are left out of consideration.

[37] As will be discussed in section 7, example (54) cannot be explained even in this way.

[38] As with *бросится* , all these verbs can also be used without an infinitive. In such sentences, the 'ingressiveness' is probably slightly less prominent. Cf. (66), for an example of *пойти*, and the next two sentences:
(I) *Боцман кинулся было вниз, /.../ но изрешеченный пробоинами "Страшный" уже сам стал быстро погружаться носом в воду.* (Степ.)
(II) *- виноват, батюшка Кирила Петрович, я было рано пустился в дорогу, да не успел отъехать и десяти верст, вдруг шина у переднего колеса пополам - что прикажешь?* (П: Д 192.19)

[39] Cf. a similar use of *начинаю* (in *praesens historicum*) in example (36).

[40] It is interesting to note that a number of other verbs are used with the same function, although, with the exception of *заикнуться*, they have only an indirect connection with the notion of inception:
(I) *Раненько, Ваишество /.../ заикнулся было Павел Трофимович.* (Салтыков-Щедрин; Boyer/Spéranski 1921/05: 253)
(II) *Часть солдат, приняв это обращение за приветствие, гаркнула было: "Здрав..., но, не поддержанная другими, тут же сконфуженно замолчала.* (Степ.)
(III) *Так вот что... промолвил было я и прикусил язык.* (Тургенев; Nilsson 1967: 48)
(IV) *- Едем в морг на опознание. - А... - я было раскрыл рот, толком не зная, что спросить, и потому замолк на полуслове.* (Незн.)
Apparently the combination *раскрыл было рот* can be used only when the speech has hardly begun (cf. "*замолк на полуслове*"), or is not yet begun, cf.:
(VI) *Мазер обвел глазами присутствующих, давая понять, что он хочет поговорить со мной наедине, и я было уже раскрыл рот, чтобы выпроводить лейтенанта Гречанника и майора Погорелова, как вдруг вперед, по-петушиному, выступил Гречанник и произнес: /.../.* (Незн.)

[41] Cf. the comment of Borras/Christian on example (94): "the note was written but the logical result of it having been written - its dispatch and receipt - was frustrated" (1971/59: 139).
It might be objected that the notion of its destruction does not necessarily imply that the document was finished. However, in the cases where an unfinished document is destroyed, apparently the verb *начать* is used instead of *написать*, cf. the following examples from Turgenev, given by Nilsson (1967: 48):
(I) *Базаров начал было письмо к отцу, да разорвал его и бросил под стол.*
(II) *Он начал было письмо к Верочке, к Петру Васильевичу - и тотчас разорвал и бросил начатые листы.*

[42] Another possible interpretation is that the text was read by the addressee, but did not prevent his flight.

[43] Forsyth's translation - "Dampfer was just going to sit down..." - accords with his view that the action cannot be carried to its conclusion. It is, however, possible that Dampfer did sit down, but only very briefly.

[44] Nilsson (1967: 51-52) discusses an example of the same combination taken from Turgenev: *раскрыл было книгу*. Here it is less clear whether or not the subject had already managed to look at the contents of the book.

[45] Some other interesting examples of this type (from Turgenev) are discussed by Nilsson (1967: 52-54), who comments that the use of *было* in such cases seems "outside the usages described in the grammar".

[46] Cf. the definition of Černov who even uses the Russian equivalent of the term *terminus*: "конечный предел" (A16).

[47] The combination *едва не* has a similar function, cf. the following examples:
(I) *Бедняк от радости едва не помешался.* (Крылов; Saenkova 1971: 301)
(II) */.../ и вдруг сильный толчок едва не сбросил меня в море.* (Лерм.)
Although in principle it seems possible to combine this particle with *было*, examples from literary texts are lacking. The only example at my disposal is given by Šaxmatov:
(III) *он едва было не ударил меня* (1941/25-27: 485)
For this reason, constructions using *едва не* are left regarded as outside the scope of this article.

[48] In SJaP *чуть было не* is treated as a variant of *чуть не*. In Puškin's works, the relative frequency of these variants in sentences with a perfective preterite is as follows: 11 cases of *чуть было не* vs. 32 cases of *чуть не*.

[49] This does not mean that I regard a further analysis of *чуть не* impossible. As is well known *чуть* is not always accompanied by a negation and it might well be that it is possible to formulate a 'general meaning' for both components that can account for all their uses.

[50] Example (161) must be excluded here because it is almost a repetition of (160).

[51] See Forsyth (1970: 104) and Rassudova (1982: 70) for a discussion of the notion of expectation, associated with negated perfective forms. This is exemplified in sentences such as: *Он споткнулся, но не упал.*

[52] These two types of use of negated perfective preterite forms reflect the distinction that is usually made between the "аористическое значение" and the "перфектное значение" of this form (cf. Bondarko 1971: 95). In the latter case, the past event characterises a later time (typically the 'moment of speech') that serves as a kind of orientation-point. The cases of "aorist-function" are usually defined negatively as the absence of such a typical link with the orientation-point of the speaker. In my opinion, however, the action in these cases is linked with something more: it is presented as part of a certain "chain of events", in which it is linked with previous and/or subsequent events. The notion of expectation which is often present in sentences with a negated perfective preterite form results from the linkage with a previous situation.

In my opinion, both the linkage of events in the "aorist-function", and the special linkage with the orientation-point in the "perfect function" result from a common feature that is an essential element of the meaning of the perfective aspect in Russian. I have labelled this element "(contrasting) sequential connection" (cf. Barentsen 1985: 60). It presupposes two other features. The first I label "event-unit". This signifies that the meaning of the given verb is such that the event is associated with a certain discrete unit, that the boundaries of the event are relatively clearly defined, and so it is clear what kind of change a complete event brings about. (This notion of an "event-unit" closely corresponds to the property that is usually denoted by terms such as "terminativity" or "boundedness"). The second feature is "totality": the presentation of the event-unit as a single whole, a totality (which implies the attainment of the "terminus"). The deciding feature "(contrasting) sequential connection" implies that this event-unit, which is itself viewed as a whole, is also presented as a specific link in a greater whole: in this way, the changes that are brought about by the completed event are emphasised.

[53] In view of the elliptical character of this sentence, it is not clear whether the example must be regarded as an instance of a было-sentence with single imperfective preterite form, or as an instance of the more common construction of imperfective preterite + infinitive.

[54] The two было-sentences containing a perfective present form - (40 and (41) - and the one example with an imperfective present form - (42) - are the only other examples I know of было-sentences referring to a repeated event.

[55] The 'conative' character of (16) is recognised by Mazon, who uses the term "prétérit imperfectif de tentative" (1914: 180). With respect to (163), Nilsson tries to explain the imperfective aspect by referring to its 'durative' character. In his article, the following comment precedes the presentation of this example: "Было is usually encountered in connection with perfective verbs. That this should be so is easy enough to understand. For the normal function of было is to indicate that the act which would ordinarily have been initiated and then carried through to full execution is being interrupted. But there are also examples showing the particle used in connection with imperfective verbs, signifying that an act which would under normal circumstances have been carried through for an indefinite period of time will suddenly be discontinued. The following provides a characteristic example:" (1967: 47; emphasis mine - A.A.B.). In my opinion the notion of 'duration' is more likely to be regarded as derivative of the notion of 'conation'.

[56] In my material, the different combinations are represented as follows: попытался + pf inf - 10, попробовал + pf inf - 3, пытался + pf inf - 2, пробовал + ipf inf - 2, попытался, пытался and попробовал + ipf inf - one of each. The combination попытался было + pf inf clearly predominates, and it can probably be regarded as the conventional way of expressing the idea: 'he made an unsuccessful attempt to....'.

[57] A similar meaning is found in constructions of the type 'imperfective finite verb + было + infinitive'. In the next section, sentences of this type with finite verbs expressing intention are discussed. In my sample there is one example with the verb отчаиваться, that is semantically closer to verbs like бояться and думать, discussed in this section. The example has given already been given in section 2: (19).

[58] Where there is no special connection with the situation at the moment of speech, a было-construction including the perfective verb подумать is normally

used to express a thought which later proves not to accord with reality:

(I) *Оно (письмо) привлекло внимание Грязнова сначала своей чудовищной неграмотностью. Он, было, подумал, что этот замдиректора "косит" и нарочно написал с такими умопомрачительными ошибками. Но потом ему показалось, что когда-то давно он уже встречался с подобным "правописанием": /.../. (Незн.)*

(II) *До отъезда Евгений думал об Аксинье нехотя, урывками... Одно время он было подумал: "Не буду прерывать с ней отношений. Она согласится. Но чувство порядочности осилило, – решил он по приезде поговорить и, если представится возможность, расстаться". (Шолохов; Forsyth 1970: 145)*

(III) *Так вот, этот тип дал мне выпить коньяку из своей фляжки, я было подумал, что он достает из кармана револьвер, и сказал, что я вел себя как надо /.../. (Вестд.)*

(IV) *На бегу он (Грикспоор) очень сильно стукнулся головой, подумал было, что ранен, но побежал дальше под градом земли и камней. (Вестд.)*

(It is interesting to note that in the Dutch original of (II) and (III), the adverb *eerst* ('at first') is used. This is the Dutch parallel of the Russian *сперва*, which has a certain relationship with the *было*-construction, cf. section 11 and example (170).)

[59] In my sample the corresponding impersonal construction is found only once, in the following thoughts of Puškin's coffin-maker: /.../ *разве гробовщик гаэр святочный? Хотелось было мне позвать их на новоселье, задать им пир горой: ин не бывать же тому! (П: Г 92.16)*

[60] This example shows that the constructions '*хотел* + infinitive + *было*' and '*хотел* + infinitive without *было*' are very close. The reason for not using *было* in the first sentence is probably the wish to avoid an accumulation of embedded *было*-constructions.

[61] It seems that the particle *было* cannot be used with *хотел* when the aim of the subject is an activity or a change of situation in which he has only a passive role, e.g. in a sentence like: *Я хотел получить несколько экземпляров этой книги.*

[62] Cf. Rozental' (ed.) (1971: 378), where the only example of *было* given is a sentence with *хотел*: *я хотел было остаться дома, но не вытерпел и отправился к ней* (Тургенев) and the meaning of *было* is described as 'the impossibility of concluding the action' (def. A17).

[63] Cf. Unbegaun's translation of *он хотел было лишить себя жизни, да испугался*: "il était sur le point de se donner la mort, mais il a eu peur".

[64] Kirsner/Thompson use an English construction of this type - 'I had intended to give you an exam next week' - to illustrate the difference between MEANING and INFERENCE. According to them this sentence "strongly suggests that the speaker no longer intends to give the exam". But "the MESSAGE of 'non-intention in the present' is not the MEANING of *had intended* but rather an INFERENCE from that MEANING" (1976: 203).

[65] It is interesting to note the absence in my material of examples containing *захотеть* - the ingressive derivative of *хотеть* - (although there is one example of the ingressive counterpart of the impersonal verb *хотеться* (cf. note 59): *Мальчики сидели вокруг их, тут же сидели и те две собаки, которым так было захотелось меня съесть. (Тургенев; Nilsson 1967: 50)). As stated at the beginning of this section, in *было*-sentences, the verb *хотеть* has an 'active' meaning, something like: intention + preliminary activity. Apparently it is

difficult to express the notion of the emergence of this variant of intention
with the ingressive verb *захотеть*. It seems to me that in contemporary Russian,
the verb *собраться* is more or less specialised in this function. In a way,
собрался было serves as the ingressive counterpart of both *собирался было* and
хотел было. This could explain the fact that the verb *собраться* is the most
frequently used finite verb in the construction 'finite perfective verb + *было* +
infinitive' (17 percent of cases). The verb *вздумать* appears to be closely
related semantically. In the works of Puškin, this verb occurs seven times, and
here it is almost the only ingressive verb that is used in *было*-sentences expressing non-realised intention (there are no Puškin-examples with *собрался было*
at all). The other four examples of *вздумал было* in my material are all taken
from the works of Turgenev (and cited by Nilsson). Cf. (27) and the following
examples:

(I) *Буджацкие татары вздумали было нас беспокоить. Казачий полковник заманил их
     по своему в засаду. 160 были убиты, шестеро взяты в плен.* (П: ЗМ 337.10)

(II) *Для развлечения вздумал было я в клобе играть, но принужден был оста-
     новиться.* (П: Пс 950.31)

(III) *Вздумал я было ее заложить: пятится моя лошадь назад.*
      (Тургенев; Nilsson 1967: 42)

(IV) *Иные помещики вздумали было покупать сами косы на наличные деньги и разда-
     вать в долг мужикам по той же цене; но мужики оказались недовольными и даже
     впали в уныние /.../.* (Тургенев; Nilsson 1967: 42 (the first four words))

[66]   It would probably be useful to present a typology of the various types of
'disturbance', but this would exceed the scope of this article.

[67]   This term is used by Ebeling (1956: 86) in his description of the use of
the Russian imperative that is sometimes labelled 'dramatic imperative'. According to Ebeling, the general meaning of the Russian imperative "can be defined as
an action fulfilled as the result of a foreign impulse or permission." (*ibid.*)
The 'dramatic imperative' is illustrated by the following sentence from
Turgenev: *А тут еще, как нарочно, подвернись другой знакомый нам гимназист, и
начни хвастаться новыми часами.* In this sentence, "the imperative shows the
actor himself as the urging or enabling force". "Nonetheless, we may speak in
this case of a foreign impulse, because the action is presented as not in
accordance with the preceding actions, as breaking the line of events. Thus the
word "foreign" in our definition does not point solely to the actor, but to the
natural flow of events as a whole" (*ibid.*; empasis mine - A.A.B.). It is interesting to note that there is actually an example of the *было*-construction in
which the 'disturbing' action is indicated by such a 'dramatic imperative':
Только было цветы распустились, как вдруг возьми да приморозь. (Karcevski 1927:
140).

[68]   Cf. Boguslawski/Karolak (1973/70: 369). Nilsson (1967: 47-50) discusses the
various ways in which the clauses or sentences that indicate a disturbing event
can be connected with the *было*-clause. The affinity of *было* with the conjunction
как вдруг is stressed by Belošapkova (1961: 41) and OIG (1964: 239-246). According to Belošapkova, *как вдруг* expresses that the second of two events "неожиданно прерывает или сменяет первое" (l.c.).

[69]   Where a past imperfective indicates a single 'action in progress', it is
natural to apply the notion of disturbance to the action itself (cf. section
12). However, to express an action that is disturbed before attaining the
'Term.', one of the more specialised constructions is normally used: the combination of perfective aspect with *чуть не*; or the expression of the event by a
perfective infinitive, preceded by a finite form of one of a limited group of
verbs, chiefly: *хотел, собирался, собрался, (по)пытался*.

REFERENCES

AS
1895   *Slovar' russkogo jazyka sostavlennyj vtorym otdeleniem imperatorskoj akademii nauk.* Tom I. S.-Peterburg.
Astaf'eva, N.I./ Kiselev, I.A./ Kravčenko, Z.F.
1971   *Sovremennyj russkij jazyk. Služebnye časti reči. Modal'nye slova. Meždometija.* Minsk: Vyšėjšaja škola.
Barentsen, A.A.
1985   *'Tijd', 'Aspect' en de conjunctie <u>poka</u>. Over betekenis en gebruik van enkele vormen in het moderne Russisch.* Dissertation. Amsterdam.
BAS
1950   *Slovar' sovremennogo russkogo literaturnogo jazyka.* Tom I. M.-L.
Belošapkova, V.A.
1961   "Predloženija s sojuzom *kak vdrug* v sovremennom russkom jazyke", *Russkij jazyk v škole,* 1961, 6, 39-43.
Bogusɫawski, A./ Karolak, S.
1973/70   *Gramatyka rosyjska w ujęciu funkcionalnym.* Warszawa: Wiedza powszechna.
Bondarko, A.V.
1971   *Vid i vremja russkogo glagola. (Značenie i upotreblenie).* M.
1983   *Principy funkcional'noj grammatiki i voprosy aspektologii.* L.: Nauka.
Borras, F.M./ Christian, R.F.
1971/59   *Russian syntax. Aspects of modern Russian syntax and vocabulary.* Oxford: University Press.
Boyer, P./ Spéranski, N.
1921/05   *Manuel pour l'étude de la langue russe.* Paris: Librairie Armand Collin.
Buslaev, F.I.
1959/1881 *Istoričeskaja grammatika russkogo jazyka.* M.
Černov, V.I.
1970   "O priglagol'nyx časticax <u>bylo</u> i <u>byvalo</u>", *Russkij jazyk v škole i vuze* (= Uč. zap. Smolenskogo GPI, vyp. 24), 258-264. Smolensk.
Černyx, P. Ja.
1953   *Jazyk uloženija 1649 goda.* M.
Cocron, F.
1962   *La langue russe dans la seconde moitié du XVIIe siècle (morphologie).* Paris: Institut d'études slaves.
Dal', V.
1956/1880 *Tolkovyj slovar' živogo velikorusskogo jazyka.* Tom I. M.
Daneš, F.
1975   "Temporální perspektiva v sémantické struktuře sloves a její syntaktické konsekvence", *Charakterystyka temporalna wypowiedzenia* (Prace instituta języka polskiego 8), 71/75.
Demidenko, L.P./ Naumovič, A.N.
1972   *Sovremennyj russkij jazyk. Glagol.* Minsk: Vyšėjšaja škola.
Ebeling, C.L.
1956   "On the verbal predicate in Russian", *For Roman Jakobson*, 83-90. The Hague: Mouton.
Eckert, R./ Crome, E./ Fleckenstein, C.
1983   *Geschichte der russischen Sprache.* Leipzig: Enzyklopädie.
Ferrell, J.
1953   "The tenses of the Russian verb", *The Slavonic and East European Review* 32, No. 78, 108-116.

Forsyth, J.
1970   *A Grammar of Aspect. Usage and meaning in the Russian Verb.*
          Cambridge: CUP

Garde, P.
1980   *Grammaire russe. Tome premier: Phonologie - Morphologie.*
          Paris: Institut d'études slaves.

GRJa
1960/52   *Grammatika russkogo jazyka. Tom I: Fonetika i morfologija; Tom II:
          Sintaksis.* M.: Izd. AN SSSR.

GSRLJa
1970   *Grammatika sovremennogo russkogo literaturnogo jazyka.* M.: Nauka.

Gvozdev, A.N.
1952   *Očerki po stilistike russkogo jazyka.* M.

van Holk, A.G.F.
1951   "On the actor-infinitive construction in Russian",
          Word 7, 136-143.

Isačenko, A.V.
1940   "Tenses and auxiliary verbs with special reference to Slavic
          languages", *Language* 16, 3, 189-198.
1968/62   *Die russische Sprache der Gegenwart. Teil 1. Formenlehre.*
          Halle (Saale): Max Niemeyer.

Karcevskij, S.
1927   *Système du verbe russe. Essai de linguistique synchronique.* Prague.

Kiparsky, V.
1967   *Russische historische Grammatik. Band II. Die Entwicklung des
          Formensystems.* Heidelberg: Carl Winter.

Kirsner, R.S./ Thompson, S.A.
1976   "The role of pragmatic inference in semantics: a study of sensory
          verb complements in English", *Glossa* 10, 2, 200-240.

Kunert, H.P.
1984   *Aspekt, Aktionsart, Tempus: Eine Untersuchung zur Wiedergabe
          russischer Verbkategorien im Französischen.* (= Tübinger Beiträge
          zur Linguistik 245). Tübingen: Gunter Narr.

Kuznecov, P.S.
1959   *Očerki istoričeskoj morfologii russkogo jazyka.* M.

MAS
1957   *Slovar' russkogo jazyka v četyrex tomax.* Tom I. M.

Maslov, Ju. S.
1984/48   "Vid i leksičeskoe značenie glagola v sovremennom russkom
          literaturnom jazyke", *Očerki po aspektologii*, 48-65. L.
          (Originally published in: *Izvestija AN SSSR, otd. lit. i jaz.*,
          1948, t. 7, vyp. 4, 303-316.)

Mazon, A.
1914   *Emplois des aspects du verbe russe.* Paris.

Nikiforov, S.D.
1952   *Glagol, ego kategorii i formy v russkoj pis'mennosti 2-oj
          poloviny XVI veka.* M.

Nikitevič, V.M.
1963   *Grammatičeskie kategorii v sovremennom russkom jazyke.* M.

Nilsson, N.Å.
1967   "The Use of Preterite + *bylo* in Turgenev",
          Scando-Slavica 13, 39-57.

OIG
1964   *Očerki po istoričeskoj grammatike literaturnogo jazyka XIX v.
          Izmenenija v stroe složnopodčinennogo predloženija.* M.

Ožegov, S.I.
1975[10]   *Slovar' russkogo jazyka.* M.: Sovetskaja ènciklopedija.
Pedersen, H.
1916   *Russisk grammatik.* København.
Pennington, A.E.
1980   *Grigorij Kotošixin: O Rossii v carstvovanii Alekseja Mixajloviča. Text and Commentary.* Oxford: At the Clarendon Press.
Peškovskij, A.M.
1920   *Russkij sintaksis v naučnom osveščenii.* II izdanie. M.
Potebnja, A.
1888/74   *Iz zapisok po russkoj grammatike. I. Vvedenie; II. Sostavnye členy predloženija i ix zameny.* Xar'kov.
Prokopovič, E.N.
1982   *Glagol v predloženii. Semantika i stilistika vido-vremennyx form.* M.: Nauka.
Rassudova, O.P.
1982   *Upotreblenie vidov glagola v sovremennom russkom jazyke.* M.: Russkij jazyk.
RG
1980   *Russkaja grammatika. Tom I. Fonetika, fonologija, udarenie, intonacija, slovoobrazovanie, morfologija; Tom II. Sintaksis.* M.: Nauka.
RJa
1979   *Russkij jazyk. Ènciklopedija.* M.: Sovetskaja ènciklopedija.
Rozental', D.E. (red.)
1971   *Sovremennyj russkij jazyk.* M.: Izd. Moskovskogo universiteta.
Saenkova, N.A.
1971   "O sootnošenii leksičeskogo i grammatičeskogo značenij u častic *čut' bylo ne, čut' ne, edva ne*", *Sovremennyj russkij jazyk* (= Uč. zap. MGPI 423[a]), 298-305.
SATG
1974   *Slovar' avtobiografičeskoj trilogii M. Gor'kogo.* Vypusk 1. L.
Šaxmatov, A.A.
1941/25-27 *Sintaksis russkogo jazyka.* L.
Sémon, J.-P.
1979   "L'acte itératif nombré et l'aspect", *IIe Colloque de linguistique russe*, 87-104. Paris: Institut d'études slaves.
SJaP
1956   *Slovar' jazyka Puškina.* AN SSSR. M.
Sobolevskij, A.I.
1907[4]   *Lekcii po istorii russkogo jazyka.* M.
Švedova, N. Ju.
1960   *Očerki po sintaksisu russkoj razgovornoj reči.* M.: Izd. AN SSSR.
Tagamlickaja, G.
1964   "K voprosu o časticax v russkom i bolgarskom jazykax", *Izvestija na instituta za bălgarski ezik*, 11, 177-195.
Tauscher, E./ Kirschbaum, E.-G.
1967/58   *Grammatik der russischen Sprache.* Berlin: Volk und Wissen.
Unbegaun, B.O.
1951   *Grammaire russe.* Lyon-Paris.
Ušakov
1935   *Tolkovyj slovar' russkogo jazyka* (red. D.N. Ušakov), Tom I. M.
Veyrenc, Ch.J.
1970   *Histoire de la langue russe.* (= Que sais-je? No. 1368). Paris: Presses universitaires de France.

68

Vinogradov, V.V.
1972/47   *Russkij jazyk (Grammatičeskoe učenie o slove)*. M.: Vysšaja škola.
1975/50   "O kategorii modal'nosti i modal'nyx slovax v russkom jazyke",
           Izbrannye trudy. Issledovanija po russkoj grammatike, 53-87.
           M.: Nauka. (Originally published in: *Trudy Instituta russkogo
           jazyka*, 1950, 38-79. M.-L.)

L'ANALYSE LOGIQUE DE LA PHRASE DU TYPE *MOŽNO KURIT'*

ANDRIES BREUNIS

La décomposition des phrases en propositions et formes de proposition, connue sous le nom d'analyse logique, est la détermination de la structure des phrases, qui est fondée sur la *langue*. Il s'agit donc d'une analyse linguistique. Une analyse qui se préoccupe au contenu des phrases, est une analyse qui est fondée sur ce qui est raconté, c'est-à-dire sur la *parole*, donc c'est une analyse textuelle. La différence entre les deux est claire: on peut employer des expressions variées dans des phrases différentes pour dire plus ou moins la même chose. Certains disent ce que d'autres préfèrent passer sous silence. Le locuteur-scripteur peut déplacer vers le fond - c'est-à-dire entre les lignes - ce qui est le centre d'intérêt de l'autre; il peut même scotomiser ce qui reste impliqué. Cependant, l'*allocutaire* peut écouter beaucoup sans l'avoir entendu. Mais les unités linguistiques sont toujours les mêmes dans tous les discours des gens parlant la même langue. La différence entre *l'arbre haut* et *l'arbre est haut* (*vysokoe derevo* et *derevo vysoko*) peut être une question d'accent du point de vue du texte, mais c'est une différence fondamentale d'un point de vue linguistique, du moins dans les langues où ces exemples sont empruntés. Sur le plan *délocutoire*, les unités linguistiques se succèdent, se chevauchent, fusionnent même, mais elles sont toujours inaltérées et inaltérables. C'est pour cette raison que la détermination du *thème* et du *rhème*, quelles que soient les terminologies textuelles employées, est autre chose que la détermination du *sujet* et du *prédicat*. Le thème et le rhème dépendent du contexte, le sujet et le prédicat dépendent des parties du discours.

La terminologie en question, sujet et prédicat, dans un sens propre à la linguistique, présuppose dans la langue une catégorie grammaticale de *verbes*, une catégorie qui diffère des autres parties du discours, comme par exemple des *noms* (substantifs et adjectifs, *nomina*) dans les langues de L'Europe Occidentale d'aujourd'hui et de l'Antiquité, à laquelle remonte cette terminologie.

En conséquence, sur le plan délocutoire, une unité avec un verbe conjugué est une unité fondamentale de la langue. Le verbe est l'*élément* ou le *membre constitutif* de cette unité. Celle-ci s'appelle *proposition*. La proposition a un sujet (*arbor floret*, "l'arbre fleurit") ou non (*pluit*, "il pleut"). Néanmoins, le verbe et le prédicat ne sont pas des concepts identiques. Le verbe, employé dans une proposition, peut être déterminé par un mot d'une autre catégorie. Le cas échéant, le verbe et ce mot constituent conjointement le prédicat. C'est pourquoi le verbe est aussi bien l'élément constitutif de la proposition, que l'élément constitutif du prédicat. Les éléments qui déterminent le verbe, sont aussi à la fois des éléments qui déterminent la proposition entière. Cette double conception de la proposition est possible, grâce à notre faculté de reconnaître une unité linguistique et en même temps les mots, les éléments distincts qui la constituent: c'est que *les caractères de l'unité se confondent avec l'unité elle-même*.

Une autre raison pour laquelle le prédicat n'est pas la même chose que le verbe, est la suivante. Un mot d'une autre catégorie grammaticale que la catégorie des verbes, peut également se présenter comme élément constitutif d'une proposition, mais seulement à certaines conditions, qui sont différentes dans toutes les langues, ayant, par ailleurs, en commun la différence entre les verbes et les mots d'autres catégories.

L'analyse dite logique à quoi sert-elle au juste?

L'analyse logique est l'analyse des *signes* pour scruter la langue. La *signification*, c'est-à-dire, l'action de faire des signes, les éléments distincts dans une chaîne d'unités

linguistiques, est produite par voie de la parole. Les signes,
impliqués dans la langue, sont *innombrables*, c'est-à-dire, ils ne
peuvent se compter. Pourtant, leur nombre n'est pas illimité. Le
nombre de signes se limite à tout ce dont on peut parler. Cela
détermine la *valeur* des termes. La valeur n'est pas la
signification d'un morceau d'un signe coupé en mots, comme dans
un dictionnaire. La valeur est la signification virtuelle dans
laquelle est caché tout ce qui est impliqué dans une production
d'un énoncé.

L'analyse logique met à l'épreuve l'analyse grammaticale et
celle-ci est nécessaire pour apprendre la valeur des termes.
C'est que la catégorisation des mots dans une langue est une
division selon la fonction syntaxique et cette dernière est un
élément sémantique commun à tous les membres de la même catégorie
grammaticale.

Après avoir constaté (le cas échéant!) qu'il existe une
catégorie de verbes dans une langue, distincte d'autres
catégories, il faut identifier tous les verbes et toutes les
autres parties du discours. Après, on peut continuer de découvrir
les genres dans les catégories et les espèces dans les genres.
Le principe de cette classification est toujours de déceler
l'élément sémantique commun à tous les mots d'une catégorie et
après, un élément sémantique commun à tous les mots d'une
catégorie dans une catégorie, etc. Cet élément commun est la
différence entre les catégories, puisque dans la différence se
trouve le sens.

Par exemple, en russe, dans la catégorie principale de
verbes, on peut distinguer deux autres catégories verbales,
à savoir, d'une part les verbes perfectifs et les verbes qu'on
peut relier à celles-là, soit les verbes imperfectifs, d'autre
part les verbes qui ne laissent pas se relier aux verbes
perfectifs. (Donc, la classification des verbes en russe ne
commence pas par la distinction des verbes perfectifs et
imperfectifs). Quant au noms, on pourrait commencer la
classification par la répartition en substantifs et adjectifs,
peut-être la classification se réaliserait après par les noms
propres.

Les propriétés morphologiques de certains mots ne sont pas nécessairement une caractéristique d'une catégorie grammaticale. Par exemple, dans beaucoup de langues, il y a des mots qui ont une désinence d'épithète et qui appartiennent à la catégorie des substantifs.

Tant que les catégories principales ne sont pas encore établies, leur répartition en catégories plus spécifiées, qui doit être réalisée sur le modèle de la répartition en catégories principales, sera impossible. Mais en même temps, on peut croire, la première catégorisation définitivement établie, tout sera simple comme effeuiller la marguerite: une catégorisation continuelle des mots dévoile les valeurs jusqu'à la dénudation totale. Constater qu'il y a des catégories grammaticales différentes, ce n'est jamais que le premier de tous les pas dans la direction de l'objectif à atteindre: l'inventaire de toutes les pensées possibles. Qu'il soit utopique, ce but, ou non, ce qui est sûr, c'est que la linguistique restera loin d'être en état d'y parvenir, à moins qu'elle ne se donne pour tâche tout d'abord d'arriver à bout des rudiments de l'analyse logique, qui est fondée sur la division en catégories grammaticales. Ces catégories ne sont pas les mêmes que les catégories de la pensée, si celle-ci est conçue comme partagée et répartie en actions, qualités et choses concrètes. Les problèmes les plus fondamentaux de la catégorisation sont insolubles, si la théorie de la langue se coince dans la grammaire latine qui devient un cercle vicieux, quand elle est imposée à d'autres langues, au lieu de servir de comparaison, ce qu'elle devrait être, d'ailleurs, pour la langue latine elle-même.

En général, l'investigateur reconnaît bien les verbes, les substantifs et les mots d'autres catégories d'une langue, parce que les catégories de la grammaire des langues classiques semblent cadrer nettement avec les parties du discours. Où certaines combinaisons fournissent des problèmes, c'est là, où l'investigation des parties du discours commence. Comme par exemple en russe, les phrases du type *možno kurit', nado rabotat', trudno govorit'*, etc. Dans un sens, R. L'Hermitte a résolu les

problèmes de l'analyse logique de ce type de phrase. Mais la
solution de L'Hermitte suggère, que la fonction syntaxique d'un
mot, c'est-à-dire l'élément sémantique commun à tous les mots de
la même catégorie, peut être le contenu de l'ordre de mots, quand
ils sont employés pour signifier. Mais ce que nous voulons
analyser, c'est la forme d'une unité contenant les parties du
discours, et cela n'est pas imposé par le contexte, mais par le
système de la langue. Qu'est-ce qu'il se passe quand une unité
linguistique fonctionne comme une autre unité, dont la première
n'a pas les mêmes parties du discours? L'emploi métaphorique d'un
mot est semblable: *gueule* appliqué à quelqu'un qui a une bouche,
réfère au fait qu'on aurait pu dire *bouche*, dont la langue dispose
aussi. De même façon, une unité linguistique, c'est-à-dire
syntaxique, employée en fonction d'une autre unité, réfère par le
lien paradigmatique à cette unité qui reste impliquée dans la
langue, et réfère à la fois à son emploi normal, n'étant pas en
vigueur dans le contexte en question. L'ordre des phonèmes dans
un mot est essentiel pour la signification, l'ordre des mots dans
une phrase est toute autre chose. Quant à l'analyse dite logique,
il s'agit de parties du discours impliquées dans la langue, non
des façons variées selon lesquelles elles peuvent se manifester
dans la parole. Donc, le type de phrase, que nous allons analyser
ici, pourquoi serait-il tantôt une proposition sans sujet,
c'est-à-dire, une phrase impersonnelle, ou tantôt une proposition
à sujet et prédicat, comme il en a l'apparence, quand la partie
contenant l'infinitif est le *thème* et la forme en *-o* est le *rhème*?
Après l'analyse de L'Hermitte, il reste encore la question de
savoir à quelles catégories grammaticales appartiennent les
éléments dans la phrase du type en question et de quelle façon ce
type de phrase diffère d'autres types dans la langue russe. Pour
déterminer la catégorie grammaticale des éléments de ce type de
phrase, il faut aussi examiner leur emploi dans d'autres types de
construction.

La catégorisation de mots se déroule de façon différente
dans toutes les langues, même dans les langues qui ont en commun
la distinction entre formes verbales et formes nominales. Ainsi,

les catégories grammaticales en russe diffèrent, par exemple, des
catégories en français. Puisque la notion de proposition existe
dans la linguistique grâce à cette distinction verbes et mots
d'autres classes, cette notion présuppose une opposition d'une
unité à élément constitutif verbal, et d'une autre unité. Dans le
russe, comme en français, c'est une unité dont l'élément
constitutif est un nom substantif. Quand cette unité-ci est
déterminée par le prédicat dans une proposition, cette unité,
nommé *groupe syntaxique*, est le sujet de la proposition. En
relation avec le groupe syntaxique, le prédicat, le membre
constitutif de la proposition, est un membre déterminant. A
l'intérieur du groupe, le membre constitutif peut aussi être
déterminé, par des adjectifs-épithètes, ou par des autres
substantifs, qui s'appellent des appositions. Mais dans le groupe,
c'est le substantif, l'élément déterminé, qui est le membre
constitutif. Les autres éléments du groupe sont des membres
accessoires. Ils sont désignés ainsi, parce que, d'un point de
vue grammatical, ils peuvent manquer; un groupe avec des adjectifs
est alors la même chose qu'un groupe sans adjectifs. Par contre,
un groupe dans lequel manque un substantif, par exemple en cas
d'un *ellipse* ou si le substantif est *sous-entendu* - si la langue
distingue des substantifs et des adjectifs - est un autre type de
groupe du point de vue de la grammaire, mais il peut être la
même chose d'un point de vue sémantique.
   En russe comme en bien d'autres langues, les groupes
syntaxiques peuvent être adéquats aux propositions à verbe
conjugué, sans qu'il y ait ellipse d'une forme verbale, ou sans
que la forme verbale soit *sous-entendue*. (Sur le plan *locutoire* le
terme proposition souvent n'a pas de sens). Quand le groupe a sa
fonction primaire, celle du groupe, l'élément déterminant est un
membre accessoire, mais il peut être le membre constitutif du
groupe fonctionnant comme proposition. (C'est-à-dire, *homme* et
petit sont le membre constitutif et accessoire respectivement,
quand ils sont liés l'un à l'autre dans un groupe; la situation
est inversée dans une proposition). Un groupe dans la fonction de
proposition contient un *temps*, le présent ou le futur de cette
proposition est exprimé par une forme de "être" (*byt'*). Dans tous

les autres cas, un groupe syntaxique est une partie d'un ensemble,
qui peut bien être employée comme unité indépendante, ayant, en
ce cas, un effet spécial, parce qu'elle est, tout compte fait,
une partie d'un ensemble (*Nuit. Bruit lointain de canons. Va-et-vient continuel de soldats*).

En russe, les groupes syntaxiques ainsi que les propositions
- abstraction faite des unités à fonction adverbiale et des autres
unités eventuelles - peuvent être constitués par un seul mot.
Des groupes: *ulica; fonar'; apteka*; des propositions: *morozit,
teplo* (mais non *vniman'e!*, c'est le plan locutoire). Si un mot
peut être lié à *est'*, alors que l'expression peut être employée
dans une proposition (par exemple *ulica* dans *ulica est'*), dans
ce cas c'est un mot qu'on peut employer dans un groupe constitué
par ce mot seulement, comme les exemples de groupes ci-dessus.
Sinon (**cholodno est'* est impossible), il s'agit d'une forme dont
la fonction primaire est le prédicat d'une proposition à un terme.
Autrement dit, non seulement les formes comme <u>morozit</u>, "il
gèle", sont des propositions, mais aussi une forme comme *noč'*,
"c'est nuit".(*Noč'. Morozit. Razbojniki sidjat vokrug kostra* sont
trois propositions). Il s'ensuit que la *valeur* du mot russe *noč'*
diffère du mot *nuit* en français, une différence qui dépasse les
bornes des catégories grammaticales de ces langues respectives.
Le *nuit* français est un substantif, le *noč'* russe, en dehors de
tout contexte, est un substantif et un verbe à la fois, puisque,
dans une proposition à un terme, il est semblable à une forme
verbale conjuguée, et il est aussi un substantif, parce que
dans *noč' nastupaet* il désigne le sujet. Dans *noč'*, comme élément
de la langue, il n'y a pas de différence entre un verbe et un
substantif. Quand dans un groupe fonctionnant comme proposition,
un substantif est le membre constitutif de cette proposition,
c'est alors une forme nominale dans une fonction verbale, une
fonction secondaire d'un nom substantif. Par contre, *noč'*
tantôt est un verbe tantôt un nom substantif, mais c'est dans un
contexte particulier seulement, que cette différence ne signifie
rien, c'est-à-dire, qu'une des deux parties de la valeur est
exclue. Il s'ensuit aussi, que la catégorisation actuelle de mots
en russe ne commence pas par la différence entre les formes

nominales et verbales. Cependant, la constatation elle-même que cette différence existe, c'était le début des études de la langue russe.

Voilà un exemple illustrant comment les catégories grammaticales en russe diffèrent du français. Pour les mêmes raisons, une catégorie d'adverbes, semblable à celle du français, n'existe pas.

Certaines formes dans la langue russe, à savoir le type *očen'*, *sliškom*, etc. sont caractérisées comme adverbes, mais, contrairement à d'autres adverbes, elles ne fonctionnent jamais comme verbe. Ces formes ne peuvent être employées que dans une combinaison avec un adjectif, un autre adverbe ou quelquefois même avec un verbe (*ja očen' uvažaju jego*); elles sont *synsémantiques*. Cela ne s'applique pas aux formes comme *zdes'*, "ici", *segodnja*, "aujourd'hui", *tam*, "là", etc. Comme les substantifs déclinés, ces formes fonctionnent non seulement comme complément du verbe (*ja zdes' rabotaju*), mais aussi comme le complément déterminatif du substantif: *položenie doma*, "la situation chez nous". Dans cette fonction ces formes peuvent constituer le prédicat d'une proposition: *otec doma*, "le père est chez lui". Cette diversité de fonctions n'implique pas que ces formes ne sont pas des adverbes. Leur fonction primaire est celle d'un adverbe, c'est dans une fonction secondaire, quand elles fonctionnent comme le déterminant d'un substantif, tout comme un substantif décliné: *interes k muzyke*. Elles ne sont jamais adéquates à un substantif dans le nominatif.

Beaucoup d'adverbes, formes dérivées de l'adjectif, ne déterminent que des formes verbales ou des adjectifs, ou des adverbes, mais ne fonctionnent jamais ni comme complément attributif, ni comme prédicat de la proposition: *bystro*, *smelo*, etc. Ce sont les vrais adverbes, qui justifient l'admission en russe d'une catégorie grammaticale distincte des adverbes. Il y a un autre groupe de formes, traditionellement désignées comme "adverbes prédicatifs", pour la plupart formes qui se terminent en *-o*. Elles fonctionnent comme le prédicat dans une proposition sans sujet, donc, dans une phrase impersonnelle, du

type *pluit, oportet*. Par exemple *cholodno*, "froidement", *nado*,
"il faut", *možno*, "c'est possible", etc. Le passé est exprimé par
l'addition de *bylo*, le futur a *budet*, des formes de "être" (*byt'*).
Les formes du passé et du futur sont des formes composées,
puisqu'on reconnaît les parties constituantes, et à la fois elles
sont des formes verbales, adéquates aux autres formes verbales
conjuguées, l'union d'une racine verbale et d'une désinence.

Beaucoup de formes de ce type d'adverbe ne peuvent
fonctionner comme prédicat que dans une combinaison avec un
quelconque complément, et elles-mêmes peuvent fonctionner comme le
complément d'un autre verbe (le type *trudno*). Parmi ces formes
il y en a d'autres qui peuvent fonctionner aussi comme le membre
constitutif d'une proposition impersonnelle à un terme (le type
cholodno). Les formes restantes (le type *nado*, aussi le type
nel'zja, "on ne peut pas") fonctionnent exclusivement comme
l'élément constitutif du prédicat, mais toujours en combinaison
avec un complément, sauf dans les tournures elliptiques ou dans
les sous-entendus.

Le type *pora*, "il est temps" aussi bien que "le temps", "la
période", est un substantif-verbe comme *noč'*, dans sa qualité de
verbe, ce type peut fonctionner comme "adverbe prédicatif" du
type *nado*.

Les formes comme *cholodno*, qui fonctionnent soit comme
adverbe, soit comme verbe (le prédicat d'une proposition à un
terme) sont d'une catégorie grammaticale particulière, la valeur
d'un adverbe et d'un verbe n'est pas différenciée dans ce type.
Leur fonction d'adverbe ou de verbe dépend du type de
construction. Le groupe de formes comme *nado*, *nel'zja*, etc.
semblent apparemment appartenir à la catégorie des *verbes*, mais
leur emploi est comme celui des "adverbes prédicatifs" comme
trudno, puisque le complément est obligatoire sur le plan
délocutoire (*Net, nel'zja!* est *locution*). Peut-être, nous verrons
plus tard si cet emploi est relevant pour la détermination de la
catégorie grammaticales des formes comme *nado*. En outre, parfois,
on dirait qu'une forme de ce type est un adjectif-prédicatif à
forme brève (*nužno*).

Avant de traiter plus à fond la question du statut

syntaxique des formes du type *nado*, *nužno*, etc., il faut d'abord
parler de la catégorie grammaticale à laquelle appartient
l'infinitif des verbes, pour retourner en fin à notre analyse de
la phrase du type *možno kurit'*.

Quel est le statut syntaxique de l'infinitif?

Récapitulons. La différence entre les catégories dites
grammaticales est la différence entre les fonctions *primaires*.
Un substantif ou un adjectif-épithète, fonctionnant comme verbe,
est une forme nominale dans une fonction *secondaire*. Le verbe
aussi a des fonctions secondaires. Les participes, le gérondif
en russe, etc. et aussi l'infinitif sont les formes de la fonction
secondaire du verbe, parce que, dans ces formes, le verbe
fonctionne comme forme nominale. Tout comme une forme nominale
ne devient pas verbale dans une fonction secondaire, le verbe
à son tour n'est pas une forme nominale quand il est employé
dans une fonction secondaire. L'évidence de cette thèse nous
est fournie, par exemple, par la différence entre un participe
et un adjectif-épithète qui est dérivé d'un participe, ce
dont il y a exemple dans plusieurs langues. En russe, la forme
de l'ancien participe en *-čij* (*stojačij vorotnik*, *brodjačaja
natura*) a survécu, grâce au fait que le participe en *-čij*
est devenu un adjectif. En français, le participe en *-ant* est
indéclinable, contrairement à l'adjectif dérivé du participe.
On rencontre des différences d'accentuation, entre les participes
et ses dérivés dans d'autres langues, comme en néerlandais
uitstékend ("excellent") et *uítstekend* (de "exceller"). L'adjectif
dérivé du participe peut fonctionner comme verbe, donc peut
constituer le prédicat dans une proposition, la function primaire
du verbe: *ja nekurjaščij*, "je ne fume pas". Ainsi, l'infinitif
aussi est une forme flexionnelle du verbe et non pas un *abstrait
verbal*, ce qui serait une forme de *dérivation*. Sauf dans le
cas d'un verbe dit *défectif*, les formes flexionnelles existent
partout, presque tous les verbes ont un infinitif; les formes
dérivées sont moins nombreuses que les formes flexionnelles
dans la langue et souvent l'abstrait verbal en russe (en *-n'e*) a
un sens limité par rapport au verbe dont il est dérivé.

Donc, l'infinitif est la forme du verbe en fonction du

nom substantif et dans cette fonction la forme d'infinitif est
liée au verbe conjugué. L'infinitif, pour ainsi dire, peut
remplacer une proposition dite subordonnée, celle-ci, donc,
est remplacée par une "proposition infinitive". L'abstrait verbal
peut aussi être consideré comme le remplaçant d'une subordonnée,
mais le lien avec le verbe principal diffère de celui entre
l'infinitif et le verbe: la différence entre *ja ljublju kurit'* et
ja lublju kuren'e est évidente: ici, comme les autres formes de
la fonction secondaire du verbe, l'infinitif est lié au sujet
seulement. L'infinitif détermine le verbe conjugué comme un
complément, de façon semblable au membre déterminant d'un composé
nominal qui détermine un autre mot, d'où le terme "Satzcompositum",
"composé propositionnelle". Le déterminant de l'abstrait verbal
est un complément attributif (*strašnoe kuren'e*), le déterminant
d'un infinitif est un complément adverbial (*strašno kurit'*).
Quelles sont les conséquences de la catégorisation des "adverbes"
dont nous venons de parler, pour l'analyse logique de la phrase
du type à infinitif et "adverbe"?

    L'analyse logique, qui est fondée sur les relations des
déterminants et des déterminés, de la phrase du type *možno kurit'*
ne présente, en raison de ce qui précède, aucun problème. Dans une
proposition comme *professor idët domoj*, *professor* est le sujet,
idët domoj est le prédicat; par conséquant, dans *professor idët
domoj obedat'*, il y a le même sujet, le prédicat est étendu par
l'infinitif, puisque, cette forme aussi, est un complément du
verbe. Comme dans *professor ljubit kurit'*, où l'infinitif est
l'objet, le complément direct, même un complément *central*,
selon la terminologie de Kuryłowicz, en opposition au complément
marginal, comme par exemple *v komnate* dans *professor ljubit
kurit' v komnate*. Donc, dans *možno kurit'* la forme en *-o*, un
"adverbe prédicatif", est le prédicat dans une proposition
impersonnelle, l'infinitif est le complément, un complément
particulier, existant dans la langue à côté de toutes autres
formes qui fonctionnent comme complément d'un autre genre,
circonstantiel, de lieu, etc.

    Cependant, dans plusieurs contextes (*kurit'? možno!*)
c'est l'infinitif qui est déterminé et c'est l'"adverbe"

qui détermine. Des savants, parmi lesquels Ebeling, même parlent
d'un sujet (l'infinitif) et d'un prédicat. Pour eux, les mêmes
termes sont en vigueur dans le cas d'autres types de phrases
impersonnelles, comme par exemple *zdes' cholodno*, dans laquelle,
d'un point de vue formel, *cholodno* est le prédicat, c'est
qu'il est le prédicat dans une proposition à un terme. L'adverbe
zdes' serait donc le membre déterminant le verbe ("complément
de lieu"), mais dans beaucoup de contextes, la situation semble
inverse. En outre, une construction avec *trudno* ou *nado*, etc.,
comme le prédicat, n'est pas complète sur le plan délocutoire,
comme s'il manquait une espèce de sujet. Dans le cas de la phrase
du type *možno kurit'*, est-il possible de désigner l'infinitif
comme *sujet*?

    Si l'interprétation de la fonction de l'infinitif comme
sujet était correcte, l'infinitif, dans ce cas, fonctionnerait
comme substantif dans le nominatif. Cela arrive dans d'autres
langues que le russe, par exemple en français, selon l'exemple
de L'Hermitte *se baigner est agréable*, différent de *il est
agréable de se baigner* (ce qui, peut-être, ne se laisse pas
comparer à cause de la préposition *de*. D'ailleurs, qu'est-ce
qu'on dit en français pour le néerlandais *het baden*? *Le baigner*?
Le se baigner?). Existe-t-il un exemple dans la langue russe d'un
infinitif remplaçant un abstrait verbal dans le nominatif?
    Dans un grand nombre de cas, tout porte à croire, que
l'infinitif est un substantif dans le nominatif. cela arrive
surtout dans l'emploi dit *disjunct*: *guljat', èto moja strast'*
Il fonctionne ici comme l'introduction d'une phrase nominale
à *èto*. L'infinitif même, comme il paraît, est le sujet d'une
phrase nominale du type *Amsterdam - stolica Gollandii*, "Amsterdam
est la capitale des Pays Bas",   dans *učit'sja - naša zadača*.
Peut-être il est le prédicat dans *naš dolg - borot'sja za mir*.
Si l'on croit que l'analyse en sujet et prédicat d'une phrase
nominale n'est pas possible, à moins que l'on sache quel est
le *thème* et quel est le *rhème*, dans l'exemple suivant on a
du moins un infinitif qui peut être le sujet et un autre qui
peut être le prédicat: *žizn' prožit' ne pole perejti* (proverbe),

à condition que ce soit une phrase nominale. Mais les exemples cités, sont-il des phrases nominales?

Comme mentionné plus haut, une phrase nominale en russe est un groupe en fonction de proposition. Une proposition contient un *temps*, le présent de *byt'*, "être". En dehors du contexte, le groupe peut être ambigu. Une construction comme par exemple *Moskva - stolica SSSR*, peut fonctionner comme proposition ("Moscou est la capitale de l'URSS"), mais en même temps c'est un groupe, par exemple quand la construction est employée comme le titre d'un livre sur Moscou ("Moscou, capitale de l'URSS"). Les proverbes ne sont pas nécessairement des phrases nominales, souvent c'est impossible d'ajouter un verbe ("autres temps étaient autres moeurs"?), ils ne sont pas en tout cas une proposition: *vek živi, vek učis'*. Quand il y a deux groupes syntaxiques dans un contexte, l'un peut déterminer l'autre, cela dépend du contexte et s'applique aux exemples cités ci-dessus avec l'infinitif. C'est la même chose dans le cas de deux propositions dont l'une détermine l'autre. Cette relation peut être exprimée par les caractéristiques spécifiques d'une proposition subordonnée, mais ces indices ne sont pas nécessaires: *Il ne vient pas. Il est malade.* = ... *parce qu'il est malade.*

Un groupe peut introduire une proposition; à cause du contexte il peut être évident, que la proposition entière détermine le groupe, c'est de nouveau l'emploi dit *disjunct*: *Moskva, ètot gorod mne nravitsja* ("nominatif proleptique"). L'indépendance du groupe introduisant une proposition est plus claire, dans *Moskva, ja ljublju ètot gorod* ("nominatif pendant").

Dans d'autres exemples de l'emploi *disjunct*, une certaine ambiguïté probablement pourrait être présente, par exemple, dans *zdes' cholodno*, "il fait froid ici". D'un point de vue formel, cet exemple est une proposition impersonnelle, le membre constitutif est *cholodno*, ce qui est déterminé par le complément de lieu *zdes'*. Mais conçue comme proposition à un terme, précédée par un groupe indépendant, la phrase, dépendant du contexte, peut être interprétée comme constituée

par *cholodno* qui détermine le groupe indépendant qui précède.
Cette interprétation, dans la conception exposée ici, dépend
du contexte. Puisque l'infinitif peut fonctionner comme groupe
introduisant une proposition, tout comme *zdes'*, l'ambiguïté
de la phrase du type *možno kurit'*, peut être expliquée de
la même façon. L'infinitif est la forme pour l'emploi *disjunct*
par excellence. C'est qu'il n'est pas une forme qui n'est
usée que dans une combinaison avec un verbe conjugué. Il n'est
pas un nom substantif, sans doute, mais il est le nom du verbe.
Sur le plan locutoire, il suffit de nommer le verbe, pour
exprimer un impératif (*vstavat'!*). Dans les dictionnaires,
l'infinitif est la forme dite conventionnelle (*conventional
citation form*) pour citer le verbe. Mais le nom d'un mot n'est
pas toujours un nominatif.

Dans *kurit' vospreščaetsja* l'infinitif n'est pas employé
clairement *disjunct*, mais il n'y a aucune preuve que cette
construction n'est pas une proposition impersonnelle. Même
la forme "passive", *kurit' vspreščeno* ne fournit aucune
indication non ambiguë de la fonction syntaxique de l'infinitif.
Il y a peu de preuve de la fonction de sujet, comme n'il y a pas
de preuve du contraire! Dans l'exemple dernier l'ambiguïté
même est plus saillante, si l'on compare à les expressions
nužno knigu (avec le complément de l'objet direct) et *nužno
čitat'*. L'ambiguïté en question est constituée par les relations
des déterminants. Si l'infinitif dans *kurit' vospreščaetsja* est le
sujet de la proposition, il est déterminé par l'élément
constitutif de la proposition, à savoir le verbe *vospreščaetsja*.
De même façon le sujet dans *roza krasna* est déterminé par le
prédicat. Mais si l'infinitif dans *kurit' vospreščaetsja* est le
complément dans une phrase impersonnelle, c'est le membre
constitutif du prédicat *vospreščaetsja* qui est déterminé par
l'infinitif.

Cette ambiguïté de relations du déterminant et du déterminé
n'est pas unique en russe. Peut-être, des autres exemples
éclaireront le problème.

Il s'agit des constructions du type *byla noč'*. Etant donné
que la proposition *noč'* est une phrase impersonnelle à un

terme, comme le latin *pluit*, ou *oportet*, le passé de cette
construction doit être de même une phrase impersonnelle.
Cependant, dans *noč' nastupaet*, *noč'* est un substantif indiquant
le sujet, c'est pour cette raison que *noč'* dans *byla noč'*
est aussi le sujet. Il s'ensuit, que *byla noč'* est ambigu,
la signification de *noč'* dans cette expression ne distingue
pas la fonction nominale et la fonction verbale. Et ce sont
surtout les relations de déterminants et déterminés qui nous
intéressent, elles sont les mêmes dans *kurit' vospreščaetsja*,
probablement différentes dans *vxod vospreščaetsja*. La double
fonction des éléments existe également dans *dožd' idët*, ce
qui se ne laisse pas analyser comme *dožd' menja razdražaet*
ou *dom stoit*. Voir *moroz* qui peut signifier la même chose
que *morozit*, et on peut comparer *segodnja na ulice veter* avec
segodnja na ulice duet veter. Découle-t-il de ce qui précède,
que dans *kurit' vospreščaetsja* l'infinitif est le sujet et
le complément à la fois? Non, il s'agit seulement des relations
de déterminants et déterminés et du fait que l'élément constitutif
de la proposition reste le même. L'infinitif russe ne fonctionne
nulle part et jamais explicitement comme substantif dans le
nominatif. C'est pour cela qu'on ne peut pas qualifier de
sujet l'infinitif dans *kurit' vospreščaetsja*. C'est une phrase
impersonnelle, donc il n'y a pas de sujet. Evidemment, il y a
une phrase impersonnelle à deux termes, spécifique pour le
russe, qui se caractérise par la double fonction des parties
constituantes. Cette double fonction se présente dans le type
možno kurit' aussi bien que dans le type *zdes' cholodno*. Il
s'ensuit que ce phénomène de la double fonction n'est pas
déterminé par le contexte, mais il appartient à l'unité
linguistique, qu'on peut nommer la phrase impersonnelle à deux
termes. Dans cette unité, ce qui doit être exprimé par le
contexte en d'autres langues, à l'aide d'un groupe syntaxique
indépendant, qui introduit une proposition, cela s'est fixé
en russe dans la phrase impersonnelle à deux termes. Seulement
si le membre constitutif de la proposition sans sujet a un
complément *synsémantique* (*očen'*, *sliškom*) la double fonction
des déterminants et déterminés ne se trouve pas. C'est intéressant

de voir, que, quant aux phrases du type *možno kurit'* et du type
zdes' cholodno, nous en concluons, dans un sens, la même chose
que l'estimé Ebeling, soit, par une voie différente, et sans qu'il
soit question, selon nous, d'un sujet en tant que tel.

L'existence de la proposition impersonnelle à deux termes
en russe explique également la raison pour laquelle certains
"adverbes prédicatifs" ne sont verbes que dans le cadre de
cette unité linguistique spécifique. Dans l'élément constitutif
de cette proposition, la différence entre un adjectif prédicatif
et un adverbe prédicatif a disparu. Seulement, dans certains
cas, la signification typique d'un adjectif bref se met à jour:
Nina, ty ne xočeš' so mnoj poguljat'? Net, guljat' žarko. S'il
est vrai, que l'infinitif, dans ce cas, préfère une position
avant le prédicat, c'est une adaption à la signification des
membres de cette unité, un phénomène accessoire, une
"Begleiterscheinung" de l'unité nommé la proposition impersonnelle
à deux termes. Par contre, il n'y a des exemples que dans les
constructions de ce genre, l'accent de mot peut différencier la
signification de l'adverbe de celle de l'adjectif. C'est toujours
la forme de l'adverbe qui apparaît. (A.G. 80, par. 978).

La double fonction des déterminants et déterminés établie,
dans *byla noč'* et dans la proposition impersonnelle à deux
termes, maintenant une analyse ultérieure des formes du passé
et du futur de *nado*, *možno*, etc. (*nado bylo*, *možno budet*), est
réalisable. Puisque les combinaisons en question ne sont pas
propositions comme *byla noč'* ou *nado rabotat'*, la double fonction
des déterminants et déterminés qu'on peut démontrer dans les
formes du passé et du futur s'est accompagnée ici d'une alternance
des membres en fonction de l'éléments constitutif. Dans la
forme *nado bylo* il y a deux membres constitutifs d'un ordre
différent de l'élément constitutif dans *nado rabotat'*. Le verbe
bylo - c'est que *bylo* est une forme du verbe *byt'* - est
le membre constitutif de la proposition dont il fait partie
et il est déterminé par *nado*. Cela est possible, parce que
dans la signification de *nado* la fonction de verbe n'est pas
distinguée de la fonction de complément déterminant le verbe.
Simultanément, exactement puisque ces fonctions ne sont pas

85

différenciées, le membre *nado* est aussi l'élément constitutif de la même proposition. Il est déterminé par *bylo*, constituant alors, à ce point de vue, le morphème du passé. Voilà, ce que veut dire la thèse, que le terme "la forme zéro de la copule" n'est approprié à la phrase nominale que du point de vue de la morphologie.

Université de Leiden

BIBLIOGRAPHIE

A.G. 80
    1980   *Russkaja Grammatika.* AN SSSR.
                Institut Russkogo Jazyka. Moscou.
Breunis, Andries
    1983   "Sur la phrase nominale en russe", *Dutch Contributions to the Ninth International Congress of Slavists. Linguistics. SSGL III,* 37-51. Amsterdam.
Ebeling, C.L.
    1958   "Subject and Predicate, Especially in Russian", *Dutch Contributions to the Fourth International Congress of Slavists, Moscow,* september 1958, 1-39. La Haye.
L'Hermitte, René
    1974   "Sujet", "Copule" et "Prédicat", *Mélanges Linguistiques offerts à Emile Benveniste. Collection linguistique p.p. la Soc.d.Ling.de Paris, LXX,* 383-388. Louvain.
Kuryłowicz, J.
    1964   *The Inflectional Categories of Indo-European.* Heidelberg. Chap. VI.
Pul'kina I.M. & Zachava-Nekrasova, E.B.
    1964³   *Učebnik Russkogo Jazyka dlja Studentov-Inostrancev.* Moscou

-*SJA* AND *SEBJA*

NELLEKE GERRITSEN

1.   Introduction

Traditionally, Russian reflexive verbs, i.e. verbs with the postverbal affix -SJA[1] (henceforth Vsja), are divided into several unrelated groups according to the presumed meanings of -SJA. The only generally recognized meaning of -SJA as a whole is "intransitivity". This is a rather unsatisfactory situation from both a theoretical and a practical point of view. Theoretically because it is plausible to start from the assumption that one form has one meaning. Practically because the lack of a unified explanation for the use of -SJA in handbooks on Russian grammar makes it almost impossible for students to choose between a Vsja, the reflexive object pronoun SEBJA, the passive participle and the non-reflexive verb without an object.

In contrast to this traditional approach I hold the view that all the so-called meanings of -SJA are essentially mere interpretations of one invariant meaning, and that these interpretations form a continuum from "true reflexive" to "passive" Vsja.

Further, in my opinion -SJA as a whole differs from the reflexive object pronoun SEBJA, the passive participle (henceforth PP), and intransitive verbs with respect to roles, participants and entities[2]. (As will appear from what follows, entities belong to the real world, participants to the language. Participants are thus "linguistic entities".) Consider the following scheme:

	ROLE	PARTICIPANT	ENTITY
V tr (act. + pass.)	2	2	2
V + SEBJA	2	2	1
V + -SJA	2	1	1
V intr	1	1	1

From this scheme we can deduce the following oppositions:
1. V tr vs V + SEBJA; difference: number of entities.
Both V tr and V + SEBJA evoke the thought of a second entity beside
the one referred to by the subject. However, in constructions with
SEBJA, the meaning of SEBJA, which is "coreferentiality", subsequently denies the existence of this second entity in the real
world. So, the one real-world-entity is depicted in language as
being split up into two different ones: there are two participants.
2. V + SEBJA vs V + -SJA; difference: number of participants.
-SJA, being an affix attached to the verb, does not refer to a
separate participant, so it does not evoke (as SEBJA does) the
thought of two entities[3]: there is only one, viz. the one referred
to by the subject of Vsja. SEBJA, as a direct object (DO) with a
patient role, ascribes to the subject the role of an agent. -SJA,
not indicating a separate participant, does not specify whether or
not the subject has a full agent role, it only says that the subject is somehow affected by the event and in addition has a second
role.
3. V + -SJA vs V intr; difference: number of roles.
The subject of an intransitive non-reflexive verb has only one
(non-patient) role. -SJA on the other hand attributes to the subject a second role, it marks the subject as being doubly involved
in the event.
4. V + -SJA vs V_{pp}; difference: number of participants and entities.
In a construction with a PP, just as in active transitive constructions, there are two roles, participants and entities. The
subject of a PP-construction is a patient, no more than that. Some
other entity (whether present in the construction or deducible
from the context) is responsible for what happens to the subject-
referent. In contrast, in "passive" reflexive constructions the
subject is more than a mere patient, although the second role may

be hardly definable. An external participant may play an agentive role that completes the one of the subject (see below).

On the basis of the above analysis, we can incorporate the continuum of -SJA interpretations in the whole of the Russian verb system. Starting on top with two participants (a subject with an agent role and a DO with a patient role) it ends below with the same number of participants with reversed order of roles: here the subject has the patient role, the agent being represented by an instrumental object. The transition between the two extremes is constituted by the -SJA-continuum, running from "true reflexive" to "passive":

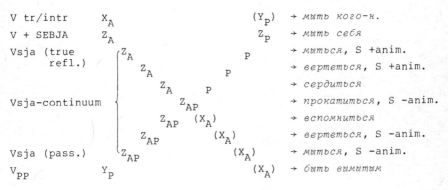

V tr/intr	X_A	(Y_P) → мыть кого-н.
V + SEBJA	Z_A	Z_P → мыть себя
Vsja (true refl.)	Z_A ... P	→ мыться, S +anim.
	Z_A ... P	→ вертеться, S +anim.
	Z_A ... P	→ сердиться
Vsja-continuum	Z_{AP}	→ прокатиться, S −anim.
	Z_{AP} (X_A)	→ вспомниться
	Z_{AP} (X_A)	→ вертеться, S −anim.
Vsja (pass.)	Z_{AP} (X_A)	→ мыться, S −anim.
V_{PP}	Y_P (X_A)	→ быть вымытым

(X, Y, Z: participants of the event;
 A, P: roles; A = agent, P = patient)

The terms "agent", "agentive" need an explanation: in the literature they are ill-defined and used in a variety of ways. My proposal is to consider "agent" a cluster of non-patient features such as +volition, +control, +responsibility, +activity, +causation etc. In the -SJA-continuum the subject has a double role. The constant factor is that the participant is affected by the event. In addition there is a second role, the character of which is to be inferred from factors other than -SJA, such as the lexical meaning of the verb and the status of the subject (animate or inanimate, cf. *Иван моется* vs *Окно моется*). With the so-called true reflexives this second role is, in general, a full agent role,

which means that the participant has the whole cluster of agentive
features. Descending along the continuum the subject gradually
loses more and more agentive features. At the same time the two
roles of the participant tend to merge until, in the middle of the
continuum, we can hardly distinguish them (cf. *Гром прокатился*[4]).
From this point on a second, external participant begins to manifest itself. This participant takes over the agentive features
which the subject has lost. Cf. *Крылья вертелись от морского бриза*,
where the wind is the causing force, but the wings are also active,
besides being affected. At the bottom of the continuum very little
agentivity on the part of the subject is left.

This article will be chiefly concerned with the opposition
between -SJA and SEBJA. It will be demonstrated that the difference between the two is indeed a matter of roles, participants
and entities.

2.   *-SJA versus SEBJA*

2.1. *Occurrence*
Possible relations between -SJA and SEBJA are:

	-SJA	"="	SEBJA
1.	–		+
2.	+	+	+
3.	+	–	+
4.	+		–

("=": the interpretation of -SJA is more or less equivalent with
the meaning of SEBJA)

Ad 1. Not every verb that can occur with SEBJA as a direct
object, can also be combined with -SJA. For instance, beside
*жалеть себя, заставлять себя, упрекать себя, ненавидеть себя,
превзойти себя*, we find no *жалеться, заставляться* (with the "same"
lexical meaning), *упрекаться, ненавидеться, превзойтись*.
The question as to when a specific verb can have SEBJA as a
DO is difficult to answer. In Russian grammars SEBJA is treated

very superficially, possibilities of occurrence not being mentioned at all. Dictionaries are not much of a help either: except
for bound phrases of verb + SEBJA, it depends on mere chance
whether an example with SEBJA is given in the lemma of a verb[5].

Janko-Trinickaja says about SEBJA (1962: 184):

Далеко не все переходные глаголы могут иметь при себе в качестве прямого
объекта возвратное местоимение *себя*: этому довольно часто препятствует лекси-
ческое значение переходных глаголов, обозначающих действия, которые нельзя
обычно произнести над собой, например: *избегать, пригласить, караулить,
встретить* и т.п.

But beside the fact that it is possible to say for instance:

Мы сам себя пригласили

if we mean to say " ... nobody else did!", on page 185 of the
above mentioned study we find an example of a sentence, in which
in my opinion all the verbs mentioned by Janko-Trinickaja could be
filled in:

... *Разве может человек сам себя обидеть?* ...

So it seems to me we could say that whenever a verb can have an
animate DO (SEBJA usually refers to a person), it can also have
SEBJA. SEBJA refers to a member of the set of entities which may
occupy the position of a DO with a particular verb.
-SJA does not refer to a member of a set of entities. So the possibility of occurrence of SEBJA with a particular verb and the
possibility of -SJA being attached to that same verb are two different things. This situation reflects my statements above about
participants and entities.

Ad 2. (and 4.). The Vsja belonging here are the so-called
"true" reflexive verbs, i.e. here the interpretation of -SJA is
more or less equivalent with the meaning of SEBJA. However, grammarians disagree about when this equivalence exists. For instance,
Peškovskij (1956[7]: 114) includes verbs like *бросаться, вертеться,
садиться*:

В них во всех, то с большей, то с меньшей натяжкой, надставка *–ся* могла бы
быть заменена словом *себя* в значении вин. пад.

although

Обычно же замена надставки *-ся* словом *себя* производит прямо комическое впечатление ...

Usually the above mentioned verbs are not considered to be
"true" reflexives. So the question is: what is a "true" reflexive?
Where does Peškovskij's "comical effect" come from?

If we take for instance *вертеть*, we know there is a participant "turning" and a participant "being turned". If we fill in
SEBJA on the place of the DO (the participant "being turned"), we
indeed get a comical picture, viz. one entity, split up into two
participants, one of them turning the other one around. *Вертеться*
in contrast does not produce a comical effect, because -SJA does
not evoke the thought of a split entity, but of a single entity,
playing two roles at a time. The subject as a whole is active and
at the same time affected by the action. So, in a construction
with SEBJA the agent and the patient are viewed as two distinct
participants, playing opposite roles, whereas in a construction
with -SJA the roles are more or less merged.

With true reflexive verbs like *мыться*, which imply movement,
the action is comparable with the action in a construction with
V + SEBJA. The subject has an agent and a patient role, which can
still be distinguished. Part of the entity is moving, part is non-
moving. With verbs like *вертеться*, also implying movement, the two
roles are already merged to a considerable degree: the whole entity
is moving (is active, and at the same time affected by the action).
Therefore these verbs cannot be considered to be true reflexives.
The degree of agentivity of the subject and the degree of merging
of the roles are deducible, as is stated above, from the status of
the subject (+ or - animate), and from the lexical meaning of the
verb. It is not signaled by -SJA. That is why -SJA can occur where
SEBJA cannot.

Whereas Peškovskij extends the boundaries of the true reflexives, Janko-Trinickaja and Veyrenc narrow them. Veyrenc (1980: 227
-230) excludes Vsja like *бриться, гримироваться, причесываться*,
which he calls reflexive verbs "à référence partielle". With these
verbs -SJA is not replaceable by SEBJA, only by a DO denoting a
particular part of the body. Janko-Trinickaja (1962: 180) calls

the same type of Vsja reflexives "включенного неодушевленного объекта", instead of "включенного возвратного объекта". She opposes *причесываться* for instance to *причесывать волосы* (as Veyrenc does), and does not oppose it to *причесывать себя/кого-н.*

With "partial reflexives" implying movement, we can establish the same type of difference as with Vsja concerning the whole body (see above). Here too SEBJA can occur if we can split up the entity into two participants, a moving one and a non-moving one, with SEBJA referring to the non-moving one, cf. *(бриться), брить щеки* and *брить себя*. If it is not possible to distinguish between a moving and a non-moving participant, SEBJA cannot be used. Cf. *уткнуться (головой), уткнуть голову, *уткнуть себя*: the subject moves by means of his head, it is the head that moves.

Some grammarians distinguish between paraphrase of -SJA with the help of SEBJA and occurrence of SEBJA in actual sentences. Staxova (1961: 304) for instance states explicitly that e.g. *одеваться* can be paraphrased by means of SEBJA, but that *одевать себя* is not used in modern Russian. In Klenin (1975: 190) on the other hand, we find that *одеваться* and *одевать себя* "may both occur (synonymously)". So it appears to be difficult to draw a clear cut boundary between 2. and 4. where true reflexives are concerned.

In my opinion the distinction between paraphrase and occurrence is an artificial one. If it is possible to paraphrase -SJA by means of SEBJA, it can be used also (although there may not be much need to do so with certain verbs, where the action is usually performed by the agent on his own body), if only in conjunction or contrast with other DO's:

Она причесала себя и дочь / себя, а не дочь

If it is not possible to use SEBJA even this way, -SJA is not paraphrasable by means of SEBJA, and Vsja cannot be considered to be a true reflexive (cf. Peškovskij's examples).

Ad 3. SEBJA means "coreferentiality", and this is the "truest" reflexivity there is. -SJA in contrast can be interpreted in many different ways. When a Vsja cannot be interpreted as a true reflexive, we cannot speak of -SJA "=" SEBJA. In this paper SEBJA will

be compared with "true reflexive", "re-agentive", "middle" and
"passive" Vsja, the difference between -SJA and SEBJA growing in
this same sequence.

Ad 4. As we have found that most transitive verbs that can
have an animate DO can also have SEBJA, this group mainly consists
of Vsja derived from transitive verbs with an inanimate DO, Vsja
derived from intransitive verbs, and Vsja tantum (i.e. Vsja beside
which no corresponding non-reflexive verb with more or less the
same lexical meaning exists).

2.2. *Differences*

SEBJA is a pronoun with an independent status. It refers to a
member of a set of entities which can occupy the syntactic position of a DO with transitive verbs. Its function is anaphoric: it
gives the hearer the instruction: "Look for the antecedent". Its
meaning is "coreferentiality": it refers to the same entity in the
real world that the subject refers to. As a DO it has a patient
role, and therefore it attributes to the subject the role of agent
(the notions of patient and agent include here also the roles of
the DO and the subject of verbs of perception, like видеть, чувст-
вовать). The verb denotes an action (or perception), not a process
or a state. The two participants (subject and SEBJA) are present
from the start, independently of whether the action is performed
or not.

-SJA has no independent status. It is an affix, constituting
a unity with the verb to which it is attached. It is not a DO,
nevertheless it blocks the occurrence of a DO with the verb[6]. It
does not instruct the hearer to look for an antecedent. The entity
to which it points is obvious: it is the subject of the verb it is
attached to (the problem of subjectless sentences with a Vsja
needs further investigation). -SJA assigns to the subject two
roles. These two roles do not appear at the same time. The second
role arises as a consequence of the event; it comes into sight
together with the verb to which it is attached, and which may
denote an action or a process. The participant becomes the bearer
of a quality in the state following the action or process, it may

be called an "object of result".

From what is said above about SEBJA and -SJA we can conclude
that SEBJA points in two directions: 1) to its own referent: "this
referent is the patient, no other referent is"; 2) to the referent
of the antecedent: "this referent is the agent, no other referent
is". -SJA does not stand in an opposition with other possible participants, it does not say: "this participant, no other one", but:
"the subject, the one participant there is, is doubly engaged in
the action".

This difference between -SJA and SEBJA is reflected in the
form. The two-syllable word SEBJA may, and often does, bear the
sentence-accent, which then does not include the verb in its scope.
If in contrast the syllable -SJA happens to carry the sentence-
accent, it includes (at least) the entire verb in its scope[7]. The
reduced form of -SJA, -S', which occurs after vowels (with the
exclusion of participles), cannot bear any accent at all.

2.3. *Examples*

The examples given below are grouped in numbered pairs of
sentences. The a.-sentences are constructions with SEBJA, the b.-
sentences contain the corresponding Vsja.
The sequence of the sentences runs parallel to the -SJA-continuum,
in such a way that the interpretation of -SJA in the first group
of sentences (group A) is true reflexive, in the second group
(group B) re-agentive, middle, and passive successively.

The semantic difference between SEBJA and -SJA is smallest in
group A. With true reflexive Vsja the verb denotes an action, as
does the verb in a construction with SEBJA, and the roles of the
subject of the Vsja (a full agent and a patient role) are still
distinguishable. SEBJA may be used instead of -SJA if one wishes
to evoke a contrast with other (possible) patients. If it is necessary to emphasize the fact that the subject-referent himself is
also the patient of the action, because the verb denotes an action
that is usually directed to some entity other than himself, the
verb can often only have SEBJA, not -SJA (cf. the verbs mentioned
in section 2, ad 1.).

In group B the subject of the Vsja is not a full agent any
more, it gradually loses its agentive features. To express the
fact that the subject of the verb is a full agent, SEBJA is needed.
Within the construction with SEBJA, there is an opposition between
the subject-referent and other possible agents.

Group A is subdivided into Aa.: physical actions, performed
on the whole body of the subject or part of it; Ab.: total actions
(i.e. not only physical, nor only mental) concerning the whole
person or "parts" of him, like qualities, thoughts, ideas, words,
his name, etc.; Ac.: physical actions concerning part of the body
or the whole person, which produce a negative effect on the subject.

Group B is subdivided on the basis of the different interpretations of -SJA: Ba.: re-agentive, Bb.: middle, Bc.: passive.

A   -SJA: true reflexive interpretation; SEBJA: opposition with
     other (possible) patients

Aa. Physical actions

These actions are generally performed by the subject on its
own body, more often than on other persons' bodies. The semantic
difference between SEBJA and -SJA is small, the main function of
SEBJA, as opposed to -SJA, being a syntagmatic one, viz. to make
possible the conjunction or contrast with other DO's in the sentence. With -SJA this possibility does not exist without repeating
the verb, because -SJA, not having a separate status, cannot be
part of a compound object.

Part of the body:

(1) a. *Я мою себя, а потом буду мыть сина.* (Norman 1972: 94)
     b. *я моюсь.*

The a.-sentence is a clear example of contrast with another DO,
present in the sentence.

Combination with other DO's even makes the use of SEBJA possible in sentences with a causative interpretation:

(2) a. *Борис бреет отца и себя у парикмахера.* (Walther 1983: 427)
     bl *Борис бреется у парикмахера.*

b2 *Мать собиралась помыть свою дочь, но дочь не захотела мыться.* (Nedjalkov 1979: 59)

In the b.-sentences SEBJA cannot replace -SJA, so the only possibility for using SEBJA in such cases is conjunction or contrast with other patients, present in the sentence.

The other entities with which SEBJA is contrasted need not always be present in the sentence. If they are not, SEBJA only evokes the thought of them:

(3) a. *Он не умеет брить себя.* (Cranmer 1976: 54)
   b. *Он не умеет бриться.* (ibid.)

In (3) a. we learn that the person, denoted by the subject, cannot shave himself, but he may be able to shave other persons. In b. no such thought comes to the mind of the hearer: the person mentioned just cannot perform the action of shaving (himself)[8].

If the referent of the subject usually did not perform the action on himself all by himself, *сам* can, in conjunction with SEBJA, evoke the opposition with other participants:

(4) a. *Сегодня ребенок умыл себя сам в первый раз.* (Babby 1974: 318)
   b. *Ребенок умылся, оделся, и ...*

In (4) b. we are only interested in what happened, not in who did it, or to whom.

The fact that -SJA does not evoke the thought of any other participant than the one present in the sentence, may lead to a shift in the way the action is viewed. As we can see in the following pair of sentences, the construction with SEBJA depicts an action with an agent and a patient, whereas the construction with -SJA gives us the picture of the participant as an object of result. The participant is in a certain state as a result of (in this case) his own actions:

(5) a. *Она очень сильно мажет себя.* (Cranmer 1976: 49)
   b. *Она очень сильно мажется.* (ibid.)

These sentences are translated by Cranmer as: a. 'She heavily makes-up herself' and b. 'She wears heavy make-up', which confirms the above analysis.

The independent status of SEBJA may have further consequences:

(6) a. *Он (Дибич) ощупал себя клейкой ладонью. Кобура револьвера
        была пуста.* (Staxova 1961: 301)

     b. *Часа через полтора лейтенант проснулся. Он ощупался, сдер-
        нул платок.* (SRJ II: 736)

In (6) a. we could consider the referent of *ладонью* to be a third
participant, beside those of the subject and SEBJA. -SJA in b.
does not involve a separate participant, so there is no question
at all of splitting up into two participants, let alone into three.
That is why the instrumental object *ладонью* cannot be added here.
Of course, -SJA can occur with an instrumental object denoting a
part of the body, cf. *уткнуться головой.* But then the instrumental
object does not perform an action on something else, as in (6) a.,
it is moving as a whole, representing the subject (see above,
section 2, ad 2.).

The whole body:

(7) a. *Он отряхивал себя.* (Staxova 1961: 303)

     b. *Вступив на палубу, он отряхнулся от воды, как выкупавшийся
        пес, и огляделся.* (SRJ II: 709)

Verbs like *отряхивать/отряхнуть* allow two types of second valence.
In this case these valences are 1) the entity that is shaken (the
patient), and 2) the material that is shaken out (dust, snow,
water etc.). If SEBJA, referring to the entity shaken, is present,
the material that is shaken out cannot be present. As -SJA is not
a DO, in b. *от воды* can be present.

(8) a. *Рагозин вырвал себя из неподвижности, охватил мальчика за
        руку и подвел к рисункам.* (Staxova 1961: 293)

     b1 *Елена вырвалась из моих объятий.* (SRJ I: 276)

     b2 *Как я рад, что наконец вырвался из города.* (ibid.)

The common element in these sentences is the adjunct with *из.*
There is however an important difference. The adjunct in the a.-
sentence is part of the subject-entity, it represents as it were a
third participant (1: *Рагозин*, 2: *себя* , 3: *неподвижность*). The
adjuncts in the b.-sentences on the other hand are not manifestations of the subject, they are places from where the subject (as a

whole) moves away. In both b.-sentences the participant is the object of result. He performs an action and as a result is in a certain state, viz. free, away.

Ab. Total actions

The actions in this section are not predominantly performed by the referent of the subject with himself. Therefore SEBJA may be needed to emphasize that it is (part of) the person, denoted by the subject, that is the patient of the action.

"Part" of the person:

(9) a. *Чайковский подошел, назвал себя. Трощенко спросил: - Чем могу служить?* (SRJ II: 354)

    b. *До свиданья... Простите, имени вашего не знаю. Я назвался. - Иван Тимофеевич? Ну, вот и отлично.* (ibid.)

In these sentences the "part" is the name of the subject-referent, but by means of SEBJA this name represents the whole person. In the a.-sentence the information about the object is new, the part of the sentence preceding SEBJA making clear that someone enters and mentions something/someone. The place of the DO after the verb could be occupied by different objects, among them, as a member of this set of entities, the referent of SEBJA. In the b.-sentence someone is asking for the name of the subject of the Vsja, so the situation is clear before the verb appears. There are no other possible objects except the referent of the subject, so SEBJA would give too much emphasis to the object.

(10) a. *В партии он был известен под именем Ивана Несчастной жизни, как он называл себя на допросах у следователей.* (Staxova 1961: 301)

    b. *(Самозванец:) Я бедный черноризец; ... Явился к вам; Димитрием назвался.* (SRJ II: 354)

The interpretation of *назвать* in these sentences is somewhat different from the one in (9). In (9) it is 'name oneself, mention one's own name', in (10) 'give oneself a name'. In a. SEBJA is used to emphasize the fact that the *следователи*, for instance, did not give the subject-referent the epithet, he himself did it. The opposition here is thus one concerning the agent. The reason why this sentence is not placed under group B (see below) is the fact that Vsja has a true reflexive interpretation here, -SJA and SEBJA being almost synonymous. And, as can be concluded from the -SJA-continuum, the difference between -SJA and SEBJA grows, descending from true to passive reflexives. It will be clear that there is no question of clear cut boundaries where we speak of a continuum. Between different groups there are areas where they overlap, they gradually shade off into one another.

In the b.-sentence again there is no opposition regarding participants. The emphasis is on the name, not on the person.

(11) a. *Художник выразил себя в этой картине.* (Cranmer 1976: 53)

   b. *Студент выразился хорошо в школьном сочинении.* (ibid.)

The "part" of the subject-referent meant by SEBJA in this case is the personality, the "soul", the ideas of the person. SEBJA is the answer to the question: "What did he express?". Regarding b. one cannot ask such a question, one can only ask: "How did he express himself, what kind of words did he use?". The adverb of manner is obligatory here, the emphasis is on the action.

   In the next pair of sentences V (the verb from which -SJA is derived) and Vsja are usually considered to have different lexical meanings: V means 'to deceive someone/oneself', Vsja 'to be mistaken'.

(12) a. *Он (Степан Аркадьич) не мог обманывать себя и уверять себя, что он раскаивается в своем поступке.* (Vil'gel'mina 1963: 129)

   b. *(Он не мог обманывать себя, но) он мог обманываться.* (ibid.)

In my opinion the difference only concerns the participants. In (12) a. again the thought of other possible participants is evoked. *Он* could perhaps deceive other persons, but not himself. In sentences like (12) b. the process of deceit takes place within the person denoted by the subject. Part of him (e.g. his subconsciousness, his observations) deceives another part of the same person (e.g. his consciousness, his intellect), and as a result the person arrives at the wrong conclusions.

The whole person:

(13) a. *Я защищаю себя, а не вас.* (Townsend 1967: 198)

    b. *Спасибо ... Я как-нибудь сам защищусь!* (SRJ I: 598)

The a.-sentence is a clear example of contrast with another DO, which contrast is absent in b. In b. *сам* evokes a contrast with other possible agents: the subject performs the action all by himself, without the help of other persons.

    Another example with the same verb demonstrates again the fact that the referent of SEBJA is conceived of as an independent entity, whereas the referent of -SJA is not:

(14) a. *Мама не позволяет Володе защищать себя от злых собак.*
      (Klenin 1975: 189)

    b. *Мама не позволяет Володе защищаться от злых собак.* (ibid.)

In a. it is not clear who is the antecedent of SEBJA. Both *мама* and *Володе* could refer to the entity that is coreferential with the entity referred to by SEBJA, so the sentence is ambiguous. This confirms what is said before, viz. that the hearer is instructed to look for the antecedent, as it is not always obvious. When SEBJA is replaced by -SJA, however, this ambiguity disappears, because -SJA does not involve a separate participant, but points to the subject of the verb it is attached to ((14) b.).

    Another consequence of the separate status of SEBJA is the possibility of its being conjoined with an adjective:

(15) a. *Вижу себя всего в зеркале.* (Norman 1972: 127)

    b. *Смотрюсь в зеркало, молодой и красивый.* (ibid.)

In a construction with -SJA the adjective can only determine the subject, as is the case in (15) b.

(16) a. *Я унизил себя до неверья, я унизил тебя до тоски.* (Janko-
      Trinickaja 1962: 187)

    b. *В меня вселится новый бес, и Фебови презрев угрозы, уни-
      жусь до смиренной прозы.* (ibid. 186)

These examples speak for themselves. So do the following sentences:

(17) a. *Ивану хочется хвалить себя.* (Veyrenc 1980: 286)

    b. *Плотно поев, бойцы курили и хвалились друг перед другом.*
      (SRJ IV: 594)

where in a. the person denoted by the subject wants to praise himself because apparently nobody else does, or because he always
praises other people and now it's his turn to be praised (by himself). In b. the emphasis is on what the persons mentioned were
doing.

(18) a. *В самой науке, в ее одушевленных лекциях (...), теперь
стало ему заметно везде желание выказаться, хвастнуть,
выставить себя.* (Staxova 1961: 298)

   b. *Теркин не хотел поднимать истории. Он мог отправиться к
капитану и сказать, кто он. Надо тогда выставляться, назы-
вать свою фамилию, а ему было неудобно в ту минуту.* (ibid.)

In a. we have a clear example of a split entity. The persons involved want to point to themselves as if these were separate persons:
"this person is me, here is someone you cannot overlook". In b.
the person denoted by the subject has to come forward, as a whole
person, the entity is not divided into two participants.

(19) a. *Целый год сидел он за ним (портретом), не выходя из своей
кельи, едва питая себя суровой пищей.* (SRJ III: 127)

   b. *Он питаться стал плодами, и водою ключевой.* (ibid. 128)

In both sentences in (19) there is an instrumental object, but it
has a different status in a. and b. In a. it can be omitted. What
is important here is the patient who undergoes the action of feed-
ing. In b. the emphasis is not on the patient (there is no DO with
a patient role), but on the way the action is performed, and on
the result of this for the person involved. He is the object of
result, the food mentioned is the means to achieve this result.

(20) a. *Он отдал себя любимому делу и немалого добился.* (SRJ II:
673)

   b. *Я отдался целиком общественной жизни.* (ibid. 674)

The difference between the two sentences is here hardly percepti-
ble, but nevertheless the difference between the separate participants referred to by SEBJA and the undivided person referred to by
-SJA is still present.

(21) a. *Я на знакомства очень осторожен - я берегу себя.* (Janko-
Trinickaja 1962: 186)

   b. *- Здесь глубоко, берегитесь! - с испугом вскрикнула Маша.*
(SRJ I: 80)

In a. the emphasis is on the participant who has to be taken care
of, guarded. In b. it is on something else: 'beware of ... !'. So,
although the referent of the subject in b. will be affected by the
action, the attention is on something else.

(22) a. *Однако при первой же встрече он держал себя так, как будто
ничего не случилось.* (Vil'gel'minina 1963: 130)

b. *Она винила себя в том, что держалась с ним недостаточно
строго.* (ibid.)

SEBJA in a. leads to the projection of two persons, one of them
the real person, the other one the person as he presents himself.
In b. the person WAS not strict enough, there is no question of
his presenting himself in a certain way.

Ac. Actions with a negative effect on the subject
     The actions introduced in this section are usually presented
in order to show the difference between SEBJA and -SJA where they
seem to be semantically equivalent. In the literature this difference is claimed to be a matter of (in)voluntariness of the action.
It concerns only physical actions, because psychological or social
actions cannot be performed accidentally.
     However, if we compare

(23) a. *Играя пистолетом, который он считал незаряженным, он за-
стрелил себя.* (Staxova 1961: 292)

b. *Потеряв все, он впал в отчаяние и застрелился.* (ibid.)

and

(24) a. *Он поранил себя ножом (преднамеренно).* (Isačenko 1960: 392)

b. *Он играл ножом и поранился.* (ibid.)

it appears that it cannot be (in)voluntariness which differentiates between SEBJA and -SJA, as the involuntariness in (23) is
expressed in the a.-sentence (SEBJA), and in (24) in the b.-sen-
tence (-SJA)!
     If we deal with these sentences on the basis of the present
analysis, however, (23) and (24) acquire a natural explanation:
(23) a.: If someone plays with a pistol, the pistol can go off,
and any member of the set of entities present in its environment,
the person playing included, could be hit. In this sentence SEBJA

emphasizes the fact that it is indeed the latter who is the victim.

(24) b.: If on the other hand someone plays with a knife, the
most likely object to be injured is the person playing, so there
is no opposition with other possible objects, no emphasis. This is
a motivation for using -SJA.

(23) a.: The situation described in the part of the sentence preceding the verb, makes it clear that the action affects the referent of the subject. No thought of other possible patients is
evoked.

(24) a.: To injure oneself with a knife is a rather unusual action,
so SEBJA is present to show that it is indeed the entity referred
to by the subject that is injured, not any other entity.

(25) a. *Он случайно порезал себя бритвой.* (Cranmer 1976: 49)

   b1 *Он случайно порезался бритвой.* (ibid.)

   b2 *Даронин наскоро (...) побрился. При этом дважды порезался.*
   (SRJ III: 302)

In all three sentences an involuntary action is expressed, whether
SEBJA or -SJA is used. In a. we get the picture of an action, in
b1 of the result of an action. Sentence b1 could be the answer to
the question: "What happened to him? There is blood on his cheek!".
In b2 the affected person is obvious from the preceding sentence,
he need not be stressed by means of SEBJA.

(26) a. *Половина их в течение десяти лет гибла, кто вешая себя,
   кто сжигаясь.* (RG 1982: 617)

   b. *От стыда и горя он решил расстаться с жизнью и повесился.*
   (Staxova 1961: 292)

Of the two events mentioned in the second part of the a.-sentence,
one is described by means of V + SEBJA, the other with a Vsja. The
reason why SEBJA is used in the first event is that *вешать* has an
obligatory agent[9]. So either the subject or someone else did the
hanging. To emphasize that it was the person, denoted by the subject, SEBJA is used. *Сжигать* on the other hand has an optional
agent, so *сжигаясь* means that they got burnt to death. What matters is the "result", not how it happened, or who did it. In b.
the circumstances under which the hanging took place are given in
the preceding part of the sentence. Agent and patient are obvious,

so there is no opposition with other possible participants.

(27) a. *Кирилла не утешил холодный душ, которым он окатил сам себя.* (Staxova 1961: 304)

    b. *Кирилла не утешил холодный душ, которым он окатился.* (ibid.)

The combined *сам себя* underlines the clumsiness of the hero, the comical situation he is in. In b. the event is described without special accents on who was responsible, who was whose "victim".

(28) a. *Он рассмеялся и ударил себя ладонью по колену.* (Isačenko 1960:391)

    b. *Проходя по темной комнате, он ударился коленом об стол.* (ibid.)

In (28) a. the one real-world entity is referred to not two or three, but four times: twice regarding his agentive role, through *он* and *ладонью*, whose referents are moving, and twice regarding his patient role, through SEBJA and *колену*, whose referents are non-moving. In b. the knee is not referred to as a separate participant, as is the case in a., nor does it perform an action on something else as does the instrumental object in a. (*ладонью*). The undivided participant moves, part of him is hit. He is hit with respect to his knee.

(29) a. (continuation of the b.-sentence) *Отравила себя, чтобы казнить этим другого!* (Walther 1983: 417)

    b. *Не могу допустить, чтобы она отравилась ... Боже мой, если ваше предположение справедливо, то ведь ... это жестоко, бесчеловечно.*

SEBJA in a. is opposed to *другого*, although the verbs of which they are the DO differ. *Отравиться* (b.) can be interpreted both as true reflexive and as middle (*отравить* has an optional agent: cf. for instance *отравиться угарным газом*). But that is not what matters here. What is expressed is that the referent of the subject is in a certain state as a result of an event (whether or not the person performed the action himself; that he himself indeed was the agent follows from the next part of the sentence).

(30) a. *Мария Годунова и сын ее Феодор отравили себя ядом.* (SRJ II: 704)

    b. *Я отравился и отравил вас, вместе того чтоб быть просто и прямо счастливым.* (Janko-Trinickaja 1962: 184)

The first sentence speaks for itself. Nobody else poisoned the
persons mentioned, nor did they poison anybody else, they themselves poisoned themselves. In the second sentence there are two
affected persons, so we might expect SEBJA (*u вас*). In that case
however the event would be presented as one action with two affected objects, and that is apparently not what is meant here. Here
we have in fact two events: 1) something happened to the referent
of the subject; 2) the subject-referent performed an action with
someone else. Whether or not the subject-referent is responsible
for what happened to himself (first event), is not made clear.
What matters is the state he is in, and the fact that he was not a
pure passive undergoer (the double role). For what happened to the
other participant he indeed is responsible, he is the agent who
performed an action with a patient.

(31) a. *Он убил себя выстрелом из пистолета.* (Isačenko 1960: 392)
     b. *Он упал с пятого этажа и убился.* (ibid.)

In contrast to *застрелить* (cf. (23)), *убить* has an optional agent.
So, because *убиться* means 'to get killed' (as is the interpretation in b.), SEBJA has to be used if the speaker wants to indicate
suicide. Although the subject-referent in b. seems to be a mere
patient, the second role is still there. On the one hand something
happens to him, but on the other hand he "does" something: he
dies.

The sentences (29), (30) and (31) form the transition from
group A to group B (see below).

B   -SJA: other interpretations; SEBJA: opposition with other
     possible agents

Ba. -SJA: "Re-agentive"
     The term "re-agentive" is used to indicate that the referent
of the subject does not perform an action, but reacts on certain
stimuli in or outside himself. The result of this with respect to
the described events is an opposition between action (SEBJA) and
process (-SJA)[10]. As to the agent, we have two oppositions:
1) within the construction with SEBJA there is an opposition
between "this agent" and other possible agents; 2) between the

construction with SEBJA and the one with -SJA there is an opposition between a subject with a full agent role (SEBJA) and a subject which is, beside being affected, only a re-agent (-SJA). The participant reacts to certain stimuli and as a result gets into a certain state.

From this point of view the following examples as a matter of fact speak for themselves:

(32) a. *Нехлюдов никак не мог настроить себя, чтобы быть любезным.* (SRJ II: 401)

b. *Я собирался ехать в областную партийную школу и давно настроился на учебный лад.* (ibid.)

(33) a. *Настрой себя на деловой лад.* (Staxova 1961: 297)

b. *Настройся на деловой лад.* (ibid.)

The use of the imperative mood in (33) might seem to contradict the above analysis, but does not really do so. In a. the order is: "Perform the action", in b.: "See to it that you get into that state".

(34) a. *Он (Степан Аркадьич) не мог обманывать себя и уверять себя, что он раскаивается в своем поступке.* (Vil'gel'minina 1963: 129)

b1 *Он начал постепенно уверяться в правоте своего поступка.* (ibid.)

b2 *Чтобы действительно увериться, что он не пьян, майор ущипнул себя так больно, что сам вскрикнул.* (SRJ IV: 449)

The a.- and b1-sentences are clear without further comment. Whether the state the participant in b1 gets into is caused by his own or someone else's activities, or by other events, is left undecided. In b2 the participant performs a volitional act (SEBJA) to arrive at the state of being convinced (-SJA).

(35) a. *Ты очень сильная женщина, Поля, ты - настоящая. Как ты согнула себя, ты, такая гордая, а?* (SRJ IV: 179)

b. *Мне было обидно, что мать немела и тряслась перед дедом, что отец с трусливым озлоблением сносил его самодурство. А теперь и Катя вот согнулась и замолчала.* (ibid. 180)

The opposition action - process ((35) a. - (35) b.) with a verb like *согнуть* is only possible in a non-literal (non-physical) sense. In the literal, physical sense this verb is of the same type as *вертеть*, where SEBJA cannot be used (cf. also (42) below).

(36) a. *Он все успокаивал себя мыслю, что ... (SSRLJ 16: 938)*

    b1 *Успокоясь сими мыслями, кои казались мне самою достовер-*
    ною догадкой, я то ходил вдоль забора, то сидел на лавке,
    попевая и насвистывая веселые песни. (ibid. 939)

    b2 *Она попробовала улыбнуться, успокоиться, но подбородок ее*
    дрожал и грудь все еще колыхалась. (SRJ IV: 522)

In b2 the participant did not try to perform an action, but performed an action to try to get into a state (cf. (34) b2).

(37) a. *Так утешал он себя, ...*

    b1 *... но никак не мог утешиться. Воспоминание это жгло*
    совесть. (Janko-Trinickaja 1962: 186)

    b2 *Увы! Утешится жена, и друга лучший друг забудет.* (ibid.)

The situation in a. and b1 corresponds to the one in (36) a. and
b2, the action being expressed in a. and the (absence of) the
result in b1. As to b2, it is not clear whether the participant
referred to by the subject will perform the action, or whether
someone else will. -SJA leaves this undecided. What is clear is
that the participant will be in a certain state as a result of the
action.

Bb. -SJA: "Middle"

    Further downwards along the continuum, the subject again
loses one agentive feature: he is an actor without being responsible (or: with the responsibility not being expressed), or he is
responsible without being active, in that he possesses certain
qualities which bring about the state he is in.

(38) a. *Советский Союз превратился, точнее превратил сам себя во*
    вторую промышленную державу в мире. (Janko-Trinickaja 1962:
    187)

    b. = first part of a.

Точнее in a. confirms what is said above about the non-expressed
responsibility of the participant in the sentence-part with Vsja.
SEBJA is more precise in that it designates the referent of the
subject as the one responsible for what happened to him (*сам* reinforces this effect). In the first part of the sentence (b.) -SJA
only points to the double role. The participant is active in that
it changes, and at the same time is affected by the change.

(39) a. *Теория оправдала себя.* (Isačenko 1960: 398)

    b. *Теория оправдалась.* (ibid.)

Althouth SEBJA refers most of the time to a person, it may also refer to an inanimate entity. This has consequences with respect to the agentivity of the subject, which cannot have the feature +volition. But still it is responsible, in such a way that it appeared to be strong enough to justify itself, it needed no one to do that. In b. we learn only that the justifying has happened, although here also the external agent (whoever it was) could not have established its correctness without certain qualities (the "agentive" role) of the *теория*. (Sentences such as those under (39) show that when the difference between -SJA and SEBJA increases, less context is needed to recognize it.)

(40) a. *Он-то считает себя умным,* ...

    b. *... а у окружающих считается круглым дураком.* (Vinogradov 1947: 631)

Считаться (b.) is often considered to have a passive interpretation. In passive constructions an external participant is fully responsible for the action. In b. however -SJA, assigning a double role to the subject, attributes to the one participant present part of the responsibility, and we could say that in this sentence the qualities of the subject-referent are the reason that he is looked upon in a certain way.

(41) a. *Но душа требовала отзива, и Карась окружил себя особого рода дураками.* (Janko-Trinickaja 1962: 186)

    b. *Он, окружась толпой врачей, на ложе мнимого мученья, стоная молит исцеленья.* (ibid.)

The a.-sentence, like all the a.-sentences in both the A- and B-groups, is explicit with regard to the agentivity of the subject. The b.-sentence however is not. We do not learn from the b.-sentence who caused the state the subject-referent is in: he himself or someone else. But if someone else did it, the subject-referent bears at least part of the responsibility. He is not a mere patient of the action (in that case a passive participle would have been used), his share in the action having been at least a permissive one.

Bc.   -SJA: "Passive"

With the passive interpretation of -SJA we have arrived at
the bottom of the continuum. The difference between SEBJA and
-SJA has grown to such an extent, that there is little use in comparing them. Verbs that can have SEBJA in the place of the DO, but
also can derive a passive Vsja are for instance: *ловить/поймать,*
обвинять, принудить, проклинать.

Passive Vsja bear a certain resemblance to passive participles, therefore they can be more usefully compared with the PP
than with SEBJA. The subject of reflexive versus analytical passive will be dealt with in a subsequent article.

Bd.   -SJA: Other interpretations

Besides true, re-agentive, middle and passive interpretations, other interpretations of -SJA exist. These interpretations,
and the exact place of such interpretational groups in the continuum, need to be further investigated. For the time being it
does not look as if they offer new interesting data for the comparison with SEBJA. Yet I would like to mention one example:

(42) a. *Кирилл сидел неподвижно, точно ему требовалось крайнее*
         усилие воли, чтобы возвратить себя из бесконечной дали
         к тому, что находилось перед его взором. (Staxova 1961:
         293)

      b. *Дети возвращались домой.*

Возвращаться is a Vsja with a "non-causative" interpretation. The
term "non-causative" is used to indicate that the Vsja has lost
the causative element which is present in the meaning of V, which
meaning is: 'to cause Vsja'. So V is a causative verb. Generally
spoken SEBJA cannot be used with such causative verbs. But this
rule appears to apply only to the literal sense of the verb. As we
can see in the a.-sentence, in a metaphorical sense V + SEBJA can
occur. The a.-sentence shows that the referent of SEBJA is a member of the set of entities that are possible patients of V. The
participant that is the agent forces another participant (being
the same real-world-entity) to return. In a literal sense this
would not be possible, because the whole undivided entity is involved in the act of returning. Only -SJA is possible in that case

and the subject has its double role: the participant is active and at the same time bears the result of the action, is the object of result.

3. Conclusion

The example-sentences under A and B can be considered to support the hypothesis that the difference between -SJA and SEBJA is a matter of roles and participants:
1. in a construction of the type S + V + SEBJA there are two distinct participants, each with its own role (the subject has a full agent role, SEBJA a patient role);
2. in a construction consisting of S + Vsja there is only one participant, but it plays a double role.
In 1. V denotes an action, it is the action itself that is depicted, whereas in 2. an action or process is depicted complete with its result. In connection with the latter one of the two roles of the participant in the Vsja-construction is "object of result". The other one is an agentive role, but seldom a full one (only with true reflexives). The degree of agentivity does not depend on -SJA, but is to be inferred from other factors.

University of Leiden

NOTES

This research was supported by the Foundation for Linguistic Research, which is funded by the Netherlands Organization for the advancement of pure research, ZWO.
I wish to thank Dr C.E. Keijsper for valuable ideas, criticism and support at various stages of research and writing.

[1] For technical reasons the forms -SJA and SEBJA are given throughout the article in transliteration.
[2] A similar point of view is held by Xrakovskij (1981: 5-38), but his elaboration differs considerably from mine.
[3] Cf. Klenin (1975: 190): "*Zaščiščat' sebja* and *zaščiščat'sja* differ in essentially one way: the former has an expressed object, the latter does not. The other differences are subordinate to this one."
[4] Precisely in these cases -SJA is often left out, and *Гром прокатил* is used beside *Гром прокатился*.

⁵ Cf. Isačenko (1975: 463): "Leider werden diese Fälle in der russischen Grammatik gewöhnlich nicht besprochen, auch fehlen sie meist in den Wörterbüchern."
⁶ There are a few exceptions to this rule, cf. *бояться команду, слушаться маму, дождаться подругу*. With SEBJA, being a DO, such a combination is forbidden.
⁷ For the notion of "scope": see Keijsper elsewhere in this volume.
⁸ My interpretation of b. differs essentially from Cranmer's: "... *он* does not know how to shave anyone, including himself.". In my opinion the word "anyone" should be omitted here. If the speaker had meant to say what Cranmer thinks he did, he would have used the non-reflexive *брить*.
⁹ Cf. Babby 1974: 320-321, who explains the difference between verbs like *повеситься* ("=" *повесить себя*) and *лишиться* ("≠" *лишить себя*) on the basis of the notions "obligatory agent" and "optional agent".
¹⁰ This is confirmed by what we find in the dictionaries: to paraphrase this type of Vsja, verbs like *становиться/стать* are used, whereas the meaning of the corresponding V is usually described with verbs like *делать*.

REFERENCES

Babby, L.H.
1974   "A transformational analysis of transitive -SJA verbs in Russian", *Lingua* 35, 1975, 297-332.
Cranmer, D.J.
1976   *Derived Intransitivity: a Contrastive Analysis of Certain Reflexive Verbs in German, Russian and English*. Tübingen.
Isačenko, A.V.
1960   *Grammatičeskij stroj russkogo jazyka v sopostavlenii s slovackim. Morfologija II*. Bratislava.
1975³   *Die Russische Sprache der Gegenwart. Formenlehre*. München.
Janko-Trinickaja, N.A.
1962   *Vozvratnye glagoly v sovremennom russkom jazyke*. Moskva.
Klenin, E.
1975   "The Pronoun *sebjá*, Particle *sebe*, and Affix *-sja*", *Slavic and East-European Journal* 19, 2, 188-199.
Nedjalkov, V.P.
1979   "O refleksivnom glagol'nom slovoobrazovanii", *Slovoobrazovanie i frazoobrazovanie, Tezisy dokladov naučnoj konferencii*, 59-61. Moskva.
Norman, B.Ju.
1972   *Perexodnost', zalog, vozvratnost' (na materiale bolgarskogo i drugix slavjanskix jazykov)*. Minsk.
Peškovskij, A.M.
1956⁷/1935   *Russkij sintaksis v naučnom osveščenii*. Moskva.
RG
1982   *Russkaja grammatika. Tom I. Fonetika, fonologija, udarenie, intonacija, slovoobrazovanie, morfologija*. AN SSSR. Moskva.
SRJ
1981²   *Slovar' russkogo jazyka v četyrex tomax*. AN SSSR. Moskva.
SSRLJ
1950-65   *Slovar' sovremennogo russkogo literaturnogo jazyka*. AN SSSR. Moskva-Leningrad.

Staxova, G.A.
1961   "Glagoly sobstvenno-vozvratnogo zalogovogo značenija v sovremennom russkom jazyke", *Issledovanija po leksikologii i grammatike
russkogo jazyka*, 288-306. Moskva.
Townsend, Ch.E.
1967   "Voice and Verbs in -*sja*", *Slavic and East-European Journal* 11,
2, 196-203.
Veyrenc, J.
1980   *Études sur le verbe russe*. Paris.
Vil'gel'minina, A.A.
1963   *The Russian Verb. Aspect and Voice*. Moskva.
Vinogradov, V.V.
1947   *Russkij jazyk. Grammatičeskoe učenie o slove*. Moskva-Leningrad.
Walther, G.
1983   "Zur Semantik des reflexiven Affixes -SJA in der russischen
Sprache der Gegenwart", *Zeitschrift für Slawistik*, 28, 3, 413-437.
Xrakovskij, V.S.
1981   "Diateza i referentnost' (K voprosu o sootnošenii aktivnyx, pas-
sivnyx, refleksivnyx i reciproknyx konstrukcij.)", *Zalogovye konstrukcii v raznostrukturnyx jazykax*, 5-38. Leningrad.

THE GEMINATE PALATALS AND AFFRICATES IN CSR

B.M. GROEN

0   *INTRODUCTION*

Much has been written about the geminate palatals (and affricates) in contemporary standard Russian, and all kinds of analyses have been made. There are descriptions in which these sound complexes are described as separate phonemes, the monophonematic interpretation, as found in e.g. Avanesov (1984:60, and earlier publications), Reformatskij (1967:1655f.), Pilch (1967:1562), Panov (1967:passim) and the Academy's latest Russkaja Grammatika (AkGr 1980, tom 1, 18-19).

Other investigators present biphonematic solutions: Trager (1934:335), Halle (1959:47, 51-52), Isačenko (1971:51-52), Shapiro (1972:406f.) and Kortlandt (1973:76), to mention only a few. There are also 'mixed' opinions about the phonemic status of the geminate palatals; they are found in, for example, Bulygina (1971) and Thelin (1974).

The variety of analyses we find in the literature on the geminate palatals indicates their complex nature. The various authors have chosen quite different arguments for their analyses, such as phonetic, functional-phonemic, morphonemic, morphological, dialectal, diachronical, or even orthographic arguments, and all kinds of combinations of these.[1]

There are very few purely functional-phonemic analyses, based on Trubetzkoy's theory of phonology, the most recent one, as far as I know, being Kortlandt's "Phonetics and Phonemics of standard Russian" (1973). This analysis is, however, much too condensed for the complex phonetic facts of the geminate palatals.

For the phonetic data of the following exposition, I have

based myself mainly on Avanesov (1948(1970) and 1984), Barinova
(1966), Borunova (1966), Panov (1967), Drage (1968), Ganiev (1971),
Isačenko (1971), Comrie & Stone (1978) and the Academy Grammar of
1980.

1   SOFT LONG [š':] WITHIN A MORPHEME

1.1   Soft long [š':] occurs within a morpheme: щука, пища, вещь.
In Avanesov 1984 (112f.) a pronunciation with a 'very soft plosive
element' in the second part of this sound complex (transcribed as
[ш'ᵀ'ш']) is also considered possible, but this plosive element
should not be too strong in order to not sound dialectal. From
Barinova (1966:46) it appears that a pronunciation [š't'š'] as a
realization of щ within a morpheme is still relatively frequent
among Muscovites, although it is rapidly decreasing among younger
generations.[2] From Krysin (1974:96ff.) the same can be concluded:
some 30% of those interviewed pronounced [š't'š'] within a morpheme
(older people much more than younger; Muscovites much less than
others). On the basis of these sources and others[3], I come to the
conclusion that the pronunciation [š't'š'] within a morpheme is not
at all very marginal and cannot be ascribed to dialectisms only[4];
it should be accounted for in the phonemic system.
    The variant [š't'š'] is probably very rare in pre- and post-
consonantal positions, but there is very little information about
this in the literature. In Barinova (1966:46-47) we find for вообще
10% [š't'š']-pronunciation for the oldest generation, but zero
for the two younger generations.

1.2   Length of [š':] is usually lost (in elliptic speech) in a
number of positions:
1. in final position: товарищ, борщ;
2. in postconsonantal position when the preceding consonant belongs
to the same syllable: гардеробщик, упаковщик, община, сообщник.
This rule is formulated by Avanesov (1968:81, 1972:83, 1984:113f.),
but he also lists words like комплиментщик [n'š'], where [n'] may
belong to the preceding syllable, надсмотрщик [tr̥š'], where [r̥] is
syllabic. If Avanesov follows the rules for syllable division given

in the AkGr (1980:23), then his statement on length optionality in postconsonantal position is needlessly complicated, because these rules state that sonorants in the first position of a cluster may belong to either the preceding or the following syllable, all other consonants always belong to the following syllable. There is thus no restriction of syllable division effective.[5]

3. in preconsonantal position: мощный, сущность. In this position shortened [š'] tends to be hardened to [š]. However, this is considered wrong by Avanesov (1984:114)and other authors. Only in the words помощник, всенощная and всенощно short hard [š] is sanctioned by orthoepists (Shapiro 1968:29, Isačenko 1971:46). The orthography of these words should then be considered archaic.

As a consequence of the loss of length in these positions minimal pairs arise in CSR: рощь [roš'(:)] ~ рожь [roš] (Pilch 1967: 1557).

1.3   Both [š':] and [š't'š'] are possible pronunciations in words which have, synchronically, no longer a morpheme boundary: счастье, считать, счет, исчез, чересчур (Avanesov 1984:179). However, [š't'š'] occurs here very often, in the latter two words even more frequent than [š':].

1.4   As a consequence of vowel syncope the words тысяча and сейчас are realized as [týš':ə] and [š':as]. Such a kind of syncope with comparable result may occur in colloquial speech (across morpheme boundaries) in patronymics and many other words and constructions: Борисович [bʌr'íš'(:)], записочку [zʌp'íš'(:)ku], прежде чем [pr'éš':ʋm] (Flier 1980:308).

1.5   The word дождь may be pronounced [doš'(:)] (according to the old Muscovite norm) or [došt']. Both pronunciations belong to CSR and "may occur in the speech of one and the same individual". (Shapiro 1968:2, 29) (See further section 4.2).

2   *SOFT LONG* [š':] *ACROSS A MORPHEME BOUNDARY*

2.1   On the boundary of a root and a suffix the orthographic

clusters -сч- (-зч-, -здч-, -жч-, -стч-, -щ-) are realized as [š':]
or [š't'š']: заносчивый, смазчик, громоздче, мужчина, режче,
хрустче, слаще.[6] The frequency of the one pronunciation against the
other seems to vary from word to word; in разносчик hardly [š't'š'],
in бороздчатый hardly [š':].[7]

2.2 The most frequent realization of -сч- on the boundary of a
prefix and a root is [š't'š']: расчертить, бесчестный.

In Avanesov's opinion (1984:179) the exclusive realization of
-сч- (or -зч-) on the boundary of a preposition and a following word
should be [š't'š']: из части, без чувств, с честью.

From Avanesov's data one would be inclined to conclude that a
pronunciation [š':] on these boundaries is more of an exception and
limited to certain words. Field research, however, led to a different
conclusion.

Borunova (1966) tried, by means of an experiment among young
Muscovites, to determine which factors influenced the pronunciation
of [š't'š'] or [š':] across the prefix/preposition boundaries. She
concludes that assimilation of [s] with [t'š'] across a morpheme
boundary is far more developed in frequent combinations than in
rare constructions such as с чартизмом, where [š':] is hardly imag-
inable, while [sč'] (without any assimilation) does occur relatively
speaking, quite often. In a word like бесчопорность only 1% pronounced [š':], while in расчетливый this was 96%. This probably
explains, for example, the difference between [š':] in расческа 78%
and in расчесать only 14%. Borunova considered words with a pronunciation of [š':] for 70% or more of the informants as unprefixed
words, for less than 50% the words were clearly prefixed, and for a
percentage between 50 and 70 she considered the process of simplification of the morpheme structure as not yet accomplished. These
percentages seem to be chosen rather arbitrarily, but the process of
change Borunova signals is certainly going on, and we should realize
that it is not in all relevant cases possible to determine whether
a morpheme boundary should be considered present or not.

A difference between the boundaries of a prefix and a root,
or a preposition and a following word is that, according to
Borunova's findings, in the latter case the percentage of a [š':]-
pronunciation does not exceed 12, while in the former case this

percentage lies, depending on (the frequency of) the word, practically between 0 and 100.

During field research among Moscow-born factory workers Ganiev (1971:50-51) found that the pronunciation [š':] across morpheme boundaries was much more frequent than [š't'š'].

A pronunciation of [s't'š'] with assimilation of the first sibilant as to softness only also occurs, but most (Russian) authors consider this a spelling pronunciation and therefore wrong (Barinova 1966:27, Panov 1968:84, Borunova 1966:60ff.). Ganiev in his above-mentioned research also found a pronunciation [st'š'] (бесчестно) or even [sš'] (брусчаткой, on the boundary of a root and a suffix), but he supposes that these latter pronunciations were 'occasional', the result of 'literal reading', by which he clearly intends to disqualify them as wrong.

For our point of view these orthoepic deviations do not play a role because they do not create an opposition of the type [s't'š'] or [st'š'] ~ [š't'š'] or [š':].

Although Avanesov considers the fricative pronunciation [š':] instead of affricative [š't'š'] on the boundary of a prefix/preposition to be "просторечие" ("and even dialectal"; 1984:179) it nevertheless occurs so often that it should be accepted as part of the phonetic reality of CSR.

2.3   The pronunciation of [š':] on the boundary of two 'full' words seems to be impossible; in вырос чудесный сад only 18% pronounced [š't'š'], while 82% reproduced a sound complex without any assimilation: [st'š'] (Borunova 1966:69).

2.4   СЩ

A sound complex on the boundary of a prefix ending in [s] and followed by a root beginning with [š':] is, according to Avanesov (1984:114, 177), either realized as double long [š'::] or 'normal' long [š':]: рассчитывать, расщемить.

I did not find any support in the literature for the existence of double long consonants, but, on the contrary, many sources which discuss this cluster analyse it in terms of a 'normal' long consonant. The AkGr (1980, tom 1, 29,44) states that -сщ- on the boundary of a prefix and a root is pronounced [š':]. In careful speech a pronun-

ciation of two separate short [š'] is considered possible. Isačenko
(1971:40) quotes forms like без щуки and расщупать and analyses
them with loss of the final consonant of the prefix or preposition.
Panov (1967:87) explicitly rejects the possibility of 'more than
long' consonants and cites examples such as этот хлыщ счастлив,
where the complex -щ сч- results in only one [š':].[8] On the basis
of this literature it is not very realistic to assume such double
long consonants.

2.5   We come to the conclusion that there is a continuing process
in which within a morpheme [š':] secures its position, while across
morpheme boundaries [š't'š'] gradually drives out [š':] (Glovinskaja
1971a:25), but at the same time we must conclude that either within
a morpheme, or within an accentual unit across morpheme boundaries,
both the fricative as well as the affricative variants occur; the
difference lies in their frequency of occurrence.[9] This means that
the presence or absence of a boundary is of no importance.

     Kortlandt (1973) uses the notation /Σš/[10] for [š':] (within a
morpheme) and /Σ-č/ for [š't'š'] or [š':] (across boundaries).
Observing the phonetic facts described above I note /Σč/[11] for both
[š'(:)] and [š't'š'] within or across morpheme boundaries.

     It should be realized that loss of length in the cases
described above (section 1.2) has nothing to do with optionality
of the kind meant by Ebeling (1967). Length opposition of [š':] ~
[š'] exists in only one position: after [t'] which is not preceded
by [š'] (see below 2.6); in all other occurrences this opposition
is neutralized: in final position or immediate consonantal environment both [š':] and [š'] are possible; initially and intervocali-
cally only long [š':] (or [š't'š']) occurs.

2.6   ТЩ
     According to Avanesov (1984:114) the cluster тщ, found within
as well as across morpheme boundaries, is pronounced [t'š'::]
([ч̥'ш̥'ш'] in Avanesov's transcription) or [t'š':]. Here again a
case of supposedly double long consonants (see above 2.4). If we
reject the double long variant as not realistic, we have [t'š':],
which is a closure followed by a long fricative: тщательно, от щуки.[12]
Phonemically this is /čč/; the archiphoneme /č/ is neutralized for

hard/softness only, not for voice, because *[dž'] does not exist.

Length is distinctive in this position: тщетно ~ честно:
[t'š':] ~ [t'š']. Length is very probably not optional in this
environment.

3   HARD LONG [š:]

Hard long [š:] occurs only when a morpheme boundary is involved:
root and suffix: влезший; prefix and root: бесшумный; preposition
and root: с шумом.

Length of [š:] is distinctive because of the existence of
minimal pairs like шить ~ сшить or вымерший ~ вымерзший.

In the words сумасшедший and масштаб the cluster -сш- is
realized as a single [š]; the orthography must be considered archaic
(Avanesov 1984:178).

The sound [š:] can be phonemicized as /Σš/. It would be incorrect to indicate the morpheme boundary in this cluster because
this is not a relevant factor; /Σš/ is opposed to /Σč/ by the phonological feature of fricativeness/occlusiveness, the occurring
phonetic manifestations are predictable from these phoneme clusters.

4   SOFT LONG [ž':]

4.1   Soft long [ž':] is, according to Avanesov (1984:180), still
the literary norm for the pronunciation of зж or жж within a
morpheme: визжать, поезжай, вожжи, сожженный.

It is clear, not only from other sources but also from
Avanesov's own text, that this norm leads an artificial existence.
Avanesov must admit that there is a growing tendency which replaces
[ž':] by [ž:] (see Barinova 1966:49, Avanesov 1984:239f., Comrie &
Stone 1978:30); he also remarks that in the word можжевельник hard
[ž:] is the normal pronunciation and therefore must be permitted,
but nevertheless soft long [ž':] remains the standard pronunciation.

Again from the experiments of Barinova we learn that the hard
pronunciation is proportionally more than twice as frequent among
the younger generation as compared to the older generation (1966:50).
According to Shapiro (1968:29), soft long [ž':] "is maintained with

any consistency only in the speech of the oldest generation, whereas [ž:] appears exclusively or in free variation with [ž':] in the speech of all but the oldest generation of standard speakers".

In Krysin (1974:84ff.) the pronunciation of жж or зж within a morpheme has been investigated on the basis of 12 words.[13] It appeared that the hard pronunciation occurred twice as much as the soft pronunciation. But the difference in hard or soft for the various words was considerable: in дрожжи the proportion was 1:1, in можжевельник 6(hard):1. On the basis of these figures one must conclude that the realizations of hard and soft are not consistent for most of the speakers of CSR. One and the same speaker might pronounce [ž':] in дрожжи on the one hand and [ž:] in можжевельник on the other (the other way round is less probable), or [ž':] in визжать and [ž:] in жжется.[14]

The AkGr (1980:18) permits both soft [ž':] and hard [ž:], but the words дрожжи and вожжи should be pronounced with soft [ž':] only.[15]

4.2 The oblique cases of дождь and its derivatives have [ž':] (old Muscovite norm) or [žd']: дождя; дождливый [ž'(:)l'] or [ždl']. Long hard [ž:] should be considered dialectal (AkGr:18). (See also section 1.5).

4.3 Length of [ž':] is optional before consonants: дождливый.

5 *HARD LONG* [ž:]

5.1 Hard long [ž:] occurs on prefix/preposition boundaries: разжег, сжег, изжога; без жены, с женой, из жара.

5.2 Concluding, we determine that both [ž':] and [ž:] are possible realizations within a morpheme, but [ž:] is the only one possible across morpheme boundaries.

This is exactly the state of affairs as described by Ebeling (1967:135): The feature softness is optional in forms like поезжай. Soft [ž':] can always be substituted by hard [ž:]. The opposite is not true: substitution of [ž:] by [ž':] results in an existing form

only when no morpheme boundary is involved. This leads to the
following phonemicization: [ž:] ← /Σž/ and [ž('):] ← /Σẕ̌'/, where
the phoneme /ẕ̌'/ represents a heavy phoneme.

6 SOFT [t'š'] VERSUS HARD [tš]

6.1 Orthographic ч is (mostly) realized as soft [t'š'][16] and
opposed to тш which is always hard [tš]. The first only occurs
within a morpheme, while the latter occurs across morpheme boundaries,
but also within a morpheme in, as far as I know, only one Russian
root[17] : обветшать which forms an (almost) minimal pair with отвечать.
Owing to this one pair we cannot account for the difference between
the two sound complexes by means of the presence or absence of a
morpheme boundary. Moreover, the sound complex [t'š'] cannot be
represented by a sequence of the phonemes /t'/ and */š'/, because
soft [š'] does not occur independently but only after [t'] (or in
certain positions as a variant of long [š':]; see above 1.2). We are
thus obliged to accept the existence of a separate phoneme /č/
manifested in [t'š'] and opposed to /Tš/ realized as [tš]. Examples:
часто, очутиться, кричать, врач ~ отшутиться, ухудшать, выцветший,
музыкантша. In the examples with -тш- a morpheme boundary runs across
this cluster. The sequence /Tš/ does not occur initially or finally,
because initial /t/ (or /T/, see below) does not constitute a
morpheme. Final /š/ constituting a morpheme is only found in the
verbal flexion for 2sg present tense which is always preceded by a
vowel.

   The description of /Tš/ so far is valid for explicit, carefully
articulated, speech. It is remarkable that in more elliptic variants
the fricative segment is lengthened (Avanesov 1984:188). This results
in [tš:] which is presented phonemically as /TΣš/, where /Σ/ represents an optional archiphoneme. The archiphoneme /T/ is the product
of neutralization of the features hard/soft and voiced/voiceless.

6.2 In the word лучший (and derivatives of the same root) the
consonant cluster is pronounced hard or soft. Avanesov (1984:188)
transcribes this as hard [чш] which is in my transcription [tš:], or
soft [т'ч'] which equals [t':š']. The hard pronunciation of -ч-

within the root is due to assimilation before hard -ш-; the soft
realization must equally be ascribed to assimilation, but now after
soft -ч-. The difference between the two realizations lies in the
direction of the assimilation: regressive in the former, progressive
in the latter case. The hard cluster [tš:] should be described as
/T̲Σš/, the soft cluster [t':š'] as /T̲č/, resulting in a phonological
doublet for this root.[18]

6.3   ТЧ

The graphic combination -тч- (or -дч-) consists phonetically
of a long closure followed by a soft fricative (Avanesov 1984:188,
Il'ina 1986:41): [t':š'].[19] It is found within as well as across
morpheme boundaries: отчество, ветчина; летчик, отчаянный, находчи-
вый, подчеркнуть, под часами. According to Avanesov (ibidem) the
closure of [t] may be hard in bookish style, instead of soft, when
this sound complex occurs on a prefix/preposition boundary. This
results in [tt'š']. This is, however, subphonemic, because there is
no hard/soft opposition of dentals before dentals/palatals
(Kortlandt 1973:78). Phonemically the above discussed clusters
result in /T̲č/.[20]

6.4   ТЩ VERSUS ТЧ

According to Avanesov (1948/1970:334f.) the opposition between
[š':] and [t'š'] after [t'] is neutralized: тщательно, летчик. This
would mean that there is no opposition between the fricative and
occlusive element in the middle of the clusters [t'š'š'] ← /č̲č/ and
[t't'š'] ← /T̲č/. Avanesov does not confirm this statement about
neutralization in his later publications. Nor have I found any other
indication about its existence.

6.5   ЧЧ

The realization of -чч-, only occurring in loan words, is (in
Avanesov's transcription, 1984:173) long soft [ч':] with optional
length.[21] There are at least two interpretations for the symboliza-
tion of this complex sound: with a long closure [t'(:)š'] or with a
long fricative part [t'š'(:)]. The first interpretation is phonemically /T̲č/, the second /č̲č/; the doubly underlined phonemes are
optional.[22] Examples: пиччикато, каприччио.

7   [dž:]

Orthographic -дж-, occurring within a root only in loan words but also across morpheme boundaries in Russian constructions, is phonetically realized as [dž(:)] with optional length[23] (Avanesov 1984:209, AkGr 1980:44, Panov 1967:90). Phonemically this results in /T̲Z̲ž/, in which /Z̲/ represents an optional archiphoneme. Examples: джем, арпеджио; поджидал, от жены.

8   [ts]

8.1   In Avanesov's description (1984:115) always hard [c], graphic ц, only occurring within the boundaries of a morpheme, is the same as [t] and [s], that is [t͡s], but at the same time [c] must be distinguished from [ts], graphic тс, only occurring across a morpheme boundary, which may be pronounced [cs]: поцарствовать ~ подсаживать. From this not very efficient description we are inclined to conclude that if there is a difference at all between ц [ts] and тс [ts:], it is only optional. Avanesov makes, however, a distinction between different positions in which -тс- occurs (1984:181f.):
- on the boundary of a root and a suffix: [ts]: советский, детство;
- on the boundary of a flexional desinence and the reflexive postfix: [t:s]: бояться, боится, боятся; несется, несутся;
- on a prefix/preposition boundary: [ts(:)][24]: отсадил, под стеной.
  The phonemic representation is then:
- [ts] ← /T̲s/: occurring within a morpheme and on the boundary of a root and a suffix;
- [t:s] ← /T̲T̲s/: occurring on a flexional boundary. I did not find an indication about the optionality of length in this position[25];
- [ts(:)] ← /T̲S̲s/: occurring on the prefix/preposition boundary, where /S̲/ indicates an optional archiphoneme.

8.2   There is also a soft cluster [t's']: отсидеть; [t's'] ← /T̲s'/ opposed to оценить [ts] ← /T̲s/.

In the root цвет the cluster [t's'] is also soft, but this is due to the environment.

8.3   Orthographic -тц- (or -дц-) is realized as a long closure

followed by a fricative [t:s], phonemically /T̲T̲s/: отца, двадцать[26]
This implies that братца and браться have identical phonetic and
phonemic forms.

8.4   Long [c:] (Avanesov's transcription, 1984:173), orthograph-
ically -цц-, occurring in loan words, permits two interpretations:
[t(:)s] + /T̲T̲s/ or [ts(:)] + /T̲S̲s/. It is not clear whether both
are correct, or only one of the two. From Glovinskaja's experimental data (1971b:64) one would conclude that length is optional (the
doubly underlined archiphonemes). Examples: интермеццо, палаццо.

9   [dz]
     The clusters [dz':], [dz:] with optional length (or without
length before consonants) (Avanesov 1984:209, AkGr 1980:29) occur
in onomatopoeic forms, in specialistic terminology, in loan words,
in (originally foreign) family names and in Russian constructions
only across morpheme boundaries. Phonemically the clusters result
in: /T̲S̲z'/: надзиратель, под зеркалом, дзинь, дзеканье;
     /T̲S̲z/: муэдзин (hard transcription in Avanesov 1984:209);
     /T̲Sb/: отец бы, Гинцбург.
The doubly underlined archiphonemes are optional.

10   *SOFT* [š'] *AND* [ž'] *IN LOAN WORDS*
     In words of foreign origin soft (short) [š'] and [ž'] occur:
пшют [pš'ùt], жюри [ž'ür'í]. This results in the marginal phonemes
⟨/š'/⟩ and ⟨/ž'/⟩. Since there are other loans where a 'normal'
hard [š] is pronounced (брошюра, парашют), the feature of softness
might be optional. In that case we have to do with the marginal
heavy phonemes ⟨/š̲'/⟩ and ⟨/ž̲'/⟩ (Avanesov 1984:118; Glovinskaja
1971b:62).

11   *SUMMARY*

11.1   We recapitulate with a survey of the phonemicization of the
sounds and sound clusters discussed above. Capitalized and/or

single underlined symbols are archiphonemes, double underlining
indicates optional or heavy phonemes, cornered brackets stand for
marginal phonemes:

пища	[š':]/[š't'š'] ← /Σč/	позже	} [ž':]/[ž:] ← /Σž̲'/
товарищ	[š'(:)]/[š't'š'] ← /Σč/	можжевельник	
счастье	}		
разносчик			
расчертить	[š't'š']/[š':] ← /Σč/		
с честью			
расщупать			
влезший	}	сжег	}
бесшумный	[š:] ← /Σš/	без жены	[ž:] ← /Σž/
с шумом			
отшуметь	[tš(:)] ← /T̲Σš/	джем, джин	[dž(:)] ← /T̲Σž/
очуметь	[t'š'] ← /č/		
тщательно	[t'š':] ← /č̲č/		
кабатчик	[t':š'] ← /T̲č/		
пиччикато	{ [t'š'(:)] ← /č̲č/		
	[t'(:)š'] ← /T̲č/		
цель	}		
немецкий	[ts] ← /T̲s/		
браться	}		
братца	[t:s] ← /TTs/		
отсылать	[ts(:)] ← /T̲Ss/	под зонтиком	[dz(:)] ← /T̲Sz/
палаццо	{ [t(:)s] ← /TTs/		
	[ts(:)] ← /T̲Ss/		
пшют	[š(')] ← ⟨/š̲'/⟩	жюри	[ž(')] ← ⟨/ž̲'/⟩

11.2 Note that although before palatals (/š ž č/) there is neutral
ization between dental and palatal fricatives, this neutralization
does not take place before dentals:

сцена	[sts]	←	/S̲Ts/
мышца	[šts]	←	/Š̲Ts/
вещстол	[š'(:)st]	←	/Σčst/
кэмбриджцы	[tšts]	←	/T̲Š̲Ts/
кэмбриджский	[tšsk']	←	/T̲Šsk'/

University of Leiden

NOTES

[1]   A good example of analyses in which a great variety of considerations freely play their role is Thelin (1974) and Flier (1980) and their very hybrid discussion which followed in subsequent issues of Russian Linguistics. Cf. also the discussions in Bulygina 1971 and Veyrenc 1966.

[2]   The figures mentioned in Barinova 1966 are obtained by means of two experiments. In the first experiment the informant was invited to describe his own pronunciation of words containing щ (and сч and the like); in the second the informant was asked to read a text on tape. In both cases subjective judgments, hypercorrect forms and orthography may have influenced the results.

[3]   Cf. also Shapiro (1968:29) and Il'ina (1986:42).

[4]   According to Kortlandt (1973:112) the "difference between [š':] and [š'č'] is dialectal". Apart from Avanesov's remark which is ambivalent in his text, I did not find this affirmed in the various Russian sources.

[5]   Flier (1980:313) speaks of loss of length in "postobstruential environments", thus excluding nasals and liquidae. Panov (1967:88) makes the same restriction. Shapiro (1975:51) speaks of neutralization "in syllable coda position", without explaining this notion. See for another restriction section 2.6.

[6]   Avanesov also lists in this context words without a morpheme boundary: дощатый, вощанка, песчанка, (1984:179); cf. Tixonov 1985.

[7]   Although more than 60% of the informants pronounce [š't'š']in a word like брусчатый (Krysin 1974:97), Avanesov remarks that this pronunciation is less preferable (1984:179). But on the same page he writes that the word бороздчатый may be pronounced in both variants, although the factual occurrence of [š't'š'] in this word is, according to Krysin's information, much lower than in брусчатый. This illustrates the arbitrariness of Avanesov's judgment in this case.

[8]   Cf. also Shapiro 1972:410.

[9]   See for an indication (of limited importance because of the small number of informants within a limited region) Barinova 1966 and Flier 1980:307.

[10]   /Σ/ is an archiphoneme of /s z s' z' š ž/, that is an archiphoneme in which the features voiced/voiceless, hard/soft and dental/palatal are neutralized. See Kortlandt 1973:76.

[11]   See for the discussion of the phoneme /č/, section 6.

[12]   The wide-spread hard pronunciation [tš] of this cluster must be considered against the norm of CSR (Avanesov 1984:114).

[13]   See for the description of the experimental investigation, p.28ff. The number of interrogated people was considerable: between 3,000 and 4,300 people, spread all over the country, old and young, of all social classes.

[14]   Cf. Kortlandt (1974:112): "The difference between [ž':] and [ž:], which is subphonemic, is optional in the standard language (though some speakers use exclusively either the first or the second variant)".

[15]   The facts contradict the second part of the statement: hard pronunciation in дрожжи: 31% youngest generation (Barinova 1966:51), 60% (Ganiev 1971:51), 44% (Krysin 1974:85).

[16]   There is a tendency among members of the Moscow intelligentsia, without any

doubt speakers of CSR, to pronounce [š'] instead of [č'] in consonantal environments, and in initial and final positions (Paufošima 1971:268/9). This tendency might be understood as being in line with the phenomenon, that in the position after [š'] the difference between [t'š'] and [š'] is subphonemic. See 2.5.

[17] [tš] also occurs in loan words: *бридж, Кэмбридж*.

[18] Kortlandt (1973:78) transcribes this sound complex as [tš] ← /Tš̱/ neglecting the length of either of the constituent parts. Panov's transcription (1963:28) of this sound sequence is [č'] followed by hard [š]; this would result in the phoneme sequence /čš/. But is the sound sequence [č'š] a realistic one in CSR?

[19] Shapiro (1972:408) transcribes here [č':] in e.g. *мати*. How to interpret this: a short closure followed by a long fricative, i.e. [t'š':]?

[20] I have not found any indication about the optionality of length in this cluster. Compare below 6.5.

[21] More precisely, Avanesov's transcription misses the comma for softness, but I consider this a printing error.

[22] See Ebeling 1967:134ff.

[23] As is the case with [tš(:)] (see 6.1) length is present in elliptic speech, whereas in explicit, more carefully articulated, speech the cluster is realized without length of the fricative segment.

[24] This realization is, here again, typical of elliptic speech; in the more explicit code [ts] is normal. Cf. section 7.

[25] Shapiro remarks that "More regularly maintained are geminates in position immediately following a stressed vowel, whereas immediately preceding stressed vowels they are more susceptible to simplification" (1968:32).

[26] Very often in *двадцать, тридцать* the long closure is omitted. This is, in Avanesov's opinion (1984:182), not recommendable. This is at least some indication about potential optionality.

BIBLIOGRAPHY

AkGr
  1980   *Russkaja Grammatika*. Tom 1. Akademija Nauk,M.
Avanesov, R.I.
  1948/1970   "O dolgix šipjaščix v russkom jazyke", *Doklady i soobščenija
              filologičeskogo fakul'teta MGU;* vyp. 6, 23-29. (Reprinted in:
              A.A. Reformatskij, *Iz istorii otečestvennoj fonologii*. Izd. Nauka,
              M. 326-335).
  1968[4]   *Russkoe literaturnoe proiznošenie*. M.
  1972[5]   *Russkoe literaturnoe proiznošenie*. M.
  1984[6]   *Russkoe literaturnoe proiznošenie*. M.
Barinova, G.A.
  1966   "O proiznošenii [ž':] i [š':]", *Razvitie fonetiki sovremennogo
              russkogo jazyka*. Izd. Nauka, M., 25-54.
Borunova, S.N.
  1966   "Sočetanija [š'č'] i [š':] na granicax morfem", *Razvitie fonetiki
              sovremennogo russkogo jazyka*. Izd. Nauka, M., 55-71.
Bulygina, T.V.
  1971   "O russkix dolgix šipjaščix", *Fonetika. Fonologija. Grammatika.
              K semidesjatiletiju A.A. Reformatskogo*. Izd. Nauka, M., 84-91.

Comrie, B. and G. Stone
    1978   *The Russian Language since the Revolution*. Oxford.
Drage, C.L.
    1968   "Some Data on Modern Moscow Pronunciation", *The Slavonic and East European Review* 46, 353-382.
Ebeling, C.L.
    1967   "Some premisses of phonemic analysis", *WORD* 23, 122-137.
Flier, M.S.
    1980   "The sharped geminate palatals in Russian", *Russian Linguistics* 4, 303-328.
    1982   "The Russian sharped geminate palatals in functional perspective", *Russian Linguistics* 6, 277-291.
Ganiev, Ž.V.
    1971   "O proiznošenii rabočix-urožencev g. Moskvy", *Razvitie fonetiki sovremennogo russkogo jazyka. Fonologičeskie podsistemy*. Izd. Nauka, M., 33-53.
Glovinskaja, M.Ja.
    1971a   "O grammatičeskix faktorax razvitija fonetičeskoj sistemy sovremennogo russkogo jazyka", *Razvitie fonetiki sovremennogo russkogo jazyka. Fonologičeskie podsistemy*. Izd. Nauka, M., 20-32.
    1971b   "Ob odnoj fonologičeskoj podsisteme v sovremennom russkom literaturnom jazyke, *Razvitie fonetiki sovremennogo russkogo jazyka. Fonologičeskie podsistemy*. Izd. Nauka, M., 54-96.
Halle, M.
    1959   *The Sound Pattern of Russian. A linguistic and acoustical investigation*. The Hague.
Il'ina, N.E.
    1986   "Proiznošenie v moskovskom kamernom teatre", *Russkoe sceničeskoe proiznošenie*. M., 34-50.
Isačenko, A.V.
    1971   "Morfonologičeskaja interpretacija dolgix mjagkix šipjaščix [š':], [ž':] v russkom jazyke", *International Journal of Slavic Linguistics and Poetics* 14, 32-52.
Kortlandt, F.H.H.
    1973   "Phonetics and Phonemics of Standard Russian", *Tijdschrift voor Slavische Taal- en Letterkunde* 2, 73-83.
    1974   "Optional features in contemporary Russian", *Dutch Contributions to the 7th International Congress of Slavists. Warsaw 1973*. The Hague-Paris, 107-114.
Krysin, L.P.
    1974   "Dolgie mjagkie šipjaščie", *Russkij jazyk po dannym massovogo obsledovanija*. M., 84-102.
Panov, M.V.
    1963   "O stil'jax proiznošenija (v svjazi s obščimi problemami stilistiki)", *Razvitie sovremennogo russkogo jazyka*. Izd. Nauka, M., 5-38.
    1967   *Russkaja fonetika*. M.
    1968   *Russkij jazyk i sovetskoe obščestvo. Fonetika sovremennogo russkogo literaturnogo jazyka*. M.
Paufošima, R.F.
    1971   "O proiznošenii č v literaturnom jazyke", *Razvitie fonetiki sovremennogo russkogo jazyka*. Izd. Nauka, M., 268-269.
Pilch, H.
    1967   "Russische Konsonantgruppen im Silbenan- und Auslaut", *To Honor Roman Jakobson*, Vol. II, 1555-1584.

131

Reformatskij, A.A.
  1967   "⟨ž̧⟩", *To Honor Roman Jakobson*, Vol. II, 1650–1656.
Shapiro, M.
  1968   *Russian phonetic variants and phonostylistics*. Berkeley and Los
                Angeles.
  1972   "Consonant syncope in Russian", *The Slavic Word. Proceedings of
                the International Slavistic Colloquium at UCLA, September 11-16,
                1970*. The Hague, 404-425.
  1975   "Markedness as a criterion of phonemicity", *Phonologica 1972*.
                München, 49-54.
Thelin, Nils B.
  1974   "On the phonological status of the Russian geminate palatals",
                Russian Linguistics 1, 163-176.
  1981   "On the phonemic status of the geminate palatals in Russian - one
                more time", *Russian Linguistics* 5, 301-313.
  1983   "The Russian geminate palatals in a processual and more realistic
                functional perspective, ...", *Russian Linguistics* 7, 167-192.
Tixonov, A.N.
  1985   *Slovoobrazovatel'nyj slovar' russkogo jazyka v dvux tomax*. M.
Trager G.L.
  1934   "The phonemes of Russian", *Language* 10, 334-344.
Veyrenc, J.
  1966   "Un ou deux phonèmes? Le cas de щ en russe", *La Linguistique* II,
                111-123.

ON THE PASSIVE PAST PARTICIPLE: ITS MEANING AND USAGE IN THE MIDDLE RUSSIAN FIRST CHRONICLE OF NOVGOROD

JADRANKA GVOZDANOVIĆ

1.   INTRODUCTION

The choice of the topic of this investigation, the meaning and usage of the passive past participle in Middle Russian, was motivated by more general considerations: those of semantics of passive sentences as compared with their active counterparts, which might be termed a corner-stone of linguistic theories. Elucidation of a part of this semantics might contribute towards evaluating current theories, which, however, will fall outside of the scope of this paper.

In the period of Russian which will be under consideration here, namely that of the 13th through 15th centuries, which is termed Middle Russian, passive participles were the main means of forming passive sentences. And of the two passive participles, the present participle was very infrequently used, attested mainly as due to Old Church Slavonic influences (cf. Borkovskij & Kuznecov 1963: 276).

The choice of the language data, two copies of the same part of the same chronicle, the first dating from the 13th century and the second from the 15th century, was motivated by the conception that language variation within one speech community at one period of time, and between two periods of time, is restricted by the organization of the language system of that community and thus indicative of the place of a given unit (*in casu*: the passive past participle) within the system. This holds both for variation within one system, also called variability, and variation between two systems such that the later one

arises from the former one through language change (cf. also
Gvozdanović 1985).

2. MEANING OF THE PASSIVE PAST PARTICIPLE IN RELATION TO
    ITS USAGE IN THE FIRST PART OF THE FIRST CHRONICLE OF
    NOVGOROD

A linguistic unit is defined on the basis of a systematic
association of a (set of) form(s) with a (set of) meaning
(variants). As to the passive past participle in the period
under investigation, it used to be formed by means of the suffix -n- or -t- added to verbal stems; -n- (preceded by the
thematic vowel -e-) was used with infinitive stemd ending in a
consonant or -i-, and -t-, with infinitive stems ending in a
vowel (cf. Borkovskij & Kuznecov 1963: 276). In Borkovskij &
Kuznecov's (1963: 274) opinion, passive participles denoted,
as they still do today, that the person or object affected by
the action expressed by means of the verbal stem followed by
the passive participle suffix, does not bring this action
about, but rather undergoes it as brought about by somebody
or something else. In addition to this formulation about the
general meaning, Gorškova & Xaburgaev (1981: 351) mention a
usage of the passive past participle as characteristic of dialogues with the meaning of *"passive perfect"*, i.e. that of a
present state which is the result of an action (in the given
case, a causing action), completed before the speech moment.
    How does this usage, characteristic of dialogues, relate
to the meaning of the passive past participle in the system
of Middle Russian? Is this one of the meaning variants, and
if so, is its relation to the other one(s) either that of
complementarity or of overlapping? Or can it be considered
to constitute the general meaning of the passive past participle?
    In search of an answer, we can best start from a meaning
postulate based on the description given above, because it is
specific enough for being tested. By this meaning postulate,
a passive participle suffix means that an entity is charac-

*terized by the state which is the effect of the action expressed
by means of the verbal stem*. In the case of the passive *past* participle, the action *precedes its orientation point in another situation expressed within the immediate context,* and in the case
of the passive *present* participle, it is *going on at its orientation point.* The entity characterized by the state as defined
above will henceforth be called *'Goal'*, and the one controlling
the action, *'Agent'*.

The passive past participle suffix was most frequently combined with perfective verbal stems, and the question that must
be asked now is that of delimitation between the meaning contributed by the perfective aspect and that contributed by the
passive past participle suffix. Specifically, is the part of
Gorškova & Xaburgaev's (1981: 351) definition which refers to
'the result of an action' a necessary part of the meaning definition of the passive past participle itself, or an interpretational result of its most usual combination with the perfective
aspect? This question can be answered only against the background of an aspect definition which has been formulated independently of this problem. Such a definition for the contemporary Russian system (and the Middle Russian one was less developed, but of the same type) can be found in Barentsen's (1985:
59ff. etc.) work, according to which the category *'aspect'* is
applicable to verbs whose lexical meaning is characterized by a
'unity of action'. The perfective aspect is characterized by an
effectuation of this unity through reaching its *'terminus'* and
*'binding it sequentially onto a subsequent and/or preceding
situation'*. It is now possible to assume that the passive past
participle in combination with the perfective aspect always
referred to the effect of the termination of the action, inter-
pretable as its result. Only if this interpretation possibility
is found also in combination with the imperfective aspect, can
this be viewed as a necessary part of the passive past participle meaning indeed.

On the basis of the meaning postulate formulated above, the
following predictions concerning usage can be formulated:
- the passive past participle will not be likely to occur if

the context preceding it concentrates on the Agent of the
action;
- the passive past participle will not be likely to occur
  if the immediate context concentrates on the action preceding its terminus.

These predictions must by necessity be formulated as
tendencies. In spoken language, violations are possible given
the appropriate parsing and contrast expressed by means of
intonation, and written language can refer to these means
given sufficiently clear inference.

In a contemporary language, predictions based on a
meaning postulate can be tested and possibly falsified with
native informants. In case of falsification, one proceeds
either by formulating an additional postulate or by refor-
mulating the original one, depending on the outcome.

For a previous, only documented, language stage, no
full testing of a definition of a unit within the system
is possible, but only testing on the basis of a preserved
corpus. And in cases where the writers have not identified
themselves, one can only rely on a single handwriting as an
indication of a single system. If different copies of a
manuscript are found, they ought to be treated as different
language systems, unless the outcome of the analysis proves
that they belong to the same language system.

In order to test the prediction concerning usage possibilities of the passive past participle in the early periods of Russian in which passive participles were the main
means of forming passive sentences, as formulated above, I
have chosen the First Chronicle of Novgorod as written in the
13th century and the 15th century. The first copy is known as
Sinodal'nyj spisok (henceforth 'S'; it is preserved at the
manuscript department of the *Gosudarstvennyj istoričeskij
muzej v Sinodal'nom sobranii,* № 786), and the second copy is
known as *Komissionnyj spisok* (henceforth 'K'; it is preserved
at the Leningrad department of the Institute of history,
Archaeological committee, № 240). The manuscripts have been
published by the *Akademija nauk SSSR, Moskva/ Leningrad* 1950,
under the title *'Novgorodskaja pervaja letopis' staršego i*

mladšego izvodov'. The present investigation has been based on the published edition.

S was written partly in the 13th century (in two hand-writings, the first one, ending on page 123, from the beginning of the 13th century, and the second one, from page 123 until page 236, from the middle of the 13th century) and partly in the middle of the 14th century (cf. Ljapunov 1900: IV). K dates from the first half and/or middle of the 15th century. The parts of the text corresponding with the first handwriting in S, have been written in K by three different hands, the second of which (on sheets 7 - 13) can be dated paleographically in the middle of the 15th century, and the remaining ones either at the beginning or in the middle of the 15th century. The text contained in the first 123 pages of S, written by the same hand at the beginning of the 13th century, forms the basis of the investigation to be presented here. It reports on Russian clerical, political and social history from the year 6524 (i.e. 1016) until the year 6708 (i.e. 1200).

If the number of transitive finite verbs in S governing the accusative case of the Goal and used in the active form is compared with the number of passive participle forms, we find the following ratio: 346 active vs. 27 passive and 1 present passive. Given the fact that the Agent, directly involved with the action, could in passive sentences be referred to by means of the instrumental case, whereas the *от(ъ)* + genitive case construction was used for expressing an entity not entirely involved with the action (such as nature forces, e.g. lightning, or a parliament decision causing an action to be carried out), we can now further state that out of the 27 attestations of the passive past participle, in only 5 of them the Agent has been specified, next to the Goal. Let us examine those 5 examples in more detail, taking their immediate context into account as well.

(1)   Usage of the passive past participle with a specified
      Agent in S:
    - ВЪ ЛѢТО 6547. ОСВЯЩЕНА БЫСТЬ ЦЕРКЫ СВЯТЫЯ БОГОРОДИЦЯ
      ВОЛОДИМИРОМЬ.

'In the year 6547. There was sanctified the church of
the Holy Virgin by Volodimir.'
- ВЪ ЛѢТО 6553. СЪГОРѢ СВЯТАЯ СОФИЯ, ВЪ СУБОТУ, ПО ЗА-
УТРЬНИИ, ВЪ ЧАС 3, МѢСЯЦЯ МАРТА ВЪ 15. ВЪ ТО ЖЕ ЛѢТО
ЗАЛОЖЕНА БЫСТЬ СВЯТАЯ СОФИЯ НОВѢГОРОДѢ ВОЛОДИМИРОМЬ
КНЯЗѢМЬ.
'In the year 6553. There burnt down the Holy Sophia,
on a Saturday, after the matins, around three o'clock,
in the month of March on the 15th. In the same year
there was founded the Holy Sophia in Novgorod by Volo-
dimir the monarch.'
- ВЪ ЛѢТО 6581. ЗАЛОЖЕНА БЫСТЬ ЦЕРКЫ ПЕЧЕРЬСКАЯ ФЕОДОСОМЬ
ИГУМЕНОМЬ.
'In the year 6581. There was founded the Pečer'skaja
church by Theodosius the abbot.'
- ВЪ ЛѢТО 6597. СВЯЩЕНА БЫСТЬ ЦЕРКЫ ПЕЧЕРЬСКАЯ ИОАНОМЬ
МИТРОПОЛИТОМЬ; ТОМЬ ЖЕ ЛѢТѢ ПРѢСТАВИСЯ.
'In the year 6597. There was sanctified the Pečer'skaja
church by John the metropolitan; in the same year he
passed away.'
- ВЪ ЛѢТО 6617. ... И КОНЦЯША ТРЬПЕЗНИЦЮ ПЕЧЕРЬСКАГО
МАНАСТЫРЯ. ВЪ ТО ЖЕ ЛѢТО ЗАЛОЖЕНА БЫСТЬ ЦЕРКЫ КНЯЗЕМЬ
СВЯТОПЪЛКОМЬ КЫЕВѢ.
'In the year 6617. ... And they finished the dining
room of the Pečer'skij monastery. In the same year there
was founded a church by the monarch Svjatopolk in Kiev.'

We can see on the basis of these examples of passive with
a specified Agent that the immediately preceding context does
not concentrate on the Agent indeed:
- in the first example above, there is no immediately preceding
  context, and Volodimir had been at issue 19 years before;
- in the second example above, the immediately preceding context concentrates on the church of the Holy Sophia, not the
  Agent;
- in the third example above, the Agent Theodosius the abbot
  is being mentioned for the first time in the given example;
- in the fourth example above, the Agent John the archiepiscope
  is being mentioned for the first time in the given example

as well, and
- in the fifth example above, the Agent Svjatopolk had been
  at issue 14 years before, but not in the immediately preceding context.
In the remaining examples of the passive past participle,
there is no specified Agent.

On the basis of the document from the 13th century investigated here, the first usage prediction formulated above
cannot be rejected. We are consequently justified in further
assuming that the passive past participle in the Middle Russian system of the writer of that manuscript could be used
either without a specified Agent or - if the Agent is specified - unless the immediately preceding context concentrates
on the Agent. Apart from this consideration of contextual
congruence, the writer was apparently free in choosing either
an active or a passive form, with the corresponding meaning
difference, as illustrated by the two sentences in the fifth
example above. It was apparently - as it presumably still is -
a matter of choosing the perspective from which the participants in the state of affairs are viewed and presented accordingly, as already understood by various analyses of synchronic
language data.

But is it only a matter of presenting the perspective from
which the participants in the state of affairs are viewed, or
also the perspective from which the action itself is viewed?

The second prediction formulated above was based on the
assumption that by adding a passive past participle suffix to
a verbal stem, the perspective is shifted from the action expressed by means of that verbal stem onto its effect, presented
as a state characterizing the participant which has undergone
the action. Can it be shown then that the passive past participle views the action from the perspective of its effect, not
the process producing the effect?

Within the investigated manuscript, the second prediction
cannot be rejected. A test case for it is provided by the fourth
example mentioned above, as compared with the first one. In both
examples, there is a passive past participle of 'sanctify', but
in the first example it is combined with the perfective verbal

aspect (formally expressed by means of the prefix *o-*), and in
the fourth example, with the imperfective verbal aspect. In the
first example, the meaning is clearly that of a characteristic
of the Goal resulting from the action. And in the fourth example? We can see that the immediately following context there
concentrates on the Agent's passing away at a later point of
that year, when the Agent was - next to the Goal's being in the
state which is the effect of the action - characterized by
having brought about this effect in his lifetime. Also in the
fourth example, with the imperfective verbal aspect, there is
consequently no reference to the process of the action itself,
only to its effect.

The same holds for the other available examples of the
passive past participle in the same manuscript, as illustrated
by the following examples of coordination.

(2)   Usage of passive in coordinated sentences in S:

- ВЪ ЛѢТО 6673. ПОСТАВЛЕНЪ БЫСТЬ ИЛИЯ АРХИЕПИСКОПЪ НОВѢ-
ГОРОДЬСКЫЙ ОТ МИТРОПОЛИТА ИОАННА, ПРИ КНЯЗИ РУСЬСТѢМЬ
РОСТИСЛАВѢ, МѢСЯЦА МАРТА ВЪ 28, НА ВЬРЬБНИЦЮ, И ПРИДЕ
НОВУГОРОДУ МѢСЯЦА МАИЯ ВЪ 11, ПРИ КНЯЗИ НОВГОРОДЬСТЕМЬ
СВЯТОСЛАВѢ, А ПРИ ПОСАДНИЦЕ ЗАХАРИИ.
'In the year 6673. There was nominated Eliah the archi-
episcope of Novgorod by John the metropolitan, at the
time of the Russian monarch Rostislav, in the month of
March on the 28th, on Palm Sunday, and he came to Nov-
gorod in the month of May on the 11th, at the time of
the Novgorod monarch Svjatoslav, and the governor
Zachariah.'

- ВЪ ЛѢТО 6685. ... ВЪ ТО ЖЕ ВРѢМЯ СЛЕПЛЕНЪ БЫСТЬ МЬСТИ-
СЛАВЪ КНЯЗЬ СЪ БРАТОМЬ ЯРОПЪЛКОМЬ ОТ СТРЬЯ СВОЕГО ВСѢ-
ВОЛОДА, И ПУСТИ Я ВЪ РУСЬ; ВЕДОМА ЖЕ ИМА СЛЕПОМА И
ГНЮЩЕМА ОЧИМА, И ЯКО ДОИДОСТА СМОЛЬНЬСКА ...
'In the year 6685. ... At the same time there was
blinded Mstislav the monarch with his brother Svjatopolk
due to his uncle Vsevolod, and he let them two go into
Rus'; as they were led blind and ailing at their eyes,
and as they arrived at Smolensk ...'

These examples, as well as all of the other ones, show
that the passive participles were indeed used with the meaning
of a state which is the effect of the action expressed by
means of the verbal stem, an action preceding its orientation
point in the case of the past participle, as illustrated by
both examples above, and an action at its orientation point in
the case of the present participle, as illustrated by *ВЕДОМА*
'as the two of them were led' in the second example. No case
of reference to the process itself producing the given effect
can be established, only to the state equalling the effect.
The term *'effect'* appears to be preferable to *'result'*, because
'effect' is applicable to all the interpretation possibilities
of passive participles, both past and present ones, and irres-
pectively of the verbal aspect. The interpretation of *'result'*
may indeed be viewed as due to the most frequent combination of
the passive past participle suffix with perfective verbal stems,
as assumed at the beginning of this investigation.

We can conclude that the predictions which follow from the
meaning postulate of the passive past participle suffix formulated at the beginning of this investigation, cannot be rejected on the basis of this manuscript, which means that the
meaning postulate can be taken as an acceptable solution.

Finally, it could be asked whether the usage of the passive
past participle established for the first part of S is an idiosyncratic characteristic of that manuscript, or of that period,
or a more general characteristic of Russian. The last possibility can best be investigated first, because a positive answer to
this question makes the other possibilities superfluous.

In order to investigate general applicability of the solution established to be acceptable for S, we propose to compare
S with K, the latter containing basically the same text, but
with additions, and written two centuries later, as stated above.

In connection with the passive past participle, there are
only two differences between S and K, such that S (taken as basic) has the passive past participle and K has the aorist, an
active past tense, of the same verbal stem, as shown below.

(3)   Differences between S and K in connection with the passive past participle:

S: - ВЪ ЛѢТО 6552. ПОГРѢБЕНА БЫСТА 2 КНЯЗЯ, СЫНА СВЯТОСЛАВЛЯ: ЯРОПЪЛЪ, ОЛЬГЪ; И КРЕСТИША КОСТИ ЕЮ.

ВЪ ЛѢТО 6553. СЪГОРѢ СВЯТАЯ СОФИЯ, ВЪ СУБОТУ, ПО ЗА- УТРЬНИИ, ВЪ ЧАС 3, МѢСЯЦА МАРТА ВЪ 15. ВЪ ТО ЖЕ ЛѢТО ЗАЛОЖЕНА БЫСТЬ СВЯТАЯ СОФИЯ НОВѢГОРОДѢ ВОЛОДИМИРОМЬ КНЯЗѢМЬ.

'In the year 6552. There were burried 2 monarchs, sons of Svjatoslav: Jaropol, Oleg; and they christened their bones. In the year 6553. There burnt down the Holy Sophia, on a Saturday, after the matins, around three o'clock, in the month of March on the 15th. In the same year there was founded the Holy Sophia in Novgorod by Volodimir the mo- narch.'

K: - В ЛѢТО 6552. ХОДИ ЯРОСЛАВЪ НА ЛИТВУ; А НА ВЕСНУ ЖЕ ВОЛО- ДИМИРЪ ЗАЛОЖИ НОВЪГОРОД И СДѢЛА ЕГО.

В ЛѢТО 6553. ЗАЛОЖИ ВОЛОДИМИРЪ СВЯТУЮ СОФИЮ В НОВѢГОРОДѢ.

'In the year 6552. There went Yaroslav against Lithuania; and in that Spring Volodimir founded Novgorod and built it up. In the year 6553. There founded Volodimir the Holy Sophia in Novgorod.'

S: - ВЪ ЛѢТО 6579.

ВЪ ЛѢТО 6580. ПѢРЕНЕСЕНА БЫСТА БОРИСА И ГЛѢБА СЪ ЛЬТА ВЫШЕГОРОДУ.

'In the year 6579. In the year 6580. There were transferred Boris and Gleb from L'to to Vyšegorod.'

K: - В ЛѢТО 6579. ... ГЛѢБЪ ЖЕ, ВЫИМЯ ТОПОРЪ, РОСТЯ И, И ПАДЕ МЕРТВЪ; И ЛЮДЬЕ РАЗИДОШАСЯ. ОН ЖЕ ПОГИБЕ ДУШЕЮ И ТѢЛОМЬ, ПРЕДАВЪСЯ ДИАВОЛУ.

В ЛѢТО 6580. ПРЕНЕСОША СВЯТАЯ СТРАСТОТЕРПЦА БОРИСА И ГЛѢБА. ...

'In the year 6579. ... Gleb then, taking out the axe, stroke him, and he fell down dead; and the people dis- persed. That one perished with body and soul, having surrendered to the devil.

In the year 6580. They transferred the holy sufferers
Boris and Gleb.'

Both differences between S and K appear to correlate with
the respective immediately preceding contexts, which are different too. In the first example of difference presented above,
K concentrates on the Agent Volodimir in the immediately preceding context, and apparently applies the same consideration
of textual congruence by not using a passive construction if[1]
the immediately preceding context concentrates on the Agent.
In the second example of difference presented above, K concentrates on Gleb and another male participant, different from
Boris, in the immediately preceding context. It was presumably
due to this partial overlapping between the Goal in the sentence
under consideration and the participants in the immediately preceding context, that it was for the sake of clarity preferable
not to set the perspective on the Goal and thus also not to use
a passive construction (which is in part determined by this perspective, as shown above).

On the basis of the investigated manuscript, there is no
reason to assume for the 15th century that the passive past participle was used according to principles different from those
valid two centuries earlier. On the basis of this usage, there
is no reason to assume that its meaning was different either.

3.   CONCLUSION

In this investigation, a meaning postulate of the passive
past participle in Middle Russian was tested by formulating
restrictive predictions about its usage in the written language
and testing them on the basis of two mutually comparable manuscripts. On the basis of nonfalsification within the investigated
manuscripts, we may now assume that it is plausible indeed to
proceed investigating the passive past participle in Russian
against the background of the meaning postulate formulated above
by which *an entity (in casu: Goal) is characterized by the state
which is the effect of an action preceding its orientation point*
(whereas the passive present participle can be postulated to mean

that *an entity (in casu: Goal) is characterized by the state
which is the effect of an action at its orientation point)*.

On the basis of this investigation it is plausible to state
that the meaning of the passive participles in Middle Russian
was not that of *'an action (affecting a Goal)'*, but rather that
of *'a state as the effect of an action (predicated to a Goal as
its characteristic)'*. This means that passive sentences based on
these participles differed from the corresponding active sentences not only on the basis of the perspective from which the
participants in the states of affairs are viewed (such that the
Goal determines the perspective in passive sentences, and the
Agent in active ones), but also on the basis of the perspective
from which the predicate is viewed, as either a state (in passive sentences containing a passive participle) or an action
(in the corresponding active sentences).[2] A linguistic theory
must be able to account for the established meaning differences
in a principled way in order to be adequate.

University of Amsterdam

NOTES

[1] Note that *'textual congruence'* does not equal *'predictability from the
context'*.
[2] Reflexive constructions, which were the other means of passivization, did
not occur with a specified Agent in the investigated manuscripts. This restriction already points to a semantic difference as compared with their
active counterparts.

BIBLIOGRAPHY

Barentsen, A.A.
  1985   *'Tijd', 'Aspect' en de conjunctie poka (Over betekenis en gebruik
            van enkele vormen in het moderne Russisch)*. Amsterdam.
Borkovskij, V.I., O.J. Kuznecov
  1963   *Istoričeskaja grammatika russkogo jazyka*. Moskva: Akademija Nauk.
Gorškova, K.V., G.A. Xaburgaev
  1981   *Istoričeskaja grammatika russkogo jazyka*. Moskva: Vysšaja škola.
Gvozdanović J.
  1985   *Language System and Its Change (on Theory and Testability)*.
            Berlin/ New York/ Amsterdam: Mouton de Gruyter.
Ljapunov, B.M.
  1900   *Issledovanie o jazyke Sinodal'nago spiska 1-oj Novgorodskoj leto-
            pisi*. Sanktpeterburg: Imperatorskaja Akademija Nauk.

MULTIFUNCTIONALITY IN ASPECTUAL DETERMINATION
IN RUSSIAN

H. HAMBURGER

1. *INTRODUCTION*

When Daneš (1976) in his perspicacious article on the indirect
passive voice (voice of the recipient) shows the relationship of
voice and functional sentence perspective, he is actually dealing
with the relationship between different functions of language. In
doing so he continues the tradition set by the Prague school
which in the thirties founded the theory of the so-called 'func-
tionalism'. The concept of function was further elaborated by
Halliday (1970).

Halliday (op.cit.:140ff.) distinguishes in language three
universal grammatical relevant functions: (1) the ideational
function, (2) the interpersonal function, (3) the textual function. The first function refers to what is usually called cog-
nitive or referential meaning, whereas the second function bears
reference to modal meaning. In our opinion the interpersonal
function should not be limited to modality but also include deictic meaning, so that it embraces all speaker-linked categories.
These two functions agree with the Groot's definition of the
spoken sentence (1964^2:51) as a "self-contained auditive gestalt
by which the speaker expresses his attitude towards something".
By 'something' de Groot understands an element of referential
meaning. His definition of the sentence already shows that the
ideational function is basic and that the interpersonal function
is second important.

Halliday's third function concerns the sentence perspective
(theme-rheme structure) and the information structure (new-
given). The third function presupposes the second and the first

one. The functions occur in a cluster. An utterance contains a
complete cluster, but not each part of the utterance necessarily
shows the presence of the second or the third function.

Halliday takes as an example the three kinds of subject: the
logical subject, the grammatical subject, and the psychological
subject. The logical subject refers to the ideational function,
the grammatical subject serves the interpersonal function - which
shows that deictic meaning belongs to the domain of this function -, and the psychological subject represents the textual function. Halliday demonstrates that the three subjects may coincide
or may occur separately, but he does not mention the fact that the
grammatical subject and the psychological subject are applied to
an element of the ideational world, i.e. that they too presuppose
the ideational function.

Since aspect is determined by indicators belonging to the
three functions, confusion may arise about which function is determining the aspect of a particular process. This confusion may
be eliminated by supposing that the three functions usually determine the aspect simultaneously.

2.   FUNCTION AND ASPECT

Before we shall try to establish the relationship between the
above-mentioned functions and aspect in Russian we must point out
our views on the Russian aspect.

Generally a process is represented in Russian in two variants:
1. a variant that fits into a 'whole' context (the 'whole' or perfective process) and 2. a variant that fits into a 'non-whole'
context (the 'non-whole' or imperfective process). 'Whole' and
'non-whole' are the meanings of the perfective and the imperfec-
ive aspect, respectively. Both are semantically marked (cf. Šeljakin 1976:21). 'Wholeness' and 'non-wholeness' should not be confused with ideational 'completeness' and 'incompleteness'.'Počital',
for instance, is a 'whole' and 'incomplete' process, whereas čital
in *Ja uže čital ètu knigu* is 'non-whole' and 'complete'. (cf.
Hamburger 1983, 1984a en 1984b). This aspectual dichotomy is characteristic of the way in which in Russian processes are embodied

in the lexical material and are presented in the utterance.

Since process and context are in a relationship of mutual interaction (cf. Bondarko, Lehmann, Bourke, Rassudova and many others), aspect concerns both the process and its context. The process as well as the context contains aspectual determinators. This idea corresponds with Lehmann's concepts of *innere* und *äussere Determination* (1977: 131).

As an example we take the sentence *On pročital dva časa*. The 'wholeness' of *pročital* is determined by the perdurativity of the process as well as by its context *dva časa*. The above implies that, in principle, there does not exist real aspectual competition. Hence we suppose that, when the aspectual opposition is illustrated with the aid of minimal pairs, the contexts are insufficiently elaborated.

In earlier investigations we tried to demonstrate that a process determines aspect not directly, but through a cluster of semantic *Aktionsarten* (AAs). Although they do not clearly keep apart semantic and morphologically characterized AAs, Bondarko, Maslov, Šeljakin, Rassudova and other slavists have underlined the importance of the AA as an aspectual determinator. Rassudova's following remark agrees very well with our concept of semantic AA[1]:

"Under Aktionsart we understand the general characteristics of the lexical meaning of a verb which reflect the nature of the progress of an action and the distribution of an action in time" (1984: 20).

The semantic AA corresponds with the processual structure as a whole, or - more often - with one of its components, the temporal component among them. The AA is usually realized in either aspect, be it generally in a relationship of aspectual dominance (cf. Hamburger 1984a and 1984b). The same is true for the various meanings in the context. They also determine aspect in a relationship of dominance. Contrary to Lehmann we do not consider the semantic AAs and the contextual meanings aspectual meanings, because aspectual meaning is, in our opinion, restricted to 'wholeness' and 'non-wholeness'. The meanings in process and context, however, determine the aspectual usage by

showing their preference for one of the two aspects. As Lehmann
says: "Nur eine Minderheit der Indikatoren korreliert unbedingt
mit einem bestimmten Aspekt" (op. cit.: 150).

Aspectual determination does not always proceed in a sphere
of harmony: there is agreement or conflict between the aspectual
determinators in the AA-cluster and also within the context. In
the case of a conflict a hierarchy is developed. There is also a
conflict possible between the aspectual determination of the
process and the determination of the context. Maslov (1974) and
Rassudova (op. cit.: 51 and 55), too, are concerned with the
hierarchy of aspectual determinators of different degrees of importance. Maslov distinguishes *konsequente, inkonsequente,* and
relative Aspektantonymie and *synonymische Aspektkonkurrenz,*
whereas Rassudova speaks of strong and weak oppositions of determinators. As examples of a strong opposition she mentions the
opposition between the concrete-factual and the concrete-processual meanings and between the iterative and the singulative
meanings, whereas she calls 'weak opposition' the opposition
between the indefinite-iterative and the aggregate meanings and
between the concrete-factual and the general-factual meanings.

The aspectual determinators in the context serve the above-
mentioned three functions. The relationship between process and
context with their determinators on the one hand and aspect on
the other are depicted in fig. 1.

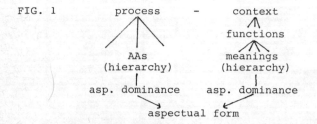

FIG. 1

Unfortunately not much work has been done in the field of sta-
tistics of aspectual usage. In determining the aspectual dominance we have mainly used the figures given by Forsyth (1970),

which are partly based on Štejnfel'dt's word count. In the remaining cases we have drawn on our own experience. The reliability of the indications of dominance used in this paper should be enhanced by extensive statistical research.

Below a survey is given of the semantic AAs distinguished by us. Some of the names of the AAs have been changed in the course of the various research projects in order to strip them as much as possible from ambiguous and redundant connotations.

1. The AA of the independent predicate. This AA indicates the combination of a causing event and the corresponding caused event.
2. The eventive AA. This AA indicates the caused event.
3. The instrumental AA. This AA indicates the causing event.
4. The processual (conative) AA. This AA indicates an unfinished caused (or seldom causing) event. Applied to a terminative process it indicates a predicate in which the terminative boundary has not been reached.
5. The terminative AA. This AA indicates a predicate in which the terminative boundary has been reached.
6. The aterminative AA. This AA indicates a predicate of a verb in which there is no inherent terminative boundary.
7. The ingressive AA. This AA indicates the beginning of a predicate.
8. The iterative AA. This AA indicates a predicate of which the temporal component has an iterative character.
9. The singulative AA. This AA indicates a predicate of which the temporal component has a singulative character.
10.The AA of the establishment of fact. This AA indicates a predicate without its temporal component.

Some AAs are mutually exclusive, like the singulative AA and the iterative AA, the terminative AA and the aterminative AA, the terminative AA and the processual AA, whereas other AAs are compatible, like the terminative AA and the singulative AA, the terminative AA and the iterative AA, the terminative AA and the kf-AA, the processual AA and the singulative AA, etc.

For the purpose of this investigation the speaker-linked

verbal categories, such as mood, tense, and voice are regarded as contextual aspectual determinators.

Although, in principle, the meaning of the various AAs has its counterpart in the context (cf. Lehmann's concept of *Kookkurrenz* (op. cit.: 150)), this is not always indicated in the diagrams for ease of survey. For this reason only the most relevant AAs and contextual meanings have been mentioned.

In the diagrams the relevant dominances are indicated by an arrow.

The following abbreviations are used in the diagrams:

appr	= apprehension	it	= iterative AA
at	= aterminative AA	kf	= establishment of fact
backgr	= background	M	= interpersonal function
co	= processual AA	nec	= necessity
cpl	= complete	p	= perfective
d	= dominant	part	= partial
dur	= duration	poss	= possibility
ev	= eventive AA	pot	= potentiality
frgr	= foreground	prhb	= prohibition
fut	= future tense	prt	= past tense
gvn	= given	rslt	= result
I	= ideational function	sg	= singulative AA
i	= imperfective	sim	= simultaneity
id	= independent AA	succ	= succession
ig	= ingressive AA	T	= textual function
imposs	= impossibility	te	= terminative AA
in	= instrumental AA	vol	= volition

3. THE IDEATIONAL FUNCTION AND ASPECT

The most relevant ideational meanings expressed by perfective forms are result and ingressivity. Ideational meanings belonging to the temporal component of the process, such as succession, singulativity, delimitivity, perdurativity, are discussed in 3.8. Less central ideational meanings are suddenness, partitivity, etc. These meanings occur as semantic AAs and/or contextual meanings.

The most relevant ideational meanings expressed by means of imperfective forms are processuality (conation) and stativity. Ideational meanings belonging to the temporal component, such as simultaneity, iterativity, etc. are discussed in 3.8. Less important meanings are the general-factional meaning, the 'cancelled' process, etc.

3.1.   RESULT

'Result' is closely connected with the terminative AA. It is predominantly expressed by the perfective aspect (see (1)). When 'result' is dominated by iteration, it is realised by the imperfective aspect (2).

> (1) *My postroili ètot dom za god*
> (2) *My vsegda stroili takoj dom za god*

In turn 'result' may dominate iteration, namely, in the case of the aggregate meaning (see 3.8.5).

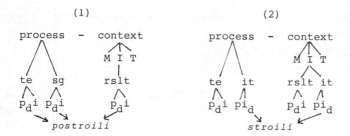

In (1) there is agreement within the AA-cluster and between the process and the context. in (2) there is a conflict in the AA-cluster and in the context, which conflicts are both won by 'iteration'. Thus there exists agreement between the determination of the process and its context.

3.2.   INGRESSIVITY

In Russian 'ingressivity' is usually expressed by perfective forms, either synthetically (3) or analytically (e.g. *stal čitat'*). An example of an imperfective ingressive process is depicted in (9).

(3) *On zažeg sveču*

(3)

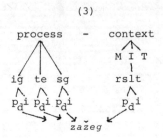

That 'inception' also in the context predominantly determines the perfective aspect is demonstrated by Rassudova (op. cit.: 59).

3.3. SUDDENNESS

The contextual meaning 'suddenness' is illustrated by the following sentences:

(4) *On vdrug vstal i nalil stakan čaju*
(5) *On, byvalo, vdrug vstaval i nalival čaj*

In (4) there is no conflict within the AA-cluster, nor between process and context. In the AA-cluster of (5), however, there is a conflict between the terminative AA and the iterative AA, which is won by the latter. The now existing conflict between process and context is won by the process: iterativity dominates 'suddenness'.

(4)   (5)

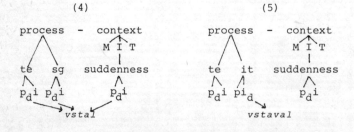

3.4. THE PARTITIVE CONTEXT

The partitive determinator is illustrated in (6) and (7).

(6) *On vypil čaju*

(7) *Každoe utro on pil nemnogo čaju*

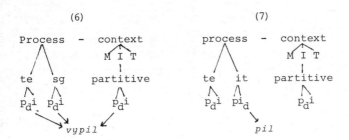

In (6) there is no conflict, but in (7) there is a conflict within the AA-cluster, which is won by the iterative AA, which also wins the conflict with the context.

3.5. THE PROCESS IN PROGRESS

The processual AA marks the process in progress, which is also called 'process in development', 'unfinished process', 'concrete-processual' process. It includes proper conative processes, durative processes, commencement (*pristup k dejstviju*). This AA has a strong preference for the imperfective aspect. Perfective realizations of this type of process may have a delimitative or perdurative character (e.g. *počital, pročital*)(see 3.8).

(8) *Vedro napolnjalos' medlenno*

(9) *On zažigal sveču, no ne mog zažeč' ee, tak kak dul veter*

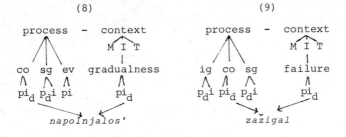

In (8) there is a tendentive-conative process, i.e. a process in which only the caused event is being realized. The processual AA has won the conflict in the AA-cluster and the process is in agreement with the context.[2]

In (9) there is a proper conative process. A 'failing activity' in the context corresponds with conation in the process.

3.6. *THE STATIVE PROCESS*

Stative and other aterminative processes are mostly expressed imperfectively. Perfective aterminative processes are delimitative or perdurative (see 3.8).

(10) *On ležal dolgo v posteli*

(11) *On bil ego*

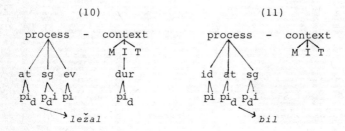

The process in (10) represents the final phase of caused event, the process in (11) is an independent single-phase process. In both processes the conflict in the AA-cluster has been won by the aterminative AA.

3.7. *THE ESTABLISHMENT OF FACT*

In the process presented as a fact *(konstatacija fakta)*, also called 'simple denotation' (Forsyth), 'general factual' process (Maslov, Bondarko, Rassudova), the temporal component is absent.

(12) *Vy uže čitali ètu knigu?*

(12)

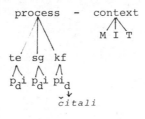

In (12) in the AA-cluster the kf-AA dominates the terminative and the singulative AAs.

The 'cancelled' *(annulirovannyj)* process has been replaced by a second process and has become its context.

(13)   *Vy brali moju gazetu? Ona smjata.*

(13)

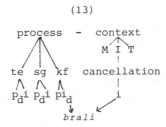

In (13) the kf-AA dominates the AA-cluster. 'Cancellation' is considered a variant of the general-factual meaning.

The kf-process must be distinguished from the conative process with the meaning of commencement[3], although they have much in common: a process in progress is little more than just an activity and is closely related to a fact (cf. 4.2 and 5.4).

(14)   *Vy uže perevodili ètot tekst?*

(14) can be translated in two ways: (a) Did you (ever) translate this text?, (b) Have you already been translating this text? The context of the latter interpretation may be a 'failure'! *Da, a ne perevel ego do konca,* which is incompatible with (a), because this interpretation implies the completion of the translation.

(14b)

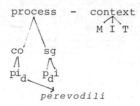

perevodili

Rassudova's examples with the general-factual meaning (op.cit.:
58ff.) show the close connection between the establishment of
fact and the anaphoric use of the imperfective aspect (see 5.4).
This demonstrates the multifunctionality in the determination of
Russian aspect.

3.8. *THE TEMPORAL COMPONENT*

The temporal component contains the semantic time that a process
needs to run its course. It is of a single or an iterative nature.
Besides, the temporal component is part of the context. It embraces heterogeneous contextual meanings, such as 'succession',
'simultaneity', indications of singulativity, iterativity,
clock-time, calendar time, etc.

In the first instance the temporal component serves the
ideational function. But ideational time does hardly exist without being affected by the interpersonal function. It is interpreted deictically by the introduction of a point of orientation,
the moment of speech, which is by itself an element of the context. As a result of this the distinction of past, present and
future arises, which corresponds with the distinctions
'yesterday', 'today' and 'tomorrow' in the context. Most of
the above-mentioned temporal meanings are considered aspectual
determinators.

Ideational temporal meanings that are relevant to the perfective aspect are 'succession', 'singulativity', 'delimitativ-
ity', 'perdurativity', etc., whereas 'simultaneity' and 'iteration' are determinators for the imperfective aspect.

157

3.8.1. SUCCESSION

'Succession' is a typical contextual determinator. We take as
examples the following sentences:

(15) *V ètot den' on vstal rano, pozavtrakal i pošel v institut*
(16) *V èti dni on vstaval rano, zavtrakal i šel v institut*

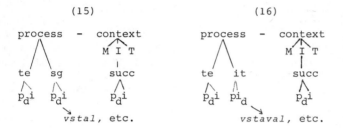

In (15) there is no conflict between the determinators; in (16)
in the AA-cluster the iterative AA dominates the terminative AA
and subsequently the process dominates the context.

3.8.2. SIMULTANEITY

Just as 'succession' 'simultaneity' involves more than one predicate. The processes involved in 'simultaneity' are divided
into imperfective background processes, which contain the processual AA or the aterminative AA, and processes in the foreground.
The latter type of process is either imperfective (complete
simultaneity) or perfective (partial simultaneity).

(17) *Kogda solnce podnimalos', ono osveščalo gory*
(18) *Kogda ona gotovila obed, ee muž prišel domoj*

In (17) we have to do with complete simultaneity: the processes
involved cover the same period of time. In (18) the simultaneity
is only partial. Here we deal with the so-called *Inzidenz* (cf.
Lehmann op.cit.: 143).

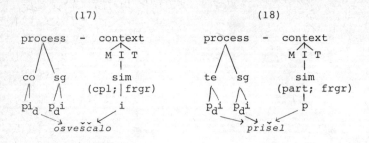

In the temporal clause introduced by *poka* 'succession' is expressed by perfectivity, whereas 'simultaneity' is realized by imperfective forms.

    (19) *My sideli doma, poka ne končilas' burja*

    (20) *Poka on čital, ja razgljadyval al'bom*

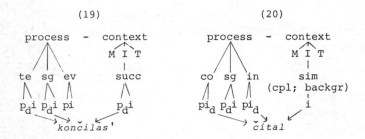

3.8.3.   *TEMPORAL DELIMITIATION*

The contextual meanings 'succession' or 'result' may affect the process by delimiting its temporal component and thus determine the perfective aspect. In Russian this finds expression in the morphologically characterized perdurative, delimitative, and semelfactive AAs. Examples are found in (21), (22), and (23) resp.

    (21) *On promachal platkom neskol'ko minut i ušel*

    (22) *On pomachal platkom i ušel*

    (23) *On machnul platkom v znak soglasija*

159

(21, 22, 23)

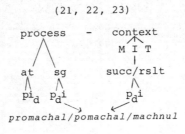

In (21, 22, 23) the context dominates the process.

3.8.4.   THE SINGULATIVE PROCESS

In the foregoing examples we have demonstrated that a process is
singulative or iterative. The single process is predominantly
perfective. Rassudova remarks:

"The main function of the P is the expression of single actions. This is
not the case with the I; although the I is not precluded from conveying
single actions, it is used for this purpose less frequently, and in this
sphere it plays 'second fiddle', as it were" (op. cit.: 16).

3.8.5.   ITERATIVITY

Although iterativity is mostly expressed imperfectively, a context of 'succession' or 'result' evokes perfective iterativity.
This type of iterativity is known as the aggregate meaning
(summarnoe značenie). Veyrenc (1980: 131ff.) too puts emphasis
on the bi-aspectual nature of iterativity.

> (24) *On tri raza perečital stichotvorenie i togda znal ego*
>   *naizust'*

(24)

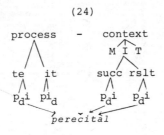

In (24) in the AA-cluster iterativity dominates terminativity as
usual, but with the aggregate process the context is dominant. Also
vyšli in *Vse vyšli na ulicu* is regarded to be an aggregate process
(cf. Šeljakin 1976: 22). Šeljakin sets this *vyšli* against *vychodili*
in the same context, where *vychodili* expresses the indefinite
iterative meaning.

3.9. THE INFINITIVE

The distinction finite verb - infinite verb is mainly a question
of surface structure: the infinite verb is a transposition of a
finite verb. Both synonymous expressions often exist side by side:
*trava načala zelenet'/trava zazelenela, on uspel vyučit' sticho-
tvorenie/on vyučil stichotvorenie, tebe tuda ne vojti/ty tuda ne
vojdeš'*, etc.

According to the type of auxiliary the infinitive construction can be divided into an ideational and a modal subtype. In
this section we shall discuss infinitive constructions containing
an ideational auxiliary predicate.

Generally speaking the auxiliary predicate is a context for
the infinitive concerned and vice versa. The ideational auxiliary,
however, usually does not represent the context but is part of the
predicate structure.

(25) *On stal igrat'*
(26) *On uspel dostat' gazetu*
(27) *On prodolžal čitat' knigu*

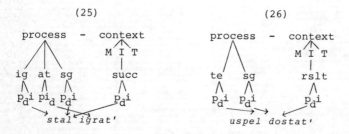

(27)

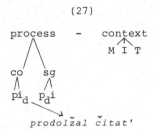

process - context
                M I T

co   sg
pi_d P_d^i

prodolžal čitat'

Although in these examples the auxiliary predicate and the infinitive are considered a unit, the determinators may determine either
the auxiliary or the infinitive. In (25), for instance, the ingressive AA and the singulative AA determine the infinitive. In
(26) and (27) such a distribution is less obvious.

4.   THE INTERPERSONAL FUNCTION AND ASPECT

In 3 we restricted ourselves to the ideational function and its
role in aspectual determination. In the example chosen the other
functions were less relevant for several reasons; all examples
contained, for instance, a past tense predicate and the past tense
is a poor aspectual determinator. The examples were also unmarked
from the point of view of the textual function.

Now we shall discuss the interpersonal function and the way
it affects the determination of the aspects.

4.1.   THE TENSES

Tense serves both the ideational function and the interpersonal
function. This is illustrated especially by the relative tenses,
such as pluperfect and future II. These tenses have not only a
deictic meaning (past and future, respectively) (interpersonal
function), but they also imply succession (ideational function).

Much has been written about the relationship between tense
and aspect, but unfortunately this is not or unsufficiently supported by statistical data. As far as the past tense concerns it
is difficult to distinguish a particular preference for one of
the aspects. However, the moment of speech may be a relevant

contextual determinator, because the (partial) coincidence of the past (and future) process with the moment of speech is accompanied by a dominance of the perfective aspect. On the contrary the dissociation from the moment of speech goes either with the perfective aspect (aorist) or with the imperfective aspect (kf or processual AA).

There is an overwhelming dominance of the imperfective aspect with the present tense[4]. Actual present tense predicates must be considered processual.

(28) *Ona pečet tort*

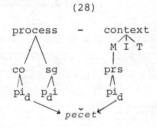

4.1.1. THE FUTURE TENSE

It is assumed that there is a dominance of the perfective aspect with the future tense (cf. Forsyth op.cit.: 122n.), which is apparently caused by the numerous modal meanings combined with the future tense. From the following examples from Waring (1980: 166) it appears that a future tense may or may not be accompanied by an extra modal meaning (see (29) and (30), respectively).

(29) *Zavtra my izroem ètu ploščadku* (shall)

(30) *Takoj sposob ne goditsja: my izroem vsju našu ledjanuju ploščadku* (may)

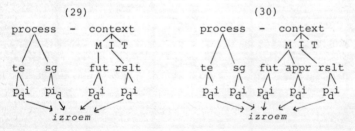

'Apprehension' is a variant of 'potentiality'. A similar contrast without or with an extra modal meaning in the context - this time 'impossibility'- is found in (31) and (32) resp., although (31) may be interpreted with an element of volition.

(31) *On tuda ni za čto ne vojdet* (will)

(32) *On tuda ne vojdet, tak kak dver' zaperta* (can)

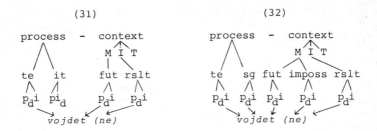

(31) illustrates that pronouns and adverbs of the *ni*-type in combination with the future tense usually have the aggregate meaning (see 3.8.5; cf. Rassudova op. cit.: 53).

Other types of contextual modal meaning are contained in (33), (34), and (35), more precisely 'prohibition', 'necessity', and 'unwillingness' resp.

(33) *Sejčas ty est' ne budeš'!*

(34) *Vy dvoe ponesete ego v avtomobil'!*

(35) *Ja ne budu delat' ètogo!*

The predicates in (33) and (34) are closely related to the imperative (see 4.3.1).

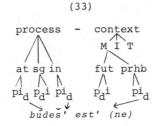

In (33) 'prohibition' as a determinator is obviously stronger than the future tense.

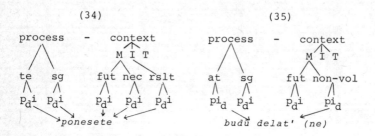

(34)   (35)

In (35) 'non-volition' dominates within the context and the context dominates the process.

When 'potentiality' is combined with 'iteration' it belongs to the so-called 'graphic-exemplary meaning' *(nagljadno-primernoe značenie)* (cf. Maslov op. cit.: 118; Rassudova op. cit.: 114ff. and 153ff.). Here repeated processes do not take up all the time indicated by the predicate, but only part of the time.

(36) *On vsegda pridet tebe na pomošč'*

In (36) the agent will help from time to time, when the occasion arises. The context (potentiality) dominates the iterative AA in the process (see also Lehmann's example (op. cit.: 131) *Ja vsegda povtorju ego vam)*.

(36)

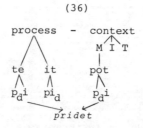

The relationship between future tense and aspect is furthermore illustrated by the following sentences:

(37) *Esli ja najdu ego adres, ja napišu emu* (succession)
(38) *Kogda on budet uchodit', vyzovite menja* (partial
simultaneity)

The AA of the establishment is found in the AA-cluster of (39).

(39) *Zavtra ego budut choronit'*

(39)

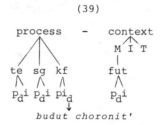

The kf-meaning both in the process and in the context dominates
the other meanings. Here the ideational function is stronger than
the interpersonal function.

4.2. THE INFINITIVE

In 3.9 we pointed out that the auxiliary predicate is a context
for the infinitive and vice versa. This holds especially for the
modal auxiliary. Both auxiliary predicate and infinitive contain
aspectual determinators. Whereas the infinitive reflects the ideational function, the modal auxiliary serves the interpersonal
function. In this investigation we shall consider the auxiliary
process only an aspectual determinator.

Because of the enormous quantity of material offered by the
infinitive constructions we have been forced to make a choice
that represents as well as possible the various arrangements of
meaning in the process and its context.

(40) *On chočet izučit' russkij jazyk*
(41) *On chočet izučat' russkij jazyk*

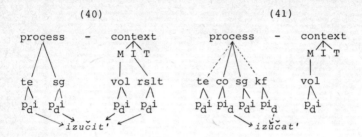

In (41) the verbal lexeme of the infinitive allows an interpretation with a co-AA or with a kf-AA. In that case co must be substituted by te.

(42) *On ne chotel otkryt' dver'*
(43) *On ne chotel otkryvat' dver'*

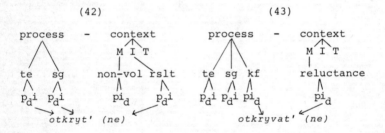

'To open' is a process of short duration. Hence the presence of the co-AA in the AA-cluster of (43) is less plausible. In (42) the conflict in the context is won by 'result'.
Auxiliaries characterized by the meaning of 'reluctance' are *nadoest', ustat',*

(44) *My spešim, čtoby ne opozdat'*
(45) *Zimoj nado odevat'sja teplo*
(46) *Moroz! Nado odet'sja teplo*

167

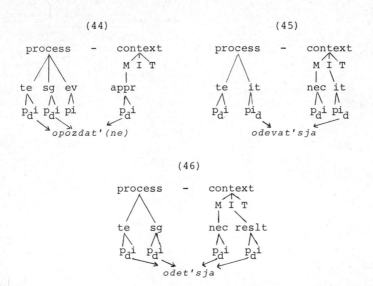

In (45) iteration dominates necessity in the context.

(47) *Možno li pročitat' vaše sočinenije?*

(48) *Ja ne mogu perevesti ètot tekst*

(49) *Ja ne mogu perevodit' ètot tekst*

(50) *Ja mogu ne perevesti ètot tekst*

(51) *Ja mogu ne perevodit' ètot tekst*

(52) *Nel'zja perevodit' ètot tekst*

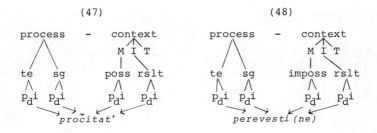

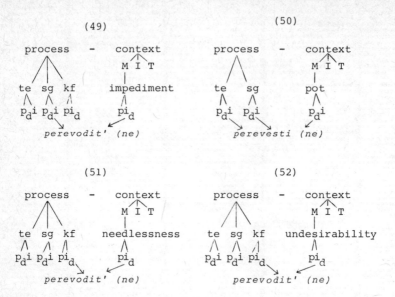

In (49) kf and 'impediment' dominate the other meanings. 'Impediment' is much related to 'reluctance', 'needlessness' and 'undesirability' (see (43), (51), and (52) respectively). These four contextual meanings correspond with the kf-AA in the process.

(53) *My možem rešat' ètu problemu segodnja*

(53)

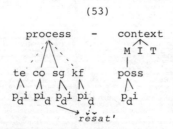

In (53) the conflict between the process and the context is won by the former. Since *rešat'* does not preclude the completion of the process of solving *(možet byt' ja rešu ee)*, the kf-AA is regarded as an alternative interpretation (cf. (41)). In that case co must be substituted by te.

(54) *V ètich uslovijach mogut razvit'sja bakterii*

(54)

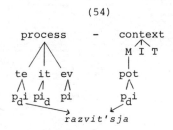

(54) is an example of the potential variant of the graphic-exemplary meaning (cf. (36)), which is mainly restricted to the infinitive and the future tense (cf. Rassudova op. cit.: 159f.). The perfective infinitive in (54) indicates limited iteration, whereas the imperfective infinitive in the same context would refer to unlimited iteration.

(55) *Ja pošel kupit' (ètot) kostjum*
(56) *Ja pošel pokupat' kostjum*

(55)   (56)

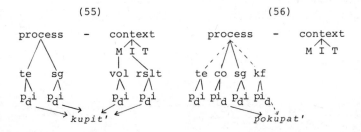

(55) implies a particular suit, which has been selected before, whereas in (56) *kostjum* refers to any suit. *Pokupat'* indicates here only the process of selecting (commencement).

Generally speaking the processual meaning in the imperfective infinitive (conation, duration, commencement) and the establishment of fact are hardly distinguishable. Because the infinitive is a category without tense and the dependent infinitive

does not even indicate time, the infinitive is eminently suitable
to express the kf-meaning. This is especially true for the imperfective infinitive, which lacks any marked information about completion, result and limitation. Rassudova (op. cit.: 133) supposes
that the infinitive preferably fulfils the function of simply
naming. In the past tense the processual meaning and the establishment of fact can be distinguished more easily (see 3.7).

4.3. THE INTERPERSONAL FUNCTION AND MOOD

Mood, too, serves the interpersonal function and may be an aspectual determinator. Forsyth (op. cit.: 244), for instance, points
out that the affirmative subjunctive predicate is predominantly
perfective, whereas the negated subjunctive predicate is in general imperfective. Of the moods we shall restrict ourselves to
the imperative mood.

4.3.1. THE IMPERATIVE

'Volition' is not restricted to the subjunctive predicate, the
infinitive construction and the future tense; it is also present
in the imperative. In fact the imperative is regarded as the
direct speech representation of a compound proposition with a
volitive object clause: *Go away!* is based on 'I want you to go
away'. On the analogy of the affirmative volitive infinitive construction a dominance of the perfective aspect is assumed with
the affirmative imperative and of the imperfective aspect with
the negated imperative (cf. Mazon 1908: 242).

(57) *Ostudite kompot, pered tem kak ego podavat'!*
(58) *Pridi v ljuboj moment!*
(59) *Ne opozdajte!*
(60) *Ne opazdyvajte!*

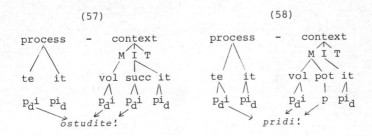

In (57) 'succession' is the strongest aspectual determinator, so
the context dominates the process. The imperative in (58) is an
example of the potential variant of the graphic-exemplary meaning (cf. (36) and (54)).

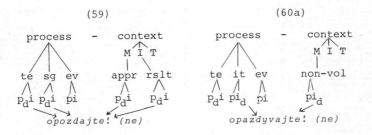

In (60a) 'non-volition' refers to 'prohibition', in (60b) to a
negative request. In (60b) kf and 'non-volition' dominate the
terminative and the singulative AAs. Rassudova (op. cit.: 191)
too shows that an example like (60a) may be interpreted as a
single process: *Ne opazdyvajte zavtra, v našem rasporjaženii budet očen' malo vremeni* (cf. (60b)).

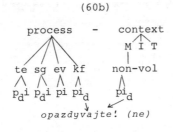

In the imperative diagrams we have in general restricted ourselves to the registration of the interpersonal determination. In the next section we shall discuss the contribution of the textual function to the determination of the aspect.

5. THE TEXTUAL FUNCTION AND ASPECT

As we mentioned before, the textual function presupposes the ideational function and, usually, also the interpersonal function. As far as the textual function concerns we restrict ourselves to the information structure of the utterance (cf. Halliday op. cit.: 162ff.; Bondarko/Bulanin 1967: 169ff.). This structure consists of a part with 'new' information and a part with 'known' information ('given'). The information structure plays a not insignificant role with respect to the determination of aspect. This has been noticed by many slavists. Whereas Mehlig (1976) calls 'given' *Proform*, Salnikow (1980) uses the feature *vorerwähnt* to indicate 'known' information. Bourke (1976: 58) speaks of 'presupposition' when the information assumed by the speaker is to be shared by him and the hearer, and of 'focus' when this is not the case. We shall use the concepts 'new' and 'given as aspectual determinators.

5.1. THE PAST TENSE

In Russian the perfective aspect is used to express the 'new' predicate, whereas the imperfective aspect ususally expresses the 'known' predicate.

To begin with the textual function is relevant in those utterances in which a particular constituent is brought to the foreground, such as the agent, the place, the reason, the time, etc. (cf. Rassudova op. cit.: 75ff.). In these cases the process is 'given' and it is expressed by imperfective forms.

(61) *Kto šil ètot kostjum? Ja chotel s nim pogovorit'*
(62) *Kto sšil ètot kostjum? Kostjum mne očen' nravitsja*

173

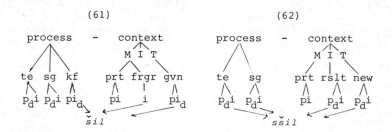

In (61) the agent is in the foreground. It makes the process to
be 'given'. Bourke's examples (op. cit.: 67) *Gde vy kupili/poku-
pali apel'siny?* show a similar opposition: *pokupali* is 'given',
because the place of the buying of the oranges has been brought
to the fore.

'Given' has often the kf-AA as its counterpart, but the opposite is not necessarily true: *čitali* in *Vy čitali ètot roman?*,
for example, contains the kf-AA but is 'new'. The frequent cooc-
currence of 'given' and the kf-AA, however, is not accidental,
because a 'known' process is easily reduced to a fact.

Other examples of aspectual determination by the textual
function in combination with the past tense are found in (63) and
(64).

    (63) *Vy pozvonili emu? Vy ved' namereny byli sdelat' èto?*
    (64) *Ja tuda ne pošel, chotja ja nameren byl*

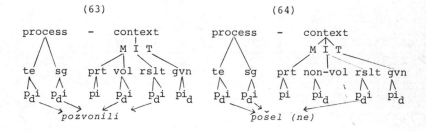

In (63) and (64) 'given' is dominated by other determinators.
These examples show that textual determinators, too, are related
to the aspect in a relationship of dominance. The idea of the

anaphoric meaning of the perfective predicate is confirmed by
Rassudova (op. cit.: 60f.). Lehmann (op. cit.: 139) speaks in
this connection of the *neutral markierte anaphorische Bedeutung* of
the imperfective aspect and the *expressiv markierte anaphorische
Bedeutung* of the perfective aspect.

5.2. THE FUTURE TENSE

The textual function plays also a role in the determination of the
aspect of the future tense. First in the case of the deictic type
of context in which one of the constituents is placed into the
foreground (cf. (65)).

    (65) *Gde Vy budete uznavat'?*

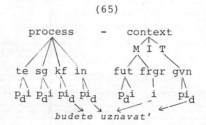

In (65) it is the 'place' which is emphasized. This 'emphasis'
presupposes the process to be known to the hearer.
    The next type of future predicate the aspect of which is
determined by a meaning serving the textual function is the predicate of the morphologically characterized AA of the *pojti*-type
(66). This is in contrast to the predicate of the undirectional
verb of motion (see (67)).

    (66) *Zavtra ja pojdu na rynok*
    (67) *Zavtra ja idu na rynok*

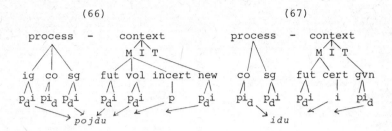

(66)   (67)

In (66) 'new' is combined with 'incertitude', whereas in (67) 'given' goes with 'certitude'. In (67) the hearer is supposed to be informed about the agent's going to the market.

(68) *Čto Vy budete zakazyvat?*

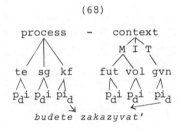

(68)

In (68) the waiter expects the agent to order something. This is the decisive factor in the determination of the aspect. Here 'given' corresponds with kf.

5.3.   *THE IMPERATIVE*

It is in the imperative that the multifunctionality in aspectual determination emerges most clearly. Here all of the three functions are usually relevant.

(69) *Vstan' požalujsta! Èto mesto zanjato.*

(70) *Pora! Vstavaj!*

(71) *Posidite!*

(72) *Sidite!*

(73) *Vojdite!*

(74) *Vchodite!*

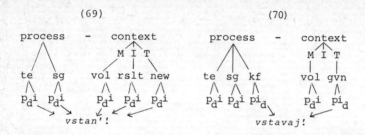

(69)   (70)

The conflict between the aspectual determinators in (70) is won by
the combination kf- given. The process may also be considered to
possess the processual AA instead of the kf-AA. In the imperative
these AA-meanings easily coincide.

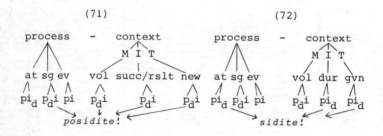

(71)   (72)

In (71) the determination of the context suppresses the influence
of the aterminative AA.

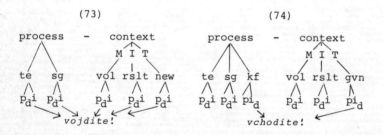

(73)   (74)

In (74) the combination 'given'-kf suppresses the influence of the
te-AA.

In the imperative 'new' and 'given' offer an explanation for

177

the connotations 'non-emotional' and 'emotional', respectively, which are often mentioned in Russian grammar. An unknown appearance unlikely evokes emotionality.

5.4. *THE INFINITIVE*

Rassudova (op. cit.: 139ff.) gives many examples of the general-factual meaning in the infinitive. It is evident that in all these examples the infinitive is used at the same time anaphorically, in other words, serves the textual function (cf. 3.7).

The meaning 'given' may also be combined with the processual AA in its variant 'commencement'.

(75) *Možno nalivat' čaj?*
(76) *Pora odevat'sja*

(75)

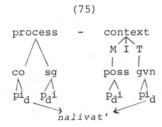

In (75) the process of pouring tea is expected by the hearer, the process in (76) is part of a 'program'. The co-AA in (75) may be replaced by the kf-AA and the te-AA. The same holds for (76).

6. *CONCLUSION*

In the past few years much attention has been paid to the connection between aspect and context in Russian (Bondarko, Rassudova, Lehmann, Bourke, etc.). It has become evident from these investigations that aspectual determination originates not only from the process itself, but also from its context.

In the present investigation we have tried to throw some more light on the nature of the aspectual determinators, their

mutual relationship, and on the connection between determinators
and aspect.

The aspectual determinators in the process itself are the
semantic *Aktionsarten* which are actually components of the semantic processual structure. The determinators in the context are its
various meanings. These contextual meanings serve three linguistic
functions (cf. Halliday): the ideational (=referential) function,
the interpersonal (= modal and deictic) function, and the textual
function (refers to the information structure), which usually
operate simultaneously. In other words the aspectual context is in
principle multifunctional.

Thus an aspectual form is determined not by one but by several determinators at the same time. The determinators are of a
different nature, of a different origin (process or context) and
serve different functions.

A determinator has its own statistical relationship with the
two aspects: as a rule it prefers one of the two, not excluding
the other.

Both the process and its context contain a number of aspectual determinators, which often present a contradictory determination. Hence the determination of a particular verbal form is ef-
fected only after the conflicts between the determinators have
been solved and a hierarchy has been established between them.
Such a hierarchy may exist between the determinators in the process, the context, and/or between the determinators of the process
and the context.

We have tried to visualize the determination of aspect by
means of diagrams. Unfortunately little statistical information
is available about the relationship between the determinators and
the aspects. The reliability of the diagrams will be enhanced,
when more statistical material has been produced.

University of Groningen

NOTES

[1] Our semantic AA corresponds in many respects with Lehmann's *aktionale Bedeutung*, which also includes processual meanings *(Verbal-Charakter)* and morphologically characterized AAs. Both semantic AAs and *aktionale Bedeutungen* are bi-aspectual.

[2] Without further statistical research it is not possible to determine whether there is an aspectual dominance with the independent AA and the eventive AA.

[3] By the meaning 'commencement' we understand 'a period of initial activity in a process'. 'Commencement' must be distinguished from 'ingression' which implies the transgression of a boundary (cf. Hamburger 1983). Rassudova uses the term 'commencement' mainly with respect to the infinitive (op. cit.: 135 ff.), although she mentions examples with a negative past tense: *Ja ešče ne čital ètu stat'ju* (op. cit.: 85f.). Especially in the negative past predicate the processual AA and kf coincide.

[4] A variant of the present tense is the so-called present-potential meaning *(Ja ne pojmu čto vas tam deržit* (Lehmann, op. cit.: 144)). Here the interpersonal function through the determinator 'impossibility' determines the perfective aspect.

REFERENCES

Bondarko, A.V.
  1971   *Vid i vremja russkogo glagola*. Moscow.
Bourke, M.K.
  1976   *A semantic re-examination of aspect and manner of action in Russian*. Ann Arbor, Mich.
Daneš, F.
  1976   "Semantische Struktur des Verbs und das indirekte Passiv im Tschechischen und Deutschen", in: Lötsch, R., and R. Růžička (eds.), *Satzstruktur und Genus verbi*, 113-124. Berlin.
Forsyth, J.
  1970   *A Grammar of Aspect*. Cambridge.
Groot, A.W. de
  1964[2]   *Inleiding tot de algemene taalwetenschap*. Groningen.
Halliday, M.A.K.
  1970   "Language Structure and Language Function", in: Lyons, J. (ed.), *New Horizons in Linguistics*, 140-165. Harmondsworth.
Hamburger, H.
  1983   "Conation and Aspect in Russian", in: van Holk, A.G.F. (ed.), *Dutch Contributions to the Ninth International Congress of Slavists*, 109-134. Amsterdam.
Hamburger, H.
  1984a   "*Aktionsart* and Aspect in Russian", *Russian Linguistics* 1984-2, 129-146.
Hamburger, H.
  1984b   "The absolute use of the Verb in general and in Russian in particular", in: Baak, J.J. van (ed.), *Signs of Friendship*. 145-163. Amsterdam.
Lehmann, V.
  1977   "Vorschläge zur Erklärung des russischen Aspekts", in: Girke, W., and H. Jachnow (eds.), *Slavistische Linguistik 1976*, 129-166. München.

Maslov, J.S.
  1974   "Zur Semantik der Perfektivitätsopposition", *Wiener Slavisti-
              sches Jahrbuch* XX, 107-122.
Mazon, A.
  1908   *Morphologie des aspects du verbe russe*. Paris.
Mehlig, H.R.
  1976   "Der imperfektive Aspekt als Proform", in: *Proceedings of the
              Fourth International Congress of Applied Linguistics* Vol. I,
              177-186, Stuttgart.
Rassudova, O.P.
  1984   *Aspectual Usage in modern Russian*. Moscow.
Salnikow, N.
  1980   "Funktionale Satzperspektive und Verbalaspekt im Russischen",
              Zielsprache Russisch Heft 3, 86-96.
Šeljakin, M.A.
  1976   "Lingvističeskie osnovy obučenija inostrancev upotrebleniju
              vidov russkogo jazyka", in: Rassudova O., and M. Scheljakin
              (eds.), *Die russischen Verbaspekte in Forschung und Unterricht*,
              21-40. Dortmund.
Šeljakin, M.A.
  1977   "Osnovnye problemy sovremennoj russkoj aspektologii", *Voprosy
              russkoj aspektologii* II. Tartu.
Veyrenc, J.
  1980.   *Etudes sur le verbe russe*. Paris.

CONJUNCTION REDUCTION IN RUSSIAN
A CATEGORIAL ANALYSIS

PETER HENDRIKS

1. *INTRODUCTION*

In this paper we will discuss a number of problems related to
the analysis and description of sentences that are elliptical,
i.e. incomplete in some respect. We will concentrate primarily on
ellipsis in coordinative sentences. The phenomena in question have
been treated in the literature under various more specific names
such as conjunction reduction, gapping, and non-constituent conjunction. There is disagreement as to whether these notions apply
to distinct linguistic processes or not.

One of the goals will be to investigate the relevance of the
above-mentioned distinctions to the linguistic analysis of modern
Russian, or, conversely, to investigate whether there is linguistic evidence in Russian in support of these notions.

One of the most salient characteristics of conjunction reduction is its very general nature. Most categories of a language can
be involved in ellipsis. In spite of this, the omissibility of
linguistic material from sentences usually does not get very much
attention in linguistic descriptions. Questions of ellipsis have
been the subject of debate in recent years mostly because the data
presented difficulties for a particular model of description. In
transformational grammar, for example, the problem was to postulate the most suitable underlying structures from which elliptical
sentences could be derived by means of various transformations.

The different kinds of rules set up in studies of ellipsis
often lead to the introduction of one or more zero elements at
some point in the representation. There is no general agreement on
the status of zero elements in linguistic analyses, and many lin-

guists do not find it necessary to introduce them in the first place. It has been suggested, for example, by Apresjan e.a.(1978), that syntactic zero should be distinguished from several other kinds of ellipsis. Syntactic zero is characterized by the obligatory omission of linguistic elements, which are not retrievable.

One of the main goals of this paper is to demonstrate that various types of incompleteness of sentences, such as ellipsis, Gapping, and non-constituent conjunction, can be handled in a uniform way in a flexible categorial grammar.

In the next paragraph we will give a short introduction to a recent variant of categorial grammar. In the remainder of this paper we will apply the rules of this grammar to a number of typical examples of ellipsis in Russian.

An important source of information on ellipsis and reduction in Russian is Padučeva (1974). We will use a number of her examples and observations for the sake of comparison. Although categorial grammar is generally used as a basis for semantic analysis, we will not give logical translations or model-theoretical interpretations of the categorial structures. It must be stressed, however, that for most adherents of this type of grammar the possibility of a parallel development of syntactic and semantic rules is the quintessence of this approach.

2. FLEXIBLE CATEGORIAL GRAMMAR

2.0. Categorial grammar (CG) analyzes sentences in terms of functor-argument relations. In the categorial lexicon each lexeme or morpheme is defined either as a basic or as a derived category. The latter are usually called functor categories. We will take S and NP as basic categories. All other categories are derived from the basic categories by means of a recursive definition. The analysis of a sentence (or part thereof) starts by assigning the appropriate category definition to each element. It is possible for a lexeme to have more than one categorial definition. The rules of the grammar can now operate on this initial sequence of categories. The rules try to combine adjacent elements into an ever larger segment, until the input sentence has finally been reconstructed. For obvious reasons the rules of combination are gener-

STUDIES IN SLAVIC AND GENERAL LINGUISTICS 8: Dutch Studies in
Russian Linguistics - ERRATA:

page: line:

18	1	for:	Accoring	read:	According
	5		некоторм		некотором
19	7		autor's		author's
26	7		psoetd		posted
30	21		some		some preparations
31	17		opposite		the opposite
35	24		все веселой		всей веселой
36	6		договременное		долговременное
44	6		фо		во
63	15		далше		дальше
75	17		morozit		*morozit*
80	25		cela		Cela
109	3		Althouth		Although
118	21		[sč']		[st'š']
154	19		of caused event		of a caused event
161	14		the example chosen		the examples chosen

162 (diagr. (29))   for: $\overset{sg}{\overset{\wedge}{P\ \ i_d}}$ read: $\overset{sg}{\overset{\wedge}{P_d\ \ i}}$

165	4		establishment		establishment of fact
166	22		*ustat'*,		*ustat'*, etc.

168 (diagr. (49)) $\overset{sg\quad kf}{\overset{\wedge\ \ \wedge}{P_d\ i\ p\ \ i_d}}$ $\overset{sg\quad kf}{\overset{\wedge\ \ \wedge}{P_d\ i\ p\ \ i_d}}$

222	5		represemt		represent
224	3		-- NP$_1'$		⟨--⟩ NP$_1'$
280	17		this person, it is		this person), it is
319	26		vision.) Nevertheless		vision).) Nevertheless
325	19		which is at yet		which is as yet
415	14	for:	9.2 180 106-80 -4.9	-27.1	I
		read:	9.2 u.v. 89-106 3.0	u.v.	I
428	7	omit:	3.1, 3.2,		
	12	for:	a total of 53	read:	a total of 51
506	31		et identique		est identique

ally called reduction rules. Whether two elements are combinable depends on their categorial definition. If, for example, a functor is contiguous with an appropriate argument, the two can be combined. The functor is then said to apply to its argument. Functor categories are categories looking for the argument specified in their definition. The definition of a functor category specifies the required argument as well as the resulting category. For example, the functor S/NP denotes the category of elements that need an NP in order to form a sentence, i.e. intransitive verb phrases. A distinctive feature of CG is that functor category labels contain explicit information on the syntactic behaviour of the expressions involved. We will now briefly go into a few aspects of CG that have remained implicit sofar.

2.1. *Generative vs. recognition grammar.*
CGs are usually formulated as recognition grammars, although the generative formulation is straightforward. The same rules are operative in both types. In this paper the analytic variant is used. The input to the reduction rules is a linguistic expression; the result of applying the rules is a derivation tree showing the step by step reduction of the expression to its resulting category. A final functor category indicates that the expression in question is incomplete.

2.2. *Composition.*
Originally, the only way to concatenate ex-pressions in CG was the application of functor expressions to argument expressions. Unfortunately, many linguistic expressions are not amenable to this rather restricted type of grammar. An important extension of CG is the introduction of functional composition, allowing the concatenation of adjacent functor categories. The functor determining the resulting category is called the main functor. The addition of composition greatly enhances the recognizing power of the grammar, in particular with regard to discontinuous elements and word order.

2.3. *Type-shifting rules.*
Another unwelcome limitation of early CG was the rigid assigment

of categories to the elements of linguistic expressions. The initial categorial assigments were not allowed to be changed during the application of the reduction rules. Recent variants of CG have abandoned this restrictive view by introducing type-shifting rules. The empirical signifance of category-changing rules is a point of debate in the current literature. In any case it seems certain that the unrestricted use of such rules is highly undesirable. We will only make use of the type-raising rule, already introduced by Montague (1974), stating that an expression of category X can be raised to category Y/(Y/X). The effect of type-raising is the reversing of the functor-argument relationship: an argument becomes a functor looking for an argument 'that would have applied to it before type-raising' (cf. Dowty: 1985). In the majority of cases, raising does not have a semantic effect. Its main purpose is to avoid type-clashes (cf. Moortgat: 1985). Type raising also is a major factor in providing a categorial grammar with considerable flexibility. It has been assumed so far that the generative capacity of the system is not influenced by this rule.

2.4. *Directionality*.

We have said nothing sofar about the order in which application and composition may operate. The slash in functor category labels has generally been used to indicate the direction in which arguments are to be sought. The forward slash is then used for right-oriented functors, whereas the backward slash indicates left-oriented functors. If a CG uses the slashes to indicate the orientation of functors, the system is called directional.

Because of the relatively free order of words in Russian, it seems more appropriate to adopt a non-directional categorial system (This means that in our notation the slash will not indicate directionality. It will only serve to separate arguments and resulting categories). If a directional system were to be used, a great many items in the lexicon would have two categorial definitions, a left- and a right-oriented one. This seems highly undesirable from a descriptive point of view. Non-directional definitions do justice to the characteristic freedom of word order.

It is clear, however, that the system we have set up, is capable of accepting expressions which violate regular word order.

The recognizing power of the grammar will therefore have to be constrained somehow. Since the syntactic properties of the lexemes will be contained mainly in the individual entries in the lexicon, that would also seem the appropriate place to include specific word order constraints (or other idiosyncrasies, for that matter). One can also set up lexical rule schema's applying to particular classes of lexemes. Another, more general possibility is to introduce a convention stating which word order should be tried first, when trying to find the argument for a particular functor. Such a convention could be based on the structure of the categorial definition of the word in question (cf. Flynn 1983). Conventions for word order would be particularly valuable for parsing purposes. It goes without saying that nearly all of this research remains to be done.

The arguments of functors will normally be encoded in a fixed order in the lexicon. It would be possible to specify a preferred order for individual lexemes. However, the order in which arguments are concatenated is not essential. The last rule that we will add to the grammar is the transitivity rule (or relation-inversion rule), which allows us to reverse the arguments of a functor (cf. Bouma 1985).

2.5. *Constituency*.

The flexibility of this particular system of categorial grammar is such that, if an expression can be reduced to a particular category, that reduction can be obtained using all possible bracketings of its members. The groups of elements that are formed as a result of the application of the reduction rules do not have the status of constituents as they would be defined by some form of rewrite rules. An important aspect of the reduction process is that the intermediate groupings have a precise interpretation in terms of the semantics that is being applied.

2.6. *Surface grammar*.

The analysis presented here hugs the syntactic surface closely. There is no deep syntactic level of representation. It can be described as a single-level synctactical system. There are no devices such as transformations. Each sentence is derived directly

by means of a single set of rules. There are no intermediate
structures that are used as input to a different set of rules.

2.7. *Morphology.*

Any precise description of syntactic structures in Russian has to
deal with the rich morpho-grammatical structure of the language.
Eventually, it will be necessary to introduce grammatical features
into the categorial definitions. It is to be expected that the addition of features to the system will play a major role in resol-
ving questions concerning the directionality of functors. It may
be expected that inclusion of grammatical features in the category definitions makes up, so to speak, for the non-directionality
of the system.

So far categorial grammar has only been applied to fairly
small fragments English and a few other West-European languages.
There do not seem to exist any extensive studies of languages with
a much more complex inflectional morphology than, for example,
English.

2.8. *Summary of rules.*

We will now summarize the rules that have been discussed above and
that will be applied in the next section. As for the notation of
functor categories, arguments are written to the right side of the
slash, resulting categories to the left. There is not yet a standard notation for categories.

CONCATENATION RULES:

RIGHT-APPLICATION (RA): X/Y Y ==> X
LEFT-APPLICATION (LA): Y X/Y ==> X
RIGHT-COMPOSITION (RC): X/Y Y/Z ==> X/Z
LEFT-COMPOSITION (LC): Y/Z X/Y ==> X/Z

CATEGORY-CHANGING RULES:

TYPE-RAISING (TR): A ==> B/(B/A)
TYPE-DIVISION (TD): X/Y ==> (X/Z)/(Y/Z)
RELATION-INVERSION (RI): (X/Y)/Z ==> (X/Z)Y

187

3.   COORDINATION AND CONJUNCTION REDUCTION

3.0.   We will first discuss a number of decisions we have made
with respect to the categorial analysis of specific Russian   words
and constructions.

In categorial descriptions of, for example, English and
Dutch, common nouns are usually assigned to a category CN or   N.
Adjectives take nouns as their arguments in order to form NPs.
Their category is therefore something like NP/N. Now in Russian
common nouns can function by themselves as NPs, because the language does not have an article system. For this reason we will
assign all common and also proper nouns to the category   NP.   The
consequence for adjectives and other determiners is that they   are
of category NP/NP. The assignment of adjectives to category NP/NP
is not adequate for all adjectival forms, however. Only the long
forms of adjectives are used as pre- or post-nominal modifiers and
in predicates. The short forms occur only in a predicative position. The (partial) complementary distribution of the long and
short adjectival forms suggests that they can be assigned to different categories from the categorial point of view. We will treat
them as intransitive verbs and assign them to the category   S/NP
(cf. Siegel 1976).

Conjunctions have the very versatile property of being able
to join sentence parts of almost any type. Since enumeration of
possible types of conjuncts is not really feasible, the best one
could do in a categorial grammar is to assign a generalized functor category to conjunctions. The most general form of this category is (X/*X)/X. According to the definition, a conjunction looks
for a sequence of some type X and produces a sequence that in turn
looks for one or more word sequences of the same type. The resulting sequence will be of the same category as its conjuncts.   In
order to simplify the categorial representation and the reduction,
we will, following Dowty (1985) use a coordination schema:

(CS)   { X* conj X } ===>   X

This schema will allow us to combine identical conjuncts, which turns out to be very useful in describing various types of incomplete sentences. Provided it is possible to produce identical conjuncts via raising, the conjunction schema will allow their combination. Most examples of Paduĉeva's (symmetric) reduction types should not present great difficulties for our flexible framework. Besides the most common conjunction и "and", we will take into account other conjunctions such as а 'and, but' and но 'but'.

On the basis of the preliminary morphological analysis we may have to distinguish zero elements in various contexts. But most of these instances will not all occur explicitly in the syntactic or semantic representation. The representation that is subject to syntactic analysis will reflect the output of the morphological rules in the sense that the elements of a sentence will be accompanied by tuples of morphological features (in a comprehensive analysis, at least). The question with respect to the syntactic analysis is which linguistic facts should be given an explicit zero representation. The present tense forms of быть 'to be' are a reasonable candidate. They can be said to present a case of syntactic zero.

It is interesting to note that Dowty does not introduce a zero element in the sentences he analyzes, whereas Van der Zee (1982) does in his categorial analysis of Gapping in Dutch. It seems that this is due to the rules they employ in their respective categorial systems.

3.1.   *Term conjunction.*
It seems appropriate to consider conjoined NPs non-elliptical if the verb does not distribute over its conjuncts (e.g., in the case of reciprocal verbs). Semantically speaking, the NPs involved in term conjunction only have a collective interpretation. For example:

(1) точность и краткость - вот главные достоинства прозы
    'preciseness and succintness are the main qualities of prose'

The coordinative NP in (1), for example, can only have a collective interpretation. In other words, this sentence does not have a reading 'preciseness is the main virtue and succinctness is the main quality of prose'.

Paraphrases of certain types of coordinative structures reveal that their conjoined constituents do not consist of common elements that have been factored out, so to speak. But we cannot use this information directly in our derivations because of the strictly surface approach. However, the peculiarities of these structures are often due to lexico-grammatical idiosyncrasies of the lexemes involved. This means that the characteristic features of these coordinative structures can often be captured by inserting appropriate categorial definitions in the lexicon. Let us look at a few examples.

(2) прямая X и прямая У пересекаются
    'the straight lines X and Y intersect'

The definition of the reflexive verb пересекаться will have to contain the information that the subject NP either expresses plural number or is a coordinative NP.

The following sentence is an example of term conjunction in the direct object (For the convenience of non-Slavists word by word translations will be given for analyzed sentences. Sequences that are presented as prefabricated constituents or those that are combined on the basis of the rules, are underlined).

'he compares the old bounds of Moscow with its present bounds'

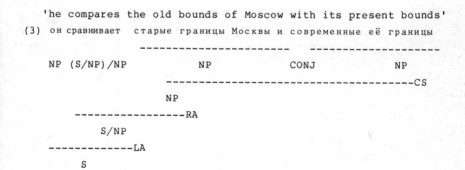

```
(3) он сравнивает   старые границы Москвы и современные её границы
                    -----------------------  ---------------------
NP (S/NP)/NP              NP             CONJ              NP
                    -------------------------------------------CS
                         NP
         --------------------RA
             S/NP
    -------------LA
        S
```

The verb сравнивать 'compare' expects two NPs that represent the items of comparison. The NPs can be coordinated by и 'and', or the second NP can be dominated by the preposition с 'with'. The verb сравнивать can also occur with one (plural) complement. In any case, it does not seem correct to regard this sentence as elliptical: its meaning is not 'he compares the old bounds of Moscow and he compares its contemporary bounds'.

Sentence (4) is interesting in that it seems to combine features of term-conjunction and reduction.

(4) точки A и B принадлежат, соответственно, множествам M и N
    'points A and B belong to sets M and N, respectively'

The occurrence of the word соответственно 'respectively' is intimately connected with the occurrence of the coordinated NPs in this type of sentence. Without going into exhaustive detail here, it is worth pointing out that a categorial analysis of this adverb will force us to specify the syntactic (and indirectly, semantic) role it plays. For example, соответственно combines with 2-place verbs, which means that its argument position can be specified as (S/NP)/NP. Since the combination of соответственно and a verb is also a 2-place verb, this adverb can be assigned to the category ((S/NP)/NP)/((S/NP)/NP). Further, there are restrictions on the structure of the two argument NPs. These conditions could be included as feature specifications to the NP labels in the lexicon.

Sentence (5) is another example of term-conjunction. The conjoined NP refers to one triangle that has both properties denoted by the adjectives. The conjunction is intersective, because both properties are essential in order for the predication to be correct. The singular form of the noun треугольник 'triangle' is an indication that there is a single referent.

(5) равнобедренный и прямоугольный треугольник имеет угол в 45°
    'an isosceles and right-angled triangle has an angle of 45 '

An interesting case of non-agreement of conjoined adjectives with the head noun can be seen in (6):

(6) старый и новый варианты 'the old and the new variant'

191

This NP is elliptical in sofar as the noun has to combine with both adjectives semantically, in order to get the right interpretation. The singular form of the adjectives indicates that two variants are involved. This fact is also signaled by the plural noun. The conjunction of the adjectives must have a collective interpretation here. If the noun is in the singular, the conjoined adjectives have an intersective interpretation. I do not as yet have a precise solution to this problem in categorial terms, but there are several attractive possibilities offered by the present framework. On the one hand, the noun варианты, which belongs to the argument category NP, could be raised to the functor category NP/(NP/NP). On the other hand, there is the possibility of distinguishing different types of "and"-conjunction to account for the collective vs. intersective interpretation. A reasoned description of these facts will depend on the formulation of an adequate feature-passing mechanism.

Sentence (7) is unambiguous in the sense that the eating of one and the same melon is excluded. This is indicated by the prepositional phrase governed by the preposition по used in its distributive sense. We will therefore want to regard the PP as a complement of the verb. To what category should по then be assigned? The required argument is clearly a NP. The resulting distributive PP constitutes a category looking for a transitive verb. This combination will in turn result in an intransitive VP. Putting all this together gives us ((S/NP)/((S/NP)/NP))/NP, or using abbreviations: (IV/TV)/NP. Assuming the formation of NP and PP, the derivation is:

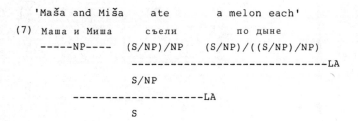

3.2. *Simple conjuncts.*

Conjuncts can belong to a wide range of grammatical categories, but given the conjunction schema and the rules of our CG, many types of sentences with symmetric conjuncts can be descibed in an elegant way. This is true even of complex cases such as non-constituent conjunction, as we shall see below. Let us first look at a few examples of simple conjuncts. The unreduced versions of such sentences can generally be obtained by simple insertion of the factored out element(s).

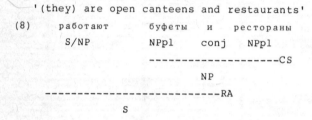

'(they) are open canteens and restaurants'
```
(8)      работают        буфеты    и     рестораны
         S/NP            NPpl    conj    NPpl
                         --------------------CS
                              NP
         --------------------------------RA
                    S
```

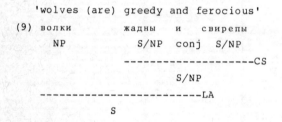

'wolves (are) greedy and ferocious'
```
(9) волки          жадны    и    свирепы
    NP             S/NP   conj   S/NP
                   --------------------CS
                        S/NP
    ------------------------LA
              S
```

Perhaps it should be stipulated by metarule that conjunction is to be performed first (or as soon as possible). Otherwise we could get incorrect results, for example, if we allow волки to combine with the sequence (Ø + жадны) first.

Besides the latent element due to reduction, this type of sentence contains another empty place, viz. the not overtly marked present tense form of быть 'be'. In view of the relevant linguistic facts, we must there introduce a zero into the representation that forms the input to the syntactic rules. The question is, to what category this zero or the overt members of the paradigm can be assigned?

It has been observed that the short adjectival forms are si-

milar in function to intransitive verbs. This means that they can
be assigned to the category S/NP. Let us now assume that we can
distinguish between the copula 'be' and the 'be' of identity on
semantic grounds, and that the copula 'be' is used with short
forms of the adjective. We can then establish a categorial definition for the copula. Since a copula combines with one or more elements that function as a one-place predicate to form a one-place
predicate, it seems correct to define it as (S/NP)/(S/NP).
Padučeva does not introduce a zero copula in these examples (although she does in other positions). Example (1Ø) is analogous to
the previous one, but the zero is represented:

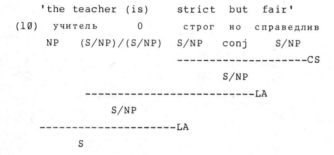

The following example demonstrates Padučeva's rule stating
that if two conjuncts have the righthand element in common, that
element may be omitted in the left conjunct:

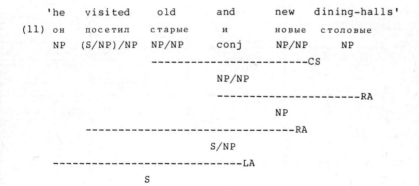

In the following example the conjuncts differ with respect to their members. However, functional application produces the required identity of the conjucts. The verb 'study' is here taken as denoting a non-specific activity. Therefore it is defined as a one-place verb.

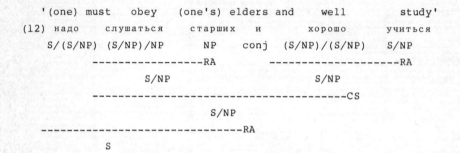

```
      '(one) must    obey    (one's) elders and     well        study'
(12)  надо     слушаться    старших    и      хорошо      учиться
     S/(S/NP) (S/NP)/NP      NP    conj (S/NP)/(S/NP)   S/NP
     ------------------RA              --------------------RA
           S/NP                                S/NP
     -------------------------------------------------CS
                          S/NP
     ------------------------------RA
           S
```

3.3. *Reduced vs. elliptical sentences.*
Coordinative sentences and the corresponding non-symmetric variants can sometimes be converted into each other by a simple change of word order. Cf., e.g.:

'he was tired not only physically, but also mentally'
(13) он устал не только физически, но и духовно
    'he was not only physically tired, but also mentally'
(14) он не только физически устал, но и духовно
      '(we) found boletus mushrooms and honey agarics'
(15) попадались подберезовики и опята
      'boletus mushrooms (we) found, and honey agarics'
(16) подберезовики попадались, и опята

Padučeva calls sentences (13) and (15) coordinative, and (14) and (16) elliptical. She apparently restricts the term coordination to sentences with symmetrical conjuncts. Semantically, however, the verb distributes over both conjuncts in these sentences: it is understood in the second conjunct.

It should be noted that the word order in (15) is not caused by the coordinative construction: попадались подберезовики is per-

fectly acceptable as a sentence. The difference in word order is
due to a difference in the topic/comment structure. Sentences like
(13) and (15) do not present a problem for the categ. rules.

(17) попадались подберезовики и опята
    (S/NP)/NP   NP   conj   NP
                     ------------------------CS
                      NP
    ------------------------RA
        S/NP

The resulting functor shows that this sentence is complete
except for the NP that is the first complement of the verb. This
result of course depends on the category assigned to the verb. If
it is also given an intransitive, "impersonal" definition, sentences such as (17) could be considered cases of situational ellipsis: the person(s) involved, are to be inferred from the context
or situation.

    Paduċeva admits that the borderline between what she calls
coordination and ellipsis is not always clear. One of her examples
is:

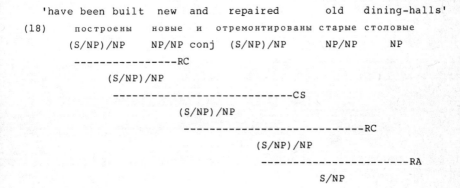

'have been built new and repaired old dining-halls'
(18)   построены   новые   и   отремонтированы старые столовые
       (S/NP)/NP   NP/NP conj (S/NP)/NP   NP/NP   NP
      ----------------RC
         (S/NP)/NP
           ------------------------------CS
           (S/NP)/NP
             ------------------------------RC
              (S/NP)/NP
                ------------------------RA
                S/NP

It should be noted that this analysis is not the only one
possible for this sentence. However, a remarkable feature of this
analysis is the strict left-to-right order in which the reduction
takes place. In view of the fact that constituent structure does

not play an essential role in categorial systems, this one-pass
type of analysis, which appears to be possible in many cases, can
be regarded as a valuable additional property of this system (cf.
Ades and Steedman, 1982).

The other borderline cases mentioned by Padučeva are examples
of so-called non-constituent conjunction. Let us look at this type
of sentence first.

'for ever left Herzen Russia, and Einstein Germany'
(19) навсегда покинули Герцен Россию а Эйнстейн Германию
'he says today one (thing) and tomorrow something else'
(20) он говорит сегодня одно, а завтра другое

In (19) and (20) the conjuncts are indeed adjacent, but their
grammatical composition is not homogeneous: they do not contain
elements of one specific category. Unlike homogeneous coordinated
phrases, conjoined phrases of the above type cannot occur in a
different position in the sentence. The plural form of the verb,
however, seems to be more in accordance with (homogeneous) coordination. Another point that can be made about (19) is that it is
unambiguous in contrast with the non-elliptical version:

(19') навсегда Герцен и Эйнштейн покинули Россию и Германию

As for the categorial analysis of (19), the incomplete right
conjunct contains two remnants; they are not directly in construction. As might be expected, they cannot be combined on the basis
of their initial NP assignments. In order to be able to combine
the NPs in the conjuncts, it is necessary to type-raise them. By
way of illustration, case markings have been included to show how
the reduction rules could take morphological features into account. NPa is raised to (S/NPa)/((S/NPn)/NPa) and NPn to
S/(S/NPn). By functional composition we can now obtain the functor
categories for each of the two conjuncts: S/((S/NPn)/NPa). In tree
form:

Герцен	Россию	а	Эйнштейн	Германию
NPn	NPa	conj	NPn	NPa

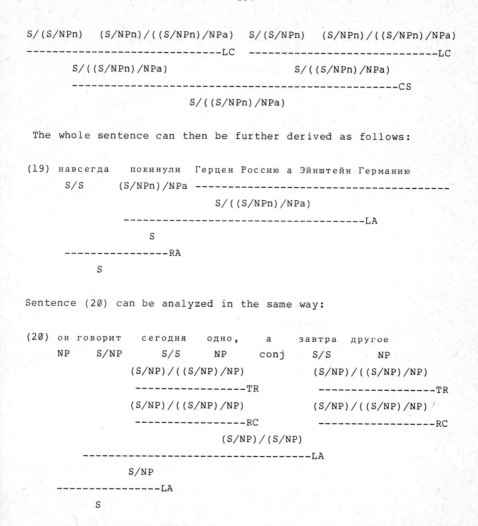

```
S/(S/NPn)   (S/NPn)/((S/NPn)/NPa)   S/(S/NPn)   (S/NPn)/((S/NPn)/NPa)
----------------------------LC   ----------------------------LC
     S/((S/NPn)/NPa)                    S/((S/NPn)/NPa)
     ----------------------------------------------CS
                    S/((S/NPn)/NPa)
```

The whole sentence can then be further derived as follows:

```
(19) навсегда    покинули  Герцен Россию а Эйнштейн Германию
     S/S        (S/NPn)/NPa -----------------------------------
                            S/((S/NPn)/NPa)
                 -----------------------------------LA
              S
     -----------------RA
       S
```

Sentence (20) can be analyzed in the same way:

```
(20) он говорит   сегодня    одно,    а    завтра  другое
     NP   S/NP     S/S       NP     conj   S/S     NP
               (S/NP)/((S/NP)/NP)        (S/NP)/((S/NP)/NP)
               -----------------TR       -----------------TR
               (S/NP)/((S/NP)/NP)        (S/NP)/((S/NP)/NP)
               -----------------RC       -----------------RC
               (S/NP)/(S/NP)
     ----------------------------------LA
              S/NP
     -----------------LA
        S
```

Note that these analyses produce intermediate structures that few linguists would consider constituents in their theories. The term 'phantom constituents' describes them fairly well (cf. Dowty 1985).

Example (21) is peculiar in various respects. For example, it is longer than its non-reduced counter-part никто ничего никому не давал. The two conjoined pronouns differ in syntactic function and in grammatical case. I would, albeit somewhat hesitatingly, like

to propose an analysis using type-raising and composition. The
pronouns ничего and никому will first be raised to their
appropriate categories, viz. (S/NP)/((S/NP)/NP) and
((S/NP)/NP)/(((S/NP)/NP)/NP), respectively. For simplicity we will
abbreviate them as IV/TV and TV/TTV. The effect of raising is that
the two NPs are reanalyzed as elements that, combined with an n-
place verb, will result in an (n-1)-place verb. Given their different syntactic roles in this sentence, they should not be col-
lapsed by the conjunction schema. This can be achieved by allowing composition to take place. In the folowing derivation the negative particle has already been combined with the verb:

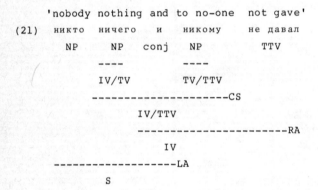

```
      'nobody nothing and to no-one  not gave'
(21)  никто  ничего  и   никому    не давал
        NP     NP   conj   NP        TTV
              ----        ----
             IV/TV      TV/TTV
            --------------------CS
             IV/TTV
            -----------------------RA
               IV
        --------------------LA
         S
```

Gapped sentences are likely to be problematic for a CG using
the rules given above. Unlike sentences with non-constituent conjunction, Gapped sentences do not contain symmetric conjuncts. The
common elements of the coordination are in the left conjunct,
whereas the right side is characterized by the Gapped element(s).
Sentence (19) shows that in Russian the much greater freedom of
word order makes the difference between non-constituent conjunction and Gapping even smaller than in English. In Russian, just as
in English, Gapped sentences differ from sentences with conjunction reduction by their intonation pattern (cf. Padučeva (1974)
and Dowty (1985)). Sentences (22) and (23) are not reducible to
the category S by the means we have introduced sofar. The resulting category now indicates that a NP is missing. In itself, this

might not be such an unacceptable solution. However, if we want elliptical sentences to be recognized by the CG, we will have to include a stronger mechanism into our rule system. An attractive candidate could be the type of WRAP convention proposed by Bach (1983). We will leave this point for the future.

```
      'love   my  lives in Kazan', and I on the river Moscow'
(22)  милый мой живет в Казани, а я на Москва-реке
      'Pete  loves  this song, but I hate'
(23)  Петя любит эту песню, а я ненавижу
```

We will, however, give one example of a sentence generally regarded as elliptical, which can be handled by this system:

```
     'I    liked    and     continue    to like    mathematics'
(24)  я     любил     и      продолжаю    любить     математику
      NP (S/NP)/NP conj (S/NP)/(S/NP) (S/NP)/NP      NP
                         ----------------------RC
                         (S/NP)/NP
     -------------------------------CS
          (S/NP)/NP
                   -------------------------------RA
               S/NP
     ---------------------------LA
           S
```

3.4.   I hope to have demonstrated in this paper that flexible categorial grammar is a powerful tool for the analysis of lan-guages, in particular, those that are characterized by free word order and discontinuous constructions. Ellipsis and conjunction reduction are notorious test cases for any theory. It may come as a surprise that many of these complex structures can be tackled successfully in a surface syntactic approach using only a minimum set of rules.

University of Leiden

BIBLIOGRAPHY

Ades, Anthony E. and Mark J. Steedman
    1982   "On the order of words", *Linguistics and Philosophy* 4, 517-558.
Apresjan, Yu.D., I.L.Iomdin, N.V.Percov
    1978   "Ob"jekty i sredstva modeli poverchnostnogo sintaksisa russkogo
              jazyka", *Makedonski Jazik* 29, 125-171.
Bach, Emmon
    1983   "On the relationship between word-grammar and phrase-grammar",
              Natural Language and Linguistic Theory 1, 65-89.
    1984   "Some generalizations of Categorial Grammars", in Fred Landman
              and Frank Veltman (eds.), *Varieties of Formal Semantics* 1-23,
              Dordrecht.
Benthem, Johan van
    1985   "The Lambek Calculus", to appear in W.Buszkowski e.a. (eds.)
              Categorial Grammar, Amsterdam.
Bouma, Gosse
    1985   "Kategoriale Grammatika en het Warlpiri", *Glot* 8, 227-257.
Dowty, David
    1985   "Type Raising, Functional Composition, and Non-Constituent Con-
              junction", to appear in the Proceedings of the Tucson Conference
              on Categorial Grammars.
Flynn, Michael
    1983   "A categorial theory of structure building", in Gazdar, Klein &
              Pullum (eds.), *Order, Concord, and Constituency* 139-174,
              Dordrecht.
Lambek, Joachim
    1958   "The mathematics of sentence structure", *Amer. Math. Monthly* 65,
              154-169.
    1961   "On the Calculus of Syntactic Types", in *Structure of Language and
              its Mathematical Aspects*, 166-178, Providence.
Matthews, P.H.
    1981   *Syntax*, Cambridge.
McCawley, James D.
    1981   *Everything that Linguists have Always Wanted to Know about Logic*,
              Chicago.
Montague, Richard
    1974   *Formal Philosophy*, edited by R. Thomason, New Haven.
Moortgat, Michael
    1985   "Mixed Composition and Discontinuous Dependencies", to appear in
              the Proceedings of the Tucson Conference on Categorial Grammars.
Padučeva, E. V.
    1974   *O semantike sintaksisa: materialy k transformacionnoj grammatike
              russkogo jazyka*, Moskva.
Siegel, Muffy
    1976   "Capturing the Russian Adjective", in B. Partee (ed.) *Montague
              Grammar*. New York.
Zee, Nico van der
    1982   "Samentrekking, een kategoriaal perspektief", in *Glot* 5, 189-217.

ON THE SEMANTICS AND SYNTAX OF DISCOURSE
A Text-Linguistic Approach

A.G.F. VAN HOLK

1. INTRODUCTION

One recent topic in the linguistics of discourse is the study of semantic, syntactic and pragmatic universals of texts in terms of their grammatical correlates in specific languages[1]. In order to ensure a reliable link between the observed surface structure of a text and those most abstract deep structures by which literary themes of texts appear to be implemented, at least one intermediate level of analysis will have to be introduced, which may be tentatively labeled the level of p a r a p h r a s e . Indeed, supposing the structures of individual sentences can be captured in terms of a finite set of possible 'slots' and 'filler classes' (cf. the critical discussion of the tagmemic model of the text in Gülich and Raible 1977: 97-115), the question arises whether the same description might be applied to the paraphrasing structures of suprasentential units like paragraph and text, and under which conditions a sequence of two or more constructions of the form $S = NP\ VP$ can be reduced to a single paraphrasing construction $S' = NP'\ VP'$.
In this paper I propose to approach this problem by studying the possible c o n n e c t i o n s between any single sentence of a given construction and its preceding or subsequent c o n t e x t within a suprasentential unit. As I hope to show, these connections can be described by the same magnitudes as the constructions of single sentences, in the frame of the linguistic model of thematic content developed in some of my earlier papers (Van Holk 1975, 1980, 1984).

We begin our discussion with a few observations on the place of thematics in the linguistics of discourse (section 2); this is followed by an account of so-called elementary constructions (section 3), which provide the ultimate components of literary themes; the main body of the paper is then devoted to the internal composition of these constructions and their behaviour in the context of suprasentential units (sections 4-8).

2.   THEMATIC CONSTRUCTIONS IN TEXT LINGUISTICS
2.1. The term "thematic constructions" is introduced to indicate certain recurrent configurations of universal class meanings which serve the expression of literary themes[2]; these constructions determine the so-called "microstructure" of texts, i.e. the sum total of text-internal semantic constraints between individual sentences and their parts. To this may be opposed the so-called "macrostructure" as the totality of text-external factors which determine the *situation of discourse* referred to by a particular text or collection of texts[3]. We describe these situations by projecting onto them those functional levels of linguistic expression which the comparative study of language has shown to be of universal applicability. The set of basic levels (from which an indefinite number of others can be derived) may be chosen as follows (cf. Van Holk 1983: 172-180):

(1)(i) the level of the s i g n function, of the form "a stands for b", and supposed to hold between the linguistic expression consisting of b o t h sound form and content, and the world of referents, in particular the material objects of a culture;

   (ii) the basic case relations between subject and predicate, predicate and direct object, predicate and indirect object, which are taken to represent three perpendicular axes of s e m i o t i c   s p a c e;

   (iii) the functional level of the realisation of linguistic expression, supposed to represent the axis of s e m i o t i c   t i m e.

These functional levels appear to suffice for the description of those situations which can be studied regardless of their presentation in a particular narrative text; such situations, which we call *referential systems*, include the coded action strings of weddings, burials, battles, or an official's daily business program. For all such forms of behaviour the analysis aims at establishing a one-to-one correspondence between some actant's successive states in semiotic space and the chosen units on the time axis of a text, and deriving from this relationship possible other functional dimensions, such as the causative coherence between events (cf. Xolodovič 1969). In this connection it may be added that there appear to be many more types of referential systems beside action strings. Among these, those systems deserve particular interest in which a large number of individual action strings are m i x e d in a random way, a state of affairs which obtains whenever a text or collection of texts is taken as the reflex of a society (or culture) in a given period of its history. A rather complex case is provided by the performance of a dramatic text, a social happening confronting an audience with the thematic content of its own time. The random mixture of action strings in the social structure underlying a text carries another variety of coherence, which is closely associated with the a c o u s t i c side of language, which covers, among others, the effects of s p e e c h upon the syntax of action strings.

Should it be requested to include in our research program the process of communication, such as the narrative or argumentative "superstructure" of a text (Van Dijk 1978: 155ff.), the two complementary functions of *topic* and *comment* should be added to those listed in (1), in order to capture the properties of linguistic expression known as "functional sentence perspective" and "grounding" (these two terms, incidentally, seem to mean the same phenomenon). The close interaction between the functions of topic and focus at the sentence level and the roles of subject and predicate at the level of phrase and clause[4]conduce us to consider the class-marking and position-marking functions of morphemes in thematics as "converted" from the topic-focus pair. Unlike the sound form of lexical items, the suprasegmental features of phrase stress (prominence), word order, and sentence intonation operate on the s y n t a c - t i c pattern of linguistic expressions, bringing about an ordering of the word material into a functional perspective of "backgrounded" and "foregrounded" stretches, as well as the emphasis of one portion of a sentence by suppression of constituent boundaries in another (cf. the notions of "tonically positive/negative" parts

of a sentence in De Groot 1949; 1964). The reshuffling of an action
string (comparable to the *fabula*) into a narrative string (the
sujet) results in a network of constraints known as "cohesion"
(i.e., pronoun-based coherence)[5]. However, the role of pronouns in
general is still far from clear[6]. The outcome of this brief discussion may be presented in the form of a diagram (2).

(2)

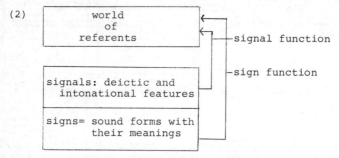

2.2. While the macrostructure of a text is the linguistic expression of macrosituations in the world of discourse, the microstructure is rooted in those entities of the same world of discourse which correspond to c l a s s meanings of morphemes and
their lexical subcategorisations. In thematics, then, the entities
denoted are of the same order of magnitude as the elements of the
linguistic expression used to investigate their behaviour. The main
consequence of this state of affairs is the coincidence of functional dimensions which in narrative structure are independent.
While in an action string every particular situation will normally
be determined by its position on the string's time axis, in thematic constructions only a single track can be measured at a time:
for instance, the level of coherence (rank; section 3.2) unites
under one dimension such features as the 'position' of a character
in the situation and the 'degree of complexity of the predicate'.

This peculiarity of thematic constructions may be exemplified by Daneš's
representation of the 'donative' construction in the form
    A(x) (xPz) T (yPz),
which reads as 'x is the agent A of a process of transition T by which
the possession P of an object z passes from x to y' (Daneš 1973: 130).
In thematic analysis the transition T from one state to another is not
represented as part of the construction itself, but rather reflects the
internal dynamics of the construction in terms of a change of state of
the microsituation. As a result, a situation in which the hero does *not
yet* or *no longer* possess a certain object or experience a certain state,

nonetheless may be captured by a thematic construction determining the relation between hero and object or state; e.g., in Ryleev's poem Bogdan
Xmel'nickij the theme of 'freedom' is expressed by the successive states
of 'imprisonment', 'being liberated', and 'having acquired freedom'
(Ryleev 1971: 156-159).

2.3. Thematic constructions fall into elementary and compound constructions, the latter being made up of the former in varying combinations. The difference between the two types may be stated as
follows. We speak of an *elementary construction* (EC) if the meaningful elements of every sentence of a text are arranged about a
single nuclear constituent, for which it is most convenient to
choose the subject (cf. section 3). If the meaningful elements are
grouped around two or more nuclei we register a *compound* construction. Thus a sentence like

   (3) *Zloj mal'čik ukral serebrjannuju korobočku u staroj*
                                                       tetuški

may be analysed as a single nucleus *mal'čik* with a certain number
of modifiers of different types (*zloj, ukrast'*, ...), or we may
posit three nuclei, as shown in (4) below, each with its own modi-
fier(s).

   (4)

      zloj mal'čik ukral serebrjannuju korobočku u staroj
                                                      tetuški

Each NP in (3) may in turn become the subject of a construction,
say *tetuška lišilas' korobočki, korobočka byla ukradena u tetuški*,
while the verb (together with the preposition: *ukral + u* ....) in
this type of construction functions as a n o d e (as in dependence grammar; cf. Gülich and Raible 1977: 128-130). In what follows, we shall concentrate on single plot lines and the constructions by which they are described (for a discussion of compound
plot analysis the reader is referred to Van Holk 1980, 1984).
The choice for one or the other analysis -and a given number of
nuclei in case of a compound construction- is dictated by the nature of the microsituation: in particular, if we wish to investigate the behaviour of a single actant of a definite type the construction to be selected will be elementary; if the situation involves the interlocutors disputing the possession of a sought-for
object the semantic material will be arranged about at least

t h r e e nuclei (more if the disputed object reveals itself as complex).

In what follows we shall concentrate on the functional dimensions and internal composition of EC's, with a view to establishing the way these properties are manifested in the textual surface.

3. ELEMENTARY CONSTRUCTIONS: INTERNAL COMPOSITION AND CLASSIFICATION

3.1. In order to capture the linguistic properties of textual microstructure it proved useful to introduce the notion of *elementary construction* (EC), mentioned above, and defined as a configuration of modifier-modified connections between the constituents of a sentence, all originating in one and the same central noun or noun-phrase. Each EC is uniquely determined by the n u m b e r of modifier-modified connections of its nucleus; the nuclear features corresponding to the modified terms of connections specify a universal morphologic class, and are accordingly called *class markers*. The features contributed by modifiers specify a particular position in the sentence - subject, predicate, object, adverbial, etc.-, and are called *position markers* (or *connectives*). The classes obtained in this way are each associated with a syntactic construction; thus the class of transitive verbs is based on the construction 'verb + direct object noun phrase' (more precisely, the construction NP_0 VTra NPObj), where the accusative suffix in Russian (or a feature of word order in other languages) indicates the direct-object position of a noun phrase relative to the verb as the modified term. Class markers may also be implemented by separate morphemes; so in the verb phrases *zarabotat' bol'šie den'gi, zaslužit' nagradu, razbit' steklo*, the preverbs *za-, raz-* are class markers of transitivity on the verb, while the accusative suffixes *-i, -u, -o* indicate, as before, the object position. The division of labour between the features is the same as registered before for topic and focus expressions (section 2.1). However, class markers normally occur jointly with referential features, which bring about a lexical subcategorisation of morphologic classes, while position markers, being contained in a modifying expression, normally operate at a structural distance from the nucleus.

The nucleus-modifier connection may be implemented by an expression of any structural type - attributive, predicative, adverbial, etc. -, where the construction S = NP VP is taken to be the basic variety: indeed, the predicate includes a modifier agreeing in person, number, gender with the subject nominal, yet the combination as a whole is traditionally regarded as e x o-
c e n t r i c (Bloomfield 1933: 194ff.). In thematics, indeed, the exocentric relation is not part of the construction, but belongs to its *realisation* in a particular context, which includes the intonation contour (and its corresponding 'tonal' function) of the sentence. As pointed out in earlier papers (Van Holk 1963, 1982), this function is the effect of c h a n g e in the state of a deictic construction, such as the topic-comment pattern of narrative and argumentative strings (cf. section 2.1). As a result of the above considerations a l l nucleus-modifier connections will be regarded as variants of the s a m e basic connection NP...VP'. This connection may be identified as Ebeling's "parallel" relation (Ebeling 1954: 211; 1978: 147), i.e. the relation between semantic elements pointing at the same portion of reality. Thus parallelism is the basis of thematic coherence or "isotopy" (Kallmeyer *et al.* 1974: 147-149).

To sum up, then, an EC consists of a nucleus made up of a definite number of class markers functioning jointly with referential subcategorising features, and an equal number of position markers, connected with the nucleus by a relation of parallelism. The connections on closer examination turn out to be hierarchically arranged into two dimensions, called r a n k and e x -
t e n s i o n. In the next sections (3.2-3.5) these fundamental notions will be explained.

3.2. The notion of r a n k as used here (and in my earlier work) is due to Bloomfield (1933: 195, 222) and especially De Groot (1949: 236-237; 1964: 99-100), and was recently resumed by the team of investigators around Seiler (1985). It is meant to capture the insight that the word order of modifiers within nominal or verbal phrases is the reflex of an underlying relationship of *semantic coherence* between the nominal (or verbal) nucleus and its modifiers within the same sentence. However, despite the striking resemblance in this respect between languages of different stock, word order on the whole remains too whimsical a feature for our present purpose. In search of a more reliable criterion we hit upon a fact which so far seems to have passed unnoticed, to wit, the fact that an n-th rank modifier appears to be linked to its modified nucleus by an n-fold relational network, or, alternatively, by a construction of n nodes. The diagrams (5) show a few relational networks and their nodes for constructions of the third rank.

(5)(i)

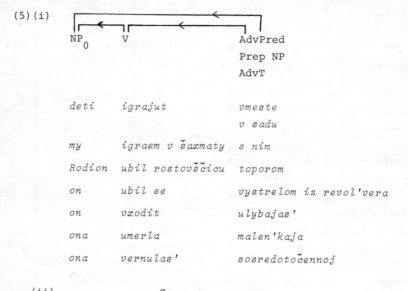

NP_0	V	AdvPred
		Prep NP
		AdvT

deti	*igrajut*	*vmeste*
		v sadu
my	*igraem v šaxmaty*	*s nim*
Rodion	*ubil rostovščicu*	*toporom*
on	*ubil ee*	*vystrelom iz revol'vera*
on	*vxodit*	*ulybajas'*
ona	*umerla*	*malen'kaja*
ona	*vernulas'*	*sosredotočennoj*

(ii)

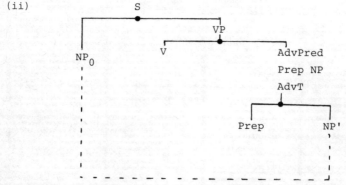

209

The underlying idea of this analysis is that the presence in any
expression of certain types of modifiers p r e v e n t s the
division of the word material into a series of binary parsings.
Thus in an expression containing an instrumental or comitative
phrase, say *ona ubila ego mečom, ona igrala s nim v šaxmaty*, the
fact that these expressions are convertible into, respectively, *ee
meč ubil ego* or *ona ubila ego, deržá meč v ruke*, and *oni s nim
igrali v šaxmaty* or *on igral s nej v šaxmaty*, make it impossible
to divide the predicate as VP ⟶ VP' + instrumental/comitative
Prep NP, because this parsing requires the presence of the feature
[plural] on the subject NP, which already has been severed from
the predicate by S ⟶ NP VP. In all these examples, then, we register a case of interference of semantic features between constituents already obtained at an earlier stage of the analysis. As
pointed out before (section 3.1), this consideration also holds
for constructions of lower rank; thus, in particular, in S = NP VP
the relation of parallelism cuts across the boundary of the exocentric combination NP VP, so that we obtained S = $(NP...VP')_S$.

We conclude this section with an example of a construction
dividing directly into f o u r constituents, as indicated in
(6).[7]

(6)(i)

(slabyj) mal'čik   ne uspel   podnjat'   (tjaželyj) kamen'
cf. *slabost' mal'čika prepjatstvoval emu v podnjatii kamnja*

(ii)

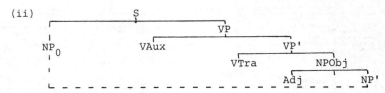

This construction makes explicit the role of qualitative modifiers in the sentence *(slabyj mal'čik, tjaželyj kamen')*. The
left-hand representations (5i, 6i) differ from the corresponding
right-hand ones in showing that, in a construction of rank *n*, in
fact a l l the constituents participate in (*n* - 1) relations

to the other constituents, to which we should add the one relation
between each constituent and the remainder of the sentence, the
relation corresponding to the node S of the right-hand representations (5ii, 6ii). The difference has to do with the fact that,
when realising an EC in discourse (sections 4 ff.), only o n e
constituent at a time can be chosen as the subject, which then
will be connected with the most distant constituent of the sentence through n nodes but only o n e predication.

3.3. The second dimension in the classification of EC's, called
extension (§ 3.1), may be defined as the number of different positions within the sentence covered by a given EC. Within a given
rank, EC's may be divided, first, into (i) constructions covering only *attributive* modifiers in the subject, and (ii) constructions covering, in addition to the subject, one or more *predicative* modifiers. Among the latter, we first distinguish, an *inner*
layer of intransitive modifiers (the main verb itself and possible
predicative adverbials bearing on the subject), then an intermediate layer of nominal modifiers related to the subject by active-
passive transformations (direct/indirect object), and finally an
outer layer of modifiers linking their clause to another clause or
to the moment of utterance (modifiers of aspect and tense).

Since the relation of the sentence to the speaker obviously
marks a natural l i m i t on sentence structure, the tense modifiers may be said to have maximal extension within a given rank,
and to c l o s e the set of possible EC's of that rank (cf.
Bloomfield 1933: 196 ff., 223, 268 on 'closure'). The set of expressions in (7) illustrates the principle of extension (we use
the arrow notation to distinguish nuclej and modifiers of each
phrase).

(7)

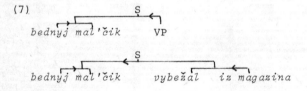

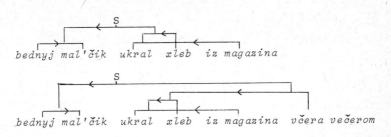

3.4. The final step in the classification of EC's is the division
of each class defined by rank, level of predication, and orientation,
into two subclasses according to the single or double "case line"
(Fillmore 1969: 117) connecting the modifier with its nucleus.
Pending the more detailed discussion below (section 5) we note that
two such expressions as (i) *John moved the stone* and (ii) *the stone
moved* (cf. Lyons 1969: 350ff.) differ in such a way that, if NP and
VP in (ii) are connected by a certain number, say k, of case lines,
then in (i) we have to posit $k + 1$ case lines in order to capture
the fact that *John* in (i) not only functions as the subject of VP
(as it would in, say, *John is ten years old*), but in addition brings
about a change of state of the included subject *the stone*; in other
words, the subject in (i) is an object in (ii), the subject in (ii)
is the subject of (1) p l u s the role of initiator, from which the
additional case line emanates. In deviation from the subject, the
agent-initiator may in suitable expressions have the roles of initiator and object of (i), as in *John swang himself into the river*, cf.
R. *on brosilsja v reku, on otpravilsja na vokzal*, G. *er begab sich
zum Bahnhof.*

It seems to have hitherto passed unnoticed that this distinction pervades the entire inventory of expressions in any language,
witness the difference between expressions involving or not the
source of the utterance, corresponding to 'perfect' and 'past' in
English, e.g. 'leaving' vs 'having left' on the one hand, and *he
leaves/left/he has/had left* on the other; likewise, the difference
between factitives like *burja razbila stekla* and experiential-bene-
factive expressions like *burja razognala ee ugrjumost'/razognala u
nee ugrjumost'....*, boil down to this very distinction between
single or double case line, or, more in general, between odd and
even numbers of case lines.

In order to obtain the total system of EC's one essential observation concerning the building-up of EC's should be added here.
Since the sentence sets an absolute limit to the extension of an
EC, the only way to obtain EC's of higher rank than the one at hand
is e m b e d d i n g the sentence into a noun phrase. This
is the well-known principle of recursive nominalisation (cf. Lyons
1969: 225 on "recycling", and 265), which in the present context
may be formulated as follows: the construction of l a r g e s t
extension in rank n is included in the construction of l e a s t
extension in rank $n + 1$. Hence the nominals of, say, rank $n = 3$,
in extension class I, are supposed to be derived from an underlying
largest extension construction of rank $n = 2$; accordingly, such
countable nouns as *stol, stul, meč, topor, kover, dom, izba, postrojka*, etc., or *čelovek, syn, doč', učitel'*, etc., will be described as the e n d products of a process referred to in a construction of the form NP_0 *makes/builds/forges, weaves/bears/gets/
appoints/...* NP', as shown in diagram (8).

(8)

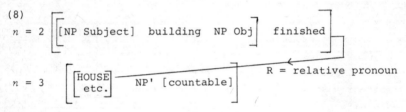

$n = 2$ [NP Subject] building NP Obj finished

$n = 3$ [HOUSE etc.] NP' [countable]

R = relative pronoun

The fact that the underlying creative process has to be accomplished in order to obtain the resulting 'object' or 'person' is
captured in the description by requiring that the underlying construction shall contain the modifier of 'result' (*zakončit' stro-
enie --› postrojka*, etc.) and a device such as the relative pronoun
R (cf. diagram 8) by which the original independent clause is
converted into an attribute; cf. *dom* = NP *postroennyj*, where the
'tense' marker of *dom byl (budet) postroen* is replaced by the suffix of the attributive participle.[8]

The system of EC's is shown in (9) for the first three ranks;
the emphasis is on the principle of classification, no details
about individual EC's are provided.

(9)

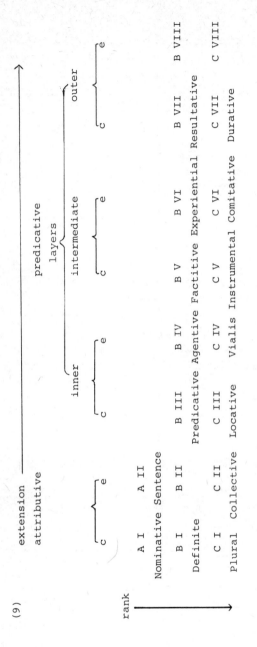

extension ⟶

attributive   predicative layers

inner   intermediate   outer

rank ⟶

A I   A II
Nominative Sentence

B I   B II   B III   B IV   B V   B VI   B VII   B VIII
Definite   Predicative Agentive Factitive Experiential Resultative

C I   C II   C III   C IV   C V   C VI   C VII   C VIII
Plural Collective Locative Vialis Instrumental Comitative Durative

Legend: c --> concentric; e --> eccentric
A,B,C,... --> ranks $n = 1,2,3,...$
Labels are attached to the most common categories

214

4. ELEMENTARY CONSTRUCTIONS IN DISCOURSE

4.1. Although an EC as an element of the thematic system (9), i.e. in its b a s i c stylistic state, covers no more than at most o n e sentence, under suitable stylistic circumstances it may happen that the distance between nucleus and modifier, or alternatively, the parallel connection between them, extends over a certain number of nodes contributed by intermediate sentences (10).

(10)
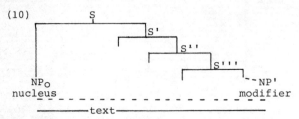

We speak of a *paraphrasing* EC to indicate the case that an arbitrary EC whose basic state would be specified by a given value of n, occasionally covers a suprasentential expression of rank $n'>n$.

   Recalling our analysis of the exocentric sentence construction in section 3.2 as $S = (NP...VP')_S$, we may regard even a single sentence as a minimal discourse, and consequently describe its structure by t w o states of the same EC, one the initial state of the EC as a topic, the other its final state as a focus. For comparison, notice the representation of emphatic sentences like *pobedil Petr* by two constructions in the diagram discussed by Dahl (1969: 18):

(11)
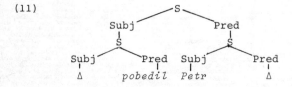

For the moment we shall assume that an arbitrary EC figuring at a given position in a text may have to be described as the t r a n s i t i o n from the EC's topical state to a focal state of higher rank, the number of nodes being determined by the set of indispensable intermediate sentences of the context converging on the given EC. Thus while rank within the sentence is a possible measure of coherence by bringing together all indispensable constituents of its construction, so in discourse rank will measure coherence by uniting all indispensable predications from intermediate sentences in one paraphrasing construction.

For our present purpose we shall concentrate on the role of rank as the parameter of coherence in the text. To exemplify, let us take a relatively short text, such as Krylov's fable *Vorona i lisica* 1969: II,7; Hamburger 1981) or its French original from La Fontaine. We proceed by setting up the construction of all the constituents which are directly involved in the action or event depicted by the text; this leads to a paraphrase such as *Lisica lest'ju dostala syr ot vorony, zastavljaja ee spet', tak čto syr vypal u nee iz zoba*. This is a construction in which the subject *lisica* is connected with *vorona, syr, golos/spet'*, and *zob*, in the way indicated in (12).

(12)   ⌐lisa⌐⟨*dostala* [*syr*]⟩ —— *ot* [*vorony*] ————————
                                         iz [*zoba*] ———
         ⟨*lest'ju zastavljaja* ⟨[x'] *spet'*⟩⟩—⟨*tak čto* [y"] *vypal*⟩

which may be rewritten for greater clarity as $n = 4$. tetragram:

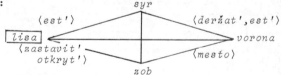

Notice that the focal tetragram (12) brings about a network of semantic constraints between all the meaningful expressions of the text, in the sense that each expression is determined by one or more of the 4 x 4 relation terminals, called *classemes*[9] established by the tetragram; thus *lisa* contains the classeme [agent of event], [recipient of cheese], [flatterer of crow] and [admirer of crow's voice], while *vorona* contains the classeme [victim of fox], [loser of cheese], [possessor of voice] and [recipient of flattery], and so on for the other constituents of the paraphrase.

Under suitable stylistic conditions, in particular if our text can be taken to belong to the sum total of the same author's fables, the same material may have to be re-analysed by a paraphrase of higher rank. In general, therefore, to the extent that an arbitrary sentence happens to be embedded in a larger context, the topical state of an EC assigned to a single sentence will pass into an entire s e t of paraphrases, of rank n' = 2,3,..., as the initial sentence is incorporated in ever more complex environments. There does not seem to exist any restriction, however, on the number of nodes that can be added under one predication. This can be inferred from the fact that the semantic network measured by the rank n of an EC's state may increase both by anticipation, and retrospectively within a single sentence. Thus in the first paragraph of Dostoevskij's novel *Igrok* the content of *Nakonec*... is developed by the entire passage, especially by the sentences in capitals in (13) below, and the last sentence *Mnogo nakopilos'* summarises this content in a similar way.[10]

(13) *Nakonec JA VOZVRATILSJA IZ MOEJ DVUXNEDEL'NOJ OTLUČKI.*
    NAŠI UŽE TRI DNJA KAK BYLI V RULETENBURGE. Ja dumal, čto
    ONI I BOG ZNAET KAK ŽDUT MENJA, ODNAKO Ž JA OŠIBSJA.
    General smotrel črezvyčajno nezavisimo (...). Mar'ja Fi-
    lippovna byla v črezvyčajnyx xlopotax i pogovorila so
    mnoju slegka; DEN'GI, ODNAKO Ž, PRINJALA, SOSČITALA I
    VYSLUŠALA VES' MOJ RAPORT. (...) POLINA ALEKSANDROVNA,
    UVIDEV MENJA, SPROSILA, ČTO JA TAK DOLGO? i, ne doždav-
    šis' otveta, ušla kuda-to. RAZUMEETSJA, ona sdelala èto
    naročno. Nam, odnako ž, ob"jasnit'sja. Mnogo nakopilos'.
                                                    (Dost. V, 208)

The foreword and backward pointing functions of the opening and closing expressions of a passage may be compared with the cataphoric and anaphoric functions of pronouns within the sentence.

    Recalling that in the basic state the EC's constituents are arranged about a single nuclear expression, the subject, we now apply this principle to the paraphrasing EC's of a suprasentential sequence (as proposed by Metzeltin and Jaksche 1983: 26ff.): the subject of the sequence will then be assigned a certain state of coherence, which, for the first rank, amounts to just o n e

classeme; in the focal states of the given EC this one classeme
will become divided over the n^2 classemes of the text, so that
each of these contributes in a proportion of $1/n^2$ to the realisation of the subject's semantic potential. Since every classeme
owes its existence to a semantic constraint known as "Rekurrenz"
or "Isotopie" (Kallmeyer *et.al.* 1974: 143 ff.), the magnitude $1/n^2$
is a suitable measure of coherence in the sense commonly attributed to the term in text linguistics (cf. esp. De Beaugrande and
Dressler 1981: 5, 88 ff.).

4.2. The central character of a plot line, represented by the subject of a sequence of sentences, may be connected with one or more
other entities of the situation of discourse at a given stage of
the narrative. Even if these entities do not participate in the
plot as independent sources of other plot lines (this would lead
to *compound* constructions; cf. section 2.3), they will as a rule
affect the complexity of plot structure by introducing one or more
'target' entities into the paraphrase. Owing to the linear nature
of linguistic expression, these connections will not be given all
at a time in the initial stage of the narrative; rather, they arise
in due course, along with the development of the semantic network
into higher levels of coherence. The result is a paraphrasing construction whose predicate is marked by a definite degree of diathetic complexity. To every predicative EC of rank $n>2$ we accordingly assign a level of predication $l>1$, whereas the attributive
constructions inside NP are assigned the level $l=0$. Higher levels
of predication arise with the appearance of novel entities in the
situation of discourse, as shown for a few typical cases in (14).

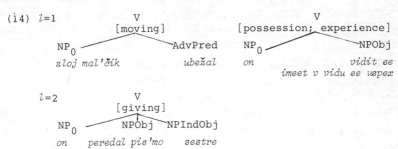

(14) $l=1$

218

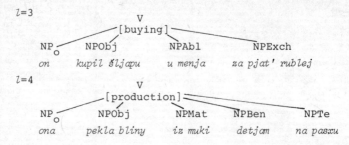

$l=3$

V
[buying]

NP$_0$ NPObj   NPAbl   NPExch
on   *kupil šljapu*   *u menja*   *za pjat' rublej*

$l=4$

V
[production]

NP$_0$ NPObj   NPMat   NPBen   NPTe
ona   *pekla bliny*   *iz muki*   *detjam*   *na pasxu*

Note that in an EC of the form $\underset{NP\ VP}{S}$ we have o n e node ($n=1$), so that subject and predicate cannot be differentiated; this construction is therefore also assigned a level of predication $l=0$.

> We recall in this connection that there are t w o EC's of the first rank: one concentric EC, represented by the sum total of nominals with no pertinent internal composition (this EC corresponds to the "Nominative" or "Objective" of case grammar; cf. Fillmore 1968: 25, Anderson 1971: 37-39; Moskey 1979: 7 ff.), and one eccentric EC, represented by the class of expressions performing both the referential function of the included nominal and the additional function of the source or speaker, so that between the latter and the content of the construction a double case line is established: one representing the subject of the narrated event, the other the narrator.

4.3. It is important to note that every novel NP$_i$ beside the subject NP$_0$ is to be introduced by a separate predication, when the paraphrasing construction of a plot is realised in a given sentence. Thus in a sentence like *Petja polučil ot nee novyj mjač* the object *novyj mjač* introduces a new entity and functions as the focus, whereas in *Petja polučil ètot mjač ot sestry* the ablative phrase is the focus introducing a new item in the situation. These well known facts of functional sentence perspective lead to a concept of step-wise introduction of NP's into the predicate, each leading to a higher value of the predicate level l. It is also possible to r e m o v e an entity from the situation of discourse. Thus in *On poprosil njanju ostavit' ego odnim* the EC covering the expression *on/ego...odin/odnim* included in the given specimen, is the result of diminishing the diathetic complexity of *on poprosil ee ob ètom* from state (l, $n=2$) to state (l, $n=1$). In general, then, it appears that the level of predication can only be raised or lowered by one unit at a time. Referring once again to the passage from *Igrok* quoted above, we register a single predication leading from *Nakonec* as a topical adverb to the remainder of the passage as a focus, while in *Mnogo nakopilos'* this predication is u n d o n e , the paragraph being temporarily closed, although the lexical meaning of *nakopilos'* anticipates on new potential complications waiting ahead.

The significance of the predicate level l for discourse thus consists in *delinearising* the plot, while a predominantly linear plot will be represented by a n-gram with low l-value, being concentrated upon the hero's solitary adventures.

5. A NOTE ON MULTIPLICITY

5.1. Comparison of the two sentences

(15)(i) *Na ee lice igrala lukavaja ulybka*

(ii) *Odnu partiju ona so mnoj igrala celyj čas*

tells us that the common structure NP VP conveys two different predications, one implying the subject's potential initiative, the other simply establishing a subject-predicate connection.[11] The difference at issue may be further elaborated by the plot line: in (16i) the mere event, its beginning, continuation or termination is depicted, while in (16ii) the agent is represented as capable of initiative, intentions, social interaction, etc.

(16)(i) *Na ee lice igrala ulybka, potom isčezla, a k koncu večera ee lico daže prinjalo kisloe vyraženie...*

(ii) *Ona sela za stol, a k koncu večera, proigravši poslednie kopejki, v užase vybežala von iz komnaty...* etc.

We interpret the difference in question following Fillmore (1969: 117) by assigning a single "case line" to the construction established by *igrat'* in (15i) or (16i), and a double "case line" to the construction *igrat'* in (15ii) or (16ii). From the form of expressions like *Ona otpravilas' na vokzal*, and their French or German translations *Elle se rendit à la gare*, *Sie begab sich zum Bahnhof*, with their substitutes *Je me rendis...*, *Tu te rendis...*, *Ich begab mich...*, *Du begabst dich...*, etc., which disambiguate the Russian originals *Ja otpravilsja...*, *Ty otpravilsja...*, etc., the subject and predicate are connected in all such expressions by a t w o f o l d grammatical agreement. These two connections, however, cancel eachother in the sense that, if one is active-transitive *(otpravit' kogo na vokzal)*, the other undoes this directivity by letting the agent become its own object. Therefore we assign o p p o s i t e directivities to the position markers on which each case line terminates.

The t o t a l directivity of the position markers may remain z e r o regardless of the presence of a direct object. This is immediately evident for a language like Ancient Greek, where active-middle pairs such as (17) occur.[12]

(17) (i) *'O iereús thúei tòn boûn*
'The priest sacrifices the ox'
(ii) *'O stratēgós thúetai boûn*
'The commander sacrifices an ox',

whereas in Russian the object position is blocked in reflexive constructions; other combinations, however, such as those listed in (18), are altogether common:

(18) (i) *On ženilsja na molodoj devuške* (cf. *He married a young girl)*
(ii) *On ottolknul ee ot sebja*
(iii) *Ona zapaslas' pšenicej na zimu* (cf. *Elle se procura du froment pour l'hiver)*

The difference between the Ancient Greek and the Russian examples vanishes in the corresponding deep structures, if we consider that the position of the reflexive-medial suffix *-tai* in (17) in deep structure is n o t that of a direct object, but rather of a benefactive (like *se* in the French example, 18iii), whereas in the passive function of *-tai* the object is likewise excluded *(paideúetai/epaideúthē tòn teknón,* etc.).

From this brief scrutiny it seems plausible to postulate the existence of another type of eccentric constructions, in which the two position markers would be pointing in the s a m e direction. The constructions of this type will contain an agent NPe_0, with a status identical to that in the reflexive expressions *(Ona otpravilas' na vokzal,* etc.), and a second constituent

with the status of a so-called counter-agent (Fillmore 1969: 116),
i.e. a personal direct object; the predicate in this type of expressions contains a direct object or preposition phrase of abstract signature, as in the examples (19).

(19) (i)   *On peredal ej izvestie*
      (ii) *Ona pišet emu pis'mo*
      (iii) *On poprosil ee ostat'sja*
      (iv) *Ona umoljala ego o pomošči.*

Even in expressions like *Mazepa nakazal Kočubeja, Ona udarila ego
v lico*, we have to take into account such transformations as *On
naložil na nego nakazanie, Ona dala emu poščečinu*, which go to
show that the verb phrase linking agent and counter-agent contains an abstract noun phrase as a direct object; this nominal
belongs to the total predicate, and is therefore closer in the
situation of discourse to the counter-agent than to the agent, as
indicated in (20), where the expression to the left is rewritten
in more explicit form to the right as the left-hand side (20).

(20)   *Mazepa---naložil---nakazanie*
      Mazepa nakazal Kočubeja →   *na Kočubeja*

The expressions (19) and (20) reveal a common construction of
'donative' or 'communicative' type[13], which we write as

(21) NPe_1 VDon/VCom NPe_2 NP_3
     [agent] [verb of donation [recipient] [object]
             or communication]

the only point of difference between the above examples being
the predicate level $l=1$ in (20) as against $l=2$ in (19).

In an earlier paper (Van Holk 1963) I proposed to assign
half-integral values to the individual position markers of an EC,
on the grounds that a concentric predication always requires the
cooperation of two constituents, the subject NP_0 and the predicate nominal NP', of which one is 'definite', the other 'indefinite'. In an eccentric EC these features converge in a reflexive
or donative-communicative predicate. So we introduce the new magnitude of *directivity* of the position markers, with values $s=\pm\frac{1}{2}$.

The total state of an EC will then be specified by the following magnitudes:

(22) (i) the value of l for each individual parallel connection between class marker and position marker (section 3.1), hence $L = \Sigma l_i$ will represemt the sum of l values for the total EC;

(ii) the total directivity $S = \Sigma s_i$, where $S = s = \frac{1}{2}$ for a concentric NP with o n e position marker and $S = 0$ or 1 for an eccentric EC with t w o position markers;

(iii) the sum $J = L + S$ representing the *total diathetic state* of an EC, which for $S = 1$ will have three values to account for the constituents of the conative-communicative construction; this is achieved by considering J as the v e c t o r a d d i - t i o n of L and S (as shown for a few cases in diagram 23i below).

Since a single EC normally does not simultaneously participate in more than one predication[14], we are entitled to put $L = l$ for our present purpose.

(23) (i) counter-agent   direct object   subject-agent

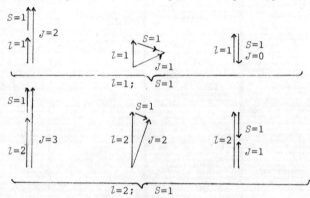

(ii)

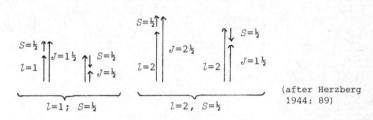

(after Herzberg
1944: 89)

5.2. In the light of the above considerations the state of a
concentric EC with a single position marker will be specified by
a half-integral value of its position marker's directivity. So,
indeed, in an expression like *On byl bolen*, the finite verb esta-
blishes a connection between the 'definite' subject *on* and an
'indefinite' predicate *bolen*; likewise, in (15i) *Na ee lice igrala lukavaja ulybka*, the verb *igrala* connects the 'definite' topic
na ee lice with the 'indefinite' focus *lukavaja ulybka*. In the
subject *on* we have to do with a non-predicative expression of
predicate level $l=0$, and a directivity value $s=\frac{1}{2}$; in the second
example the construction is of level $l=1$ and comprises the two
different directivities $s=\pm\frac{1}{2}$, so that $J=L+S=l+s$ assumes the
values $\frac{1}{2}$ for the topic and $1\frac{1}{2}$ for the focus (cf. diagram 23ii).
In a construction of the donative type (21) we register
t h r e e different directivities, associated with the agent,
the indirect object and the direct object (speaker-receiver-mes-
sage): the total directivity being in this case s_1+s_2 (both
pointing in the same direction), the vector addition illustrated
in (23i) below shows that we obtain $j=0$; $j=1$; $j=2$.

6.   MULTIPLICITY IN DISCOURSE
6.1. Applying the analysis developed so far to the thematics of
the plot, we observe that the plot line content covered by an EC
with one or two position markers may be built up according to one
of two mechanisms, which correspond to concentric and eccentric
EC's in the following way:

(24)(i)   the sentences of the plot line are of the form
          (NP VP), so that the intersentential connections
          in general are of the form (NP VP) (NP' VP');

(ii) the sentences are of the form (NP_1 VDon/Com NP_2 NP_3), so that the intersentential connections in general are of the form (NP_1 VDon/VCom NP_2 NP_3) -- NP_1' VDon/VCom' NP_2' NP_3').

We are now going to discuss these intersentential combinations in more detail.

6.2. Let us first consider the simplest case, a plot line covered by a concentric EC with a single position marker. The f i r s t possible transition to be registered for such a plot line should somehow correspond to the fundamental division S → NP VP. This structure may be described as a transition emanating from an arbitrary initial expression, say S, of a narrative, with l=0, and leading up to a construction (NP VP), with predicate level l=1, with two distinct directivities, NP' the topic, VP' the focus. Remembering that every EC, when realised through the sentence as a minimal text, is bound to undergo a change of state, the transition NP → NP'VP' is the simplest one, in which the EC' nucleus is specified by the lexical minimum of one class marker; examples are such typical 'first sentences' of narratives as *Delo bylo osen'ju*, *V dalekom gosudarstve žil-byl car'*, etc. This transition is diagrammed in (27i) below.

The next more complex intersentential combination holds for all the transitions in the plot except the first, which starts from NP. These transitions lead over from an intransitive construction (NP'VP') to a transitive-causative construction {NP VP (NP' VP')}, the result of the transition (24i); examples are expressions like *On sdelal ee nesčastnoj*, *On pogubil ee*, *On osčastlivil ee*, *On ubil protivnika*, *v rekrutskoe prisutstvie priveli ego razdetogo* (Nekrasov), etc., all involving an explicit or implicit object predicate. The transitions at issue may be specified as follows. Taking as the initial state of the construction the nominals NP_1 as the subject, NP_2 as the object, and the 'causing' and 'caused' predicates VP_1, VP_2 as components of the terminal state, we then obtain the following two groups of connections (25):

(25)(i) NP_1 combines with VP_1;
   (ii) NP_2 combines with VP_1 as its object, and with VP_2 as its subject.

These transitions are diagrammed in (27ii) below); the object
predicate results from a subdivision of the intransitive predicate,
therefore VP_1 and VP_2 are drawn closer together in the diagram than
NP_1 and NP_2.

> An alternative notation of the same transition would take (NP VP) as the
> initial state of the construction, and (NP' VP') as the terminal state.
> Component (25i) then becomes the combination of NP' through a transitive
> verb with NP', whereas components (25ii) become the combinations of VP
> with NP' as an object, and with VP as the object predicate. The difference
> in notation does not alter the basic structural fact that the ergative
> agent is connected o n l y with the transitive-causative verb as a
> whole, while the object is connected b o t h with the transitive verb
> and with the (intransitive) object predicate.

6.3. Essentially the same considerations apply to the donative-
communicative plot line. Having obtained a construction of the
form NP_1 VDon/VCom NP_2 NP_3 from an agentive subject NP_3 we now
proceed to examine the transition from the donative construction
to an included object-clause construction. Let the initial state
of the construction be given by the three participants of action -
the source of the message NP_1, its receiver NP_2, and the message
itself NP_3, while the terminal state will consist of the three
corresponding predicates - the act of communication VP_1, the
action VP_2 assigned to the receiver, the event VP_3 expliciting the
content of the message. The required transition will then consist
of the three components listed in (26).

(26) (i) NP_1 combines with VP as the source of an utterance,
command, request or other communicative act *(On
govorit, čto èto tak; On zaxotel poexat' k nim; On
poprosil ee ostat'sja doma]*;

(ii) NP_2 combines with VP_1 as the recipient of an utterance, command, request, etc., and with VP_2 as its
subject *(on poprosil ee ostat'sja* beside *ona ob"ja-
zana ostat'sja]*;

(iii) NP_3 combines with VP_1 as the object of an act of
communication, with VP_2 as the object of an act of
reception, and with VP_3 as the content of the message *(pis'mo pišetsja, pis'mo polučaetsja/čitaetsja,
and pis'mo o tom, kak popali v stolicul.*

These three groups of connections are diagrammed in (27iii). The
components $V_{1,2,3}$ are drawn closer together than $NP_{1,2,3}$ to capture the fact that the V_i's are subdivisions of the basic donative-
communicative predicate.

The alternative notation suggested above for the transition
(27ii) can also be applied to those of (27iii). Taking NP_1 VDon/Com
NP_2 NP_3 as the initial state, we may sever from it the three components NP_1 as the s o u r c e of volition (intention, etc.) or of
an utterance, VDon/Com as the address to a recipient NP_2, and NP_3
as the message to be transmitted; the terminal state NP_1' VDon/Com'
NP_2' NP_3' will then result from the following partial transitions:
NP_1 combines with NP_1' as the executor of the intended action;
VDon/Com NP_2 combines with NP_1' as the intended performer-addres-
see, and with VDon/Com' NP_2' as the predicate center or "nexus
field" of the message (cf. Diderichsen 1946), and with NP_3' as its
"content field" (ibid.). The alternative notations perhaps can be
conventionally associated with the d i r e c t i o n of the
transition (cf. section 4.2-3), opposing notations of the form
(NP VP) $\rightarrow$ (NP' VP') to such of the form $(NP_1\ NP_2) \leftarrow (VP_1\ VP_2)$.

It should be noted that certain transitions (indicated by
dotted lines in 27), are p r o h i b i t e d. Thus in (27ii) the
transition from NP' to VP" is forbidden, which captures the fact
that in *On sdelal ee nesčastnoj* the object predicate cannot be
parallel with the subject. Likewise, in (27iii), the transitions
from NP_1 to VP_2' and VP_3' are forbidden in accordance with the
fact that in *On prikazal soldatam postroit' most* the issuer of
the command himself is not forced or obliged to build a bridge,
nor building one, and the transition from NP_2 to VP_3' is forbidden
because the so-called "content field" of the message (cf. Diderichsen 1946) is not connected with the verb of reception, witness the inacceptability of expressions like *Ona uslyšala (uz-
nala, ponjala, uvidela, ...) stolicu* as transformations of *Ona
uslyšala* etc. *o tom, kak my popali v stolicu* (26iii), with *v
stolicu* as the content field of the message (this is also the
reason why a sentence cannot be embedded into a matrix except
through a noun).

(27)(i)

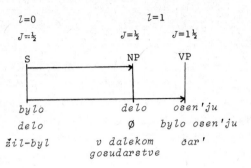

$l=0$ $l=1$

$J=\frac{1}{2}$ $J=\frac{1}{2}$ $J=1\frac{1}{2}$

S   NP   VP

bylo   *delo*   *osen'ju*
delo   Ø   *bylo osen'ju*
žil-byl   *v dalekom*   *car'*
             gosudarstve

(ii) $l=1$ $l=2$

$J=\frac{1}{2}$ $J=1\frac{1}{2}$ $J=1\frac{1}{2}$ $J=2\frac{1}{2}$

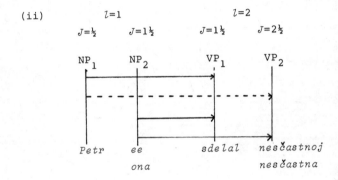

NP_1 NP_2 VP_1 VP_2

Petr   *ee*   *sdelal*   *nesčastnoj*
       ona   *nesčastna*

228

(iii)   *l*=1   *l*=2
    J=0   1   2   *J*=1   2   3

    NP₁ NP₂ NP₃   VP₁ VP₂ VP₃

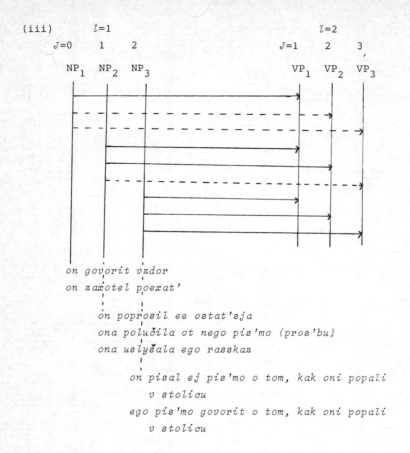

on govorit vzdor
on zaxotel poexat'

    on poprosil ee ostat'sja
    ona polučila ot nego pis'mo (pros'bu)
    ona uslyšala ego rasskaz

        on pisal ej pis'mo o tom, kak oni popali
          v stolicu
        ego pis'mo govorit o tom, kak oni popali
          v stolicu

These observations may be accounted for by means of s e -
l e c t i o n rules on the values of *l* and *J*. We have already
seen that the predicate level *l* can change only by one unit at a
time and never remains unchanged (section 4.3), so that we may
write $\Delta l=\pm 1$ for the selection on *l*. As the diagrams (27) tell
us, the value of *J* can either remain unchanged, or go up or down
by one unit, so that on this variable the selection rule
$\Delta J=0, \pm 1$ appears to be valid.

7. CONCLUSIONS

In this paper we developed a text-linguistic model designed
to account for the thematic content of plot lines, and based on
certain well-known facts of the semantics and syntax of the Russian sentence. The outcome seems to justify the conclusions that
the same magnitudes of coherence, predicate level and directivity
describing the construction of individual sentences can indeed be
applied to suprasentential expressions. In particular, it could
be shown that there is a close link between the number of position
markers within an EC (as indicated by the groups I through VIII in
the system given in 9) and the type of connections found to occur
between the sentences of a sequence. While the EC's with an o d d
number of position markers have e v e n multiplicities, those
with an e v e n number of position markers have o d d multiplicities; moreover, for the EC's of group II, the intersentential
connections fall into t w o subtypes: the one corresponding to
active-reflexive plot lines having only s i n g l e connections,
the one corresponding to donative-communicative plot lines having
t r i p l e connections.

It may be added that the r a n k of an EC in the system (9)
does not affect the multiplicity, although the coherence networks
become more complex, due to the addition of morphologic constraints. This problem, however, calls for a separate investigation.

Slavic Institute Groningen

NOTES

[1] So far, such studies have concentrated on the role of tense and aspect in
discourse,and,more recently, on the role of transitivity as a plot-advancing
factor (of particular interest is the work of Hopper, 1982a,b and Chvany 1985).
I further refer to the panel on 'Aspect in Discourse' at the Third World Congress of the AEES in Washington (November, 1985). Much further research is
needed for the inclusion of other universals, such as 'number', 'reciprocity',
'instrumental', etc., in a consistent linguistic model of the text.
[2] The condition of 'literariness' merely means to rule out for the time
being texts and themes pertaining to strictly technical disciplines. The text-

linguistic approach proposed here does not claim to have an answer to the
question of 'literariness'; it merely takes as 'literary' all those texts
which deal with human situations and adventures in the form of narrative
strings (e.g., the semantics and syntax of expressions referring to the 'honest
merchant' in Ostrovskij's *Bednost' ne porok* or to the theme of 'sale' in
Chekhov's *Višnevyj sad*; Van Holk 1986).

[3] I am aware that my use of the term "macrostructure" does not quite fit its
common employment in text linguistics, which seems to emphasise the suprasentential size of macrostructure, whereas in my conception the term captures the
sum total of cultural (social, ethnological, etc.) text-external factors determining a situation (cf. Gülich and Raible 1977: 53 ff.; 253 ff.).

[4] One should remember the crucial role of the distinction between sentence
and clause levels in the work of contemporary Russian syntacticists (cf.
Zolotova 1982; Lehfeldt 1984).

[5] De Beaugrande and Dressler (1981: 50 ff.) use the term "Kohäsion" for the
sum total of grammatical conventions by which dependences in the textual surface are established; they do include, however, the use of pro-forms in anaphoric or cataphoric functions among those conventions.

[6] I am inclined to treat the pronominal elements and their functions in the
frame of a grammar of communication as o p e r a t i o n s on syntactic
structures; thus the definite article (in Bulgarian), or the long forms of the
adjective and participle in OCS, may be described by their effect on predicative structures, viz. the incorporation of the latter in an attributive noun
phrase by suppression of the "plot-advancing" capacity of the predicate (cf.
Van Holk 1982, 1983b).

[7] An analysis like (6) will be generally required if the paraphrase of a
text contains a non-deletable qualitative attribute. Thus in Van Dijk's example *A girl in a yellow dress passed by* (Van Dijk 1978: 55), if the yellow
colour is pertinent to the text as a whole (turning up later on in the narrative, etc.), the construction at issue will be analysed as follows:

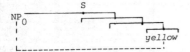

Cf. the well-known Dutch poem by Melis Stoke about the woman in a yellow
dress, where at least the classeme of 'colour' is relevant, witness the following citation:

> Waar ik reis, waar ik ga, waar ik sta, sinds dien dag
>   ontmoet ik aan iedere trein
> die vrouw in het geel met haar zonnige lach,
>   en ik gis maar: wie kan ze toch zijn?
>   (*Liedjes van de Rails*, 1939)

[8] The present treatment meets the criticism on Fillmore's "singularity principle", requiring "one case per simple sentence" (Abraham 1978: 696; cf.
Apresjan 1974: 27) by restricting this principle to the i n t e r n a l
structure of an EC, whereas multinuclear constructions as pointed out above
(section 2.2), may very well consist of two or more i d e n t i c a l EC's
(cf. Van Holk 1980, 1985, 1986).

[9] I am aware that my use of this term may not exactly coincide with
Greimas', but it proved difficult to find a better term for this important
notion (Greimas 1966: 50 ff.; Vet 1973; Kallmeyer *et al.* 1974: 147).

[10] This analysis pertains to a lower level of abstraction than the narrative
strings discovered in this passage by Wijzenbroek (1985), using a method
based on Genette.

231

[11] Cf. *igrat'* (1)*"sverkat', sijat', perelivajas' raznymi ottenkami, otrazat'-sja"*; (2) *"...provodit' vremja v kakom-nibud' zanjatii..."* (Ušakov)
[12] Cf. Lyons (1969: 373-374); in *Loûomai xitona* 'I am washing (my) shirt', the "implication of the use of the middle voice rather than the active is that the action is being carried out by the subject for his own benefit or in its own interests" (373).
[13] The close resemblance between the two types of constructions has been noticed by Klimonov (1972).

BIBLIOGRAPHY

Abraham, Werner
    1978   "Valence and Case: Remarks on Their Contribution to the Identi-
              fication of Grammatical Relations", in W. Abraham (Ed.), *Val-
              ence, Semantic Case and Grammatical Relations*, 695-729. Benja-
              mins: Amsterdam.
Anderson, John M.
    1971   *The Grammar of Case. Towards a Localistic Theory*. UP: Cambridge.
Apresjan, Ju. D.
    1974   *Leksičeskaja semantika. Sinonimičeskie sredstva jazyka.*Izd.
              Nauka , Moskva.
Beaugrande, Robert-Alain de, Wolfgang Ulrich Dressler,
    1981   *Einführung in die Textlinguistik*. Niemeyer: Tübingen.
Bloomfield, Leonard
    1933   *Language*. Holt: New York.
Chvany, Catherine V.
    1985   "Foregrounding, 'Transitivity', Saliency (in Sequential and
              Non-Sequential Prose)", *Essays in Poetics* 10,2, 1-27.
Dahl, Östen
    1969   *Topic and Comment: A Study in Russian and General Transforma-
              tional Grammar* (= *Slavica Gothoburgensia, 4*). Almqvist &
              Wiksell: Stockholm.
Daneš, František, Zdenek Hlavsa, Jan Korenský,
    1973   "Postavení slovesa v strukture české vedby", in: *Československé
              prednášky pro VII mezinárodní sjezd slavistu, 129-139*. Varsava.
Diderichsen, Poul
    1946   *Elementaer dansk grammatik*. København.
Dijk, Teun A. van
    1978   *Tekstwetenschap. Een interdisciplinaire inleiding*. Het Spectrum:
              Amsterdam.
Dostoevskij, F.M.
    1973   *Polnoe sobranie sočinenij v tridcati tomax*. Izd. Nauka :
              Leningrad.
Ebeling, Carl L.
    1954   "On the semantic structure of the Russian sentence", *Lingua* 4,
              207-222.
    1978   *Syntax and Semantics. A Taxonomic Approach*. Brill: Leiden.
Fillmore, Charles J.
    1968   "The Case for Case", in: Emmon Bach and Robert T. Harms (Eds.),
              Universals in Linguistic Theory. Holt, Rinehart and Winston:
              New York etc.
    1969   "Types of Lexical Information", in: Ferenc Kiefer (Ed.), *Studies
              in Syntax and Semantics*. Reidel: Dordrecht.

Geerts, G., W. Haeseryn, J. de Rooij, M.C. van den Toorn
1984   *Algemene Nederlandse Spraakkunst*. Wolters-Noordhoff: Groningen; Wolters: Leuven.
Greimas, A.J.
1966   *Sémantique structurale. Recherche de méthode*. Larousse: Paris.
Groot, A.W. de
1949   *Structurele syntaxis*. Servire: Den Haag.
1964   *Inleiding tot de algemene taalwetenschap*. Wolters: Groningen
Gülich, E., und W. Raible
1977   *Linguistische Textmodelle. Grundlagen und Möglichkeiten*. Fink: München.
Hamburger, H.
1981   *The Function of the Predicate in the Tales of Krylov. A Text-Grammatical Study*. Rodopi: Amsterdam.
Harweg, Roland
1968   *Pronomina und Textkonstitution*. Fink: München.
Herzberg, Gerhard
1944   *Atomic Spectra and Atomic Structure*. Dover Publ.: New York.
Holk, André van
1963   "Definite and Indefinite in Old Church Slavonic : A Contribution to the Theory of the Linguistic Sign", in: *Dutch Contributions to the Fifth International Congress of Slavists*. Mouton: The Hague.
1975   "Textual Categories and Russian Morphology", *Russian Linguistics* 2, 223-257.
1980   "The Open Message. On the Syntax of Envy in A.S. Puškin's *Mozart and Salieri*", *Russian Linguistics* 5, 1-54.
1982   "Reflections on the Syntax of the Russian Infinitive", *Russian Linguistics* 6, 255-276.
1983a   "Impersonal Structures in Russian and other Slavic Languages", in: André van Holk (Ed.), *Dutch Contributions to the Ninth International Congress of Slavists (Kiev 1983)*, 145-212. Rodopi: Amsterdam.
1983b   "On the Syntax of Conditional and Object Clauses in Russian", in: B.J. Amsenga, A.H. van den Baar, F. Suasso, M.D. de Wolf (Eds.), *Miscellanea Slavica. To Honour the Memory of Jan. M. Meijer*. Rodopi: Amsterdam.
1985   *Aspect in Textual Deep Structure (On the Message Theme in Puškin's Mednyj vsadnik*. Publications of the Slavic Institute, Nr. 16, UP: Groningen.
1986   *On the Syntax of Sale in Čechov's THE CHERRY ORCHARD*. Publications of the Slavic Institute, Nr. 24. UP: Groningen.
Hopper, Paul J. (Ed.)
1982a   *Tense-Aspect between Semantics and Pragmatics*. Benjamins: Amsterdam.
1982b   "Aspect between Discourse and Grammar", in Paul J. Hopper (Ed.), *Tense-Aspect between Semantics and Pragmatics*, 3-18.
Kallmeyer, W., W. Klein, R. Meyer-Hermann, K. Netzer, H.J. Siebert
1974   *Lekturekolleg zur Textlinguistik*. Athenäum: Frankfurt/Main.
Klimonov, V.D.
1972   "Die inhärente semantischen Merkmale des Verbs und die Struktur der Verbalphrase im Russischen (am Beispiel der semantischen Unterklasse der Verben des Gebens)". *Zeitschrift für Slawistik* XVII (1972), 685-693.

233

Krylov, I.A.
1969   Sočinenija. Izd. Xudožestvennaja literatura : Moskva.
Lehfeldt, Werner
1984   "'Rektion.' Ein Beitrag zur Begriffsgeschichte", in J.J. van Baak
            (Ed.), Signs of Friendship, 203-224. Rodopi: Amsterdam.
Lyons, John
1969   Introduction to Theoretical Linguistics. UP: Cambridge.
Metzeltin, Michael, und Harald Jaksche
1983   Textsemantik. Ein Modell zur Analyse von Texten. Narr: Tübingen.
Moskey, Stephen T.
1979   Semantic Structures and Relations in Dutch. An Introduction to
            Case Grammar. Georgetown UP: Washington.
Ryleev, K.F.
1971   Polnoe sobranie stixotvorenij. Sovetskij pisatel': Leningrad.
Seiler, Hans-Jakob
1985   "Invariance and Variation: The dimensional model of language
            universals" (paper for the First International Roman Jakobson
            Conference at New York, October 10-13, 1985).
Thelin, Nils B.
1984   "K tipologii glagol'noj prefiksacii i ee semantiki v slavjanskix
            jazykax", Revue des Etudes slaves LVI/2, 225-238.
1984   "Komposition, Perspektive und Aspekt in Puškin's Prosa: Entwurf
            einer poetisch-linguistischen Methode", in: J.J. van Baak (Ed.)
            Signs of Friendship, 257-294. Rodopi: Amsterdam.
Vet, J.P.
1973   "Linguistiek en literatuurwetenschap: de semantische theorie
            van Greimas", Forum der Letteren 14, 181-199.
Wijzenbroek, Anita
1985   Hermeneuse van een literaire structuur: Dostoevskij's SPELER.
            Diss. Groningen.
Xolodovič, A.A. (otv. red.)
1969   Tipologija kauzativnyx konstrukcij. Morfologičeskij Kauzativ.
            Izd. Nauka , Leningrad.
Zolotova, G.A.
1982   Kommunikativnye aspekty russkogo sintaksisa. Izd. Nauka,
            Moskva.

REFLECTIONS ON THE RUSSIAN REFLEXIVE POSSESSIVE PRONOUN *SVOJ*

WIM HONSELAAR

0. *INTRODUCTION*

In Russian there is a great number of lexical units containing the morpheme -*svoj*-, for instance: (adjectives) *svoj* 'one's own',
svojskij 'homely', *svoevol'nyj* 'self-willed', *svoevlastnyj* 'despotic';
(adverbs) *po-svoemu* 'in one's own way', *po-svojski* 'ditto'; in a familiar way', *vosvojasi* '(at) home'; (nouns) *svojstvo* 'property', *svojst-
vennik* 'relative-by-marriage', *svojak* 'brother-in-law'; (verbs) *pri-
svoit'* 'appropriate, award', *usvoit'* 'acquire' (Tixonov,1985:81-2). In
all of these units -*svoj*- has an invariant meaning which interacts
with the meaning of the other constituents of the unit. Therefore,
an analysis of the semantics of the morphologically uncomplicated
lexical unit *svoj* will considerably contribute to the understanding
of the meaning of the more complex units.

However, as the linguistic literature shows, the morphological
transparency of *svoj* goes hand in hand with semantic intransparency.
Even Padučeva(1985), in spite of the fact that it deals extensively
with *svoj* (and the personal reflexive pronoun *sebja*) and the relevant literature, restricts itself to a rather fragmentary discussion on the semantics of *svoj* .

From a methodological point of view, the most obvious strategy
in analyzing the meaning of *svoj* is a paradigmatic confrontation
with personal possessive pronouns (*moj* 'my', *tvoj* 'your', etc.) in
appropriate contexts (cf. Andreevskij(1973) and many others). This
strategy has resulted in numerous valuable observations on the effects that replacement of reflexive possessives by personal ones,
and vice versa, has on the content of an utterance. At first glance,
the effects of both reflexive and personal possessives do not seem

to cohere greatly: they constitute sets of widely divergent observations. On closer investigation, it seems to be possible to give an explanation for this diversity on the one hand and the creative and productive use of these pronouns on the other, by assuming that every time a reflexive or personal possessive is used, its invariant meaning receives a particular interpretation due to the influence of contextual and situational factors. In this paper I will present invariant meanings for *svoj, moj*, etc. and try to show how the various effects can be explained on the basis of these meanings.

A number of linguists has been focussing their attention on other aspects of the use of *svoj*: the antecedent/controller (e.g. Peškovskij(1956), Timberlake(1980.b)), reference conditions on reflexivization (e.g. Timberlake(1980.a)) and constructions in which *svoj* occurs (e.g. Padučeva(1985)). Ideally, the findings from these studies will be confirmed by the semantic analysis of *svoj* in this paper.

1. *USAGE OF* svoj

The general rule, to be found in numerous textbooks, says that one has the option of using either *svoj* or *moj* 'my', *tvoj* 'your sg.', *naš* 'our', *vaš* 'your plur.' in the case of a first/second person antecedent in the same clause, and that *svoj* is obligatory in the case of a third person antecedent in the same clause; e.g. (from Tauscher,Kirschbaum(1974:224-25)):

(1) *ja$_i$ vižu svoju$_i$/moju$_i$ mat'*
     'I see my mother'

(2) *ty$_i$ vidiš' svoju$_i$/tvoju$_i$ mat'*
     'you see your mother'

(3) *on$_i$ vidit svoju$_i$/*ego$_i$ (ego$_j$) mat'*
     'he sees his mother'

Of course, optionality does not necessarily mean that it does not matter whether one opts for *svoj* or *moj*, etc. As Padučeva(1985:181) puts it:

> (...) there are numerous contexts in which reflexivization is not obligatory and where one may notice - although sometimes only with great effort - differences of a semantic nature or other between reflexive and personal pronouns:
> (4) *Ja ne xotel stanovit'sja obuzoj dlja moix (≠ svoix) roditelej.*
>   'I did not want to become a burden to my parents.'

Andreevskij(1973) offers a detailed analysis of many contrasting
sentences with first and second person antecedents, and presents a
great many of the subtle differences that Padučeva has in mind.
An examination of hundreds of pages of modern Russian makes it
clear that in sentences with first/second person antecedents, *svoj*
is given preference over personal possessives to a very high degree. Given the findings of Andreevskij (who scrutinized texts
mainly from the 19th century) and my own quantitative data for modern Russian, one can only conclude that first and second person
possessives are preferred over *svoj* only in case there is a special
reason for the speaker to highlight the role of the corresponding
first or second person entity.

Within the realm of first and second person antecedents, *svoj*
is more likely to occur with second person antecedents than with
first person antecedents; my own findings in this respect correspond to Unbegaun's opinion, quoted in Andreevskij(1973:3).

With third person antecedents *svoj* appears to be the only option. However, contrary to the general rule, there are contexts
where a paradigmatic opposition of *svoj* and a third person possessive (*ego* 'his; its', *ee* 'her', *ix* 'their') is possible:

(5)   *Opjat' ètot Fernando s ego (≠ svoimi) večnymi kaprizami.*

      'Again that Fernando with his eternal caprices.' (Padučeva,1985:181)

(6)   *Soderžanie i forma, takim obrazom, suščestvujut v proizvedenii tol'ko v*
      ix (svoem) edinstve. (Herrmann,Boeck,1972:112)

      'Content and form, therefore, exist in a literary work only in their
      unity.'

By the way, Herrmann,Boeck(1972) contains a good many sentences of
the same type as (6) in which the anti-normative personal possessive appears to have replaced *svoj*.

Examples with third person possessives (instead of *svoj*) provided in Yokoyama,Klenin(1976) such as:

(7)   *Emu odnomu, predsedatelju, dostovalos' ot semenovodki. Ona soznavala*
      pročnoe ee položenie v kolxoze i komandavala pravleniem.

      'Only he, the chairman, had to take so much guff from the (female) seed
      specialist. She was conscious of her firm position in the collective farm
      and took charge of running it.'

(8)   *Ètot rastjapa poterjal ego košelek.*

      'That muddler dropped his wallet.'

are not considered impeccable Russian by Padučeva(1985:205).

Bolla,Pall,Papp(1970) points out the paradigmatic opposition
in headings of the following structure: Noun$_i$ s Possessive$_i$ Noun:
(9) *Čelovek so svoim trudom* (:322)
   'Man and his work'
Personal possessives are, however, preferred by far in this type of
context.

Given the above, one can but conclude that paradigmatic opposition of *svoj* and *ego, ee, ix* in sentences with a third person antecedent is a rare phenomenon. Both Padučeva(1985) and Herrmann,
Boeck(1972) are of the opinion that the option of *svoj* or *ego, ee, ix*
influences the content of the utterances in which they occur.

In this paper I will not be dealing with the opposition "*svoj*
vs. third person possessive", but will confine myself to the use of
svoj with first and second person antecedents. Nevertheless, my
findings must be relevant to the use of *svoj* with third person
antecedents as well.

2.   *THE MEANING OF* svoj
When *svoj* is used as an adnominal adjective it qualifies the
referent of the noun it modifies. Its meaning runs as follows:
   'being somehow related to THE prominent entity (or entities)
   referred to (or implied) by the context of the same clause'.
In this definition
- "somehow related" stands for any conceivable relation, not only
  for a possessive relation in the strict sense of the word;
- "THE" is an abbreviation for "which is most likely to be meant by
  the speaker, considering the context and the speech situation"
  (cf. Ebeling 1978:97). THE has been included on this place in the
  definition in order to cope with the situation where two or more
  entities are possible antecedents for *svoj* as in
  (10) *Murak$_i$ dolžen priznat' prava danirejcev$_j$ na svoe$_{ij}$ gosudarstvo* (Paduče-
        va,1985:197)
        'Murak must recognise the rights of the D's to his/their own state'
- "prominent" stands for the main participant in the situation referred to (for more details about the antecedent, see Padučeva
  (1985));
- the alternative "entities" copes with plural antecedents;
- the alternative "implied by" copes with cases in which no explic-

it antecedent is present such as in

(11) *S butylkoj iz-pod moloka izvestno čto delat' - sdat' ee i polučit'
obratno svoi pjatnadcat' kopeek.* (LitGazeta,8.V.1983)

'It is well-known what can be done with a milk-bottle - to return it and get back one's fifteen kopecks.'

A simple paraphrase of the meaning of *svoj* is "not somebody else's".

The meaning of *moj* (and m.m. of the other personal possessives) is:

'being somehow related to THE first-person-singular entity'.
The most striking difference between the meaning of the reflexive and the personal possessive pronoun appears in the way they qualify their head noun: with *moj* , etc. the speaker gives a straightforward qualification of the referent of the head noun by relating it to (a) participant(s) of the speech situation (i.e. to the speaker, the addressee, etc.) or a thing conjured up by the context. With *svoj* the speaker gives the instruction to stay, as it were, within the narrow context of his own words and to "continue" the reference to a prominent entity which is mentioned or implied by the context. In short, *svoj* has anaphoric qualities, *moj*, etc. has deictic qualities.

3. *INTERPRETATIONS OF THE MEANING OF* svoj

In this section I will try to show the relation between the invariant meaning of *svoj* (and *moj* , etc.) on the one hand and concrete interpretations (or types of interpretations) this meaning receives in usage on the other hand. I will be dealing mainly with Andreevskij(1973)'s observations concerning sentences with first and second person antecedents.

The majority of Andreevskij's interpretations can be summarized as follows:

stressing of the particular impact THE first/second-person--singular/plural entity has in or with respect to the noun--referent

for personal possessives, and the absence of such stressing for *svoj* : *svoj* only means that the noun-referent is not related to somebody other than the prominent entity.

This general characteristic manifests itself in a number of interpretations:

a. By his explicit reference to a first/second person referent the speaker conveys his subjective, emotional attitude towards the noun phrase referent. In the case of a first person antecedent, the speaker himself is emotionally involved; with a second person antecedent the speaker expresses his feelings about that second person's involvement. These feelings may be positive (in (12) the noun phrase referent is "beloved") or negative (in (13) the speaker may express a certain degree of disdain with respect to the addressee's shop):

(12) *I ja, kak vesnu čelovečestva, Roždennuju v trudax i v boju, Poju moe otečestvo, Respubliku moju.* (:4 (Majakovskij))

'And I sing my fatherland, my republic, like the springtime of mankind, born in labor and in battle.'

(13) *Skoro ty otkroeš' tvoju modnuju lavočku?* (:5)

'Will you soon open that mod-shop of yours?'

Replacing *tvoju* in (13) by *svoju* results in a more objective account on the addressee's shop.

Personal involvement may also manifest itself in personally experienced emotions:

(14) *Ja poselilsja v otele slučajno, v marte, posle moej tragedii, menja ostavila moja žena Elena.* (Limonov:9)

'I took up residence in this hotel by chance, in march, after my tragedy, my wife Elena had left me.'

(In (14) the word *tragedija* indicates that the personal emotion is a negative one).

With respect to (15) Andreevskij(:7) remarks that the speaker talks about his property as "about a thing which is usually called a property":

(15) *Ja do six por ee ljublju ... i otdal svoe imuščestvo ...*

'I do still love her ... and I would give away my property ...'

In a similar way *svoe delo* in (16) can be interpreted as "that what is for you your job":

(16) *Ja ponimaju, čto ty na rabote i delaeš' svoe delo.* (Neznanskij,Topol': 256)

'I understand that you are at work now and that you are doing your job.'

and *svoi žizni* and *svoi groby* in (17) as "what happened/will happen to be our lives/our coffins":

(17) *My prožili svoi žizni tak glupo ... Kogda my budem počivat' v svoix grobax ...* (Andreevskij:8)

'We lived our lives in such a stupid manner ... When we will rest in our coffins ...'

In many cases the "natural" relationship between things and human beings is not such that any personal involvement or characterization is to be expected. Therefore, *svoj* is used with the noun referring to the place you are supposed to occupy, the air plane ticket you just bought, the bag you have in your hand, the shirt you are wearing, etc.etc.:

(18) *Kogda rasdastsja zvonok, zajmite svoi mesta, každyj u svoego stolba.* (Yokoyama,Klenin,1976:263)

   'When the bell rings, take up your positions, each one at his own post'

(19) *Ja vzjal so stojki svoj bilet ...* (Neznanskij,Topol':260)

   'I took my ticket from the desk ...'

(20) *Ja proveril dokumenty v svoej ... sumočke, ...* (Neznanskij,Topol':92)

   'I checked my documents in my hand bag, ...'

(21) *... i kuskom svoej rubaxi (ja) stal vytirat' emu krov' s lica.* (Neznanskij,Topol':82)

   '... and with a piece of my shirt I started to wipe off the blood from his face.'

If, however, reference is made to loved one's, then the use of personal possessives can be expected:

(22) *U menja v kvartire nad pis'mennym stolom tože visit foto moego dvenadcatiletnego Antoški ...* (Neznanskij,Topol':94)

   'In my appartment there is a picture of my 12-year old son Antoshka on the wall above my desk ...'

(23) *I vot Morjana - tak ja zval ... moju morskuju ljubovnicu - stala ...* (Neznanskij,Topol':98)

   'And so Morjana- that's how I called my lover-from-the-sea - became ...'

b. By relating an entity to a concrete first/second person referent (by means of personal possessives) this entity is conceived as "really existing" or at least as "existing in the form of a definite plan". *Svoj* on the other hand does not presuppose or suggest existence nor definiteness of the entity:

(24) *Ne smeju moego suždenija imet'* (Andreevskij:6)

   'I don't dare to have this opinion of mine'

(25) *Ne smeju svoego suždenija imet'* (ditto)

   'I don't dare to have an opinion of my own'

The same applies to (26):

(26) *Sovetuju vpred' byt' ostorožnee v svoix donosax.* (Andreevskij:5)

'I advice you to be more careful in the future with your denuncia-
tions.'

c. Related to b is the effect of "(thought of as) separately/inde-
pendently existing" for personal possessives versus "being a
part of the antecedent" for *svoj* :

(27) ... *a ja vytiral svoe lico o ego sviter.* (Neznanskij,Topol':82)

'... and I rubbed my face dry on his sweater.'

(28) *Naprjagite svoi mozgi i ...* (Neznanskij,Topol':267)

'Cudgel your brains and ...'

(29) ..., *ja žizn' svoju gotov otdat' za tebja ...* (Turgenev:268)

'..., I am ready to give my life because of you ...'

With respect to (30) Yokoyama,Klenin(1976:260) remarks that

replacing *svoi* by *moi* produces a slightly ludicrous effect:
one imagines the speaker with a bag of physical and moral
possibilities of uncertain weight, which he takes off to a
scale to get weighed.

(30) *Vzvesiv svoi fizičeskie i moral'nye vozmožnosti, ja srazu ponjal, čto
v kafe mne ne probit'sja.*

'Weighing my physical and moral possibilities, I immediately understood
that I wasn't going to make it to the cafe.'

d. Related to b is also the effect of talking about competence (
with *svoj*) versus concrete actions (with personal possessives):

(31) *Ja svoe delo znaju.* (Andreevskij:5)

'I know what I have to do.'

(32) *Ja moe delo znaju.* (ditto)

'I know what I am doing.'

e. *Svoj* may signal passive (object-like) involvement in an action
whereas *moj*, etc. rather stresses active involvement:

(33) *Rugaj menja, ja sam kljanu svoe roždenie.* (Andreevskij:7)

'Curse me, I myself curse the fact that I was born.'

(34) *Rugaj menja, ja sam kljanu moe roždenie.* (ditto)

'Curse me, I myself curse what I have created.'

f. *Svoj* may be used in a static record, whereas personal possessives
give the impression of dynamism, change:

(35) *Ty govoriš' o svoej molodosti ...* (Andreevskij:7)

'You are talking about the fact that you are so young ...'

(36) *Ty govoriš' o tvoej molodosti ...* (ditto)

'You are talking about the time when you were young ...'

(37)   ... č'i imena byli znakomy mne po cirkovym afišam vremen moej molodosti, ... (Neznanskij,Topol':73)

'... whose names I knew from the circus-posters from the time when I
was young, ...'

g. Personal possessives may signal the particular way in which an
individual experiences his emotions or the particular character
of these emotions, whereas *svoj* is more neutral in this respect:

(38)   Čem mogu iz"javit' vam svoju blagodarnost'! (Andreevskij:6)

'How should I express to you my gratitude!'

As Andreevskij says, the use of *moj* in (38) would lead to an inappropriate utterance since its submissive tone would be im-
paired by stressing the highly personal character of the
speaker's gratitude.

If the speaker has reason to stress the individual character of his emotion he will prefer to use the personal possessive:

(39)   Pozvol'te, sudarynja, iz"javit' vam moju radost'. (Andreevskij:5)

'Allow me, Madam, to express to you my gladness (=how glad I am).'

(40)   Pozvol'te, sudarynja, iz"javit' van svoju radost'.(ditto)

'Allow me, Madam, to express to you my gladness (=that I am glad).'

In the context of (39-40), *svoj* is less appropriate than *moj*.

Observations made by other linguists reflect the same general
strategy with respect to the use of *svoj* and personal possessives
as has become clear from the discussion on Andreevskij(1973):

h. According to Barnetová,...(1979:355) (41) is preferred to (42):

(41)   Peredajte privet vašej žene.

'Give my love to your wife.'

(42)   Peredajte privet svoej žene.

'ditto'

If we compare this with (43), taken from Yokoyama,Klenin(1976:
266), we can understand why (42) is inappropriate:

(43)   Ljubi bližnego svoego!

'Love thy neighbor!'

(43) means 'Love thy neighbor, whoever he may be'; if (42) is
interpreted in a similar way, it would convey 'Give my love to
your wife, whoever she may be'. For several reasons this is an
inappropriate message: it is very unlikely that somebody would

ask to give his love to someone whose identity he does not know
or about whose identity he does not care. Moreover, it sounds
rather impolite to characterize the wife at issue as "the implied subject's wife" instead of "your wife, (dear) addressee",
or as "the person who is a wife for you".

The interpretation of (43) as a general command can be explained by the fact that the meaning of *svoj* does not contribute
a great deal to the definiteness of the noun; personal possessives, on the other hand, do contribute to definiteness by their
very reference to a concrete first/second person entity.

i. In (44) and (45) which are frequently used in Soviet newspapers,
the use of *svoj* is impossible according to Yokoyama,Klenin(1976:
267) "because the whole purpose of using such a sentence at all
is to create a sense of warmth and intimacy between the individual readers and their loving editors."

(44) *My teper' otvečaem našim čitateljam.*

     'We now answer our readers.'

(45) *My obraščaemsja k našim čitateljam.*

     'We turn to our readers.'

There may be another reason for the use of *naš* here. The performative character of (44) and (45) suggests a concrete dialogue between editors and readers. In that context, where
speaker and listeners are both present, it is rather clumsy to
use *svoj* for the result would be a description of the addressee
as somebody who is related to the referent of the subject of
the sentence, which happens to be the speaker himself; the use
of *naš* expresses the direct relationship between speaker and addressee in a straightforward manner. Compare, for the same effect, (46) and (47) which are performative sentences too:

(46) *I am asking you (,my dear,) to join me.*

(47) ?*I am asking my wife to join me.*

j. Especially with respect to sentences referring to the past and
containing a first or second person subject Yokoyama,Klenin
(1976) states that the use of *svoj* can reflect the intention of
the speaker to differentiate between the speaker (or the addressee) in the hic et nunc speech situation and the same person in
the past:

(48) *Na ètom otryvke iz Fausta na odnoj iz svoix dovoennyx lekcij ... ja razvil èlegičeskuju ideju, čto ...* (Solženicyn)

'On the basis of this excerpt from *Faust* at one of my prewar lectures ... I developed the elegiac idea that ...'

(49) *... Nedavno ja razobral svoj arxiv tex let. ...* (LitGazeta)

'... Recently I sorted out my archives of those years. ...'

In (48) reference is made to "me" in the prewar period (in distinction to "me" as the speaker of the sentence) and in (49) to "me" as a former archivist.

It is clear that the meaning of *svoj* lends itself very well to this "split personality" interpretation.

No discussion on *svoj* is complete without Peškovskij's famous example from *Boris Godunov*:

(50) *Kto ni umret, ja vsex ubijca tajnyj: Ja uskoril Feodora končinu, Ja otravil svoju sestru caricu, Monaxinu smirennuju ... vse ja!*

'No matter who dies, I am the secret murderer of everyone: I hastened Feodor's demise, I poisoned my sister the carica, The meek nun ... I (do it) all!'

Yokoyama,Klenin(1976) convincingly explains the use of *svoj* in (50) as another case of the "split personality" interpretation. Here, however, the split is not temporal but a matter of perspective: the speaker makes a difference between "me as I know myself" and "me as other people think about me", or "me from my own point of view" and "me as viewed by other people".

k. In (51), (52) and (53) the use of *svoj* produces an effect of psychological withdrawal on the part of the speaker from the world of his interlocutor, or even contempt for it:

(51) *Ešče raz skažeš' mne "ty" - sovsem golovu otorvu. Ponjal? V svoej Moskve budeš' narkotiki prodavat'. Ne u nas!* (Neznanskij,Topol':79)

'If you dare to be familiar with me once more, I will cut off your head. Is that clear? You sell your drugs in that Moscow of yours. But not here!'

(52) *Ty soveršenno sdurel na svoem Kavkaze.* (Neznanskij,Topol':120)

'You have gone completely mad in that Caucasus of yours.'

(53) *Plevat' mne na nego! Xoroniš' svoego djad'ku - xoroni sebe, mne èto do lampočki, ...* (Neznanskij,Topol':24)

'I don't care a rap about him: if you are going to bury that dear uncle of yours, please go ahead, I don't care a damn, ...'

As is always the case with *svoj*, this effect is caused by the reference to the antecedent instead of to the addressee.

1. Finally, I will deal with an effect ascribed to *svoj* versus personal possessives which is different from the effects discussed above, namely distributive versus collective (or shared) possession, see Yokoyama,Klenin(1976:261-65), Timberlake(1980.a:788-
-90), Padučeva(1985:205).

I do not consider distributive versus collective possession a direct consequence of the meaning of *svoj* vs. *moj,* etc., but rather an interpretation based on knowledge of the world, and enhanced by grammatical plurality/singularity of the possessed object, since noun phrases without a possessive pronoun can undergo the same kind of interpretation, and for many noun phrases with a possessive pronoun it is uncertain how they should be interpreted with respect to the way their referents are possessed: distributively, collectively or somewhere between these two poles:

(54) *Nikto iz nix, daže ètot Fulevyj, ne podnjalsja pomoč' svoemu sokamer-*
     niku, ... (Neznanskij ,Topol':81)

     'None of them, even not that Fulevyj, raised a finger to help their
     cell-mate, ...'

(55) *Čerez minutu, peregorodiv svoimi mašinami dviženie na šosse, my po-*
     stavili ix tak, čtoby ... (Neznanskij,Topol':110)

     'A moment after we blocked the traffic on the road with our cars, we
     put them so that ...'

(56) *... my ... , pomnja o svoix resursax, zakazyvaem oficiantku.* (Neznan-
     skij,Topol':138)

     '... remembering the state of our finances, we asked for the waitress.'

(57) *A to kak v CK dokladyvat'? Čto my v svoej strane čeloveka najti ne*
     možem? (Neznanskij,Topol':147)

     'What should we report to the Central Committee in that case? That we
     are unable to catch a man in our own country?'

4.   *CONCLUSION*

The meaning of the deictic personal possessives contains a straightforward cue to the "possessor"; the anaphoric reflexive possessive refers to the "possessor" in a roundabout or implicit way by telling the hearer that he will undoubtedly find the possessor in the immediate context. This indirect reference makes it possible for the speaker to differentiate between the possessor as a being in the hic et nunc world (the speech situation) and the pos-

sessor as projected in the mind of the speaker. As projected pos-
sessors, first and second person antecedents lose their first and
second person (situational) roles, and become objects not unlike
third person objects. As a consequence, it is not surprising that
second person antecedents are still easier to conceive as objects
than first person antecedents (and that *svoj* occurs more frequently
with second than with first person antecedents), since objectification presupposes some psychological distance; this attitude is more
likely to occur when a speaker is talking about his interlocutor
than when he is talking about himself. Personal possessives are
used when objectification (by *svoj*) would be inappropriate given
the personal involvement of the antecedent.

University of Amsterdam

REFERENCES

Andreevskij, A.V.
1973   "K upotrebleniju mestoimenija *svoj* v russkom jazyke", *Russian Lan-
          guage Journal* Vol.XXVII, 98, 1-17.
Barnetová, V. and others
1979   *Russkaja Grammatika I*. Praha.
Bílý, M.
1978   "Reflexives and the subjective ('empathic') side of FSP", *Papers
          from the Fourth Scandinavian Conference of Linguistics. Hindsgavl,
          January 6-8,1978*. Odense. 227-233.
Bolla, K., Pall, É., Papp, F.
1970   *Kurs sovremennogo russkogo jazyka*. Budapest.
Borras, F.M., Christian, R.F.
1971   *Russian Syntax. Aspects of Moders Russian Syntax and Vocabulary*.
          Oxford. (Second edition).
Ebeling, C.L.
1978   *Syntax and Semantics. A Taxonomic Approach*. Leiden.
Herrmann, J., Boeck, W.
1972   "Zu besonderen Gebrauchsweisen der Possessivpronomen *svoj* und *ego*
          im wissenschaftlichen Stil der russischen Gegenwartssprache",
          Wiss. Z. Univ. Halle XXI'72 G, H.5, 111-12.
Isačenko, A.V.
1962   *Die russische Sprache der Gegenwart. Teil I. Formenlehre*. Halle.
Padučeva, E.V.
1985   *Vyskazyvanie i ego sootnesennost' s dejstvitel'nost'ju*. Moskva.
Peškovskij, A.M.
1956   *Russkij sintaksis v naučnom osveščenii*. Moskva.
Tauscher, E., Kirschbaum, E.-G.
1974   *Grammatik der russischen Sprache*. Düsseldorf.
Timberlake, A.
1980a   "Reference conditions on Russian reflexivization", *Language* 56,
          777-96.

248

Timberlake, A.
  1980   "Oblique control of Russian reflexivization", in Chvany, C.V. and
            Brecht, R.D. (eds.) *Morphosyntax in Slavic*. Columbus. 235-59.
Tixonov, A.N.
  1985   *Slovoobrazovatel'nyj slovar' russkogo jazyka. Tom II*. Moskva.
Veyrenc, J.
  1980   "Coréférence, emphase et réflexivité", in Veyrenc, J. *Études sur
            le verbe russe*. Paris. 282-95.
Yokoyama, O.T., Klenin, E.
  1976   "The semantics of 'optional' rules: Russian personal and reflex-
            ive possessives", in Matejka, L. (ed.) *Sound, Sign and Meaning*.
            Quinquagenary of the Prague Linguistic Circle. Michigan Slavic
            Contributions no.6. 249-70.

SOURCES

Limonov, É.
  1979   *Éto ja - Édička*. New York.
Neznanskij, F. i Topol', É.
  1981   *Žurnalist dlja Brežneva ili smertel'nye igry. Detektiv*. Frankfurt/
            Main.
Turgenev, I.S.
  1981   *Nakanune*, in *Polnoe sobranie sočinenij i pisem v dvenadcati tomax.
            Tom VI*. Moskva.

ON RUSSIAN PREPOSITIONAL *BLAGODARJA*

H.P. HOUTZAGERS

"Видно тебе не довольно, что я,
благодаря тебя, ранен..."
А.С. Пушкин, "Капитанская дочка"

"...и знаком ей благодарил."
М.Ю. Лермонтов, "Кавказский пленник"

1. *INTRODUCTION*

1.1 In grammars and dictionaries of Russian[1] the form *blagodarja*
is usually regarded as representing two homonyms:
-The gerund of the verb *blagodarit'* 'thank'. Like all other forms
of *blagodarit'*, the gerund *blagodarja* takes complements in the
accusative case. Example:

> *Blagodarja sestru za podarok, on poceloval eë*
>
> thanking sister [acc.] for present he kissed her
>
> 'Thanking his sister for the present, he kissed her'

Cf. with past tense of *blagodarit'*:

> *On blagodaril sestru za podarok*
>
> he thanked sister [acc.] for present
>
> 'He thanked his sister for the present'

-A preposition which has the meaning 'thanks to' and governs the
dative case. Example:

> *Blagodarja sestre, on znaet francuzskij jazyk*
>
> thanks to sister [dat.] he knows French language
>
> 'Thanks to his sister, he knows French'

In the following I shall refer to the former homonym as 'the ger-
und *blagodarja*', and to the latter, which will be the subject of
the present article, as either '*blagodarja*+D' ('D' stands for
'dative') or 'prepositional *blagodarja*'.

250

1.2 The 1984 issue of *Linguistics in the Netherlands* contains a
paper by Jan Odijk on *blagodarja*+D, in which he attempts:

'to give tentative answers to the following questions:
  (A) Why does the gerund blagodarja take an Accusative comple-
      ment?
  (B) Why does idiosyncratic blagodarja [my '*blagodarja*+D' or
      'prepositional *blagodarja*' HPH] take a Dative complement?
  (C) Why is there a difference in Case-assignment properties
      between these forms, although they have exactly the same
      form and are obviously both historically and synchroni-
      cally related?' (1984:139)

Odijk's theoretical framework is provided by Chomsky 1981 and
1970. To my mind, the analysis proposed by Odijk is in several
respects quite unsatisfactory. The present paper consists of a
detailed critique of Odijk 1984. In §2 the main points of his
article will be summarized. I shall do so by quoting the greater
part of it, leaving out passages of lesser importance. In §3 I
shall give my comment on each of these points, in such a way that
§3.1 refers to §2.1, §3.2 to §2.2, etc.

2.   MAIN POINTS OF ODIJK 1984

2.1 'The categorial status of idiosyncratic blagodarja.
Idiosyncratic blagodarja is classified in almost all traditional
Russian grammars and grammatical descriptions as a (deverbal)
preposition (cf. a.o. Vinogradov (1947), Isačenko (1975)). We will
argue against this hypothesis and show that it is an adverb (...)
Prepositions in Russian have the idiosyncratic property that they
require third person personal pronouns to be preceded by n when
they precede them. Thus the normal forms of the third person singular male personal pronouns are ego (acc,gen), emu (dat) and im
(instr), but a n must precede these pronouns when preceded by a
preposition, cf. (5) vs. (6)
    (5)a. Ona videla ego/*nego   (6)a. ot *ego/nego
          She saw him   from him
       b. Ona pomogala emu/*nemu   b. k *emu/nemu
          She helped him   towards him
       c. Ona zanimalas' im/*nim   c. s *im/nim
          She studied it   with him
(...) When tested after adverbs, we see that the n-form is ungrammatical in this position (8), and it is ungrammatical after
idiosyncratic blagodarja as well (9) (...)
    (8) lučše ego/*nego   (9) blagodarja emu/*nemu
        better him-gen   thanks to him-dat
        'better than him'   'thanks to him'   (...)
We conclude that idiosyncratic blagodarja is an adverb, not a
preposition. If it were, we would expect emu to be ungrammatical
and nemu to be grammatical after it' (1984:139-140)

2.2 'Chomsky (1981) proposes a Case Theory in which [-N]-catego-
ries (verbs, prepositions) are Case-assigners and [+N]-categories
(nouns, adjectives) are not. This seems to be falsified immediately
by Russian, where [+N]-categories can assign Case (...) let us
review Case-assignment by [+N]-categories. First, consider (12),
which illustrates patterns of Case-assignment by verbs:

(12) a. Nom   Kollektiv rabotaet   Collective works
     b. Gen   Bojat'sja odinočestva To fear loneliness
     c. Dat   Sočuvstvovat' drugu   To sympathize with a
                                                   friend
     d. Acc   Obrabotat' zemlju   To cultivate the land
     e. Instr Zanimat'sja fizikoj   To study physics

The subject of a sentence is usually in Nominative Case (12a).
Verbs can have complements in Genitive, Dative, Accusative or
Instrumental Case (12b-e). Then consider the nominalizations
related to these verbs, in (13):

(13) a. Gen   Rabota kollektiva   Work of the collective
     b. Gen   Bojazn' odinočestva   Fear for loneliness
     c. Dat   Sočuvstvie drugu   Sympathy for a friend
     d. Gen   Obrabotka zemli   Cultivation of the land
     e. Instr Zanjatija fizikoj   Study of physics

Notice that (13b,c,e) resemble the related verb qua Case. This is
the usual situation for Genitive, Dative and Instrumental Case.
In (13a,d) we observe that the Nominative of (12a) and the Accusative of (12d) are replaced by Genitive Case in the nominalization (...) We conclude that nouns in Russian can assign Case, albeit non-Nominative or -Accusative Case.
A similar phenomenon can be observed when we consider adjectives.
Adjectives can take Case marked complements, but not Nominatives
or Accusatives (...):

(15) a. Nom -----------
     b. Gen dostojnyj uvaženija   worthy respect
     c. Dat vernyj svoemu slovu   true to ones word
     d. Acc -----------
     e. Instr nedovol'nyj synom   dissatisfies with son

Hence we infer that

(16) [+N]-categories cannot assign Nominative or Accusative
     Case in Russian' (1984:140-141)

2.3 'Adverbs in Russian can assign Case, but not Nominative or
Accusative. On the basis of this fact we assume that adverbs are
[+N]-categories. Independent evidence for this assumption can be
obtained from data originally observed by Babby (1975), who no-
tices that [+N]-categories in Russian can be Case-marked, while
[-N]-categories cannot. The fact that adverbs in Russian can be
Case-marked is illustrated by čem-phrases (comparable to English
than NP), where čem NP can be replaced by a Genitive NP:

(19) a. On rabotaet lučše čem Ivan
        he works better than Ivan
        'He works better than Ivan'
     b. On rabotaet lučše Ivana
        he works better Ivan-gen
        'He works better than Ivan'

If čem is followed by an adverb, then the phrase čem adverb can

be replaced by the adverb in Genitive Case:
(20) a. On govorit bol'še cem obyčno
      He speaks more than usually
      'He speaks more than usually'
    b. On govorit bol'še obyčnogo
      He speaks more usually-Gen
      'He speaks more than usually'
Since only [+N]-categories can be Case-marked in Russian, we
conclude that adverbs belong to the [+N]-categories.' (1984:142)

2.4 'In this section we will assume a particular historical development of Russian (...) The gerund is an adverbial form, consisting of a verbal stem and an adverbial affix (...) Given the
productivity of gerund-formation, and given its formal and semantic transparency, we will assume that the verb and the gerund are
syntactically related. In (21) the dotted line indicates the
boundary between syntax and morphology, i.e. elements on or above
this line are visible to syntactic rules, elements below this
line are not.
(21)   Adv

              --V--------Adv-----syntax-morphology boundary
              blagodar'   -a
Notice that the V-node in (21) is visible in syntax, which implies that V governs its complements. In particular V can assign
Accusative Case to an object NP.
Part of our explanation will also be the assumption that Russian
went through two stages, where in stage I idiosyncratic
blagodarja did not yet exist. Only the gerund blagodarja existed
in this stage, and it had the structure of (21). At some point in
this stage blagodarja acquired its idiosyncratic meaning 'thanks
to' in addition to its regular meaning as a gerund. Of course, we
cannot say why blagodarja acquired the idiosyncratic meaning, how
it acquired it, or why this change happened at all. Assuming that
it did, however, a number of interesting questions arise to which
we do have a tentative answer. In particular one might ask how
this new idiosyncratic blagodarja is incorporated in an internal-
ized grammar in the next stage. Although formally related to the
verb blagodarit', the semantic relationship between these two is
not regular, but idiosyncratic, as formation of the new
blagodarja from a verb like blagodarit' is unproductive. These
properties suggest that idiosyncratic blagodarja is not syntactically, but morphologically related to the verb. To represent
this, we may assume structure (21), but the boundary between syntax and morphology has been shifted upwards, as indicated in (22):

(22)   --------Adv-----syntax-morphology boundary

              V   Adv
           blagodar' -a

We claim then that the gerund blagodarja is syntactically related
to the verb blagodarit', while idiosyncratic blagodarja is morphologically related to this verb.'(1984:142-143)

2.5 'Notice one result from the historical change described here.
In (21) the category V is visible in syntax, while in (22) this
category is not. A NP-complement to blagodarja in (21) can receive Case from V, in particular it can receive Accusative Case.
In (22), however, a NP-complement cannot receive Case from V
(since V is not visible in syntax), but only from the higher Adv-
node. Since adverbs in Russian are [+N]-categories, and given
generalization (16), a NP-complement in (22) cannot receive Accusative Case. We propose that the shift of the syntax-morphology
boundary is the reason why Accusative Case cannot be assigned by
idiosyncratic blagodarja.
Since every NP must have Case due to the Case Filter (cf. Chomsky
1981), this reanalysis can take place only if the complement-NP
of idiosyncratic blagodarja receives Case somehow, and as idiosyncratic blagodarja assigns Dative Case in Modern Russian, one
might ask how this is assigned and why particularly Dative Case
is assigned, and not some other. We can make two suggestions
here. First, it might be possible that Dative Case is the unmarked Case for adjectives and adverbs to assign, just as Accusative Case is the unmarked Case for verbs in Russian and Genitive Case is the unmarked Case for nouns. Some evidence for this
hypothesis can be found in the pair tošnit' (V: Accusative complement) vs. tošno (Adv: Dative complement), both meaning 'be
nauseated'. If this hypothesis is correct, then idiosyncratic
blagodarja will assign Dative Case automatically as soon as other
Case-assignment options are unavailable. A second possibility to
account for this Dative might follow from a theory of Inherent
Case. Inherent Case is assigned by some element if it is specified idiosyncratically to this effect. Although the type of Inherent Case must be specified for each individual Case-assigner,
all sorts of (sub)regularities can be found in this domain. A
theory of Inherent Case will capture these regularities and relate instances of assignment of a specific Case to semantic,
morphological and/or syntactic properties of the assigner. Given
the fact that an adjective like blagodarnyj 'grateful', which
shares many syntactic, semantic and morphological properties with
blagodarja, takes complements in Dative Case, it will come as no
surprise that idiosyncratic blagodarja also starts to assign
Dative Case.'(1984:143-144)

2.6 'Summary
In this paper we have given an account of the development of
blagodarja in Russian. By assuming that historical changes do
not develop arbitrarily, but are constrained by properties of
UG [Universal Grammar HPH] and by properties of language specific
grammars, we were able to give an account of the properties of
blagodarja in Modern Russian.' (1984:144)

3.   DISCUSSION OF ODIJK 1984

3.1 (ad §2.1)
     The assumption that *blagodarja*+D is an adverb is of crucial
importance for Odijk's analysis. Therefore one would expect that

the categorial status of *blagodarja*+D would be dealt with in a
sound and principled way. It is not, as we shall presently see.

3.1.1 Before turning to the test proposed by Odijk (henceforth
called '*n*-test'), let us have a closer look at the last sentence
of §2.1: 'We conclude that idiosyncratic *blagodarja* is an adverb,
not a preposition'. The inference made here is obviously invalid.
If the *n*-test makes it possible to decide whether or not a given
form is a preposition, then it follows from the examples in §2.1
that *blagodarja*+D is not a preposition, not that it is an adverb.
Why not some other part of speech, e.g. a verb? Though Odijk's
inadmissible inference would in itself be enough reason to lay
his paper aside altogether (remember that all further steps hang
on the hypothesis that *blagodarja*+D is an adverb), we shall not
do so. For the sake of the argument, I shall assume with Odijk
that other categories than prepositions and adverbs are excluded.

Odijk's discussion of the categorial status of *blagodarja*+D
starts from (at least) the following two assumptions:
a) the existence of the categories 'preposition' and 'adverb';
b) the validity of the *n*-test.

3.1.2 Ad a) It is well-known that in traditional grammars adverbs
constitute a morphologically and syntactically most heterogeneous
category. As Isačenko puts it:

'So gleicht denn der dem Adverb gewidmete Abschnitt mancher Grammatik einer Rumpelkammer, in die man alle Wörter steckt, mit
denen man nichts Rechtes anzufangen weiss.' (1968:176)

Forms traditionally called 'adverbs' show more dissimilarities
among themselves than common characteristics, and one even won-
ders if they have any common characteristic at all. Lyons is
probably right that

'it is doubtful whether any general theory of syntax would bring
together as members of the same syntactic class all the forms
that are traditionally described as "adverbs"' (1968:326)

As regards Chomsky 1981, to which Odijk refers as the theoretical framework within which he is working, nothing is said about
adverbs constituting a separate syntactic category (cf. also

Babby 1975:84). It is not clear whether Odijk wishes to bring together all traditional 'adverbs' as members of the same class,
but there can be no doubt about the following two points:
-he assumes, without any comment, a syntactic category 'adverb';
-he assigns to the category 'adverb' such forms as *tošno* (see
§2.5) and *blagodarja*+D, which are not (or not unanimously) regarded as adverbs in traditional grammars[2], therewith giving
Isačenko even more reason for his qualification 'Rumpelkammer'.
Why *tošno* should be an adverb is not told at all, in the case of
blagodarja+D, as we have seen, the only justification is that, in
Odijk's view, it is not a preposition. In this connection it is
worth noting that the internal unity of the category 'adverb' has
far-reaching consequences in Odijk's paper. To give only one example: in §2.3 Odijk's 'proof' that the adverb *obyčno* carries the
feature [+N] is used as 'independent evidence' for the hypothesis
that *blagodarja*+D is also [+N].

3.1.3 Ad a) and b) It is clear that if Odijk says that prepositions, in contradistinction to adverbs and other parts of speech,
have a certain 'idiosyncratic property', he must have some notion
of what prepositions are, and that notion must be independent of
the 'idiosyncratic property' referred to. Otherwise he would be
saying something like 'words that take *n*-forms can be distinguished from other words by their taking *n*-forms', which would be
an empty statement. In other words, even if one believes in the
validity of the *n*-test, the grammatical categories must be regarded as fundamentally different things, and the *n*-test as based
on a relatively superficial property of one of them. In view of
the importance for Odijk's analysis of the assumption that
blagodarja+D is not a preposition but an adverb, one would expect
him to justify his assumption in terms of fundamental properties
of adverbs and prepositions. One would wish to be given solid
reasons for believing that the distinction Odijk makes is not a
trivial one, i.e. that the *n*-test really distinguishes between
two grammatical categories and not merely between presence and
absence of *n*-epenthesis. The following questions could be asked
in this context:

-If the problem (sc. the distinction between prepositions and
adverbs) can be so easily solved, why did the traditional grammarians not do so?
-Could it be that they did not do so because, if they did, certain forms they regarded as prepositions would 'become adverbs'[3]
and vice versa[4]?
-If so, what happens on the adverb-side of the preposition-adverb
boundary in Odijk's theory? Is his definition of what adverbs are
loose (or empty) enough to accomodate forms having the syntactic
and semantic properties of prepositions (except the 'idiosyncratic' n-epenthesis)?

3.1.4 Ad b) The n-test is not reliable. Odijk himself clearly
illustrates this in a footnote (not quoted in §2):

'We must note that Hill (1977) observes adverbs taking n-forms in
substandard Russian. This fact does not affect our argument, however, since all these adverbs require Genitive Case. It reminds
one of 'adverbial prepositions', cf. the contrast between <u>mimo</u>
'along' (Genitive; n-form) vs. <u>soglasno</u> 'according to' (Dative;
no n-form). It appears that there is a special relation of an unclear nature between Genitive Case and n-forms.' (1984:144)

Thus: - n-forms occur also after other words than prepositions;
- sometimes the case assigned by the word preceding the n-
form is more important than the grammatical category to
which the word belongs.

Odijk's view that these facts do not 'affect his argument' seems
unjustified: it is evident that the n-epenthesis is a phenomenon
about which much is unexplained, and which itself would be an interesting subject of study. Using it as a key-stone for a theory
with far-reaching claims is highly inappropriate.

Odijk is right that there is 'a special relation of an unclear nature between the Genitive Case and n-forms'. Judging from
Hill's data on the history of Russian prepositions and the n-
epenthesis (1977), one might even consider the possibility that
since relatively recent times there has been a stronger relation
between the genitive and n-epenthesis than between prepositions
and n-epenthesis. From the earliest stages of Russian, forms
originally belonging to other grammatical categories have become
prepositions (in the 'traditional' sense). After a certain time

almost all these 'secondary prepositions' began to take *n*-forms
(in Hill's terminology:'made the transition from apparent to actual status'). However, Hill observes that

'THE LAST TIME A NON-GENITIVE-GOVERNING PREPOSITION MADE THE
TRANSITION FROM APPARENT TO ACTUAL STATUS WAS A CENTURY AGO (...)
(Compare this with the very large number of genitive-governing
prepositions which have made the transition in the same period).'
(1977:300, original capitals)

At the same time we see a growing tendency towards *n*-epenthesis
after comparative adverbs and adjectives, which assign the genitive case (Hill 1977:201-220). Given all this, it is doubtful
whether the fact that such words as *blagodarja*+D and *soglasno* do
not take *n*-forms has much significance, or rather, whether it
signifies what Odijk claims it does.

3.2 (ad §2.2)

It is questionable whether within the theories of Chomsky
1981 Odijk's examples (13)a-d contain any real instance of case-
assignment by nouns[5]. In (13)b, c and e, case is assigned by the
verb that is present in D-structure (cf. Chomsky 1981:51), in
(13)a and d the genitive is probably due to some general principle comparable to Chomsky's Genitive Rule and/or his of-insertion
(e.g. *John's reading the book*, *the city's destruction/destruction
of the city*; 1981:49-51). What remains to be explained, of
course, is that somewhere in the derivation of such sentences as
(13)d the accusative is blocked. Hence, Odijk's conclusion that
'nouns in Russian can assign Case, albeit non-Nominative or
-Accusative Case' lacks support. It is worth noting that, although Odijk is a generative grammarian, his reasoning is based
entirely on the comparison of surface structures, without reference to their derivation.

I have two further remarks on §2.2:
- 'This seems to be falsified...' (2nd sentence). This assertion
betrays careless reading on the part of Odijk. On page 50 Chomsky writes: 'In other languages [sc. than English HPH], categories other than [-N] are Case-assigners.'
- If (12)a *Kollektiv rabotaet* is an example of Case-assignment
by verbs (see however note 5), why not fill in (15)a by

devuška krasiva
girl beautiful
'the girl is beautiful'
(Note that the copula is not a full verb: Chomsky 1981:272; cf.
also Babby 1975:76ff.)

3.3 (ad §2.3)

In §2.2 Odijk concluded (as we have seen on highly questionable grounds) that [+N]-categories can assign case, but not nominative or accusative. In §2.3 he proceeds:

'Adverbs in Russian can assign Case, but not Nominative or Accusative. On the basis of this fact we assume that adverbs are
[+N]-categories'

Odijk's inference is of the following type:

tables have four legs
my dog has four legs
———————————————————
my dog is a table

Now the reader might object that Odijk lives in a world where the
only four-legged objects are tables, in other words that there
are only [+N]- and [-N]-labelled forms and that [-N] being excluded, adverbs must be [+N]. However, such is not the case:
Chomsky 1981 also allows for forms labelled [+V], without reference to the feature [±N] (p. 55). The purpose of my remark is not
to suggest that adverbs should be labelled [+V], but to show to
the reader the inaccurate reasoning which is so characteristic of
Odijk's article.

'Adverbs in Russian can assign Case, but not Nominative or
Accusative. On the basis of this fact...'. What fact? The only
examples of adverbs he has given us so far are *lučše* 'better' and
blagodarja+D, the categorial status of which is under discussion
in his paper. Apparently Odijk has not searched for adverbs with
accusative complements. However, under his strict definition of
prepositions (see §2.1), *blagodarja*+D is not the only form to
'become an adverb' because of the absence of *n*-epenthesis; so do
the other 'gerund prepositions', some of which take accusative
complements, e.g.[6]

259

nas bylo četvero, sčitaja ego/*nego i ego sestru
us [gen.] was four counting him [acc.] and his sister
[acc.]
'we were four, counting him and his sister'
Now let us take a look at the 'independent evidence' Odijk
gives. On the basis of the fact that the sentences *on govorit
bol'še čem obyčno* and *on govorit bol'še obyčnogo* are both correct
in Russian, he concludes that adverbs can be case-marked. I have
two remarks to make on this issue:
- The possibilities to replace *čem* + adverb by 'the adverb in the
Genitive Case' are very restricted in Russian. As a matter of
fact, I have tried in vain to find another pair of sentences of
the type presented by Odijk. In such sentences as
Ona poët krasivo a on bolee čem krasivo
She sings beautifully and he more than beautifully
On xorošo igraet a ona bolee čem xorošo
He well plays and she more than well
On často xodit v teatr a ona bolee čem často
He often goes to theatre and she more than often
replacement of *čem* + adverb by a corresponding genitive form was
not acceptable to my native informants.
- The fact that the sentences presented by Odijk are both grammatical in Russian does not imply that one is derived from the
other (remember that such pairs of sentences are rare). Why
should *obyčnogo* not be the genitive neuter singular of the adjective *obyčnyj*[7]? Consider the following examples, in which, in contradistinction to *obyčnyj-obyčno*, the adverb is not derived from
the adjectival stem:
on vygljadit lučše čem prežde
he looks better than before [adv.]
on vygljadit lučše prežnego
he looks better than previous [adj.gen.neutr.sing.]
on vygljadit lučše čem včera
he looks better than yesterday [adv.]
on vygljadit lučše včerašnego (colloquial)
he looks better than yesterday's [adj.gen.neutr.sing.]

I wish to stress that I am not aiming at refuting 'adventurous or bold ideas with unexplained data' (Chomsky 1982:45), but it is evident that saying 'If čem is followed by an adverb, then the phrase čem adverb can be replaced by the adverb in the Genitive Case' is obscuring the facts in an inadmissible way.

3.4 (ad §2.4)

Now that we are nearing the final part of Odijk's account, it is useful to return to the last of the three questions quoted in §1:

'(C) Why is there a difference in Case-assignment properties between these forms, although they have exactly the same form and are obviously both historically and synchronically related?'

I agree that the gerund *blagodarja* and *blagodarja*+D are obviously historically related. It would be too much of a coincidence if two homonyms with so similar meanings would have arisen independently of one another. But why are they 'obviously synchronically related'? Why should a synchronical grammar not accept two unrelated homonyms with an evident historical relationship? Must all historical relationships be accounted for in a synchronical grammar?

Even if we assume that both *blagodarja*s are synchronically related, the question remains strange, because Odijk, following Chomsky 1970, allows for a type of synchronical relatedness which he calls 'morphological relatedness' and which has no implication whatsoever for the syntactic environments in which the related forms may occur. So if we isolate the 'synchronic part' of Odijk's question (C), we see that 'why is there a difference in Case-assignment properties between these forms, although they have exactly the same form and are obviously synchronically related?' is answered by 'because synchronical relatedness does not necessarily say anything about case-assignment', which is rather an empty answer.

If we concentrate on the 'historical part' of Odijk's question (C), we see that 'why is there a difference in Case-assignment properties between these forms, although they have exactly the same form and are obviously historically related?' is an-

swered by: 'at some point in time *blagodarja* acquired its idiosyncratic meaning and the syntax-morphology boundary was shifted
upwards, so that idiosyncratic *blagodarja* and the verb
blagodarit' were no longer syntactically related'. The latter answer is less empty, but it is no more than a complicated way of
saying what everyone had already guessed: at some point in time
the gerund *blagodarja* acquired a 'second', idiosyncratic meaning,
so that then there were two homonyms *blagodarja*. The 'second',
idiosyncratic *blagodarja* became isolated from the paradigm of
blagodarit'.

3.5 (ad §2.5)

Since from a synchronical point of view *blagodarja*+D is not
in any non-empty sense a form of *blagodarit'*, it is not self-
evident that it should take the accusative case. On the other
hand, as I have shown in §3.3 (*ščitaja* 'counting' with accusative), there is also no a priori reason why it should *not* assign
the accusative (as a matter of fact, Hill (1977:221) and
Čerkasova (1964:232) observe that in past centuries it often
did[8]).

Let us assume for a moment that there is a special reason
why *blagodarja*+D should not assign the accusative case. Why does
it assign the dative? Odijk gives two suggestions. The first
('the dative is the unmarked case for adjectives and adverbs to
assign') is not sufficiently elaborated to say anything about it.
Remember that in the present discussion we have seen adjectives
and 'adverbs' with complements in all cases except the prepositional. Of course one can always call one of these cases 'unmarked' and the other ones 'marked'. It is not clear to me why
especially *tošno* and *tošnit'*, which appear in a very specific
and limited type of construction (see note 2), should be examples of 'unmarked' case-assignment[9]. The second suggestion ('inherent case') is a complicated way of saying that the case-
assignment of *blagodarja*+D could be idiosyncratic and that related words are known to have related idiosyncrasies, which is not
something new and for which we did not need the whole story about
[+N] and [-N].

Perhaps the most striking thing about Odijk's 'explanation' of the historical development of *blagodarja*+D is that no use whatsoever is made of historical data. I even doubt whether he gathered any such data, because if he had, the problems to be solved and the type of answer to be found in his paper would probably have been different. From easily accessible sources[10] he could have obtained the following information:

- In past centuries the verb *blagodarit'* has, at least for a certain period (late 18th and early 19th century), assigned both accusative and dative case. There has probably always been a statistical preference for the accusative. After approximately 1830, *blagodarit'* with dative case became obsolete.

- Prepositional *blagodarja* probably arose in the 18th century and was then predominantly used with the accusative. In the early 19th century use of the dative after prepositional *blagodarja* rapidly gained ground and after approximately 1830 prepositional *blagodarja* with accusative case became more and more rare.

Thus, the dative after *blagodarja*+D is not a total surprise and we do not have to discover new principles of universal grammar to account for it. Apparently in the early 19th century there was a tendency toward reducing the case-assignment possibilities after *blagodarit'* and *blagodarja* (cf.Čerkasova 1964:234). The question which remains to be answered is: why did, out of the two possibilities, prepositional *blagodarja* 'choose' the dative, whereas the verb *blagodarit'* 'chose' the accusative?

Although Odijk suggests that the crucial moment in the development of *blagodarja* is the moment when it acquired a second, 'idiosyncratic' meaning, the meaning of prepositional *blagodarja* does not play a central role in his explanation of the case assigned by it. Taking into account both the historical data and the difference in meaning between prepositional *blagodarja* and the verb *blagodarit'*, one can think of another type of explanation than the type of explanation (unsuccessfully) aimed at by Odijk. I shall give an example of such an explanation here, without claiming, however, that it is more than a reasonable guess. No reliable answer can be given without extensive study of the meaning of the cases, the development of case-assignment and the normative tendencies in the 18th and 19th centuries.

The semantic relation between prepositional *blagodarja* and its complement is different from that between *blagodarit'* and its complement. The complement of 'to thank' is, to witness the predominant use of the accusative through the ages, regarded as a direct object in Russian. The complement of prepositional *blagodarja*, however, is not 'someone being thanked', but a person or thing that is considered the cause of a pleasant or unpleasant event. It can be imagined that in the early 19th century, when prepositional *blagodarja* was still associated with the verb, and for that verb both case-assignment possibilities were still extant, prepositional *blagodarja* developed a preference for the case which did not have the meaning 'direct object'[11].

3.6 (ad §2.6)

As I have tried to show, the merits of Odijk's article must not be overestimated. Considering the title of the volume in which it was printed (*Linguistics in the Netherlands*), it is hardly a good advertisement for Dutch Slavistics and linguistics.

University of Groningen

NOTES

[1] E.g. Isačenko 1968, Švedova 1970, Tauscher-Kirschbaum 1980, Akademija Nauk SSSR 1981-84.
[2] The form *točno* appears in such sentences as
                    mne točno
                    I [dat.] sick
                    'I am sick'
About the categorial status of forms of this type discussion has been going on, according to Isačenko (1968:194), since Ščerba 1928. The form *blagodarja* +D is, as we know, almost always regarded as a preposition.
[3] E.g. *blagodarja*+D, *soglasno* 'according to', *podobno* 'like'.
[4] Comparative adverbs which sometimes take *n*-forms (cf. Hill 1977:201-220).
[5] Neither is (12)a an instance of case-assignment by a verb (cf. Chomsky 1981:52, 170, 259 ff.).
[6] I wish to thank Mrs. O.N. Heuvelman-Godovikova and Mr. A.V. Parchomov for giving their native speakers' judgments on the Russian sentences presented in the present section.

264

7   Babby, from whom Odijk takes his example, remarks that it cannot be mere
coincidence that in the English glosses *than usually* can be replaced by *than
usual* (1975:22).
8   Unfortunately, in Hill's and Čerkasova's examples the complements are always male persons, which in Russian have the same form for genitive and accusative.
9   In a footnote (not quoted in §2) Odijk himself explains *vidno* and *slyšno*
(exceptions to his assumption that adverbs cannot assign the accusative) by
the fact that *vidno* and *slyšno* appear in a 'special construction' (1984:144).
10 Akademija Nauk SSSR 1948-65, Akademija Nauk SSSR 1975-..., Sreznevskij
1956 (1906), Čerkasova 1964.
11 The difference with other 'gerund prepositions' as *sčitaja* is twofold:
-the complement of *sčitaja* is not wholly unlike a direct object: as in the
case of the verb itself, someone is 'being counted';
-the verb *sčitat'* never assigned any other case than the accusative to the
object being counted.

REFERENCES

Akademija Nauk SSSR
   1948-1965   *Slovar' sovremennogo russkogo literaturnogo jazyka*, Moskva.
   1975-   *Slovar' russkogo jazyka XI-XVII vv.*, Moskva.
   1981-1984   *Slovar' russkogo jazyka*, Moskva.
Babby, L.H.
   1975   *A Transformational Grammar of Russian Adjectives*, The Hague.
Čerkasova, E.T.
   1964   'Izmenenija v sostave predlogov', *Očerki po istoričeskoj
               grammatike russkogo literaturnogo jazyka XIX veka: Glagol,
               narečie, sojuzy* (red. V.V. Vinogradov), 225-276, Moskva.
Chomsky, N.
   1970   'Remarks on Nominalization', *Readings in English Transforma-
               tional Grammar* (eds. Jacobs R.A and Rosenbaum P.S.), 184-221,
               Waltham, Mass.
   1981   *Lectures on Government and Binding*, Dordrecht.
   1982   *The Generative Enterprise*, Dordrecht.
Hill, S.P.
   1977   *The N-Factor and Russian Prepositions*, The Hague.
Isačenko, A.V.
   1968   *Die russische Sprache der Gegenwart*, München.
   1975   *Die russische Sprache der Gegenwart*, München.
Lyons, J.
   1968   *Introduction to Theoretical Linguistics*, Cambridge.
Odijk, J.
   1984   'Blagodarja', *Linguistics in the Netherlands*,139-145,Dordrecht.
Sreznevskij, I.I.
   1955-1956   *Materialy dlja slovarja drevne-russkago jazyka*, Graz (reprint
               of 1893-1906, Peterburg).
Ščerba, L.V.
   1928   'O častjax reči v russkom jazyke', *Russkaja reč, Novaja serija
               II*, Leningrad.

Svedova, N.Ju.
   1970   *Grammatika sovremennogo russkogo literaturnogo jazyka*, Moskva.
Tauscher, E., Kirschbaum, E.G.
   1980   *Grammatik der russischen Sprache*, Düsseldorf.
Vinogradov, V.V.
   1947   *Russkij jazyk. Grammatičeskoe učenie o slove*, Moskva-Leningrad.

BETWEEN LINK AND NO LINK: OBSERVATIONS ON RUSSIAN <u>NE</u>

C.E. KEIJSPER

CONTENTS

CHAPTER 0

INTRODUCTION

Russian schoolchildren have to work their way through a large body of spelling exercises. One recurrent problem is the correct spelling of the negative particle *ne,* which must be written either as a separate word or as a part of a compound. For example: *ne pravda* (not the truth) versus *nepravda* (the not-truth, lie). A number of manuals for teachers attempt to explain the logic of current spelling conventions, and the issue is regularly discussed in the consultation section of language journals.

The mere existence of this practical problem throws suspicion on linguistic theories of negation which take it for granted that a sharp borderline exists between non-affixal (or syntactic) and affixal (or morphological) types of negation: the orthographic problem clearly points to a semantic problem here. And the latter becomes really interesting only at the point where spelling rules capitulate: combinations of *ne* plus verb. Whereas it is relatively easy to understand the semantic difference captured by the graphic distinction between, e.g., *ne pravda* and *nepravda,* all proposals

to express graphically a similar distinction in the case of *ne*
plus verb have been rejected; *ne* is written separately from a subsequent finite verb, irrespective of the semantic impact of the
combination, unless the verb does not occur without *ne-* (but see
4.2). This solution wisely protects children and their teachers
from additional frustrations and nervous breakdowns, but it ought
to be a challenge to linguists: why was it felt to be impossible
to arrive here at a semantically motivated rule for spelling?

The present paper explores this question, and a number of
related problems, in terms of the model of information structure
introduced in Keijsper 1985 (henceforth: K 1985). Chapter One below summarizes the features of this model which are relevant to
the issues at hand. The rest of the paper applies the model to
negative sentences; conversely, the discussion of negative sentences enables me to add some points to K 1985.

Chapter Two briefly gives some general basic information
about the functioning of *ne* in Russian. Most points are probably
redundant for Slavist readers, but I hope that such readers will
understand the necessity of restating well-known facts if a new
framework is being used.

Chapter Three examines a simple string of the form *ne - subject noun - verb*, with various accentuations and syntactic organizations. The string is simple in the sense that it allows only a
relatively small number of readings, once an accentuation has been
chosen.

Next, Chapter Four discusses the causes of the fact that the
number of readings increases if *ne* precedes the verb rather than
the subject. In so doing, the chapter explains why the spelling
problem has no real solution here. Also, the chapter calls attention to the fact that strings *adverb - ne - verb* correspond to at
least three different syntactic organizations. I hope that this
part of the reasoning contributes to bridging the gap which seemingly exists between information structure in my sense and problems of time and negation as traditionally studied by aspecto-
logists.

Finally, Chapter Five introduces three further points. First,
some examples are given of combinations of *vs-* (all) plus *ne* (in
this order); such combinations have two distinct readings, rough-

ly: "all - not" and "not - all". Secondly, the chapter explains why combinations of a negation and, e.g., *many*, have two readings: "less than many" and "the thing meant is a quantity other than many". The third point is about gradable adjectives.

The conclusion warns against a simplistic attempt to differentiate between morphological and syntactic types of negation.

The discussion in no way exhausts the problem of negation in Russian, but it hopefully provides a basis for further extensions.

As the reader will notice, my treatment of negation is quite different from traditional approaches. Basically, I hold the view that "ne" is a meaning like any other meaning which enters into various combinations. This view is diametrically opposed to the opinion that negation functions in the way a logical operator does. This difference has important consequences. For example, the question as to what is "the" negation of a given positive sentence has no role to play in my approach, although I recognize, of course, that "ne" has different effects in different constellations. Further, given the devices available for the analysis of accent and word order (K 1985), the notion "scope of negation", and the traditional distinction between "sentential" and "constituent" negation become redundant. In fact, I find these notions highly confusing, "scope of negation" because it ascribes to an innocent word what must in reality be ascribed to accents and their scope, and "sentential"/"constituent" negation because it draws a borderline which does not always correspond to the semantic distinction which is probably meant.

These fundamental differences ensure that discussing the literature on negation would be confusing rather than helpful here, so I leave this discussion for another occasion.

CHAPTER ONE:

SOME NOTIONS FROM INFORMATION STRUCTURE

1.1 Projection time

A speaker of a language X has at his disposal a permanent
stock of linguistic knowledge from which he draws when he utters a
sentence. The permanent stock of knowledge includes the meanings
of his language. Let me indicate these meanings by "a", "b", "c",
"d", etc.:

permanent stock of meanings   "a" "b" "c" "d" etc.

When the speaker utters the sentence *b d* he uses the meanings "b"
and "d" from this stock. The act of using a meaning may be compared
to making a photocopy of a picture: when we do so, we produce a
second picture, identical to the original one, but we do not de-
stroy the original picture, so that we can produce as many copies
as we wish. In the same way, a meaning does not disappear from our
permanent stock of knowledge when we use it in a given utterance.
I shall call the copies of meanings: "projections". Thus, when
uttering the sentence *b d,* a speaker copies the meanings "b" and
"d", so that he has the projections "b" and "d":

permanent stock of meanings   "a" "b" "c" "d" etc.
                                    | copying |
projections   "b"   "d"

Once we have acquired the meanings of our language, we have
them in mind until we die or become demented: our stock of meanings is timeless, as indicated by the term "permanent" used
above; all meanings are present constantly and simultaneously.
Projections, in contrast, are temporary phenomena: this moment we
have one thought, then we forget it and have another; projections
appear and disappear in time, they may follow one another or be
present simultaneously.
Projection time is the time in which projections exist.

1.2 *Accent; backward link*

A copying machine supplies a new piece of paper for every
copy we wish to make; if e.g. a whole book were copied on a single
piece of paper, the result would be incomprehensible. The flow of
projection time can be compared to this paper supply: every now
and then we need a new moment of projection time in order to put
into it the next chunk of information. The regulation of this flow,
i.e. the introduction of subsequent moments of projection time, is
basically effectuated by accents in the speech we utter. (But not
all accents introduce a new moment of projection time, and not all
moments of projection time are introduced by accents.)
The ability of an accent to introduce a new moment of projection
time is a consequence of its meaning, which is "not not". This
meaning cannot be used (copied) in isolation, just as an accent
(the corresponding form) cannot exist without something else which
carries the accent.
Let us assume that in our sentence, d is accented; this will be
indicated as: $\hat{d}$ ("^" = accent); our sentence is, then, $b\ \hat{d}$. The
combination of "not not" and "d" gives "not not d". The combination reads "not (not d)": the projection "d" combines with one part
of "not not" into "not d", and then this combination is negated,
the result being a new projection "d". This operation is capable of
introducing a new moment of projection time with respect to "b", as
indicated in the following diagram:

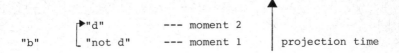

Here, the "d" in "not d" is the copy of the meaning "d"; the copy
of "not not" is the "not" in "not d" plus the upward arrow; the
"d" in moment 2 is the result of the operation:

The act of introducing moment 2 by negating "not d" may be compared to taking a new piece of paper for "d".

Since the following chapters will be about negation, it is
useful to keep in mind that during the procedure described, no
meaning "not d" from the permanent stock is copied. In fact, the
"not d" in "not (not d)" cannot be expressed in natural language:
"d" can be expressed, by *d*, "not not" can be expressed, by an
accent, but "not d" cannot be expressed; more specifically, it is
not the meaning of the English form *not d*. Moreover, "not not d"
simply states the above-mentioned procedure; it says "the negation
of the negation of d", or "$(d^{-1})^{-1}$", or "$\hat{d}$", or still another
formula in the language one uses for describing meanings. In contrast, the English word *not* is an element of a natural language
one may be describing. Thus, the present article is about Russian
ne; it is written in English; both Russian and English have the
meaning "^"/"$(\quad^{-1})^{-1}$"/"the negation of the negation"/"not not"/
etc.[1]

The effect of placing "d" in a new moment of projection time
with respect to "b" is that the information "d" is added to the
(already present) information "b", rather than the other way round.
This direction of adding "d" to "b" (rather than "b" to "d") I
call a "backward link":

This backward link may be compared to the usual procedure while photocopying: we copy "b" on one piece of paper, then "d" on the next piece of paper, and we pile the new piece of paper on top of the preceding one.

1.3 *Unaccented elements; forward link; scope*

Whereas accented elements can introduce new moments of projection time, unaccented elements are parasitic: they group with another element in some moment of projection time.
Suppose that our sentence is a $\hat{b}$ c $\hat{d}$, and that both $\hat{b}$ and $\hat{d}$ introduce new moments of projection time:

```
                    "d"          --- moment 3
      "b"           "not d"      --- moment 2   |projection time
    "not b"                      --- moment 1   |
```

In principle, unaccented elements may group with the positive or with the negative member of a pair "x"/"not x"; thus, in the example, with "b" or with "not b", and with "d" or with "not d". Let us assume that in the sentence a $\hat{b}$ c $\hat{d}$, "a" goes with "b", and "c" with "d": "a" is added to "b" in the moment defined by "b", and "c" is added to "d" in the moment defined by "d":

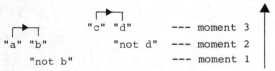

```
                    "c" "d"      --- moment 3
    "a" "b"             "not d"  --- moment 2
        "not b"                  --- moment 1
```

Here, "a" is linked forwards to "b", and "c" is linked forwards to "d": "a" goes with "b" which follows it in the sentence a $\hat{b}$ c $\hat{d}$, and "c" goes with "d" which follows "c". If "c" were grouped with "b", we would have a backward link, because "c" follows "b" in the speech chain:

```
        ┌─────◄─────┐        "d"        --- moment 3
  ...   "b"      "c"    "not d"        --- moment 2
        "not b"                        --- moment 1
```

If "a" groups with "b", and "c" with "d", the entire configuration
is:

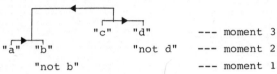

```
                        "c"    "d"      --- moment 3
  "a"    "b"                 "not d"    --- moment 2
        "not b"                         --- moment 1
```

Some terms which can be used to apply to this configuration are
the following:
Projection "a" concurs with "b", and "c" concurs with "d" (cf.
written on the same piece of paper). Further, *a* is included in the
scope of the accent on *b,* and *c* is included in the scope of the
accent on *d:* when "not b" is there (moment 1), "a" is absent, but
as soon as "b" is there (moment 2), "a" is also there; when "not
d" is there (moment 2), "c" is absent, but as soon as "d" is
there (moment 3), "c" is also there. The complexes "a b" and "c d"
are two chunks of information. For example: *My friend is ill* ("a"
= "my", "b" = "friend", "c" = "is", "d" = "ill").
Compare: *My friend is ill* (no accent on *d*):

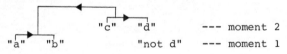

```
  "a"    "b"      "c"    "d"      --- moment 2
        "not b"                   --- moment 1
```

Here, the entire sentence is included in the scope of the accent
on *friend:* all unaccented elements concur with "b".
Further: *My friend is ill* (no accent on *b*):

```
                 "c"    "d"      --- moment 2
  "a"    "b"           "not d"   --- moment 1
```

Here, *is* is included in the scope of the accent on *ill* ("c" concurs with "d"); *my friend* is not included in the scope of the
accent on *ill:* "a" and "b" do not concur with "d" (but with "not d").

Finally: *My friend is ill:*

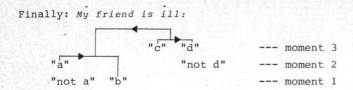

	"c" "d"	--- moment 3
"a"	"not d"	--- moment 2
"not a" "b"		--- moment 1

Here, *friend* is not included in the scope of the accent on *my:* "b"
does not concur with "a" but with "not a"; *is* is included in the
scope of the accent on *ill,* "c" concurring with "d".
In this way, the scope of an accent reflects the order of the projections involved in projection time. An element can only be included in the scope of an accent on an element to which it is
linked. The choice of link is not arbitrary (K 1985: 201-312).

1.4 *Coinciding and non-coinciding projections*

A normal copying machine has a button which we push when we
wish to make a copy of e.g. a picture. When we do so, a piece of
paper appears with a replica of the original picture. So far, we
have seen examples of this normal procedure. In e.g. *My friend is
ill* we have pushed the button twice, producing one piece of paper
with "my" and "friend" and one piece of paper with "is" and "ill";
in e.g. *My friend is ill,* we have pushed the button only once, the
result being one piece of paper with all information on it. Always,
a piece of paper appeared simultaneously with the picture reproduced on it.
In contrast to a normal copying machine, our mind is capable of
disassociating these two: we may produce a piece of paper first (a
moment of projection time), and, subsequently (in the next moment
of projection time), reproduce a meaning from our permanent stock.
Thus, two processes which normally go together, the act of producing a piece of paper and the act of reproducing a picture on it,
can follow each other in our mind. I call the normal case (two si-
multaneous processes): "coinciding projections"; the abnormal case
is called "non-coinciding projections".

The clean piece of paper which we separately produce in the non-coinciding case is a projection which has no formal correlate in
the sentence we utter; it is a non-linguistic perception of something, e.g. of an entity. Suppose, for example, that we know somebody called John. Normally, when we think of this person, we think
"John": the projection of the person and the projection "John" are
not distinguished. This is a case of coinciding projections. The
negation of "John", i.e. "not John", refers in this case to the
absence of the person:

```
┌►"person"            = "John"   ◄┐ --- moment 2
└ "absence of person" = "not John"┘ --- moment 1
```

However, when somebody points at a person he sees and asks who it
is, we first think of the person and then may identify him as John.
This is a case of non-coinciding projections, the projections "person" and "John" are disassociated, the former preceding the latter.
In this case the negation of "John", i.e. "not John", refers to
the absence of the property /John/ of the given person; the projection of the absence of the person per se already belongs to the
past:

```
                             "John"      ◄┐ --- moment 3
┌►"person without property /John/" = "not John"┘ --- moment 2
└ "absence of person"                          --- moment 1
```

Here, the projection "John" which follows "not John" fills in
the missing property of the person we are thinking of.
Non-coincidence of projections may also take the following form:

```
                             "John"    ◄┐ --- moment 3
┌►"group of persons minus John" = "not John"┘ --- moment 2
└ "absence of group of persons"             --- moment 1
```

Here, "John" fills in the person John who is missing among the
group of persons we are thinking of.
As can be seen in the diagrams, non-coinciding projections occupy
an additional moment of projection time, as compared with the corresponding coinciding case (in the example: 3 moments instead of 2).

Non-coincidence of projections plays an important role in
negative sentences, which, as is well-known, basically remove
something which is first thought to be present at least potentially. This basic idea consists of two steps (3 moments of projection
time), the first one introducing the thing involved, the second
one removing it again, either partially or entirely. Normally, the
first step already belongs to the past when the act of removal is
done; this is the so-called "presuppositional character" of negative sentences. The size of the thing which is removed varies. For
example, in *Ne Ivan čitaet* (Lit. Not John reads) (*ne/not* now being
the Russian/English word *ne/not*) we remove the property /Ivan/ of
the person who is reading but not the entire person. In *Ivan ne
čitaet* (Lit. John not reads), in contrast, we may remove the identifying property of the thing John is doing (what he is doing is
not reading but something else), but we may also remove his activity entirely (John's potential reading is absent). The interpretational possibilities are governed by a simple principle, which
will be stated in 4.1 below.

1.5   Figure/ground and part/whole organizations; attention; scope

The distinction between coinciding and non-coinciding projections enables us to describe, in terms of time and negation, some
linguistically relevant conceptual organizations which have to do
with attention. As mnemonic labels for the relevant organizations,
I use the terms figure/ground and part/whole. The terminological
distinction figure/ground is well-known from studies of visual
perception; the part/whole relation is the primitive notion of the
branch of logic called mereology.
   Looking at some picture illustrating the well-known phenomenon of figure/ground reversals, one may come to realize that the
perception of an element of such a picture as the figure equals
the idea that this element can be lifted up without affecting the
rest of the picture, and that, if we do so, the ground fills the
space which was occupied by the figure before we lifted it up. The
perception of an element as the ground equals the idea that, if we

lift up this element, the entire picture disappears. In other
words, we organize the picture to the effect that what we call
the figure is placed on top of what we call the ground. In terms
of projection time this says that the projection of the ground
precedes the projection of the figure:

	"figure"	= "ground plus figure"
"ground"	"not figure"	= "ground without figure"
"not ground"		= "absence of ground and figure"

↑ pro-jection time

A part/whole organization, in contrast, is the idea that, if we
remove the part, the rest of the whole remains, but without fill-
ing the space which was formerly occupied by the part (in contrast
to a ground):

	"part"	= "entire whole (in-cluding part)"
"whole minus part"	"not part"	= "whole without part"
"not whole"		= "absence of whole"

↑ pro-jection time

A part/whole organization results if we spread the perception of
one member of a figure/ground organization over two moments of
projection time. This spreading is the phenomenon of non-coinciding
projections introduced in 1.4 above.

We can now state the following about the person John example
of 1.4:
The person John is a figure in what may be called "the world"
("the scene", "the background", etc.); the world is the ground for
this figure. If the projections "person" and "John" are disassociated (non-coinciding projections, "spreading of perception"), it is
the person as such which is a figure in the world; the property
/John/ is a part of the person, the person being a whole. Thus,
"John" is a projection of a figure in the coinciding case (figure
= person = John; ground = world), and "John" is a projection of a
part in the non-coinciding case (part = /John/; whole = person and
figure = person; ground = world). The size of the part and of the
whole may vary; thus, on the level "group of persons", also given

in 1.4, the part is the person John, the whole is the group of
persons; this group is also a figure with respect to "the world".
The size of the combination can also be stated in terms of truth
(cf. 3.1, 4.1, 4.3 and 5.2 below).

This terminology is related to the notion of attention in
the following way. If the projections "person" and "John" coincide
("person" = "John" and "absence of person" = "not John"), the
accent on *John* focuses attention on the person John. Thus, I claim
that the act of focusing attention on the person John is the act
of negating a projection of the absence of this person John. If
the projections "person" and "John" do not coincide (if *John* fills
in a missing property of somebody we are thinking of) it is the
person as such which is the focus of attention. In other words, in
a figure/ground organization (here: ground = world; figure = person John), it is the figure which is the focus of attention. In a
part/whole organization (here: whole = person as such; part = property /John/ of this person, it is the whole which is the focus
of attention.

The issue as to what constitutes the focus of attention is
relevant, inter alia, because of its consequences for the scope of
accents. As we saw in 1.3, unaccented elements concur with some
other element in the moment of projection time defined by this
other element. Now, they concur, more specifically, with the
thought which refers to the focus of attention, i.e. with the
thought of the figure in a figure/ground combination, and with the
thought of the whole in a part/whole combination. For example, the
accent in *Ivan priechal* (John arrived) may include *priechal* in its
scope (cf. What happened?) because "Ivan" may refer to a figure
here (the person John). In contrast, the accent in *Ne Ivan
priechal* (not John arrived) does not include *priechal* in its scope
because "ne Ivan" does not refer to a figure here: we remove the
property /John/ of the person who arrived, which implies that the
person is construed as a whole and is the focus of attention (see
further Chapter Three).[2]
Further, in terms of attention, the step from *ne pravda* (not the
truth) to *nepravda* (the not-truth) consists in transferring the
focus of attention from the thing mistakenly referred to by

"pravda" to the thing referred to be "nepravda" (ibid.). Tragically, this transfer renders the combination positive. The following chapters discuss various strategies for precluding such a transfer, i.e. for ensuring that a *ne+x* combination remains negative.

In terms of a diagram of the type introduced earlier, the scope effect of non-coinciding projections is the "lowering" of a projection by one level. Consider our model-example *a b̂ c d̂*. We saw that e.g. "c" may group with "d":

$$\ldots \quad \overset{\longrightarrow}{\text{"c"} \quad \text{"d"}}$$
$$\text{"not d"}$$

This organization can occur only if "d" coincides with the non-linguistic perception of what it refers to, say with "p":

$$\ldots \quad \text{"c"} \quad \text{"d"} \quad = \text{"p"}$$
$$\text{"not d"} = \text{"absence of p"}$$

If "d" and "p" do not coincide, i.e. if the non-linguistic perception "p" precedes "d", "c" no longer concurs with "d" (but with "not d"), because it concurs with "p" (the whole):

$$\text{"d"}$$
$$\overset{\longrightarrow}{\text{"c"} \quad \text{"not d"} \quad \text{"p"}}$$
$$\text{"absence of p"}$$

Thus, although "c" is linked forwards here, it need not be included in the scope of the accent on *d* (it need not concur with "d"); it does so only if "d" coincides with "p". In either case, "c" concurs with "p": "c" is written on the piece of paper "p" also if the accent on *d*, which can in principle supply this piece of paper, fails to do so in the given case.[3]

1.6   Parallel link

The phenomenon of non-coinciding projections explained in the
foregoing affects one accent, more precisely the last accent; it
has consequences for the surrounding unaccented elements: these are
"lowered" by one level as compared with the corresponding coinciding case.

There is, in addition, an application of non-coinciding projections which affects two accents. It has the effect of "lowering"
some projection, say "x", as well as the negation, "not x". Just as
in the one-accent case, a non-linguistic projection "p" is involved.

Starting from a normal backward linking scheme, or from a normal forward linking scheme:

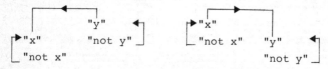

both "y" and "not y" (in the former case), or both "x" and "not x"
(in the latter case), may sometimes be lowered, so that "x" concurs
with "y" and "not x" with "not y"; a non-linguistic "p" precedes
"x" and "y":

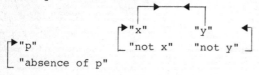

I call this configuration: "a parallel link"; its symbol is a
double arrow (see the diagram). It may be compared to taking a
piece of paper ("p") and, subsequently, putting both "x" and "y"
on this piece of paper (simultaneously). Projection "p" is a non-
linguistic thought of some state of affairs; it makes this state
of affairs the focus of attention; all other projections involved
in the sentence apply to that state of affairs.

The main field of application for parallel links is that of
negative sentences. Roughly, if one has the impression that a
negation occurring in a sentence "applies to" some element *x* while
the (surface) structure of the sentence says it belongs to an
accented element *y*, probably a parallel link is involved.

1.7 Concurrent and non-concurrent negation; word order

In all diagrams presented so far, a negation of some projection, say "not x", was written under the corresponding "x": "not
x" preceded "x" in projection time. Such a "not x" is a non-concurrent negation. A concurrent negation is a "not x" which belongs to the same moment of projection time as "x" itself:

```
      ┌──────────┐
      │          ▼               ┌──▶ "x"
   "not x"     "x"               │
                                 └── "not x"

   concurrent negation        non-concurrent negation
```

An accent which negates a concurrent negation is a "topic"-
accent, in one of the many senses of "topic"; an accent which
negates a non-concurrent negation is a "comment"-accent, in one of
the many senses of "comment". The semantic difference is the
following.
An accent negating a concurrent "not x" selects the referent of
"x" from among other referents, "not x" referring to the other
referents. An accent negating a non-concurrent "not x" negates a
projection of the absence of the referent of "x" among other referents, "not x" referring to the absence of the referent. Thus,
informally, and with an assertive type of last accent, a "topic"-
accent (concurrent negation) selects x (the referent) from among
the things in its environment; this implies that x was already
present in that environment (hence the association between "topic"
and "old information"). A "comment"-accent (non-concurrent negation) says that x is not absent in its environment, it adds, as it
were, x to its environment (hence the association between "comment"
and "new information").
    A negation of a non-concurrent negation is the basic type; it
is reinterpreted as a negation of a concurrent negation if the
meaning of word order excludes the basic interpretation. The technical details need not concern us here (see K 1985: 313 ff.); the
following example gives the main idea.

The sentence *Priechal prijâtel'* (Lit. Arrived friend) has the word
with the last accent *(prijatel')* in final position. The accent
here negates a non-concurrent negation, by virtue of the fact that
it is the last accent. Further, the meaning of word order ensures
that "not prijatel'" and "prijatel'" refer to the world of different moments: the accent introduces the friend against the background of the previous absence of the friend:

```
      ┌────────►
"priechal"  ┌►"prijatel'"      - "world at moment t₂"◄┐
            └─"not prijatel'" - "world at moment t₁"─┘
```

   Next, in *Prijâtel' priechal* (Lit. Friend arrived), the accent,
being the last one, also negates a non-concurrent negation. However, the meaning of word order ensures that "not prijatel'" and
"prijatel'" refer to the world of a single moment: the accent negates the absence of the friend in the world of a given moment,
the latter being given independently:

```
                        ┌──────────◄─────────┐
                        ├►"prijatel'"      "priechal"
 ┌►"world at moment t₂" - └─"not prijatel'"
 └  "world at moment t₁"
```

The difference is, essentially, identical to coinciding vs. non-
coinciding projections (see section 1.4 above). However, it does
not affect the scope of the accent on *prijatel'*: in both cases,
"priechal" may concur with "prijatel'". (The coincidence/non-
coincidence does not concern the level "person" or "group of persons", as it did in 1.4, but the level "world at moment t_x".)
   If we now add a second accent: *Prijâtel' priêchal* (Lit.
Friend arrived), the accent on *prijatel'* can no longer be interpreted as it is in *Prijâtel' priechal*: the accent on *priechal* ensures, given the backward link, that "not prijatel'" and
"prijatel'" refer in the same way as they did in *Priechal
prijâtel'*:

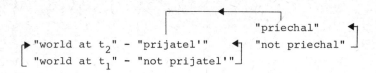

Thus, given an accent on *priechal*, the backward link has the
same effect on the interpretation of the accent on *prijatel'* as
word order had when *prijatel'* was the last word (in *Priechal
prijâtel'*). However, *prijatel'* is not the last word now, and the
meaning of word order says that it must have a negation belonging
to the same moment now. In *Prijâtel' priechal*, the "same moment"
prescribed by the meaning of word order was the same moment of
world-time (world at t_2), but in *Prijâtel' priêchal* this interpretation becomes impossible. We then give "prijatel'" a negation
in the same moment of projection time, i.e. a concurrent negation:

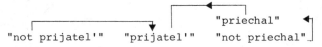

In this way, a negation of a non-concurrent negation is reinterpreted as a negation of a concurrent negation if a further accent
to the right makes it impossible to comply with the meaning of
word order in a different way.

The step from *Prijâtel' priechal* to *Prijâtel' priêchal* is
very important, inter alia for understanding negative sentences.
For example, whereas *Ne prijâtel' priechal* (Lit. Not frîend arrived) is a relatively simple sentence, we must take special measures for interpreting *Ne prijâtel' priêchal* (Lit. Not friend
arrived). In this case we must either combine "ne" with
"prijatel'" into the compound "neprijatel'" (a not-friend, an
enemy), or we must link "ne" to the entire combination of subject
and predicate:

Ne prijâtel' priêchal

This will be discussed in 3.2-3.5.

286

In addition to this case, which follows directly from K 1985, Chapter Four below introduces the same problem in application to forward links in *ădverb ne vĕrb*. Here, if we do not take special measures, "ne verb" and "verb" refer to the world at different moments, which is basically incompatible with the negative character of the sentence: the latter says that the referent of "verb" must be removed; it must obviously be removed from the same time as it was imagined to be present, so we must stop the flow of world-time in order to do the removing.

A parallel link as described in 1.6 is a means of introducing such a time-stop: the projection "p" given in 1.6 is a projection of the world at t_2; both levels in a parallel link diagram refer to that world. The parallel link option is not available in *Ne prijătel' priĕchal,* but it is available as a solution for the same problem in *ădverb ne vĕrb:* in Russian, as far as I know, only sentences with *ne* before the verb (if any) can have a parallel link.[4]

1.8   Concurrent and non-concurrent parts; identical and non-identical parts

Just as projections can belong to the same or to different moments of projection time, referents can be opposed to other referents which exist simultaneously or at different moments.
In order to understand the interpretational possibilities of quantifier-like meanings, especially in negative sentences, a distinction must be made between concurrent and non-concurrent parts. Concurrent parts are each other's complement:

The notion of non-concurrent parts can be understood by imagining a pie which becomes progressively smaller by eating parts of it:

287

The pictures just given contain non-identical parts. A pie which is cut up into pieces of equal size illustrates the notion of identical parts:

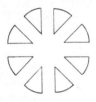

In addition to these basic distinctions introduced in K 1985 (: 278 ff.), 5.2 below gives one further distinction, for negated quantifiers; it concerns the ways in which a part can be removed if the thing from which a part is removed is, itself, a part. Section 5.4 illustrates how concurrent and non-concurrent parts can be combined. The discussion in the present paper is self-contained.

1.9   Inference

A last notion which is indispensable for understanding nega-tive sentences (as well as positive sentences) is the notion "inference". In the model applied here, an inference is a conclu-sion about the truth or falsehood of something which results from combining negations in a certain, well-defined way. For example, in *Mỷ friend is ill* the accent on *my* negates, and thereby evokes, a (concurrent) projection "not my", e.g. "your"; the accent on *ill* negates, and thereby evokes, a (non-concurrent) projection "not ill". At this point, the strict meaning of the accentuation ends. However, we often go a step further. The sentence uttered says, with an assertive type of last accent, that the combination of "my friend" and "is ill" is true:

conveyed to be true

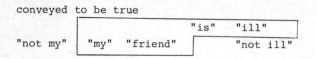

A possible inference is that the combination of the two negations involved is also true:

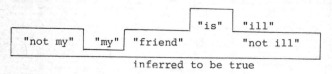

inferred to be true

That is, e.g., "Your friend is not ill" is true. It is not necessary to draw this conclusion, but the sentence spoken allows
it; it directly derives from the configuration of projections involved in the sentence. The example given here illustrates the
third type of inference as described in K (1985: 293-295). In
total, five types of inference have been formulated (K 1985: 287-
312); together with the other notions summarized here, they account for interpretations which, in other frameworks, have been
described under headings such as "negation transportation".
Section 3.1.3, below, repeats the first type of inference, in
order to give (in addition to K 1985: 288-289) the negative counterpart of this inference in 3.2.2. The second type of inference
is mentioned in 2.2. Section 5.1 illustrates the difference between the third and the fourth types of inference, in application
to Russian sentences containing *vs-* (all) and *ne* (not). Finally,
5.2-5.3 elaborates on the fourth and fifth types of inference.
In all cases, the discussion in the present paper is self-contained, but the numbering of inferences is taken from K 1985,
where the reader can find other examples and details which are
irrelevant here.

CHAPTER TWO:

NE: GENERAL REMARKS

2.1 No backward link

The application of *ne* as a separate word is frustrated by the
fact that it cannot be linked backwards. For example, it cannot be
planned as the last item of a sentence: a string like *Ona bylá ne*
(Lit. She was not) unambiguously conveys that a thought has been
broken off midway: "ona byla ne͞   ͺ...."

2.2 No second type of inference

In e.g. English, sentences can be spoken with a non-prominence-lending rise in the last syllable. This intonation is used,
inter alia, for "associating" a negation with the item which
carries the last accent. For example (with pitch contour indicated):

I don't read newspapers on Sundays (My wîfe does)

I don't read newspapers on Sundays (I buy them)

I don't read newspapers on Sundays (I only sléep/I read only bôoks)

I don't read newspapers on Sundays (I read them on Môndays)

The interested reader is referred to K (1985: 290-293) for a description of how this "association" takes place.
In Russian, the relevant non-prominence-lending rise in the last
syllable does not exist, and I have never met an example of this
type of inferential "negation association".

2.3 Moveability

Leaving aside the restrictions summarized in 2.1, *ne*-place-
ment is flexible. For example (Dahl 1979: 105):

Ne jȃ čitaju gazety   po voskresen'jam
Not I̭ read   newspapers on Sundays

Ja ne čitȃju gazety   po voskresen'jam
I   not rḙad   newspapers on Sundays

Ja ne čitaju gazȇty   po voskresen'jam
I   not read   nḙwspapers on Sundays

Ja čitaju ne gazȇty   po voskresen'jam
I read   not nȇwspapers on Sundays

Ja čitaju gazety   ne po voskresȇn'jam
I read   newspapers not on Sṷndays

Such lists are sometimes given in order to illustrate the
notion "scope of negation". This notion is redundant in my approach. For example, in application to *Ne jȃ čitaju gazety po
voskresen'jam* many authors would say that the only word in the
scope of *ne* is *ja*. Instead, I say that the accent on *ja* includes
ne in its scope ("ne" is linked forwards to "ja" here); further,
the accent does not include *čitaju gazety po voskresen'jam* in its
scope, because "ne ja" cannot refer to a figure in a figure/
ground organization (see 1.5 and Chapter Three). The word *ne* does
not have scope.

Although the list adequately illustrates the flexibility of
ne-placement, it tends to suggest that the semantic effect of *ne*-
placement and accent is identical in all sentences of the list.
This suggestion is incorrect: some types of message can only be
expressed by a sentence having *ne* before the verb. In Chapter Four
I will mainly be concerned with the latter types of message. The
semantic effect of *ne*-placement and accent in a list such as the
one given above can be derived along the lines of the model sup-
plied in Chapter Three.

2.4 Forward link vs. no link

The property of *ne* which causes the spelling problem mentioned in the Introduction (see O) is its tendency to become incorporated in the next word: alongside *ne prijatel'* (not a friend) we have the word *neprijatel'* (a not-friend, an enemy), alongside *ne dejstvitel'nyj* (not valid) we have the word *nedejstvitel'ny* (invalid), etc.; especially with adjectives, many such pairs can be formed.

The step from e.g. *ne prijatel'* to *neprijatel'* consists in eliminating the forward link from "ne" to "prijatel'":

  "ne""prijatel'"   "ne prijatel'" (no link direction)

What this amounts to semantically will be explained in Chapter Three.

Words exist which do not occur without *ne-*; for example: *nevzgoda* (ill-luck) (*vzgoda* does not exist), *neukljužij* (clumsy, unwieldy) (*ukljužij* does not exist), etc. If the rest of the sentence says that there is a link between "ne" and, e.g., "vzgoda" or "ukljužij", impossible or odd combinations are the result: *? èto nimalo nevzgoda/ne vzgoda* (? that is altogether ill-luck / that is not at all luck), *? on vovse neukljužij/ne ukljužij* (? he is altogether unwieldy / he is by no means wieldy) (Obzor 1965: 364). The non-existence of the word without *ne-* may be not absolute; in that case, only an insoluble spelling problem arises: *nikomu nevedomoe/ ne vedomoe sčast'e* (cf. ? happiness, unknown to anybody (not known to anybody / unknown to everybody)) (Ivanova 1982: 153). Such conflicts appear at least if a "ne+x" combination with no link between "ne" and "x" combines, in its turn, with the rest of the sentence by means of a parallel link; the parallel link on the higher level implies that "ne" is linked forwards to "x" (see 4.9 below).

2.5 Prosody

It would be nice if the semantic difference between forward link and no link were directly correlated to a different prosodic treatment of *ne* in the two cases. Such a direct correlation does not seem to exist, however, although a thorough study of rhythm as perceived on the basis of pitch accent distribution, pitch movement in pretonic and posttonic syllables, and degree of vowel reduction, could perhaps bring to light a tendency towards differentiation. But e.g. Ivanova's (1982: 126) suggestion that in *Bilêty nedejstvîtel'ny* (The tîckets are invâlid) "intonational underlining" of *ne-* is unnecessary, whereas in *Nêt, bilêty ne dejstvîtel'ny* (Nô, the tîckets are not vâlid) *ne* is necessarily prominent, is certainly too optimistic. On the other hand, the remark made during the 1962-1964 discussion about spelling reforms, viz. that the difference between word boundary and morpheme boundary is neutralized in the case of *ne* (see Obzor 1965: 375), may be too rash on the other extreme. Native speakers contradicting each other, this problem must be left open here.

If a word is accented, the choice of the syllable which gets the accent is not normally semantically motivated. Such a word (lexical accent unit) may include *ne*. For example, we have the paradigm *On nê byl* (He nôt was), *Ona ne bylâ* (She not wâs), etc., where the combinations *ne+byl* and *ne+byla* are single accent units (although confusingly written as two graphic words, *byl(a)* being a verb). The difference between *nê byl* and *ne bylâ* is not semantically motivated; the accent includes (at least) the entire combination in its scope in both cases. This implies that Russian cannot express semantic distinctions like that between *He wâsn't* and *He was nôt* (see Koenitz 1982: 754 for comparable remarks about Czech).

Lexically determined stress positions may be overruled by semantic considerations, just as in English. For example, although the dictionary gives *impôssible*, one may say *impossible* or *im-pôssible* in order to focus attention on the element *im-*. A Russian example (Ivanova 1982: 126): *Itak, vy želaete lučše*

byt' nêmiloserdnym, čem milosêrdnym (So you prefer being ûnchari-
table to being châritable).

On the sentential level, any word, including *ne*, can be
accented for emphasis. For example, the text analysed by Odê elsewhere in this volume contains a sentence: *Ni-čegô nê polučilos'*
(Lit. Nô-thîng nôt was-recêived), with two accents on the word
ničego, and accents on *ne* as well as the verb.
Nevertheless, it cannot be said that *ne* behaves exactly like, e.g.,
English *not,* even if it is a separate word by other criteria. For
example, consider the following dialogue:

    - *I thought he was your frîend*
    - *Nô, he is nôt my friend*

Here, *not* is accented for semantic reasons, the accent negating a
projection of the absence of *not* in the sentence. The corresponding Russian string is: *Net, on ne moj prijatel'* (without a verb).
Although an accent on *ne* and no accent on *prijatel'* (friend) would
suit the context nicely, such a pronunciation of the string is at
least awkward. It is better to put the last accent on *prijatel'*
(or, for that matter, on *moj*: he is nôt mŷ friend). Thus, although
ne can be separated from *prijatel'* by placing e.g. *moj* between
them, and although "ne" is linked forwards to "moj prijatel'"
here, it tends not to behave as a separate accent unit (but as a
proclitic element).

Needless to say, all this conspires to making the prosodic
difference between forward link and no link (if any) subtle
indeed.

2.6 *Ne and parallel links*

The feature of Russian negation which is most striking from
e.g. the English point of view can best be explained on a rough
intuitive level. Consider the sentences *They have êaten* and *They
have eaten nôthing*. As long as we have not heard the word *nothing,*
we do not know whether or not they have eaten; the verbal complex
have eaten alone does not enable us to decide this issue. In

Russian, a situation as in *They have eaten nôthing* does not arise: starting from *eli* (have eaten), the rest of the sentence cannot change the information to such an extent that we must say: "They have not eaten". If the latter should be the outcome we must say *ne eli*. In the example, the result is a so-called "double negation" construction: *Oni ničegô ne êli* (Lit. They nôthing not âte).

The converse, however, does not hold true: the combination *ne eli* alone does not exclude the possibility that the rest of the sentence changes the information to such an extent that we may say: "They have eaten". For example, *Oni mnôgo ne êli* (Lit. They mûch not âte), i.e. They didn't eat much (but they did eat).

Technically, this says that Russian sentences with a parallel link have *ne* preceding the verb (if any).[4] (But not all combinations *ne* plus verb are linked to the rest of the sentence by means of a parallel link.)

This fact ensures that Russian sentences with a parallel link are formally homogeneous (in contrast to, e.g., English and Dutch). But on the other hand, the same fact ensures that the system is at first sight awkward in terms of what is true and what is not true. In e.g. English and Dutch, parallel links have a ubiquitous relation to truth: two levels of a diagram of the type introduced in Chapter One (see 1.6) are both correct. For example, *Nôbody arríved* implies that "Everybody did not arrive" is also true (see K 1985: 302-305) (fused negation); *They didn't eat mûch (to do* plus *not)* allows the conclusion that "They ate not-much" is also true; and *Vâak kwam hij níet op tijd* (Lit. Ôften came he nôt on time) (Other element - Verb - Subject - niet) allows the reading that "Not often did he arrive on time" is correct (K 1985: 296-302). In Russian, however, there are, as far as truth is concerned, two types of parallel link. In e.g. *Niktô ne priêchal* (Lit. Nôbody not arrîved) (*ni* plus *ne*) we cannot draw the conclusion that "Everybody arrived" is correct (in contrast to the English *Nôbody didn't arríve)*; on the contrary, the Russian sentence says that everybody did *not* arrive (see K 1985: 309-312). In other sentences with a parallel link (without a *ni*-word) we can draw such a conclusion. For example, *Oni mnôgo ne êli* (Lit. They

mûch not âte) allows the conclusion that (Lit.) "They not-much
ate" is also true (K 1985: 296-302).

The development of this system can probably be explained on
the basis of the meaning of word order (as described in K 1985:
313-358), in combination with the status of the verb to be mentioned in 2.7 below.
As indicated in 1.7, *Priechal prijâtel'* (Lit. Arrived frîend)
introduces the friend against the background of his previous absence: first it was true that the friend was absent, now it is
true that the friend is present. Now, if we take e.g. "nobody" instead of "friend", this meaning must be cancelled, because it
leads to the odd idea that a person called *nobody* was first absent
and then present. Russian took the step of inserting *ne* before the
verb in order to cancel the meaning of word order (in order to preclude a thought of the absence of the referent of "nîkto" - see the
following chapters). It has the effect that the two levels of a
diagram of my type refer to the same time (parallel link), but it
reinterprets the type *Ne priechal niktô* (Lit. Not arrived nôbody)
as belonging to the type of 2.7 below. Later (see Křížková 1968:
23-25), *ne* before the verb became the rule also with Subject -
Verb order (presumably by analogy): *Niktô ne priêchal* (Lit. Nôbody not arrîved). Although the introduction of *ne* in such sentences is a natural step to take, given the rest of the system, it
has the awkward consequence that parallel links no longer have a
ubiquitous relation to truth.

In (what are now) English and Dutch, there was no basis for
introducing *ne*, because the type of 2.7 does not exist in the same
way, and the meaning of Verb - Subject order changed, to the
effect that (now) English Auxiliary - Subject order and Dutch
Verb-first order have a meaning saying that both "Aux-S-V" (English)/"V-first-S" (Dutch) and the negation of these combinations
can be true about the world of a single time (see Keijsper, forthcoming).

The exact development must, of course, be investigated more
thoroughly. As a far offspring of the different development, Dutch
needs V-S order for a parallel link in sentences like *Vâak kwam
hij nîet op tijd* (Lit. Ôften came he nôt on time); a parallel link

gives the reading "Not often did he arrive on time". If *vaak* precedes *niet* but no V-S order is chosen, as in *Hij kwam vâak nîet op*
tijd (Lit. He came ôften nôt on time), a parallel link is excluded
(only: "Often, he did not arrive on time") (the word *zo* (so) seems
to be an exception). In Russian, both Âdverb-Subject-*ne*-Vêrb and
Subject-Âdverb-*ne*-Vêrb allow (a variant of) the parallel link reading, because here *ne* before the verb, not word order, is the prerequisite for a parallel link. On the difference between these two
Russian arrangements see 4.7 below.

2.7 Absolute absence

We saw in 2.3 that *ne* can occupy various positions in a sentence, according to the message one wishes to convey. In 2.6 we
saw that, if the message involves a parallel link, *ne* must be
placed before the verb. There is yet another type of message which
requires *ne* before the verb; the two classes overlap in the
"double negation" construction, which, as far as truth is concerned, belongs here, in 2.7.

Consider the sentence *On byl ne na Krasnoj plôščadi* (Lit. He
was not on Red Square). This sentence says that he was not on Red
Square and implies that he was elsewhere (cf. 4.1 below). It cannot mean that he has never been on Red Square: his not being on
Red Square is conveyed about a specific, independently given time,
for example: when the bomb exploded, he was not there. If we wish
to convey that he has never been there, *ne* must precede the verb:
On ne byl na Krasnoj plôščadi (Lit. He not was on Red Square).
(Moreover, *on* must be in the nominative case; In *Ego* (genitive) *ne*
bylo na Krasnoj plôščadi, his absence on Red Square also applies
to a specific time.)

This status of the verb in messages conveying absolute absence has a parallel in accent placement in interrogative sentences (with the Russian type of "question intonation", i.e., in
Odé's classification elsewhere in this volume, a group C accent).
If, with the type of accent concerned, the accent is on *plôščadi*
(and the sentence is interpreted as a question), the result is a

question about his whereabouts at a given time: *On byl na Krasnoj plôščadi ?* asks whether or not he was on Red Square, for example, when the bomb exploded. If we wish to ask whether or not he has ever been on Red Square, the type of accent involved must be placed on the verb: *On bŷl na Krasnoj ploščadi ?*

Although *ne* must be placed before the verb if one wishes to convey absolute absence, it is not the case that, if *ne* is placed before the verb, the sentence necessarily conveys absolute absence.

The features of the system summarized here make it quite complicated. We will now look into some corners of the system in greater detail.

CHAPTER THREE

NE PLUS SUBJECT NOUN PLUS VERB

3.1 Prijâtel' priechal (Lit. Frîend arrived)

It follows from Chapter One that this sentence, for the time being without *ne,* has two interpretations: "prijatel'" may, but need not, coincide with the non-linguistic perception of what it refers to. I shall give these two interpretations separately.

3.1.1 Coinciding projections

In this interpretation, the sentence answers the question: What happened ?, i.e. *priechal* is included in the scope of the accent on *prijatel',* "priechal" concurring with "prijatel'":

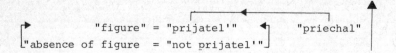

As indicated in the diagram, the accent (assuming an assertive
type) negates the absence of the friend. The "world" is the ground
to which the friend is being added. This ground contains other
figures; these constitute the environment of the friend (cf. K
1985: 171 ff.):

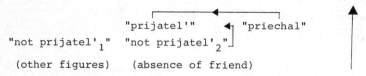

We may also represent this procedure by means of a picture. The
sentence evokes the thought of a world with a number of entities
among which the friend is absent:

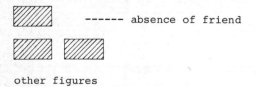

This thought is replaced by the thought of a world where the
friend is present; simultaneously ("priechal" concurring with
"prijatel'"), the friend gets the property of having arrived:

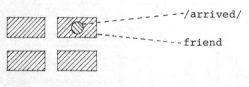

In terms of attention, the accent in this sentence focuses
attention on the person who is the friend, and "arrived" projects
a property of that person.

3.1.2 Non-coinciding projections

In this interpretation, the sentence answers the question:
Who arrived ?, i.e. *priechal* is not included in the scope of the
accent on *prijatel'*, "priechal" concurring with the thought of the
whole of which "prijatel'" projects a part:

```
                              "prijatel'"  ◄┐                      ▲
                     ┌─────────────────◄────┘                      │
"whole minus part" = "not prijatel'"┘    "priechal"               │
"absence of whole"                                                 │
```

As indicated in 1.4 - 1.5, the whole can be either a group of persons or a single entity. In the former case the (assertive type of)
accent negates the absence of the friend among other persons pictured as having arrived; in the latter case it negates the absence
of the property /friend/ of the given entity (it identifies the
entity). Thus, the size of the whole involved is not specified.
The sentence replaces

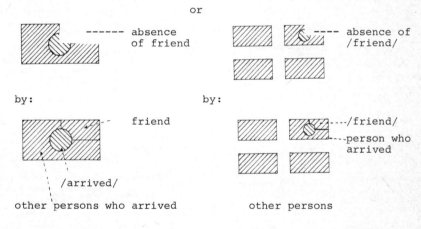

or

────── absence
       of friend

──── absence of
     /friend/

by: by:

friend

----/friend/
----person who
    arrived

/arrived/

other persons who arrived   other persons

In terms of attention, the accent in this sentence adds information about something which already is the focus of attention,
and which has the property /arrived/. Thus, whereas in the coinciding case (3.1.1) we directly focus attention on the friend, in
the non-coinciding case attention is focused on something else,
and the friend is identified with that thing (included in that

thing, mapped onto that thing). This procedure corrects an incorrect idea: it is incorrect to have the idea that the friend belongs to the environment of the thing we are thinking of, because this thing is itself the friend (includes the friend).

Note that in this description the focus of attention is the fixed point: the friend or /friend/ can be included in or mapped onto this fixed point, but the focus of attention remains where it is. This fact is essential, for understanding negative sentences, too.

3.1.3 *First type of inference, positive*

The two possible sizes of the whole in 3.1.2 can also be stated in terms of truth: if the friend is one among other persons pictured as having arrived, then these other persons may also have arrived. But if only one entity arrived, and this entity is the friend, then it is not somebody else, i.e. other potential identifications of the person are incorrect. (Cf. K 1985: 197-198, 221-222, 269, 288-289.) This incorrectness of other potential identifications can be formally stated as follows:

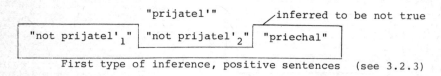

First type of inference, positive sentences   (see 3.2.3)

That is, if we map a property other than /friend/ onto the person who arrived, the result is incorrect (the person who arrived is the friend and not somebody else). This is the first type of inference; it is possible with last accents. Note that it is defined 1. on non-coinciding projections, 2. when the whole involved has the size of a single entity. This is relevant here, because we are now going to place *ne* before *prijatel'*; in that case, the (negative counterpart of the) first type of inference must be applicable, i.e. the size of the whole involved must be one entity.

3.2 *Ne prijâtel' priechal* (Lit. Not friend arrived)

3.2.1 Basic operation of negation

The addition of *ne* to the subject in our example has the effect of excluding an interpretation with coinciding projections. Further, the whole involved in the resulting non-coinciding case has the size of a single entity. Finally, instead of assigning an identifying property, the sentence now removes one.

These observations tell us that in the example a figure is transformed into a whole by the removal of a part. Representing all relevant projections separately, we arrive at the following diagram:

```
        "whole minus part"      = "ne" "prijatel'"   ↑    ----- 3
"figure" = "whole including part" =      "prijatel'"  |    ----- 2
"absence of figure"             =        "not prijatel'" | ----- 1
```

Thus, in the direction of the arrow, the levels are the following. Level 1 is the following picture:

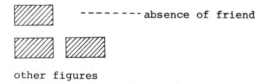

other figures

Then, the addition of the friend would give:

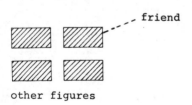

other figures

However, this does not happen entirely; the latter picture must be construed as (level 2):

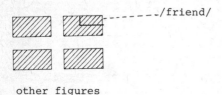

other figures

This urge is implied in the instruction that the ultimately result-ing picture be (level 3):

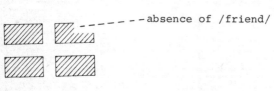

other figures

In this way, we are left with a projection of an unidentified entity. As always, the property of having arrived is mapped onto the person as such, i.e. "priechal" concurs with level 2 of the diagram.

Now, the procedure as given here must be specified further, because it consists of a number of operations: "ne" is combined with "prijatel'", and the accent on *prijatel'* performs an opera-tion; also, the diagram contains two potential jobs for the ac-cent: does it introduce level 1 and replace level 1 by level 2, as it did in 3.1.1, or does it introduce level 2 and replace level 2 by level 3, i.e. the reverse of what happened in 3.1.2?
From a comparison with other examples, it appears that the order in which the various operations are performed is relevant, and that the following holds true:
- There is, as far as I know, one case where a level 2 projection is present simultaneously with a level 3 projection. In that case the accent does its job before "ne" is added:

```
        II
   ┌─────►┐
"ne"   "x"  ◄┐
       "not x" ┘ I
```
                   --- level 2 and level 3

                   --- level 1

Here, x and ne x are simultaneously referred to, and the accent
asserts x, i.e. the accent does what it did in 3.1.1. For this
case see 4.8 below.

- Elsewhere, the accent does its job after the addition of "ne" to
"x". As long as there is a link between "ne" and "x", the negation of "ne x", i.e. the projection negated by an accent on x,
is "x":

```
     I
   ┌──►┐
"ne"   "x" ◄┐
      "x" ┘ II
```
             --- level 3

             --- level 2

(For this order of operations in positive sentences see K 1985:
241, 313, 331 etc.)

As we will see below (3.3), a combination "ne x" with no link
between "ne" and "x" has a different negation.

Thus, by linking "ne" to "x" first, the task of the accent becomes the creation of level 2 and the replacement of this level
by level 3, i.e. the operation of 3.1.2 is reversed. This says
that the step from level 1 to level 2 in the general diagram
given above, is relegated to the past by linking "ne" to "x".
(In contrast, the choice between 3.1.1 and 3.1.2 is a matter of
interpretation, contextually dependent. In e.g. *Ne prijâtel'*
priechal, a reading as the reverse of 3.1.2 is obligatory, independent of context.) In effect, the sentence gives the impression of removing something which was already there. This
impression is, of course, an illusion, i.e. "x" need not be
there before the sentence is spoken; the sentence itself says
that it was.

- Finally, the fact that in our example, only a part of the entity
is removed, viz. the identifying property /friend/, is not inherent in the use of *ne*; nor can it be ascribed to the link between "ne" and "prijatel'" or to the order of the operations. It
follows from a general principle (see 4.1). We will come across

cases where the size of the thing removed is different.
- Note that in this description, *ne* does not remove or add anything; "ne x" is just a projection of something (the last picture given above). (In other words, not *ne* but the accent has
scope.)

Summarizing for *Ne prijâtel' priechal:*

```
                                              I
                                       ┌────────────┐
           ┌►"whole minus part"      = "ne" "prijatel'" ◄┐
►"figure" =├ "whole including part" =      "prijatel'"   │ II (accent)
           └ "absence of figure"    =      "not prijatel'"◄┤(relegated
                                                            │ to the
                                                            │ past)
```

In terms of attention, this diagram says that we remove the
property /friend/ from the entity which is the focus of attention.
Thus, we cancel an identification: it is incorrect to have the idea
that the person we are thinking of (the person who arrived) is the
friend; in reality, this person is not the friend. Note that, just
as in the positive case (3.1.2), the focus of attention is the
fixed point; we remove /friend/ from this fixed point, the latter
staying where it is.

Note finally that the combination "ne prijatel'" is related
to the absence of the friend indirectly, via a projection
"prijatel'". This is characteristic of what we experience as a
negative thought.[5]

3.2.2 First type of inference, negative

The operation introduced in 3.2.1 leaves us with a projection
of an unidentified entity. We are now going to identify the entity:
we have said that it is not the friend (we have removed /friend/),
but we have not yet said who it is.
In order to arrive at a positive characterization of the person
who is not the friend, we apply the same inference as that given in
3.1.3, but instead of a combination which is inferred to be *not*
true, we now arrive at a combination which is inferred to be true:

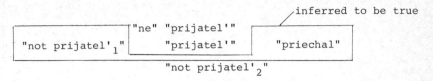

First type of inference, negative sentences (see 3.2.3)

That is, given the fact that the identification of the person who arrived as the friend is incorrect, another identification must be correct.

3.2.3 Remarks

Three points must perhaps be made explicit.
1. The combination "ne prijatel'" does not refer to the environment of the friend (i.e. it is not identical to "not prijatel'$_1$"). Even if we adopt the simplistic view that a given universe divides up into *A* and *not-A*, *A* and *not-A* comprising everything there is, *not-A* as a whole is not referred to. An expression referring to *not-A* would be an expression which, if accented, focuses attention on everything except *A*; such an expression necessarily becomes positive in the way described in 3.3 below. Elsewhere, as far as I know, we always focus attention on a specific element in a given universe. Next, we may remove /A/ from the thing which is the focus of attention, and then (first type of inference, negative) we may take another element and map it onto the thing which is the focus of attention. I think this is where many analyses of negation go wrong; as a consequence, they do not account, inter alia, for the facts of accent and scope (see also 4.1 and 4.5 below).
2. Although, for my own convenience, the diagram of the first type of inference (positive and negative) puts the entire "not prijatel'$_1$" in a box, any given application of the inference makes a choice from "not prijatel'$_1$". Indeed, e.g. *Ne prijâtel' priechal* does not lead to the conclusion that the person who arrived is everybody except the friend; instead, the person who arrived has one other identity.

3. The negative variant of the first type of inference (3.2.2)
applies only if *ne* precedes the accented element, here *prijatel'*.
In e.g. *Prijâtel' ne priechal* we may also apply the first type of
inference, but only the variant for positive sentences (3.1.3).
That is, we may interpret this sentence as: the person who did not
arrive is the friend and *not* somebody else (cf. K 1985: 289); evidently, the accent here has nothing to do with *ne*.

3.3 Neprijâtel' priechal (Lit. Not-friend (enemy) arrived)

As compared with 3.2, we now eliminate the link from "ne" to
"prijatel'": "ne""prijatel'" → "ne""prijatel'". The result is a
(positive) thought of an entity. The idea that "neprijatel'" is
somehow positive, in comparison with "ne prijatel'", originates in
the fact that in "neprijatel'" we introduce a thought of the absence of the referent of "neprijatel'", in the following way.
The procedure described in 3.2 resulted in this picture:

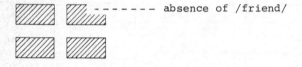

other figures

In 3.2, this picture was the result of removing /friend/, i.e. it
followed this picture:

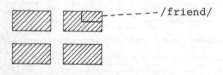

other figures

Now, the same picture, without /friend/, can also be evaluated as being the result of adding 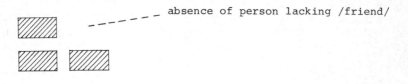 with respect to a preceding phase:

absence of person lacking /friend/

other figures

If it is this picture which is followed by the picture of a person lacking /friend/, the latter is felt as positive, and the absence of the property /friend/ is the identifying property of the person. This is what happens in *Neprijâtel' priechal*.
Thus, the step from "ne prijatel'" to "ne prijatel'" (no link) consists in introducing a projection of the absence of the referent of the complex "ne prijatel'":

> "whole minus part" = "ne prijatel'" (= new figure)
> "absence of whole minus part" = "not ne prijatel'"

In terms of attention, the accent now focuses attention on the referent of "ne prijatel'", i.e. it negates a projection of the absence of this same referent. What we have done, in comparison with 3.2, is to transfer the focus of attention: in 3.2, we removed a part of the thing which is the focus of attention; now, the referent of "ne prijatel'" itself is the focus of attention.

Neprijatel' is a single word in the sense that the negation of "neprijatel'", i.e. the projection negated by an accent on *-ja-*, is "not neprijatel'", referring to the absence of a *not*-friend.

We saw in 3.2 that two steps are needed in order to pass from "ne prijatel'" to the total absence of the referent: "ne prijatel'" - "prijatel'" - "not prijatel'" (absence of friend); such a two-step chain is characteristic of what we experience as negative. From the referent of "neprijatel'" to the absence of the referent is only one step: "neprijatel'" - "not neprijatel'" (absence of not-friend); this is what we perceive as positive (despite the fact that the entity concerned is characterized in a negative way). (Cf. K 1985: 274-276, 306-308.)

Once we have combined "ne" and "prijatel'" into the single concept "neprijatel'" we can start anew: the interpretations of *Neprijâtel' priechal* are the same as those of *Prijâtel' priechal* (see 3.1, but with "neprijatel'" instead of "prijatel'").

3.4 ? *Ne prijâtel' priêchal*

As compared with 3.2, we have now added an accent on *priechal*. The result is incoherent (unless we take *Ne prijâtel'* and *Priêchal* to be two separate sentences). The cause of the problem is the effect of the backward link described in 1.7: given the backward link from "priechal" to "ne prijatel'", the referent of the nega-tion of "ne prijatel'" is relegated to the past. This is incompat-ible with the part-whole organization involved in construing the referent of "ne prijatel'", because a part-whole organization is a means of spreading something belonging to one moment of world-time (here: an entity) over two moments of projection time (here: the entity pictured with and without its identifying property) (see 1.5 and K 1985: 151, 209-210).
The incompatibility can also be formulated in terms of concurrent and non-concurrent negations (see 1.7), which is, possibly, easier here. The effect described in 1.7 results in giving "ne prijatel'" a concurrent negation. This would imply that the accent on *prijatel'* selects the referent of "ne prijatel'" from among the things in its environment. But this implies that attention can be focused on the referent of "ne prijatel'", and the latter is con-tradicted by the link between "ne" and "prijatel'".

What saves the day in this type of conflict is a parallel link (see the end of 1.7). In our sentence this is, however, im-possible, because in Russian a parallel link requires *ne* before the verb (see 2.6). Thus, whereas *Prijâtel' ne priêchal* has a reading "the person who arrived is not my friend", such an interpretation is impossible for *Ne prijâtel' priêchal,* unless we divide the string up into two sentences: ? "somebody who is not my friend (but somebody else). Arrîved".[6]

In order to accommodate the given accentuation within one sentence we must, consequently, either eliminate the link between "ne" and "prijatel'" or choose the links in such a way that "priechal" is not linked backwards to the "ne" plus "prijatel'" combination. The former option results in the sentence *Neprijâtel' priêchal,* conveying simply that a not-friend arrived, which is not of special interest. The latter will be given in 3.5.

3.5 *Ne prijâtel' priêchal / Ne prijâtel' priechal*

This type of sentence repeats 3.2, but the referent involved is not an entity now, but a situation (the referent of the subject - predicate combination). Thus, the example says that the situation (state of affairs) meant lacks the property of being an appropriate referent of "(my) friend arrived". This information, just as in 3.2, does not provide a positive characterization of the referent; if the latter is needed, it must be added separately (first type of inference, negative variant): "(- Why are you so upset ?) (- It is) not (that) my frîend arrîved (but ...)".

Note that, in order to remove the complex property /prijatel' priechal/ from the state of affairs meant, the elements of the complex must first be put together, i.e. (for the two-accent case):

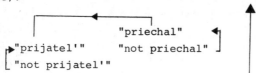

However, the link from "ne" to the complex relegates these operations to the past; it pretends that "prijatel' priechal" is already available as a single chunk of information, so that the absence of the state of affairs meant is no longer in view, and so that the last thing conveyed is:

┌►"state of affairs minus id. property" = ┌►"ne""prijatel' priechal"
└ "state of affairs incl. id. property" = └   "prijatel' priechal"
 ("absence of state of affairs")

For this last step, one accent is sufficient. The choice from *Ne
prijâtel' priechal, Ne prijâtel' priêchal*, or even *Ne prijatel'
priêchal*, creates different possibilities for the subsequent inference, as it makes available "not prijatel'$_1$" and/or "not priechal$_1$".
Note that in such complex configurations, it is hardly possible to
say whether "ne" is linked up before the accent(s) does/do its/
their job (see the levels in 3.2.1). But at least one of them must
(also) mark the last step, to the effect that a level containing
"ne" follows a level without "ne". Otherwise, the presence of the
property would be asserted at the moment when its absence is referred to; this is incoherent, except for the case of 4.8 below.
    The type of this section is frequently used in folklore texts
(tales, proverbs etc.). For example (Savel'eva 1977: 60):

Ne kukuška kukuet, a   žena gorjuet
Not cuckoo calls   but wife grieves

Ne on umer, a   smert' ego prišla
Not he died but death his came

Ne carstvo gorit, a   moja žena v korobke edet
Not Czardom burns but my   wife in box.   rides

CHAPTER FOUR

(ADVERB PLUS) <u>*NE*</u> *PLUS VERB*

4.0 Introduction

Combinations of *ne* plus verb are more heterogeneous than the
simple string discussed in Chapter Three. This heterogeneity has
three causes:
1.   We saw in 3.2 that the presence of a link between "ne" and
"prijatel'" in *Ne prijâtel' priechal* is accompanied by the interpretation that only the identifying property /friend/ of the entity is removed but not the entity itself, i.e. the sentence leaves
us with a projection of an unidentified entity rather than with a
projection of the absence of the entity.

In other combinations, among which *ne* plus verb (and *ne* plus
prijatel' when used as a predicate), we find both an interpretation where only a part is removed and an interpretation where the
corresponding whole is removed. For example, *On ne čitâet* (Lit. He
not rêads) has an interpretation "the thing he is doing is not
reading (but something else)" (removal of identifying property) as
well as an interpretation "he is not reading, i.e. his potential
reading is absent" (removal of the entire activity).

This difference between sentences like *Ne prijâtel' priechal*
and *On ne čitâet* is reflected in (at least one of the applications
of) the terms "constituent vs. sentence negation" or "special vs.
nexal negation". I think it has a simple explanation. The point
will be discussed in 4.1 below.
2.   As I mentioned in 2.7, *ne* plus verb is used for conveying
"absolute absence". The difference between *On ne čitâet* in the
sense "he is not reading now" and the same sentence in the sense
"he never reads" ("absolute absence") will be described here as a
second level of removing a part vs. removing a whole (4.3).

3.   The third complication is parallel links. It does not pertain
to *ne* plus verb per se but to the way in which this combination,
in its turn, combines with the rest of the sentence. I will use
strings of the form *adverb ne verb* for illustrating the difference
between parallel and (here) forward links (4.4 ff.).

Points 1-3 listed above all pertain to the case when "ne" is
linked forwards to the verb, i.e. the case where our example of
Chapter Three had only a single interpretation (removal of a part
on the lowest level). Just as in "ne" plus "prijatel'" there is,
in addition, the possibility of no link between "ne" and the verb
(see 4.2). In order to illustrate the difference with other readings, examples here also have the form *adverb ne verb* (see 4.4 ff.).
In the course of the discussion, we will meet the same problem as that of 3.4 (*? Ne prijâtel' priêchal*), this time in application to forward links. In *ne* plus verb the problem has a natural
solution, because here we have, besides the possibility of eliminating the link, the option of a parallel link. Moreover, the removal-of-part vs. removal-of-whole distinction on the second level
(see point 2. above) makes available a solution which neither eliminates the link between "ne" and the verb nor uses a parallel
link. It is suggested that this point is relevant to the choice of
verbal aspect in the sentences concerned. Aspect itself will not
be discussed, but my treatment hopefully explains why problems can
be expected there.
This chapter discusses only extremely simple combinations,
although some extensions will be mentioned in 4.9. It seems to me
that a precise understanding of the mechanisms involved in simple
cases is a prerequisite for investigating more complicated sentences. The latter I leave for another occasion.

4.1   Removal of part vs. removal of whole, first level

The fact that "ne prijatel'" in *Ne prijâtel' priechal* cannot
refer to the absence of the friend, whereas "ne čitaet" in *On ne
čitâet* may refer to the absence of his reading, is at first sight

very remarkable. On closer inspection, the difference appears to
be another way of stating a truth which is so obvious that it
sounds odd in explicit form: this fact tells us that the friend is
imagined to exist when "ne prijatel'" has a referent, whereas the
reading which would be there if he were reading is not there when
he is not reading.

Consider again what we did in 3.2. We removed the property /friend/
of the person who arrived, i.e. we cancelled a previous identification. Why was the identification of the person who arrived and the
friend incorrect? Because the property /friend/ is carried not by
the person who arrived but by a different person, a person in the
environment of the person who arrived. If we removed not only the
property /friend/ of the person who arrived, but the entire person,
i.e. if "ne prijatel'" referred to the absence of the person who
arrived, the friend would be absent and present simultaneously,
because he also belongs to the environment. Since a single person
cannot be absent and present simultaneously, "ne prijatel'" in *Ne
prijâtel' priechal* cannot refer to the absence of the friend.
(Note that two friends, one absent, the other present, would save
us here; this point will be used in 4.3 below.) In *ne čitâet,* however, we may remove the thing he is doing (i.e. reading) entirely:
in that case, reading does not belong to the environment where "ne
čitaet" has a referent (it is there at a different moment only).

Note that *ne čitâet* also allows an interpretation removing
only the identifying property of his activity: *On ne čitâet, a
smotrit televîzor* (He is not reading but watching television) (the
but-phrase makes explicit the first type of inference, negative
variant - see 3.2.2). We then, indeed, imagine a set of things one
can do, which is, in itself, a timeless idea. The sentence then
says: "the thing he is doing at this moment is not reading (lacks
the property of being an appropriate referent of "čitaet"), because reading is a different thing one can do (the property is
carried by a different activity)". This leaves us with a projection of an unidentified activity (the thing he is doing at this
moment); the first type of inference (negative variant) fills in
the correct identification.

In this way, the fact that *On ne čitâet* has two interpretations where *Ne prijâtel' priechal* has only one, is, in my view, not an arbitrary fact; rather, it tells us something about how we perceive different types of referent. The regularity is: "ne x" is a projection of the absence of *x* only if *x* does not exist (is imagined not to exist) at the moment when "ne x" has a referent; otherwise, "ne x" is a projection of the absence of a part of a given referent (here: the identifying property /x/ of a given entity/activity). There is one exception to this statement (see 5.2).

The rule is not restricted to the type of example given here. To give one other example, consider the difference between *On byl ne v kômnate* (He was not in the rôom) and *On byl ne v dûche* (He was not in the môod, i.e. he was in a bad mood). In the case of the room, we imagine him somewhere outside the room:

O   ☐

he   room

Since the room is imagined to exist at the moment when he is not in it (i.e. since "v komnate" has a referent), "ne v komnate" cannot refer to the absence of the place *in the room*. Instead, the place where he is lacks the property of being an appropriate referent of "in the room" (that property is carried by a different place). Thus, the sentence leaves us with a projection of an unidentified place; if we wish to identify it, we must apply the first type of inference (negative variant).
In the case of the mood, in contrast, we simply remove the mood if we are told that he is not in it:

O

he

Since the mood in which he would be if he were in it does not exist if he is not in it, "ne v duche" refers to the absence of the state *v duche*.

Now, these two examples can, of course, be brought under the same heading: we can say that in both cases, the following picture does not obtain:

room/mood

he

But a further description of the difference between the two sentences must, in my view, take into account the focus of attention. The case of the mood is simple: we remove the mood. But the case of the room is, in my view, different from what one may think at first sight. My formulation says that we do not mentally move him to some place outside the room. Instead, he is somewhere, and we mentally remove the (incorrectly assigned) property /in the room/ from this place; the latter is the focus of attention. The property was assigned to the place where he is incorrectly because the property is in reality carried by a different place (simultaneously existing).

In the same way, in *On ne čitâet* we remove either his entire activity or only the identifying property of this activity. For the reason given above, *Ne prijâtel' priechal* allows only the removal of the identifying property of the person who arrived (the focus of attention).

Next, it is important to keep in mind that we have arrived at a referent for "ne x" via the corresponding positive expression (by removing /x/ or *x*). Thus, independently of the size of the thing removed, we have the two-step procedure introduced in 3.2.1. In application to *ne čitâet*:

$$
\begin{array}{ll}
\text{activity minus identifying property /reading/} & = \text{"ne" "čitaet"} \\
\text{activity including identifying property /reading/} & = \quad\text{"čitaet"} \\
\text{absence of reading (relegated to the past)} & = \quad\text{"not čitaet"}
\end{array}
$$

removal of part, first level

```
                                              I
                                           ┌──→──┐
absence of activity reading        =   "ne" "čitaet"◄┐
activity reading                   =         "čitaet" ┘ II
absence of reading (relegated to the past) =   "not čitaet"
```

                  removal of whole, first level

The fact that we arrive at a referent for, here, "ne čitaet" by
removing part or all of his activity, is responsible for peculiarities of negative sentences as compared with positive sentences
(for some discussion see e.g. Givón 1979: 91-142). Moreover, the
two-step procedure distinguishes the cases discussed so far from
combinations without a link between "ne" and the verb (see 4.2
below).

   Note that the distinction introduced in this section cannot
adequately be covered by the terms "non-nexal" vs. "nexal" negation or "constituent" vs. "sentence" negation. For one thing, *On
ne čitáet* allows both interpretations. For another, *On byl ne v
kômnate* and *On byl ne v dûche* both have "non-nexal"/"constituent"
negation but different interpretations.

   The phenomenon that the size of a part-whole combination is
not specified by a form itself (although it may be determined by
other factors) is a regularly recurring point in the type of thing
we are talking about (cf. 1.4, 3.1.2, 3.1.3). It is very convenient because it ensures high flexibility; for logicians, however,
it is awkward because of its consequences in terms of truth.

4.2   No link between "ne" and verb

   As we saw in 3.3 in application to *Neprijâtel' priechal*, the
elimination of the forward link between "ne" and "x" amounts to
the introduction of a projection of the absence of the referent of
the "ne x" complex:

```
┌►"ne x"
└ "not ne x" = "absence of ne x"
```

In *Neprijåtel'*, the incorporation of "ne" amounts to making the referent of "neprijatel'" an entity, the accent (in the coinciding case) negating a projection of the absence of this entity in an environment of other entities.

The same possibility is available for verbs. The incorporation of "ne" makes the referent of "ne V" an activity (or state, or whatever it is) which is introduced by an accent on V against the background of the absence of this activity; the referent of "V" is a different activity (state, etc.):

"not ne V_1"   ⌐► "ne V"
(other activities,   ⌐ "not ne V_2"
including V)   (absence of *ne* V)

The fact that *V* and *ne V* are construed as different activities here has given rise to the observation, in logic-oriented linguistics, that *V* and *ne V* are contraries rather than contradictories in this case, that is (roughly), both referents can be absent: *Mary doesn't like Susan, but she doesn't dislike her either* (Tottie 1980: 103).

The difference between "ne prijatel'" and "ne prijatel'" as discussed in Chapter Three, is immediately clear intuitively, because a link between "ne" and "prijatel'" is accompanied by the interpretation removing the property /friend/ only, not the entire entity. With verbs, the difference between "ne V" and "ne V" is more difficult to become aware of, since the presence of a link does not exclude the possibility that the entire *V* is removed (see 4.1 above). The relevant difference between "ne V", removing *V* entirely, and "ne V", is that a referent for "ne V" is arrived at via "V" (by removing *V*), whereas a referent of "ne V" replaces the absence of this same referent.
For example:[7]

> (1) Ona *srâzu*   *ne ponrâvilas'* nam
>   immediately not pleased
>   (We disliked her immediately)

Here, at the moment indicated by "srazu" an event of disliking
starts: before that time, *dis*like was absent. (The sentence has in
principle also a reading involving a parallel link: "we dîdn't
like her immêdiately"; such readings will be discussed below.)
Compare also:

> (2) On ôčen' ne   ljubîl menja
>   very not loved
>   (He "disloved" me very much)

vs. (with a link):

> (3) Nenavisti k nemu u menja net, no ja ego i *ne   ljubljû*
>   not love
>   (I don't hate him, but I don't love him either, i.e. love is
>   absent as well)

A well-known type of opposition, also rendered in spelling,
is the opposition between verbs with the so-called prefix *nedo-*
and verbs with the prefix *do-* preceded by *ne: ne do-*. For example
(Skorobač 1978: 97): *Teper' pozdno nedogovarivat'* (It is now too
late to not speak to the end (to withhold information)) versus
Govorit' - i ne dogovarivat' (To speak and not to speak to the end
(to stop speaking before the end is reached)). There are about 70
of such pairs (op.cit.: 96). (Besides, there are also verbs with
nedo- which do not exist without *ne-*.)
Verbs with *nedo-* differ from combinations like that in (1) *(Ne
ponravilas'):* they are:

```
   ┌──┐
"ne do V"        (hence the name "prefix" for nedo-)
```

The meaning of *ne ponravilas'* in (1), in contrast, would more adequately be expressed if the form were *ponenravilas'*, *po-* indicating
the starting point of the event of disliking:

```
 ┌──┐──┐
"po ne V"
```

However, this order *prefix - ne* actually occurs only in verbs
which do not exist without *ne,* e.g. *voz<u>ne</u>navidet'* (to hate, perfective aspect). As we will see below (example (18)) there is
also a type

"ne do V"   (opposed to "ne do V" in e.g. *ne dogovarivat').*

4.3 *Removal of part vs. removal of whole, second level*

The removal-of-part vs. removal-of-whole distinction introduced in 4.1 (first level) is well-known and hardly requires further illustration. Roughly, the removal-of-part case on that level
is the interpretation which suggests a continuation of the sentence with a *but*-phrase: *not & but* .... The corresponding removal-
of-whole case is the reading which simply refers to the absence of
the potential event in question, e.g.

(4) V ėtot moment ja pisal pis'mo i *ne zamêtil,* kto vošêl
                                        not noticed
    (At that moment I was writing a letter and did not notice
    who entered)

Now, as is well-known, a sentence like *On ne govorit po-
kitâjski* (Lit. He not speaks Chinese) urges us to make a further
distinction (also for the corresponding positive sentence). The
example says either that he is not speaking Chinese, e.g., at this
moment, or that he speaks no Chinese at all. In both cases we remove his entire activity on the first level. (The corresponding
removal-of-part case would be, e.g. *On ne govorit po-kitâjski, a
smotrit televízor* (He is not speaking Chinese but watching television.) Nevertheless, there is a difference as to the size of the
thing which is removed. In order to state the difference in terms
of my model, so that we will be able to discuss an issue about adverbs later on, I introduce the notion of "the whole of potential
occurrences of an event". In the example, the whole consists of
all potential occurrences of the event *On govorit po-kitajski;*

every individual occurrence is a part of this whole (which consists, then, of identical parts - see 1.8). Correspondingly, we
have the time in which all occurrences are placed, say T, and the
time of every individual occurrence, say t_1, t_2, ... t_n. Of this
whole, we may remove a part, say the occurrence at t_i; alternatively, we remove the entire whole of potential occurrences from T.
Thus:

		I
whole of potential occurrences minus occurrence at t_i	=	"ne" "govorit"
whole of potential occurrences including occurrence at t_i	=	"govorit"
absence of whole (relegated to the past) =		"not govorit"

    removal of part, second level

		I
absence of whole of potential occurrences =		"ne" "govorit"
whole of potential occurrences	=	"govorit"
absence of whole (relegated to the past) =		"not govorit"

    removal of whole, second level

Note that we have retained a two-step procedure.

We saw in 4.1 that the choice between removing a part and removing a whole amounts to saying whether or not x belongs to the
environment where "ne x" has a referent. On the second level introduced now, the contrast can also be stated in terms of environment,
the environment now being all occurrences of events in T. If we remove only a part of the potential v-occurrences in T, we consider
a stretch of time larger than that from which potential v-occur-
rences are removed; in other words, v belongs to the environment
where "ne V" has a referent, v being the rest of potential v-occur-
rences. Just as before, the case when we remove the whole of potential v-occurrences in T, is the case where v does not belong to
the environment where "ne V" has a referent; indeed, we arrive at
a referent for "ne V" by removing all of v.

Yet another way of stating the same difference is one in terms
of truth. The case when we remove only a part of the potential oc-

currences of the event is the case when both the positive and the
negative sentence may be correct, namely at different moments. For
example, although he is not speaking Chinese at this moment, he
may have done so yesterday. The case when we remove the whole of
potential occurrences of the event (He speaks no Chinese at all)
is the case when only either the positive or the negative sentence
is correct; indeed, no potential occurrence is left for a different moment.
(For the first level, correspondingly: e.g. "ne čitaet" and
"čitaet" are simultaneously correct projections, namely they apply
to different activities (removal of part), vs. at a given moment
only either "ne čitaet" or "čitaet" is a correct projection (removal of whole). Needless to say, the whole on the first level is
the part on the second level.)

In 2.7 I said that, in order to convey an "absolute absence"
idea (removal of whole, second level), *ne* must be placed before the
verb. What is more precise is the observation that a corresponding
idea elsewhere is not expressed by means of *ne*. Consider, for
example, *nikto, nekto* (nominative case), and *nekogo* (other cases)
(approximately: "not somebody", see below). Of these three, only
nikto can refer to the absence of the whole of people (English
nobody basically refers to an empty part of this whole). *Nekto*, in
contrast, says (roughly): "the person referred to is not (just)
somebody, i.e. he is a certain person" (removal of part, first level,
but lexically incorporated here). *Nekogo* and other cases of the same
word does remove an entire person (removal of whole on the first
level), but it leaves the rest of the whole of people in the environment (i.e. removes only a part on the second level, lexically incorporated).
For example: *Mne   ne   s   kem   pogovorit'*
                to-me (is) not with "somebody" to-talk
                (I have nobody to talk with)
Here, we remove persons with whom I can talk but not other people.
Thus, with *kto*, the absence of the whole is expressed by *ni-*, not by
ne-. However, in order to be able to refer to the absence of the
whole, *nikto* needs, in addition, *ne* before the verb (if any), *ne*
removing the event in question. Otherwise, *nikto* refers to a person

called nobody: given a verb, only *ne* can preclude a thought of the absence of the referent of "nikto", which thought renders the expression positive (see 3.3 above and K 1985: 302–312). What is remarkable is that *ne* before the verb needs no help from elsewhere in order to be able to refer to the absence of the whole of potential occurrences of the event in question; the combination is rendered positive by eliminating the link. This is remarkable because the removal of this whole leaves us with no whole other than T to concentrate upon while we do the act of removal.

4.4 *Adverb ne verb: the problem and three solutions*

We saw in 1.7 that in a positive sentence like *Priechal prijátel'* (VŜ) the projections "not prijatel'" and "prijatel'" refer to the world at different moments, i.e. that such a sentence (with the appropriate type of accent) introduces (here) the friend against the background of his previous absence. The same meaning can be found in other combinations, among which $^{(}$ȃdverb - vêrb (K 1985: 335–336). For example, in *Ėtot podchod okončátel'no utverdílsja* (That approach definitively established itself) the fact of the establishment replaces the previous absence of that fact:

```
  ┌────────────────────►┐
├►"okončatel'no"        │
└ "not okončatel'no"├►"utverdilsja"     - "world at $t_2$"
                     └ "not utverdilsja" - "world at $t_1$"
```

Now, in negative sentences such a meaning can in principle be expected to raise problems, because with such sentences we basically remove something which is first thought to be present at least potentially. This obviously implies that no world-time should elapse while we are busy removing the thing: just as we cannot lift up an object which is in place A by going to place B where the object is not, we cannot remove an event which is imagined to occur in time A by going to time B and viewing its absence there. The time-stop which we need for the act of removing is introduced by a parallel link:[8]

323

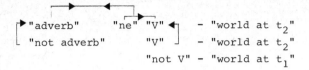

$$\begin{bmatrix} \text{"adverb"} \\ \text{"not adverb"} \end{bmatrix} \quad \text{"ne"} \quad \begin{matrix} \text{"V"} \\ \text{"V"} \\ \text{"not V"} \end{matrix} \quad \begin{matrix} - \text{"world at } t_2\text{"} \\ - \text{"world at } t_2\text{"} \\ - \text{"world at } t_1\text{"} \end{matrix}$$

The "world at t_2" to which both "ne V" and "V" apply is the projection "p" given in 1.6.

As a result of using a parallel link, the meaning we find in
okončâtel'no utverdîlsja is cancelled in *okončâtel'no ne utverdîlsja*; indeed, this combination does not convey the fact of the non-
establishment against the background of the previous absence of
this fact:

(5) Odnako posledovatel'nyj podchod ... poka čto v slavjanskom
     jazykoznanii *okončâtel'no ne   utverdîlsja*
                  definitively not established-itself
     (However, a consistent approach did not definitively estab-
     lish itself in Slavic linguistics, i.e. if some approach
     established itself, then not definitively)

To be sure, a combination *âdverb ne vêrb* may convey the fact of
not-V against the background of the previous absence of this fact,
but this idea eliminates the link between "ne" and the verb (see
4.2):

(1) Ona *srâzu   ne   ponrâvilas'* nam
         immediately not pleased
     (We disliked her immediately)

That is:

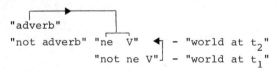

$$\begin{matrix} \text{"adverb"} \\ \text{"not adverb"} \end{matrix} \quad \begin{matrix} \text{"ne   V"} \\ \text{"not ne V"} \end{matrix} \quad \begin{matrix} - \text{"world at } t_2\text{"} \\ - \text{"world at } t_1\text{"} \end{matrix}$$

Compare (parallel link):

(6) Tol'ko Martina ne bylo, no étogo tětuški *sŕazu ne zamétili*
                                    immediately not noticed
   (Only Martin was not there, but that the aunts did not immediately notice, i.e. they may have noticed it, but not immediately)

As mentioned in 1.6, a parallel link involves two projections of
the same state of affairs; here: "srazu ne zametili" and "not-
srazu zametili". Leaving aside sentences with *ni*-words, both projections are correct: about the state of affairs referred to ("p")
we say both that noticing was absent and that noticing was there;
but the former applies only in combination with "srazu" and the
latter only in combination with "not srazu".

   These, then, are the obvious possibilities: a parallel link
between "adverb" and "ne V" cancels the meaning we find in the
corresponding positive sentences; the latter is retained by eliminating the link between "ne" and "V".
   However, there is at least one other possibility; it uses the
whole of potential occurrences introduced in 4.3.
The diagram is:

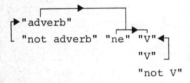

Here we arrive at a referent for "ne V" via "V" (in contrast to
cases without a link between "ne" and "V"); yet, the time-stop introduced by a parallel link is not there. In order to interpret
the sentence we need a combination of 1: "ne V" and "V" refer to
the same time (in order to remove *v* from where it is imagined),
and 2: "ne V" and "V" refer to different times (as instructed by
the forward link between "adverb" and "ne V").
Evidently, we need more than one time-level in order to resolve
this contradiction. To this aim we employ the whole of 4.3: we remove a potential occurrence or potential occurrences from, say,

t_i (so that this particular occurrence is removed from where it is
imagined); it leaves the rest of potential occurrences for other
t's (so that the absence and the presence of the event obtain at
different moments). This combination saves the link between "ne"
and "V" without recourse to a parallel link between "adverb" and
"ne V".

Note that this proposal predicts a problem for the case when we remove the whole of potential *V* occurrences from T (see 4.6 below).

   The next section gives some examples, first of the t/T trick,
then of the three types of *adverb ne verb* combination mentioned
here, in pairwise opposition.

4.5 *Examples*

   Consider what happens with *On počti spit* (He almost sleeps) if
we insert *ne* before the verb. In *On počti spit* we think of a single
occurrence of a sleeping-event: such an occurrence is almost there,
but it is as yet absent. If in *On počti ne spit* (Lit. He almost
not sleeps) we keep concentrating on a single occurrence, we necessarily construe an activity of not-sleeping (whatever that may be)
which is almost there but which is at yet absent; in other words,
we eliminate the link between "ne" and the verb. In order to prevent the creation of an activity of not-sleeping, we must broaden
our view to the effect that it embraces more occurrences of a
sleeping-event. We then interpret the sentence as saying that most
potential occurrences of this event are absent, although there is
one from time to time. This iterative effect can also be observed
in the following attested example:

(7)   Il'ja *počti   ne   žil*   doma
            almost not lived
      (Il'ja hardly ever lived (slept etc.) at home)

Interestingly, Ivanova (1982: 142) mentions *počti* among the adverbs which lead to a spelling of *ne* plus adjective as a single
graphic word (no link) e.g.

(8) ... tot smysl, kotoryj ..., *počti neperevodim* na obyčnyj jazyk
almost untranslatable

  (... that sense, which ..., is almost untranslatable into ordinary language)

Note that the adverb is interpreted differently in the two cases:
in (7) it has a "temporal" sense, while in (8) it rather indicates
a degree. With verbs, the "degree" sense does not necessarily eliminate the link between "ne" and "v"; it rather brings us to the
more subtle distinction given in 5.4 below.
Compare further:

(9) Iz-za doždej mašiny teper' *počti ne chodjat*
almost not go ("indeterminate" form)

  (Lit. Because of the rain the cars now almost do not go, i.e.
there are hardly any cars travelling)

The sentence does not mean that the cars can hardly move because
of the rain but that they travel infrequently.
An example without *počti*:

(10) Samolëty iz-za plochoj pogody *ne idut*
not go ("determinate" form)

  (Lit. Because the weather is bad the planes do not go, i.e.
they cannot fly)

Here, because there is no *počti*, we are not urged to adopt a
broader view than that of the specific journey of every plane
which is cancelled.

    In this way, the part-whole idea of potential occurrences
makes it understandable, in my view, why *On počti pročital knigu*
(Lit. He almost read the book, perfective aspect) is a normal sentence, whereas *On počti ne pročital knigu* (Lit. He almost not read
the book, perfective aspect) is unacceptable, in contrast to *On
počti ne čitâl knig* (Lit. He almost not read books, imperfective
aspect).

    Another illustrative adverb is *ešče* (yet, still):

(11) Ja *ešče ne závtrakal*
    yet not breakfasted
    (still)
    (I have not had any breakfast yet)

Compare: *Kogda on vošël, ja ešče závtrakal* (When he entered I was still eating my breakfast). If time relationships remained the same in the negative (11), (11) would mean that I was still busy with an activity of not-eating; this odd idea eliminates the link between "ne" and the verb. In order to prevent this from happening, we interpret (11) as saying that potential occurrences of break-fasting are removed from the time indicated by "ešče"; this leaves potential occurrences for after that time.

Note that I propose to treat the positive and the negative sentence in a different way. Of course, in *ja ešče závtrakal,* the meaning of *ešče* instructs us to imagine a time when the event of breakfasting will be absent, and in *ja ešče ne závtrakal* the event and its ab-sence are seemingly simply interchanged. But we need a trick in order to arrive at this idea. The point is that in *ja ešče závtrakal* the event of breakfasting is introduced against the background of its expected absence. If the negative sentence were interpreted in the same way, it would introduce not-breakfasting against the back-ground of its expected absence: the link between "ne" and the verb would be eliminated, "ne zavtrakal" referring to an event instead of to the absence of an event. In order not to evoke the thought of the absence of a (positive) event of not-breakfasting, but only of the absence of an event of breakfasting (without a further nega-tion of this absence), we must imagine the events of breakfasting which could have occurred in the time indicated by "ešče" as a part of a whole of potential occurrences, the rest of this whole being placed after the time indicated.

Note further that I have not moved an event of breakfasting from the time indicated by "ešče" to some later moment. Instead, I have introduced several potential occurrences, and removed some while leaving the others.

This procedure enables us to arrive at a referent of "ne zavtrakal" via "zavtrakal", so that the referent of "ne zavtrakal" is not opposed to its own absence. (For the proposal not to move around referents compare *On byl ne v kômnate* in 4.1.)

I think the procedure described here adequately explains the fact that, in general, *ešče* combines with a verb in the perfective aspect only if the latter is negated: the potential occurrence(s) which is (are) left for after the time from which potential occurrences are removed may be perfective, because the durative character of *ešče* applies only to the time from which potential occurrences are removed. In the positive case, however, the referent of the verb is located in the stretch of time indicated by "ešče", so that the aspect of the verb may not contradict the durative character of the adverb.

An exception to the general impossibility of *ešče* plus perfective aspect (without a negation) is the verb *ostat'sja* (to remain; see Barentsen 1979: 154), presumably because this verb is inherently negative in the sense explained in K 1985 (: 274-276), i.e. given our normal picture of the world, the interpretation of the lexical meaning of the verb involves the two-step procedure characteristic of negative sentences. This feature is relevant to the scope of accents as well as to the use of aspect here.

I now turn to some examples which put the three types of combination introduced in 4.4 into direct pairwise contrast.

A. ⌐──►─⌐──⌐ vs. B. ⌐──►─◄─⌐─►─⌐

(12) Oni *kategoríčeski ne chotját* puskat' eë v Moskvû   (A)
      categorically not want
     (They categorically do not want ("diswant") to let her go to
     Moscow)

(13) ... formy ... padežej ... *morfologíčeski ne različájutsja* (B)
                               morphologically not are-dis-
                                                        tinguished
     (The case forms are not morphologically distinguished (but
     they may be distinguished in a different way))

Here also belong (1) (*srázu ne ponrávilas'*, A) vs. (6) (*srázu ne zamêtili*, B).

B.  vs. C.

(14) Ja vas *dôlgo ne zaderžû*   (B)
           long   not shall-detain
     (I shall not detain you long, i.e. I am detaining you, but it
     won't last long)

(15) Ja teper' *dôlgo* vas *ne   uvîžu* (C)
               long   not shall-see
     (I shall not see you now, for a long time)

As described in the foregoing, the difference between the parallel
link in (14) and the forward link in (15) pertains to the way in
which the adverb is combined with the *ne*+V complex. In (14), only
"dolgo" combines with the not-detaining; the thing which lasts
not long is the detaining (not the not-detaining):

```
 ┌─► "dolgo" ----- "ne" "zaderžu" ◄┐
 └─ "not dolgo" ----- "zaderžu"    ┘
                       "not zaderžu"
```

In (15), in contrast, *dolgo* says how long the absence of seeing
will last; it will last long, but it could have lasted not long.
That is, the "not dolgo" negated by the accent on *dolgo*, as well
as "dolgo" itself, combine with "ne uvižu", "dolgo" replacing
"not dolgo":

```
 ┌─► "dolgo"
 └─ "not dolgo" "ne" "uvižu" ◄┐
                     "uvižu"  ┘
                     "not uvižu"
```

As we saw in the foregoing, such a combination removes potential
seeing-events from the stretch of time indicated by "dolgo"; it
leaves the rest of the potential occurrences for after that
time.

As is well-known, type (15) does not allow perfective aspect in
the preterite. Thus, alongside (15) (perfective aspect), we find
e.g. (16):

(16) V poslednej kvartire *dôlgo ne otkryvâli*
                          long not opened (imperfective, preterite)
    (For a long time, people in the last apartment did not open
    the door)

In the intended reading, (16) has it that potential opening-
events are removed from the stretch of time indicated by "dolgo";
this leaves potential occurrences for after that time (two forward
links). (With no link between "ne" and the verb the sentence would
mean (incoherently) that for a long time, people were busy not
opening the door. With a parallel link between "dolgo" and "ne+V"
it would mean that, if the door was opened, then for a short time
only; this idea requires *nadolgo* rather than *dolgo*.)

C. ⌐——▶——⌐——▶——⌐   vs. A. ⌐——▶——⌐——▶——⌐

(17) Medvež'ich uglôv zdes' *bôl'še ne suščestvûet*   (C)
                            more   not exist
    (Remote places do not exist here anymore)

(18) Rebënok *vsë bôl'še i   bôl'še ne doverjâl* vzrôslym (A)
             more   and more   not trusted
    (The child, more and more, distrusted adults)

Examples like (18) must be further specified as "ne do V" in
order to keep them apart from "ne do V" (see 4.2 above).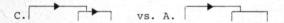
Note that the adverb *bol'še* is interpreted differently in the two
cases. In (17) it acquires a "temporal" interpretation; what
"grows" here is time: as time proceeds, the existence of remote
places is removed. In (18) it is the degree of distrust which
grows. With a parallel link, which is in principle the third
possibility, I would expect an atemporal sense of *bol'še*. Possibly,
Glovinskaja (1982: 68) alludes to the existence of this type when

she observes that in *Ból'še ja ne mogú napisat'* (Môre I cânnot
write - perfective infinitive), *bol'še* has an "object" sense.
In contrast, in *Ból'še ja ne mogu pisât'* (idem, imperfective infinitive) the "temporal" sense of *bol'še* is more likely, according
to Glovinskaja.[9]

The fact that the interpretation of the adverb changes according to the organization chosen, and the fact that an individual adverb does not necessarily occur with all organizations, makes it necessary to investigate every adverb (or type of adverb) separately.
For example, with *srazu* I found A. and B. but not C. In this case,
the gap can possibly be filled by collecting more examples or
construing the appropriate context (and choosing the appropriate
aspect), but the lexical meaning of an adverb may be too specific
to be compatible with the meaning of a certain organization. The
same holds true, of course, for the lexical meaning of the verb.
Obviously, then, the observations here do not exhaust the subject;
hopefully, they sufficiently illustrate that the use of verbal
aspect in negative sentences is related to organizations in projection time.

4.6 Removal of whole, second level: a predictable problem

Consider (19):

(19) Struktura suždenija i členenie predloženija *óčen' često ne*
                                                   very often not

    sovpadâjut ...
    coincide   ...
    (The structure of the judgement and the partition of the
    sentence very often do not coincide)

In the intended reading, "očen' často ne sovpadajut", we remove
potential occurrences of the event from the time indicated by
"very often"; this leaves the rest of the potential occurrences
for the remainder of time. (With a parallel link the sentence
would mean that *p* and *q* do not very often coincide.) As we saw in
the foregoing, the differentiation between T in which all occurrences are placed and the t's of the individual occurrences,

saves the link between "ne" and the verb.

Now, if we wish to remove the whole of potential occurrences, the appropriate adverb to use would seem to be *vsegda* (always): *p i q vsegdâ ne sovpadâjut* (Lit. p and q always not coincide). However, if such a sentence occurs (I have found no examples with the given word order), it will probably have the last accent on the adverb: *p* and *q* âlways (and not, e.g., only sometimes) do not coincide (i.e. first type of inference, variant for *positive* sentences - see 3.2.3). The reading we are looking for now, however, viz. "it is âlways the case that *p* and *q* do not coincîde", is not normally expressed by means of *vsegda*; instead, we shift to the negative quantifier *nikogda* (never).[10] Why this drastic step? Because otherwise we would need a further time-distinction in order to save the link between "ne" and the verb: besides T from which the whole of potential occurrences is removed, we would need a further T' for the rest of potential occurrences. This is obviously incoherent because there is no rest if the whole is removed and a T' level does not seem to exist in Russian. The projection "T" is the ultimate time-stop; its referent is not part of a larger whole, and we cannot arrive at a projection of the absence of T: even if there is no link between "ne" and the verb, "not ne V" does not refer to the absence of T but to the absence of the event concerned in T.

The reasoning in the foregoing makes it understandable, then, that *p i q vsegdâ ne sovpadâjut* is not a normal Russian sentence. The alternative, *p i q nikogdâ ne sovpadâjut,* must have a parallel link in order to preclude a thought of the absence of the referent of "nikogda", which thought would render the referent positive (cf. the end of 4.3). The sentence differs from our earlier examples with a parallel link in its relation to truth: whereas, e.g., *srâzu ne zamêtili* (example (6)) says that both "srazu" - "ne zametili" and "not srazu" - "zametili" are correct projections of the state of affairs referred to, a *ni ... ne* combination does not mean that both "nikogda" - "ne sovpadajut" and "vsegda" - "sovpadajut" are correct; instead, the truth of the former excludes the truth of the latter, and vice versa (see further K 1985: 302-312). In this way, Russian *ni ... ne* combinations group with "absolute absence" cases, where also only either the positive or the negative sentence is correct (4.3); this grouping takes place despite the parallel link. In English and Dutch, in contrast, fused negations (*no-*) group with other parallel links (despite the fact that the sentences concerned may convey absolute absence). To be sure, the inherent meanings of the words involved differ slightly in the two types of system (absence of whole vs. empty part of that whole); otherwise, one of the two groupings would be illogical.

4.7 A further distinction concerning parallel links

In all examples with adverbs discussed so far, the adverb preceded *ne* plus verb immediately. Many other adverb positions are possible, and they must all be examined separately, a task which I shall not undertake here. But one interesting case can be mentioned: when the adverb is in initial position. Strings *adverb - subject - ... - ne - V* can have a parallel link:

"adverb subject ... ne verb"

For example:

(20) Èti fakty ne ostalis' nezamečennymi, no *detál'no oni* do sich
                                                in-detail they
     por *ne* byli razrabôtany
       not were worked-out
     (These facts did not remain unnoticed, but so far, they have not been worked out in detail; i.e. they were worked out, but not in detail)

(21) Odnako *pôlnost'ju oni* nas *ne* *udovletvorjâjut* iz-za ...
        fully   they   not satisfy
     (But they do not satisfy us completely because of ...)

Compare (same adverb, different position):

(22) ... semantičeskaja kategorija opredelënnosti (neopredelënnosti) v russkom jazyke *pôlnost'ju ne*
                               fully   not
grammatikalizovâlas' i ...
grammaticalized
(The semantic category of definitiveness (indefinitiveness)
did not fully grammaticalize in Russian and ...)

Examples of type (20)/(21) are far more difficult to find than
cases like (22) (adverb immediately preceding *ne* plus V).
    Padučeva (1969: 21-23) suggests a semantic difference between
the two adverb positions (with a parallel link in both cases). She
paraphrases *On grômko ne rassmejâlsja* (Lit. He lôudly not lâughed)
as follows: "To li izvestno, čto on rassmejalsja, no ne gromko, to
li izvestno tol'ko to, čto on ne rassmejalsja gromko" (Either it
is known that he laughed, but not loudly, or it is known only that
he did not laugh loudly). About *Grômko on ne rassmejâlsja* (Lit.
Lôudly he not lâughed), in contrast, the author remarks: "To li on
rassmejalsja, no ne gromko, to li ne rassmejalsja voobšče" (Either
he laughed, but not loudly, or he did not laugh at all). Elsewhere
on the same pages Padučeva remarks that *Pričina tôčno ne ustanôvlena* (Lit. The cause exâctly not was-estâblished) does not presuppose any contrasts, whereas she continues *Tôčno pričina ne
ustanôvlena* (Lit. Exâctly the cause not was-estâblished) with: *a
ustanovlena li voobšče - neizvestno* (but whether it is established
at all is unknown).
    In combination with the observations cited in K 1985 (: 300-
301), viz. that *vsegda* (always), *nikogda* (never), *uže* (already),
eščë (still, yet), *srazu* (immediately), *snova* (again), and also
vsjudu (everywhere), *vezde* (everywhere), *nigde* (nowhere), do not
often occur in sentence-initial position (the list does not differentiate between various link-types and positive/negative, of
course), and in combination with my own observations, Padučeva's
remark induces me to suggest the following.
The essence of a parallel link is that the two levels of my type
of diagram refer to the same state of affairs, the latter being
pictured independently by "p" in 1.6. In comparison with forward

and backward links, this is a type of non-coincidence of projections. However, there is a lower level type of non-coincidence,
the one introduced in 1.4 (e.g. the level "person"). I think the
two adverb positions differ on this lower level, given a parallel
link in both cases: if the adverb is immediately before *ne* plus
verb, the projection introduced by the adverb coincides with the
projection of the property it refers to; if the adverb is in
initial position, the property involved is projected independently, i.e. "not adverb" does not refer to the absence of the property but to the property without its identifying property. Thus,
in the following sentence, what is left open is the possibility
that the grammatical structure has been studied; if it has been
studied, then the study lacks the property "especially":

(23) ... grammatičeskij stroj sovremennogo russkogo jazyka
     speciâl'no ne izučâlsja
     especially not was-studied
     (The grammatical structure of contemporary Russian was not
     especially studied)

If, however, the adverb is in initial position, "special'no"
would be, I think, a projection of the way in which the grammatical structure was studied; "special'no" incorrectly character-
izes the way in which the structure was studied, i.e. if we
choose "special'no", we must combine it with "ne izučalsja";
this leaves open the possibility that, if we choose a different
adverb, the way in which the structure was studied would be
characterized correctly.

    This suggestion, which must be verified by collecting more
examples, especially of adverbs in initial position, accounts for
the fact that *nikogda* and *nigde* strongly prefer the preverbal
position: they refer to the absence of the whole involved (not to
a given number of times/places of which "nikogda"/"nigde" is an
incorrect projection). Further, in preverbal position the adverb
can be unaccented (if the contrast applies to a preceding word);
this does not seem to be possible if the adverb is placed in
initial position.

Finally, the distinction being suggested here is supported by a
Dutch case to be mentioned in 5.3 below: as we saw in 2.6, Dutch
allows a parallel link only if the adverb is in initial position
(i.e. with VS order); but this possibility is restricted to the
reading expressed in Russian by *âdverb - S - ne - V̂*; in a case
which would lead to the other reading, Dutch avoids a parallel
link (see 5.3).

4.8 Poka ... ne (until; as long as not)

The conjunction *poka* has been studied in unprecedented detail
by Barentsen (e.g. 1973; 1979). For combinations of *poka* and *ne* he
found two main types. The so-called type 4 can be recognized by
the fact that it allows the inclusion of *eščë* in the sentence; for
example:

(24) Studenty uporno zanimajutsja, *poka*   ich *(eščë)*   *ne*
                                    as-long-as them yet/still not
     raspustili na kanikuly
     dismissed
     (The students work unwaveringly as long as they have not yet
     been dismissed for the vacation)

This type is covered by the distinctions introduced in the foregoing:
     "eščë ne raspustili"

That is, potential occurrences of the event "they dismissed the
students" are removed from the stretch of time indicated by "eščë"
(or "poka"), so that the rest of the potential occurrences are
left for after that time (see 4.3-4.5).

The second main type of *poka ... ne* sentence, called type 1
by Barentsen, is a special type of *ne* sentence; it has not been
treated in this chapter. Consider the following example (for ease
of comparison one with an adverb):

(25) Kogda ja perečital dannoe predloženie, ono pokazalos' mne
neumestnym, *poka*   ja *nakonec ne   pónjal*   , čto ...
             as-long-as   finally not understood
(When I reread the given sentence, it seemed inappropriate
to me, until I, at last, understood that ...)

What is special here, in my terms, is that the presence of *poka*
enables us to withhold "ne" for some time, to the effect that the
accent is interpreted in the same way as in a positive sentence,
i.e. (see 3.2.1):

```
       II
"ne"  "V"    ◄┐          --- level 2 and level 3
   "not V"  ─┘  I        --- level 1
```

Thus, the negation of "V" (negated by the accent) is "not V" here,
referring to the absence of the event. The accent asserts the
event, i.e. the event replaces its absence. Simultaneously, however, "ne V" refers to the absence of the event. This combination
is possible by virtue of the fact that "poka" enables us to relate
"ne V" and "V" to different times, so that the event can be absent
in one stretch of time while its presence is asserted for another
moment. In comparison with (24) the special point is the assertion,
the replacement of "not V" by "V" by means of the accent. In (24)
potential occurrences of the event are left for after the stretch
indicated by "poka", but they are not asserted, because "not V" is
relegated to the past by linking "ne" to "V", so that the negation
of "ne V" is "V":

```
    I
"ne"  "V"  ◄┐          --- level 3
   "V"  ─┘  II         --- level 2
   "not V"             --- level 1 (relegated to the past)
```

The traditional treatment of sentences like (25) has it that
such sentences contain the complex conjunction *poka ne* rather than
a combination of *poka* and *ne*. I see no reason to deny that "poka"
and "ne" make their own, separate contribution, but *poka* does
introduce an additional syntactic possibility for *ne* plus verb.

This case constitutes one end-point of the range of possibilities; at the other extreme are combinations without a link between "ne" and "V". In both cases an event replaces its absence in one step, but in the *poka*-case the event is the referent of "V", whereas in the no-link-case it is the referent of "ne V".

4.9 Combinations

An issue requiring further research is the question as to which types given in the foregoing may be combined in one sentence. From the discussion, only one point follows directly, in my view: a parallel link implies a forward link between "ne" and the verb. This is because a parallel link says:

```
"x" ----- "ne" "V"
"not x" -----    "V"
              ("not V")
```

In order for "not x" to concur with "V", "ne" must be linked forwards to "V"; otherwise (no link), "not x" would concur with "not ne V", which contradicts the time-stop idea of a parallel link. Thus, my analysis predicts, for example, that if we, starting from a sentence without a link between "ne" and the verb, insert a *ni*-word, which requires a parallel link (assuming that the normal interpretation of the *ni*-word is to be retained), the interpretation of the sentence changes, because the parallel link replaces "ne V" by "ne V".
For example, starting from (1):

(1) Ona *srâzu*   *ne ponrâvilas'* nam
         immediately not pleased
     (We disliked her immediately)

we replace *nam* (us) by *nikomu* (nobody) (or *ona* (she) by *nikto* (nobody)):

(26) *Nikomú* ona *srâzu*   *ne   ponrâvilas'*
    Nobody she immediately not pleased

Predictably, this sentence does not mean "Everybody disliked her immediately", nor "Nobody disliked her immediately", but "Nobody liked her immediately" (but some people may have started to like her later). The reasoning is as follows.
In (1) we start with

"srazu ne ponravilas'

Then, the *ni*-word in (26) requires

"ne ponravilas'" instead of "ne ponravilas'"

In principle, this leaves two possibilities for linking up "srazu":

"srazu ne ponravilas'" and "srazu ne ponravilas'"

But the former is incoherent, given the meaning of *srazu* and that of the perfective aspect.

The message "Everybody disliked her immediately" can be expressed by means of *vse: Vsêm ona srâzu ne ponrâvilas'* (Lit. To-all she immediately not pleased). Note that this *vs-* plus *ne* combination has quite a different interpretation from the *ni* plus *ne* combination in (26) (cf. 4.6 above and 5.1 below). It will be clear that the message "Nobody disliked her immediately" (but some people may have started to dislike her later) cannot be expressed with the given ingredients.

Sentences like (26), with two parallel links, occur regularly. One attested example:

(27) ... oni [prostye sintagmy] ... *ničêm*   *principial'no*
                                  nothing (instr.) principally
    ne   otličâjutsja   ot sintagm dvučlênnych
    not are-distinguished

(They [simple syntagms] in no respect differ fundamentally
from two-part syntagms, i.e. (approximately) they may be
different in some respects, but such differences are then not
fundamental)

What is more interesting is the question of what happens if
we combine ⌐ → ◄ ⌐ with ⌐ → ⌐ ► ⌐ . Such combinations do not seem to be excluded:

(28) ... no oni [êti sredstva] *v*   *dostâtočnoj stepeni eščë*
                          to a sufficient   degree   yet/still
  ne *izûčeny*
  not are-studied (participle)
  (But they [these means] have not yet been studied sufficiently)

Yet, questionable examples can easily be constructed.
For example, starting from

(16) V poslednej kvartire *dólgo ne otkryvâli*
                      long   not opened
  (For a long time, people in the last apartment did not open
  the door)

the insertion of *nikto* (nobody) renders the sentence uninterpret-
able:

(29) ? *Niktô dolgo(e vremja) ne otkryvâl*
    Nobody long time   not opened

The sentence can be made acceptable by replacing *dolgo* by *nadolgo*;
in that case it says: "Nobody opened the door for a long time, but
some people may have opened it for a short time", i.e. two parallel links.
Alternatively, we may place the adverb(ial phrase) in initial position; with that arrangement, the parallel chunk can be linked
backwards to the adverb, which eliminates the problem:

(30) *Dólgoe vremja niktô ne otkryvál*
Long   time   nobody not opened
(For a long time, nobody opened the door)

In this way, many messages can be imagined which would drive an informant crazy.

4.10 Spelling

As mentioned in the general introduction (0), a *ne* plus verb combination is written as two words unless the verb does not occur without *ne-* (excepting the *ne do-* vs. *nedo-* cases mentioned in 4.2). The discussion in this chapter hopefully explains why such an arbitrary rule is a wise solution. Given the fact that only two options are available for spelling (one word or two words), any semantically motivated proposal takes into account one opposition but disregards others. Clearly, a good candidate for one-word spelling is the type *Ona srázu ne ponrávilas' nam* (We disliked her immediately) or the type *Rebënok vsë ból'še i ból'še ne doverjál vzróslym* (The child more and more distrusted adults). These types more or less parallel the *neprijatel'* case of Chapter Three. One disadvantage of this solution would be that, in the imperfective aspect, no distinction is made, in that case, between *nenavidet'* (to hate), which does not occur without *ne-*, and *nenravit'sja* (to displease), which does; in the perfective aspect these would be distinguished by prefix-placement: *voznenavidet'* vs. *neponravit'sja*. Further, the present graphic distinction between "ne doV" and "nedoV" would be eliminated. But a far more serious disadvantage would be the suggested equivalence between "ne prijatel'" as used in Chapter Three and "ne čitaet". These are equivalent only if with "ne čitaet" we remove a part on the first level (He is not reading but watching television). It has been proposed that this point should be taken as the borderline, i.e. *On ne čitáet, a smotrit televízor* (two words) vs. *nečitaet* (one word) in all other cases. But then it is suggested that *nečitaet* is equivalent to *neprijatel'*, which is just as bad, because this "nečitaet" projects the absence of an event, while "neprijatel" refers to an entity, not to the absence of an entity. Also, parallel links would create a problem; these are, starting from the other side, a clear motivation for two-word spelling (as *ne* does not "apply to" the verb here). One-word spelling in the *poka*-case is, of course, monstrous. Examples not discussed here, where "ne" is linked to a whole stretch, would also be problematic.

Since the spelling problem is insoluble anyway, we'd better leave it as it is, unsolved.

CHAPTER FIVE

NOTES ON SCALES

5.0 *Introduction*

Quantifiers, especially when combined with a negation, have always interested logicians and linguists, because they seem to exhibit a number of idiosyncrasies. My suggestions in K 1985 (278-312) differ from earlier proposals in many respects. Importantly, they do not recognize the notion "scope of a quantifier". Further, they do not assume any ("deep") structures in which quantifiers and/or negations are placed elsewhere than where they are in surface structure; hence, no "transformations" such as "negation transportation" are postulated. Instead, I have applied the basic distinction between "x and its negation belong to the same moment" and "x and its negation belong to different moments", which recurs in information structure in every conceivable place, to an additional level in the case of quantifiers; this results in a distinction between concurrent and non-concurrent parts (see 1.8).

Together with five types of inference (see 1.9), which are not
restricted to quantifiers, this accounts for most relevant readings. One further distinction will be added in this chapter (5.2);
it deals with removing a part if the thing from which a part is
being removed is, itself a part. The distinction accounts for the
fact that, e.g. Jespersen's (1966: 81) *"the hill is not two
hundred feet high"* is interpreted as conveying that the hill is
less than two hundred feet high, unless the numeral is "strongly
stressed" (ibid.): *"the hill is not 'two hundred feet high, but
'three hundred"*.
This fact has worried logicians a great deal. It has even led to
the idea that, e.g., *two* means "at least two"; in Gricean pragmatics the reading "exactly two" is then derived as a Gricean impli-
cature (e.g. Horn 1978: 136-137). In contrast to this view, I do
not assume any meaning other than "two"; the possibility of two
readings has, in my view, a natural explanation.
The same point explains why logicians are inclined to call, e.g.,
Nôt many of us wanted the wâr the "sentential negation" of *Mâny of
us wanted the wâr* (see below).

Before we come to that point, in 5.1 some examples are given
of Russian sentences with *vs-* (all) and *ne,* in this order; they
illustrate the difference between my third and fourth types of
inference (K 1985: 293-302). The fourth type, i.e., e.g., *Vsê ne
priêchali* (Lit. Éverybody not arrîved) in the sense "not everybody
arrived", may be unfamiliar to the English-speaking reader, as it
is of very restricted occurrence in English *(Âll that glitters
îsn't gold)*. It must not be confused with the second type, mentioned in 2.2. The second type, which is quite normal in English,
has the last accent on the quantifier and a sentence-final intonation rise; as mentioned in 2.2, this type does not occur in
Russian. Instead, the fourth type has at least two accents and no
sentence-final intonation rise (if such a rise is present in the
few English examples it is not essential).

It must perhaps be mentioned that my inferences have little
to do with truth in the sense of traditional logic; they, inter
alia, group together readings which are treated in quite different
places in logic. One potential source of confusion is the following.

As is well-known, Jespersen (1966: 44) regarded a sentence like
Mâny of us didn't want the wâr as a case of nexal negation; in
contrast, *Nôt many of us wanted the wâr* is, with Jespersen, a
case of special negation. Logic-oriented linguists who distinguish
between sentential and constituent negation would rather call *Nôt
many of us wanted the wâr* the sentential negation of *Mâny of us
wanted the wâr*, because the truths of these sentences are incompatible, whereas the truth of *Mâny of us didn't want the wâr* is
compatible with that of *Mâny of us wanted the wâr* (e.g. Horn 1978:
133-134). In my framework, *Mâny of us didn't want the wâr* would be
described as a third inferential type from *Mâny of us wanted the
wâr*, and vice versa. In the example, the type uses concurrent
parts (complements), "many of us" in one sentence referring to
persons other than the persons referred to by "many of us" in the
other sentence. Thus, the observation that the truths of the two
sentences are compatible is, in my view, just as trivial as the
observation that $John_1$ *didn't want the war* is compatible with
$John_2$ *wanted the war*. The semantic phenomenon ensuring that logicians call *Nôt many of us wanted the wâr* the sentential negation
of *Mâny of us wanted the wâr* will be described in 5.2 below; it
is indeed the case that words like *many* allow an interpretation
which is also characteristic of, e.g., verbs (see 4.1). Hence
Jespersen's and the logician's points of view.
Further, just as "many" and "many" (in the two sentences above)
may refer to concurrent parts, "everybody" and "nobody" may. Thus,
"Everybody didn't want the war" is an inference from *Nôbody wanted
the wâr*, "everybody" and "nobody" referring to each other's complements here. (Starting from *nobody* gives the fifth type rather
than the third because of some additional complications there.)
This pair would, in logic, be treated quite differently from the
many-case, because the *everybody* - *nobody* pair consists of logically equivalent sentences. (*Everybody wanted the wâr* and *Nôbody
wanted the wâr* are contraries, etc.) The fact that *Nôbody wanted
the wâr* is necessarily true if "Everybody didn't want the war" is
true, while *Mâny of us wanted the wâr* is not necessarily true if
"Many of us didn't want the war" is true, has no role to play in
my framework (although it follows from my distinctions, of course).

Thus, the inferences state which conclusions can be drawn by a hearer on the basis of the given accent distribution and the inherent meanings of the words, irrespective of whether he must draw such a conclusion or may not do so according to logicians.

5.1 Third vs. fourth type of inference: vs- examples

In 4.6 we saw that *p i q vsegdâ ne sovpadâjut* is not a normal Russian sentence, at least in the reading "it is always the case that *p* and *q* do not coincide". Elsewhere, combinations of *vs-* and *ne* do occur; some attested examples will be given in this section. The fact that they do occur is more remarkable in Russian than it is in English because, e.g., "it is always the case that *p* and *q* do not coincide" says (third type of inference) "it is never the case that *p* and *q* coincide"; but, in contrast to English *never*, Russian *nikogda* does not refer to the complement of the *vs-*word; instead, it refers to the absence of the whole in question (given *ne* before the verb). Although Russian has no word referring to the complement of the *vs-*word, the thought of the complement can be evoked. This thought is the concurrent negation of the *vs-*word (using concurrent parts here).

The technical description of the inferences can be found in K 1985 (: 293–302). In the examples following below the third type has the following form. There is a subject containing *vs-*. The predicate contains *ne* plus verb. The sentence has a backward link between predicate and subject. It states the truth of the combination *vs-* ... *ne V*. The inference holds that the combination of 1. the complement of the *vs-*word, and 2. *V*, is also true. In effect, the sentence says *Âll x* ... *not V̂*, and the interpretation is *Nô x* ... *V̂*.

The fourth type of inference uses non-concurrent parts. (The third type is also possible with non-concurrent parts, but I have as yet found no Russian *vs-* examples of this application.) Again, the subject contains *vs-* and the predicate *ne* plus *V*. This time, the two constituents are linked up by means of a parallel link. The sentence states the truth of the combination *vs-* ... *ne V*.

346

The inference holds that the combination of 1. a non-concurrent part to the vs-word, and 2. $\hat{V}$, is also true. In effect, the sentence says $\hat{All} x \ldots not \hat{V}$, and the interpretation is $N\hat{o}t all x \ldots \hat{V}$ (not all here stands for a non-concurrent part to all, e.g. many - see the picture in 1.8).

Under every example it is indicated which reading was probably meant in the source of the example (taking into account the context).

Examples:

(31) No *vsê êto* *ne* *imelo* uspêcha
But all that not had   success
(intended reading: nothing had success; third type)

(32) Učebnikov bolgarskogo jazyka suščestvuet neskol'ko. ...
(There are several text-books for the Bulgarian language)
Vsê oni, odnako, *ne* *rasščîtany* special'no na studenta-
All they, however, not are-meant especially for student
rusîsta
of-Russian
(intended reading: no text-book is especially meant for ...;
third type)

(33) ...*vsê* êti   suščestvitel'nye *ne* *dopuskâjut* sočetânija s....
all these nouns   not allow   combination with...
(intended reading: none of the nouns allow ...; third type)

(34) *Vsê* dela / vsech del   *ne* *peredêlaes'*
All things / (genitive) not you-do
(intended reading: one cannot do everything; fourth type)

(35) *Vsê* nesobstvenno sintaksîčeskie ... otnošenija,..., *ne*
All improperly   syntactic   ... relations,..., not
svôdjatsja k aktual'nomu členeniju, ...
reduce   to actual   division, ...
(intended reading: not all ... relations can be reduced
to ...; fourth type)

(36) *Vsê* slučai, kogda ..., *ne polučâjut* dolžnogo ob"jasnênija
All cases, when ..., not receive appropriate explanation
v ramkach tradiciõnnogo ...
in framework of-traditional ...
(intended reading: not all cases ... receive ...; fourth type)

(37) ... v svjazi s čem *vsê* javlenija, svjazannye s ...,
in connection with which all phenomena, connected with...,
ne mõgut polučit' ob"jasnênija v ramkach tradiciõnnogo...
not can receive explanation in framework of-traditional ...
(intention unclear: in which connection all phenomena cannot
be explained / not all phenomena can be explained)

(38) No *vsê* oni otnjûd' *ne javlâjutsja* variantami odnogô
But all they absolutely not are variants of-single
predloženija
sentence
(intention unclear: they are all by no means variants of .../
by no means all of them are variants of ...)

Etc.

In speech, accent distribution probably helps to resolve the
ambiguity. It can be expected that the possibility of a "not all"
reading decreases if, after the negated verb, a long stretch follows, which can hardly be entirely unaccented.

According to Padučeva (1969: 19), Puškin's sentence *Vsë eščë*
ne propâlo (Lit. Everything still/yet not is-lost, i.e. not everything is already lost) is nowadays perceived as a gallicism (in
the sense indicated). This seems to be a strange characterization,
because sentences like (34)-(38) do occur, despite their lack of
clarity. Possibly, Padučeva has in mind a reading according to the
second type of inference (she indicates only the accent on *vsë*),
which is indeed non-Russian (see 2.2). But probably, it is the embedded forward link between "eščë" and "ne propalo" which makes
things worse (cf. 4.9):

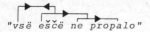

"vsë ešče ne propalo"

Interestingly, in her own generative treatment Paduceva stars out
as ungrammatical *vs-* ... *ne* combinations in the "all ... not"
reading, replacing them by *ni* ... *ne* combinations (e.g. op.cit.:
18). As illustrated by (31)-(33), things are more complicated than
that.

Although some authors incidentally mention examples like (31)
-(38), the questions raised by the data remain without an answer.
One question is: what difference exists between *vs-* ... *ne* with
the third type of inference and *ni-* ... *ne* ? I would suggest that
a close inspection of the contexts in which these alternative expressions occur could clarify this point. Note that the interpretations of the two meanings come close to each other only in some
sentences; as we saw in 4.9, circumstances exist where the two convey quite different ideas.
A second question is: what difference exists between *vse-*... *ne*
with the fourth type of inference and *ne vs-* ? In Dutch, where the
same two arrangements occur, the basic difference is the following.
Alle x ... *niet V* (all x ... not V) says: *if* some x V, then not
all x V; this leaves open the possibility that no x V. This possibility is excluded in *niet alle x* ... *V* (not all x ... V); the
latter arrangement says that at least one x V. For example, in a
context speculating on what would happen if all houses burnt down
simultaneously, if all cars were in the same street at the same
moment, etc., the following sentence appeared: *Alle huizen brânden
niet tegelijk af* (Lit. All houses bûrn not simultaneously down).
In the given context this sentence cannot be replaced by *Niet alle
huizen branden tegelijk âf* (or a different accentuation) (Lit. Nôt
all houses burn simultaneously dôwn); the latter implies that at
least some houses burn down simultaneously, whereas the author intended only to put an end to his phantasy. Probably, the difference in Russian is comparable; this would explain why people sometimes prefer the unclarity of (34)-(38) to the unambiguity of *ne
vs-:* the latter excludes more than they want to.

More complicated questions concern the possibilities of combining various types of link in one sentence (cf. 4.9).

5.2 Removing a part of a part

Recall from 4.1 the following diagram for removing a part on the first level (type: *On ne čitâet, a smotrit televízor):*

activity minus identifying property /reading/ = "ne čitaet"
activity incl. identifying property /reading/ =   "čitaet"
absence of reading (relegated to the past)   =   "not čitaet" ↑

The name "part-whole organization" used here and elsewhere in the foregoing has the sense indicated in 1.5; it abbreviates a certain relationship between organizations in projection time and the things referred to.
In *on ne čitâet, a smotrit televízor* we do not, of course, actually cut off a part of his activity; we only mentally deprive the activity of its identifying property. In the same way, in *ne prijâtel'* as discussed in Chapter Three, we mentally remove an incorrectly assigned identifying property and not, e.g., a leg of the friend: the person involved cannot lose his identity by losing a leg, so we must apply the part-whole idea on a more abstract conceptual level.

Now, if we are talking about the non-concurrent parts of a pie (see 1.8), we have a case where we can deprive something of its identity in both ways: we either mentally remove the identifying property of a piece of the pie, so that an unidentified thing remains, or we mentally cut off a part of the piece, so that a smaller piece remains. Therefore, the diagram given above has two applications here. First (the "abstract sense"):

whole (part of the pie) minus part (id. prop.) = "ne""x"
whole (part of the pie) incl. part (id. prop.) =   "x"
absence of *x*   =   "not x" ↑

This is the sense applied in e.g. *The hill is not twô hundred feet high, but thrêe hundred:* we remove the identifying property /two/ (hundred feet) of the height of the hill; this leaves us with an unidentified height; the *but*-phrase makes explicit the first type

of inference (negative variant). This case exactly parallels the
procedure for *Ne prijâtel' priechal* (see 3.2). The element from
the environment which is used for identifying the height is one of
the non-concurrent parts to *two: one, three, four,* etc. Note that
any element from the environment can be used for identification
and that non-concurrent parts are imagined in this case as things
simultaneously available in the environment (cf. 4.1); the parts
of the pie are imagined as being, themselves, indivisible things
(cf. the friend whom we cannot deprive of his identity by removing
a leg).

Secondly (mentally cutting off a part):

whole (part of the pie) minus part (part of the part) = "ne""x"
whole (part of the pie) incl. part (part of the part) =   "x"
absence of *x*   =   "not x"

This is the idea we use in e.g. *The hill is not twô hundred feet
high* in the sense "The hill is less than two hundred feet high".
We now remove some of the height of the hill, so that we are left
with a hill less high than two hundred feet. This possibility is
available because we can deprive a part of the pie of its identity
by cutting off a part, the result being a new part.

Now, the last-mentioned case is interesting. What we have applied is the diagram for removing a part, i.e. the reading chosen
if *x* belongs to the environment where "ne x" has a referent (see
4.1). But what we have construed as referents for "x" and "ne x"
is non-concurrent parts, i.e. things which do not belong to each
other's environment because they exist at different moments. For
such referents we expect the application of the diagram for removing a whole (see 4.1), i.e. e.g. *On ne čitâet* in the sense "his
potential reading is absent". We have not applied such a diagram:
it removes his entire activity, or, here, the entire part of the
pie referred to by "x" (not a part of that part). So we have combined one feature characteristic of removal-of-part cases, viz.
the fact that only part of the thing involved is being removed,
with one feature characteristic of removal-of-whole cases, viz.
the fact that "ne x" and "x" do not have a referent simultaneously.

It is the last-mentioned feature which ensures that logicians call
Nôt many of us wanted the wâr "the" (sentential) negation of *Mâny
of us wanted the wâr*.

5.3 Further discussion

The "less than" reading of 5.2 creates an interesting conflict in Dutch. I will mention it here because it clearly illustrates the exceptional status of the type.
Just like the Russian *Ne prijâtel' priêchal* (see 3.4), the Dutch
translation *Niet de vriend kwâm* is unacceptable because of the
conflict between the part-whole organization prescribed by *niet* in
the subject and the backward link between the accented verb and
the subject.
Now, if we replace *de vriend* by a word allowing a "less than"
reading, such sentences become acceptable, e.g. *Niet iedereen kwam
op tijd* (Nôt everybody arrived on tîme). Since it is, in general,
a parallel link which resolves the conflict concerned, we are inclined to say that words like *iedereen* allow a parallel link to be
chosen here. However, all related facts tell us that this is not
what happens.
In the first place, the parallel link proposal does not account
for the fact that such sentences become odd if, here, the first
accent is on *iedereen* instead of *niet*. (Moreover, we cannot choose
then between *iedereen* and *iederêen* - cf. K 1985: 301-302.)
Secondly, if *Niet iedereen kwam op tijd* had a parallel link we
would expect the same possibility for, e.g., *Niet vaak kwam hij op
tijd* (Lit. Nôt often came he on tîme). But, in contrast to English *Nôt often did he arrive on time,* where Auxiliary - Subject
order has in principle no problem with a "less than" reading in
the first part of the sentence, the Dutch sentence is odd; more
specifically, it tends to be interpreted as English S-V order
(backward link) in, e.g., *Nôt long âfter, he arrived.* This is remarkable because, as mentioned in 2.6, Dutch V-S order allows a
parallel link in e.g. *Vâak kwam hij niet op tijd* (Lit. Ôften came

he nôt on time, i.e. not often did he arrive on time).
Clearly, Dutch at least prefers to restrict the use of parallel
links here to removal-of-part cases in the "abstract" sense: in
Vâak kwam hij niet op tijd, "not vaak" (negated by the first
accent) projects an unidentified number of times; the correct
identification of that number is filled in by means of the fourth
type of inference. In *?Niet vaak kwam hij op tijd*, in contrast,
"niet vaak" does not refer to an unidentified number of times but
to a number of times smaller than that referred to by "vaak"
("less than").[11]
These and other related facts make it very unlikely that the type
Niet iedereen kwam op tijd has a parallel link. Yet, the sentence
is fully acceptable. It seems to me that in such cases, Dutch
systematically, in word order as well as in accent placement,
chooses arrangements creating the same organizations of projections as a parallel link would do, but in such a way that the
elements can also be linked up in a different way. For example,
Niet iedereen kwâm is:

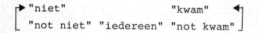

This organization can be a parallel link:

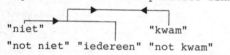

but the same organization corresponds to "overlapping constituents":

Cases where the "overlapping" option is not available because of
accent placement and/or word order are odd or unacceptable (*?Niet
iedereen kwam op tijd; ?Niet vaak kwam hij op tijd*). They would
not be odd/unacceptable if they allowed a parallel link. It would

be strange if the type *Niet iedereen kwâm (op tijd)* exceptionally allowed a parallel link. Hence it must be the "overlapping" option which applies here.

In Russian, the problem has quite a different solution. Here, the possibility of a parallel link cannot even be considered, because such a link requires *ne* before the verb, but we are talking about *ne* preceding a quantitative expression. The solution congruous with the rest of the system is: eliminating the link between "ne" and the quantitative expression. And indeed, we find, e.g., *nemnôgo* (not-much) for the "less than much" reading, vs. *ne mnôgo (a vsẽ)* (not mûch but êverything) for the other reading. But is spelling semantically correct here? That is, does *nemnôgo* indeed introduce a thought of the absence of the part arrived at by removing a part of the referent of "mnogo"? And is the further step of eliminating the link indeed not taken in, e.g., *ne vsë* (not everything), which is written as two words in both readings? With *vsë*, of course, it is less useful to keep the two apart, because the thing meant is a part smaller than *vsë* in either case, *vsë* indicating the extreme point of the scale involved. There are facts showing that spelling is surprisingly consistent here. Thus, for example, one may say *V nemnôgich strânach* (In some countries), whereas *?V ne vsêch strânach* (In not all countries) would rather be replaced by *Ne vo vsêch strânach* (Not in all countries); this shows that the connection between "ne" and "mnogie" is more intimate than that between "ne" and "vse". Also, *On nemnôgo pospâl* (Lit. He not-mûch slêpt) seems to convey the fact of his sleeping, just as *On mnôgo spâl* (Lit. He mûch slêpt) does. Compare: *?On ne vsegdâ spâl* (Lit. He not âlways slêpt), *?On ne čâsto spâl* (Lit. He not ôften slêpt), which do not parallel the positive *On vsegdâ spâl* (He âlways slêpt) and *On čâsto spâl* (He ôften slêpt). (This issue has not been discussed in Chapter Four; with the last accent on the adverb, i.e. *On ne vsegdâ/čâsto spal* the given strings are, of course, normal.)

Obviously, we have another issue for further research here. For this moment, it suffices to say that the distinction between forward link and no link is not the same as the distinction between the two readings introduced in 5.2, so there is no reason,

in principle, why we could not distinguish between, e.g.,
"ne⃗ mnogo" and "ne‾ mnogo", both for the "less than much" reading.
But evidently, the conceptual complexity of such a distinction
favours its elimination.

Elsewhere, the word *i* (in the sense "even") is used for the
"less than" reading. For example: *On i 5-i knîg ne pročital* (Lit.
He even 5̂ bôoks not read), i.e. he has read less than 5 books;
versus: *On pročital ne 5̂ knig, a 6̂* (Lit. He read not 5̂ books but
6̂ (or any other number)). Interestingly, the *i* ... *ne* construction
exceptionally allows perfective aspect in combination with a
durative expression like *za ves' večer* (during the whole evening);
e.g. *Za ves' vêčer on i dvûch slôv ne skazal* (Lit. During the
whole êvening he even twô wôrds not said). The same is possible
with *ni* (as a separate word), e.g.

(39) *Tak on polagal i ni razu za vsju svoju mnogoletnjuju*
     praktiku ne ošibsja
     (This was his assumption and not once during his many years
     of practice did he make a mistake)
(Barentsen, p.c.)

According to Rassudova (1982: 39) (she does not mention the *za*-
case) *ni* ... *ne* plus imperfective aspect conveys the absence of
the event by negating all possible occurrences; with perfective
aspect the same is arrived at by negating (the possibility of) one
single occurrence. It seems that Russian comes close to the Dutch
problem about the parallel link here (see above). As we saw in the
foregoing, *ni*-words require a parallel link (and hence *ne* before
the verb) in order to be able to refer to the absence of the whole
in question; when the absence is arrived at by removing the last
part of the whole, we have the ultimate case of the "less than"
reading.

Hopefully, the few peculiarities mentioned in this section
(others can undoubtedly be added) sufficiently illustrate the conceptual complexity of the "less than" reading, normal as it may
seem at first sight. I have argued that the complexity consists in
the fact that here we remove a part in circumstances in which a
whole is removed elsewhere.[12]

5.4 Gradable ne-compounds

In this section I would like to add two further remarks, one
about the direction of a scale, the other about a combination of
concurrent and non-concurrent parts.

As Sapir remarked in 1944 (1949: 134), "Logically, as mathe-
matically, *b increased from a = b decreased from c*. Psychological-
ly however, and therefore also linguistically, the explicit or
implicit trend is frequently in a specific direction".

At first sight, my reasoning in the foregoing seems to be
incompatible with the fact that, e.g., Russian has words like
nemalo (not-few), meaning "quite a lot" (more than few), *neplocho*
(not-bad), meaning "quite good", etc.: it seems as if we here add
rather than remove something. I think it is not negation which is
responsible for this impression, but the direction in which we
proceed along the scale involved. What I do think is that, given a
negation, moving along a scale from low to high is more complex
than descending it from high to low.
Russian is more flexible in choosing a scale-direction than, e.g.
Czech. Grygar-Rechziegel (1980: 384-385) gives examples of anto-
nymic Czech adjectives where only the "higher"/"positively
evaluated" member of the pair allows a *ne*-compound to be formed.
For example: *nebohatý* (not-rich), but not *nechudý* (not-poor).
This says, in my view, that the language does not allow us to
ascend this scale from low to high.
In "less rich than rich" we arrive at a lower point of the scale
by removing some of his wealth. If in "less poor than poor" we
retained the same scale direction, the negation would induce us
to remove a further part of his belongings, so that we fall off
the scale. In order to prevent this from happening, we must put
the scale upside down, to the effect that adding money diminishes
his poverty. This is evidently more complex than the case when
both negation and scale-direction induce us to remove (part of)
x, so restrictions can be expected here.

Finally, consider the following sentences: *Da nêt, on sovsêm
ne aktíven* (Lit. Nô, he is âltogether not âctive) and *Byl bôjkij
mâl'čik, a stal sovsêm vjâlym i neaktívnym* (Lit. He was a vivâ-

cious bóy, but he became âltogether lânguid and inâctive) (Obzor
1965: 365). The difference between *sovsêm ne aktíven* and *sovsêm
neaktívnym* here can be imagined with the help of our pie.
This time we cut off subsequent pieces of the pie in such a way
that, while the pie becomes smaller and smaller, its complement
becomes larger and larger:

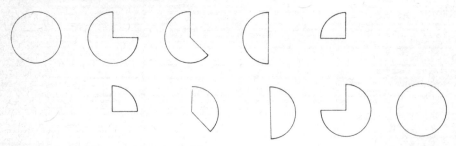

The top row represents a scale of activity. It starts at the left
with a full degree of activity and ends to the right with the absence of any activity. This rightward end-point of the top row is
referred to by "sovsem ne aktiven"; the graded property is here:
activity, and the scale runs: fully active - less active - absence
of activity.

Simultaneously with the diminishing activity, the degree of
inactivity rises; this is indicated in the bottom row (that of
the complement). The rightmost point of this scale, i.e. full inactivity, is referred to by "sovsem neaktivnym". This time the
graded property is inactivity; the scale runs: absence of inactivity - more inactive - fully inactive.

It will be clear that *ne aktiven* has a link between "ne"
and "aktiven": we arrive at a zero-degree of activity by removing
a degree of activity, and the (gradable) property of activity per
se is negated by removing the whole pie of activity (i.e. two
steps). The bottom row (the complement) corresponds to the absence of a link between "ne" and "aktivnym": the (gradable) property of inactivity is negated by removing the pie of inactivity
(one step).

As Sapir remarked in 1944 (1949: 130), "To the naive, every person is either good or bad; if he cannot be easily placed, he is rather part good and part bad than just humanly normal or neither good nor bad".

CHAPTER SIX

CONCLUSION

As a general conclusion I would like to warn against simplifications like that of Dahl (1979), who classifies approximately 240 languages according to whether they use a morphological and/or a syntactic type of sentence negation.

Criteria for classification on the morphological side are, following Dahl: portmanteau realization of the negation, prosodic unity of the negation and the verb, placement of the negation close to the root of the verb, and morphophonemic alternation in the negation morpheme. Features which favour a syntactic analysis are: moveability of the negation, prosodic independence, orthographic separation, and inflectional affixes carried by the negation morpheme.

Dahl correctly mentions (1979: 83) that the spelling criterion leads to an arbitrary classification in the case of Polish and Czech. The same holds true for Russian, which Dahl puts on the syntactic side. But the problem is worse: even the observation that e.g. Russian has both types, and that the semantic borderline cannot be detected by any of Dahl's criteria, is not worthwhile, because calling one case "morphology" and an adjacent case "syntax" contributes nothing to our understanding anyway.

University of Leiden

NOTES

1   Recently, Verhagen (1986: 87-88) has suggested that my proposal that an accent means "not not" formulates a property of all speaking rather than the additional effect of accent, because "a speaker is always talking about what he is talking about, and not about something else" (op.cit.: 87). I agree, of course, with Verhagen's statement that "the ideas evoked by the elements of an utterance are *all* 'made present' (i.e., in some sense, "not not present") simply through the act of speaking" (ibid.). In my view, this "property of all speaking" is the act of copying a meaning from the permanent stock in projection time. It is always the case that a speaker who copies some meaning, say "d", copies "d" and not "a", "b", "c" etc. For this opposition we need no accent, because it fol·lows from the fact that our permanent stock contains more than one meaning (see K 1985: 112). Therefore, the proposal that an accent means "not not" is sensible only in combination with my differentiation between permanent meanings and temporary projections (K 1985: 173).

Given this differentiation, Verhagen's proposal (ibid.), that an accent presents an idea as a relevant alternative, is close to mine. If the copied meaning involved is "d", an accent turns it into "not (not d)"; here, "not d" is that to which "d" is an alternative. By combining the copied meaning "d" with one "not" into "not d", i.e. by forming the projection to which "d" is to be an alternative, the copied meaning "d" itself is used up. Next, a projection "d" is re-introduced by means of the other "not". This procedure accounts for the ability of an accent to introduce a new moment of projection time, and for the fact that there is, in projection time, a projection other than "d" although only "d" and the meaning of accent have been copied. In other words, I agree that an accent presents "d" as a (relevant) alternative, but I hold the view that we must also account for the fact that there *is* something to which "d" is an alternative. In my proposal, this something is created in projection time by means of an accent: there is an act of copying "d", there is an act of copying "not not"; together, they give a temporary projection "not d", although no meaning "a", "b", "c" etc. is involved.

Finally, Verhagen's formulation of the two basic interpretations of an accent (op.cit.: 88) (cf. "theme" and "rheme") is closer to my point of view than he thinks it is on p. 263, note 7 (the opinion formulated in this note is not mine). Verhagen says on p. 88: "In the first case [cf."theme"], the accent is interpreted as presenting an alternative to some other idea(s) in particular: it is selected from a set of given ideas. In the second case [cf. "rheme"], the idea evoked by the accented element is interpreted as an alternative to its own negation, i.e. to its absence". Here we disagree only with respect to the last phrase: "i.e. to its absence". In my view, the "own negation" to which "d" is an alternative, i.e. "not d", is a projection (of the absence of the referent *d*), not the absence of a projection (K 1985: 195; 366-367 (note 33)). Further, the "some other idea(s)" which figure in the first-mentioned interpretation, is, in my view, also an "own negation" of "d", namely a concurrent negation instead of a non-concurrent negation (see also 1.7 below). Therefore, the formulation that an accent presents "d" as an alternative to its own negation covers, in my view, both interpretations. For the reasons explained above, I maintain that "not not" is correct, but I should have said more explicitly that it is correct only if one accepts the notion of projection time; it cannot be transplanted into some other theory without becoming nonsensical in the way explained by Verhagen.

2 There is a second level on which figure/ground and part/whole organizations are linguistically relevant (not dealt with in K 1985). This second level is usually discussed in terms of verb valences and/or semantic roles. For example, in: *John is crawling with large red ants* (Channon 1980: 136) the "semantic role" of John differs according to whether we imagine the ants on top of John (figure/ground) or as entities crawling together with John (separate figures on the same ground). Likewise, in: *This machine polishes the floor with a rotary brush* (Starosta 1978: 490) the "semantic role" of the machine depends on whether we construe the rotary brush as a part of the machine (part/whole) or as a separate figure.

This second level differs from the level discussed in K 1985 in its relation to attention: whether or not, e.g., the rotary brush is construed as a part of the machine, it is an entity on which attention can be focused. Correspondingly, the scope of an accent on *brush* is independent of whether or not the brush is conceived as a part of the machine. In other words, whether or not the rotary brush is a part of the machine, it has its own identity: if the brush is a part of the machine, the property /rotary brush/ is not the identifying property of the machine (of the whole), but only of a part of the machine.

There is as yet no established terminology for distinguishing between the two levels. For example, the article by Gerritsen elsewhere in this volume, which is concerned with the "semantic role" level, also uses the name part/whole organization.

3 My forward and backward links are not identical to Fuchs' (independently discovered) excentric and concentric types of integration (Fuchs, forthcoming); the latter are comparable to my vertical notation (order in projection time). As far as we understand each other from discussions and correspondence, our terminologies differ in the following way:
1. Fuchs' term "integration" refers to one-accent patterns only: $x + \hat{y}$ or $\hat{x} + y$. My links apply to $\hat{x} + \hat{y}$ (two accents) as well (and, for that matter, to $x + y$ (no accent)).
2. Fuchs speaks of integration only when the unaccented element in $x + \hat{y}$ or $\hat{x} + y$ is included in the scope of the accent; she considers the narrow scope readings of the same patterns separately (non-integration). My notation is intended to cover both broad and narrow scope readings. The vertical notation (order in projection time) opposes all broad scope readings (integration) to all narrow scope readings (non-integration): in the broad scope group (integration) the unaccented element concurs with the other element itself; in the narrow scope group (non-integration) the unaccented element concurs with the negation of the other element. My link direction, in contrast, differentiates between 1. the given accentuation has a narrow scope reading only (e.g. in "x̄ ȳ" with an accent on *y*, cf. *John arrived*), and 2. the given accentuation has both a broad and a narrow scope reading (e.g. in "x̄ ȳ" with an accent on *x*, cf. *Jóhn arrived*). Then, the referent of the accented element can in principle be construed as a figure or as a part; these possibilities differentiate between the two readings of e.g. "x̄ ȳ" with an accent on *x*. For example, *Jóhn arrived* and *Sómebody arrived* are both "x̄ ȳ" with an accent on *x*, but the word-inherent difference between "John" and "somebody" ensures that the scope possibilities differ nevertheless.

Formulated the other way round, the cause of a broad scope reading (integration) is, in my view, structural: the structure is such that the unaccented element is linked to the accented element. But the cause of a narrow scope reading is either structural (the accented element is linked to the unaccented element, e.g. *John arrivéd*), or word-inherent meaning (the unaccented element is linked to the accented element, but the reading is narrow nevertheless, e.g. *Sómebody arrived)*, or entirely a matter of contextually dependent interpretation *(Jôhn arrived)*. The vertical notation (order in projection time) specifies whether we are dealing with broad scope or with narrow scope (whether the unaccented element concurs with the other element or with the negation of the other element), but it does not specify whether or not the cause of the reading is structural; the latter can be seen from the type of link.

3. With Fuchs, excentric integration is an integrative accent on a modifier, and concentric integration is an integrative accent on a head (op.cit. (ms.): 7), independently of word order. Thus, broad scope *head - môdifier* is excentric integration, and broad scope *modifier - hêad* as well as broad scope *hêad - modifier* is excentric integration. In my terminology, this opposition is expressed by saying: in *head - môdifier* (excentric integration) the head is linked to the modifier; in *modifier - hêad* and *hêad - modifier* (concentric integration) the modifier is linked to the head. This corresponds to the order in projection time (vertical notation): this order is different in *head - môdifier* vs. *modifier - hêad/hêad - modifier*; the order in *modifier - hêad* and *hêad - modifier* is identical. Thus, the abstraction from word order is made in the vertical notation (order in projection time). The difference between e.g. *head - môdifier* and *modifier - hêad* (excentric vs. concentric, head linked to modifier vs. modifier linked to head) is in my framework described in terms of part-whole and figure-ground relationships (cf. *nothing rêal*, where "nothing" refers to a part, and *A real nôthing*, where "nothing" refers to a figure).

Since my notation is intended to cover accentuation as well as word order, it also opposes all forward links to all backward links. The types of link enable me to make observations like: "Russian "ne" (in contrast to e.g. English "not") cannot be linked backwards" (see 2.1). Also, in both e.g. *predicate - sûbject* and *sûbject - predicate* the predicate is linked to the subject, but the forward type is, in Russian, restricted to inherently predicative elements (other elements cannot both function as a predicate and be linked forwards); the backward type has no such restriction.

Thus, in my terminology a statement like ""x" is linked to "y"", or ""y" is linked to "x"", is independent of word order, just as Fuchs' types of integration are. A statement like ""x" is linked forwards to "y"", or ""y" is linked backwards to "x"", is not independent of word order. I need both types of statement.

4. Since in Fuchs' view, Subject - Predicate combinations cannot be analyzed as being only either *modifier - head* or *head - modifier*, the fact that only an accent on the subject can be an integrative (broad scope) accent has two explanations simultaneously (op.cit. (ms): 17 - this point is not quite clear to me). In my terms, Subject - Predicate combinations (in this order) have a backward link, and the impossibility of a forward link is explained as a consequence of the temporal meaning of a predicate. (In fact, I would adduce these constructions as an argument in favour of the view that the head/modifier terminology is useful as a temporary mnemonic device only; my distinctions cover the same area as this terminology does, but divide it up in quite a different way, which amounts to the proposal that the traditional terminology is inadequate and redundant.)

Despite these differences, Fuchs' observation that, e.g., attributive constructions Noun plus Prepositional Phrase can be integrated in an excentric way $(x + \hat{y})$ as well as in a concentric way $(\hat{x} + y)$, is concerned with the same semantic fact as my observation that such constructions can have a forward as well as a backward link. It may well turn out in the future that the present differences are a temporary inconvenience caused by the different paths which led us tc a common area.

361

⁴
One exception has been mentioned in K (1985: 331-334): a so-called predicative may take over the role of *byt'* (to be) as far as negation is concerned if unaccented *byt'* follows the accented predicative or groups with e.g. the subject preceding the predicative.

⁵
This section is intended to eliminate the simplification which I allowed in K 1985: 260-262.

⁶
The conflict described here is the same as that illustrated in Keijsper (forthcoming) in application to *only*. In the *only*-case, the conflict can be resolved by a parallel link, which is signalled in this English case by Auxiliary - Subject order (cf. 2.6 above).
The full story is slightly more complicated than I am pretending here, because in *Priêchal ne prijâtel'*, *ne* creates no conflict despite the meaning of word order: the rule (see 2.7) that, if *ne* does not precede the verb, the sentence refers to a given time, overrules word order here. In contrast, in *Priêchal niktô* (fused negation), word order was, evidently, stronger than *ni-*, leading as it did to *ne* before the verb (see 2.6). In *Ne prijâtel' priêchal* (and in other cases of this type, e.g. *only*), a backward link overrules the part-whole organization in the subject, unless this organization is incorporated in the lexical meaning involved, which is the case with quantifiers, in the languages I have considered so far. Thus, I am implicitly proposing that the conceptual steps involved are hierarchically organized. I have no explanation for this observable hierarchy; the hierarchy is language-specific.

⁷
Since I am now going to discuss an issue which has not been treated elsewhere, as far as I know, and which therefore might seem to be non-existent, I shall not go further than attested examples allow. Every example is given in the reading intended in the source of the example; some relevant accents have been added by me. Examples were taken from the following sources:

Number
of example: Source:

(1)   N.A. Lobanova: *Voprositel'nye i otricatel'nye predloženija v russkom jazyke*, 1971: 41. Izd. MGU Moskva.

(2)   Obzor 1965 (see reference section), 365.

(3)   Obzor 1965 (see reference section), 363.

(4)   Glovinskaja 1982 (see reference section), 143.

(5)   A.S. Mel'ničuk: *Porjadok slov i sintagmatičeskoe členenie predloženij v slavjanskich jazykach, Kratkaja charakteristika obščich zakonomernostej*, 1958: 4. Kiev.

(6)   A.V. Golovačeva: "Identifikacija i individualizacija v anaforičeskich strukturach", *Kategorija opredelënnosti - neopredelënnosti v slavjanskich i balkanskich jazykach*, 1979: 196-197. Moskva.

(7)   *Russkaja grammatika, tom I*, 1980: 609. Moskva.

(8)   Ivanova 1982 (see reference section), 142.

(9)   J. Forsyth: *A Grammar of Aspect, Usage and Meaning in the Russian Verb*, 1970: 341. Cambridge.

(10)   *Literaturnaja gazeta* No. 14, 1986.

(11)   *Russkaja grammatika, tom I*, 1980: 612. Moskva.

(12)   A.A. Barentsen: *'Tijd'*, *'Aspect' en de conjunctie poka, Over bete-
         kenis en gebruik van enkele vormen in het moderne Russisch*, 1985:
         311. Amsterdam.

(13)   *Pražskij lingvističeskij kružok* (ed.: N.A. Kondrašova), 1967: 264.
         Moskva.

(14)   Forsyth 1970 (see (9)), 143.

(15)   *Russkaja grammatika, tom I*, 1980: 608. Moskva.

(16)   Forsyth 1970 (see (9)), 107.

(17)   Barentsen 1985 (see (12)), 182.

(18)   Rassudova 1982 (see reference section), 66.

(19)   V.Z. Panfilov: *Grammatika i logika (grammatičeskoe i logiko-gramma-
         tičeskoe členenie predloženija)*, 1963:4. Moskva/Leningrad.

(20)   E. Kržižkova: "Zametki o meste negacii v jazykovoj strukture",
         *Edinicy raznych urovńej grammatičeskogo stroja jazyka i ich vzai-
         modejstvie*, 1969: 196. Moskva.

(21)   O.Ch. Cacher: "Problemy intonacii", *Voprosy fonetiki i fonologii*,
         1977: 8. Irkutsk.

(22)   D.I. Fursenko: "Sposoby vyraženija neopredelënnosti predmeta v
         sovremennom russkom jazyke", *Russkij jazyk dlja studentov-inostran-
         cev, Sbornik metodičeskich statej*, 1974: 41. Moskva.

(23)   A.M. Peškovskij: *Russkij sintaksis v naučnom osveščenii*, izdanie
         sed'moe, 1956: 4. Moskva.

(24)   Barentsen 1979 (see reference section), 92.

(25)   Barentsen 1979 (see reference section), 106.

(27)   Mel'ničuk 1958 (see (5)), 27.

(28)   O.I. Byčkova: "Intonacionnoe svoeobrazie rasskaza A.P. Čechova
         "Krest"", *Naučnye doklady vysšej školy, Filologičeskie nauki*,
         1982, 3, 81.

(31)   Obzor 1965 (see reference section), 118.

(32)   B.Ju. Norman: *Bolgarskij jazyk*, 1980: 20. Minsk.

(33)   Glovinskaja 1982 (see reference section), 52.

(34)   *Russkaja grammatika, tom II*, 1980: 416. Moskva.

(35)   T.M. Nikolaeva: "Aktual'noe členenie - kategorija grammatiki
         teksta", *Voprosy jazykoznanija* 1972, 2, 54.

(36)   Savel'eva 1977 (see reference section), 61-62.

(37)   Panfilov 1963 (see (19)), 37.

(38)   V.K. Čičagov: "O dinamičeskoj strukture russkogo povestvova-
         tel'nogo predloženija", *Voprosy jazykoznanija* 1959, 3, 25.

(39)   Ju. Semënov: *Petrovka 38*. 1973: 140. Moskva.

The indispensable constructed Russian examples were checked by V. Barentsen-
Orljanskaja, whom I would like to thank.

[8] At this point it may seem that the parallel scheme is redundant and equivalent to:

That is, a normal forward linking scheme with an additional level (cf. 3.2). However, in my notation this scheme says that given "V", "not adverb" is replaced by "adverb", i.e. that both "not adverb" and "adverb" link up with "V". This incorrectly describes the relevant meaning. In the meaning which I note down as a parallel scheme it is essential that the replacement of "not adverb" by "adverb" takes place simultaneously with the replacement of "V" by "ne V", i.e. that "adverb" does not combine with "V". It is, of course, not surprising that this meaning is found where a level is added as compared with positive sentences, i.e. that the parallel scheme applies mainly in negative sentences, but it is a semantic step more than just the addition of a level. Therefore, I have a special notation for it. (Elsewhere, the parallel scheme occurs, e.g., in English sentences with Auxiliary - Subject order, where the "time-stop" idea is introduced by the meaning of the order of the words; not surprisingly, words like *only* which combine with this order are often discussed in the context of negation.)
As we will see below, starting from a parallel scheme projections can be "lowered", so that again a forward linking scheme results:

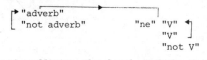

So the addition of a level, and the fact that, if "ne" is linked to "V" first, the negation of "ne V" is "V", does not automatically result in a parallel scheme. Therefore, it is a separate type.

[9] The example is questionable, however, because of the initial position of *bol'še,* which adds a further complication (see 4.7 below). But Glovinskaja's suggestion as to dependence on accent placement (I have translated her suggestion by placing the last accent on *mogu* in the perfective case and on the infinitive in the imperfective case) can probably be taken to mean that there is a parallel link in the "object" sense ("I cannot write more although I could write until now (less)").

[10] As we will see in 5.1 below, combinations of *vs-* and *ne* are not excluded per se; thus, it is not difficult to find examples of *vs- (subject) ... ne vêrb.* Also, *vsegdâ subject ne verb* is attested.
Because of such observable differences between individual *vs-*cases, I do not consider it problematic that my framework makes understandable both the fact that *ne* is inserted before the verb if a *ni-*word is used (see e.g. 2.6 on word order) and the fact that *vs-* tends to be replaced by *ni-* if the verb is preceded by *ne* (for example the *vsegda* case being discussed in the main text). I indeed hold the view that from various sides, the system conspires to the "double negation" construction, and that it is useful to keep the various sides apart because, after all, *ni* occurs without *ne*, and *ne* occurs with *vs-*. The two expressions *ni ... ne* and *vs- ... ne* are not synonymous, although their interpretations overlap (cf. also 4.9).

[11]   Things improve considerably in sentences with "ambient" *het* (it) and
"existential" *er* (unstressed there); for example (attested): *Niet altijd gaat
het om mensen met een voldôende literaire âchtergrond* (Lit. Nôt always goes it
about people with a sufficient literary bâsis).
Further, fused negations do not need word order for a parallel link; thus, e.g.,
(Nog) geen drie boeken heeft hij gelêzen (Lit. (Still/yet) not thrêe books has
he rêad) is acceptable ("he has read even less than three books").

[12]   This seems to be the end-point of the conceptual level on which accent functions. Beyond this point a drastic change takes place.
The two readings of 5.2 can also be recognized in the difference between e.g.
On ne čitâet, a smotrit televízor (mentally removing an identifying property)
and *On ne ubîl eë, a tol'ko tjažélo rânil* (He didn't kill her but only wounded
her seriously) (mentally removing the "terminus part" of the event, so that
"less" of the event remains). In cases like the latter the thing being removed
is a part and a whole simultaneously, but in different constellations. It is the
"terminus part" of the event, i.e. in the internal structure of a single occurrence of the event, but it is a whole (figure) in the system I have been dealing
with so far, i.e. something with an own identity on which attention can be
focused. In the example this entire whole is being removed. In this respect the
sentence is not different from, e.g., example (4) (4.3).
In application to entities, the same step brings us to the level mentioned in
footnote 2.
Thus, at the point where according to the regularity given in 4.1 (or its
counterpart for positive sentences), i.e. the truth-relationships it reflects
(cf. 4.3), a part-feature is combined with a whole-feature, the thing involved
is a whole as far as the relation with identity and attention mentioned in 1.5
is concerned; it is a part in a different constellation, i.e. there is a second
whole (e.g. the machine in footnote 2).
The "less than" reading dealt with in 5.2-5.3 is a borderline case, because here
the part being removed does not acquire an own identity, i.e. it is not a whole
on the level of accent. But the case illustrates the combination which triggers
the creation of two things out of one, so that the story of accent starts all
over again for each thing separately.

REFERENCES

Barentsen, A.A.
   1973   "'Vid' i 'vremja' v predloženijach, soderžaščich slovo *poka*",
               *Dutch contributions to the seventh international congress of slav-
               ists* (ed.: A. van Holk), 33-94. The Hague/Paris.
   1979   "Nabljudenija nad funkcionirovaniem sojuza *poka*", *Dutch contribu-
               tions to the eight international congress of slavists* (ed.: J.
               Meijer), 57-159. Lisse.
Channon, R.
   1980   "On place advancements in English and Russian", *Morphosyntax in
               Slavic* (eds.: C.V. Chvany, R.D. Brecht), 114-138. Columbus.
Dahl, Ö.
   1979   "Typology of sentence negation", *Linguistics* 17, 79-106.

Fuchs, A.
  forth-   "Pragmatic as against grammatical factors in the determination of
  coming   accent placement".
Givón, T.
  1979   *On understanding grammar*. New York/San Francisco/London.
Glovinskaja, M.Ja.
  1982   *Semantičeskie tipy vidovych protivopostavlenij russkogo glagola.*
        Moskva.
Grygar-Rechziegel, A.
  1980   "Some Remarks on Lexical Negation in Czech", *Voz'mi na radost'*,
        To honour Jeanne van der Eng-Liedmeier, 381-396. Amsterdam.
Horn, L.R.
  1978   "Some aspects of negation", *Universals of Language 4, Syntax* (ed.:
        J.H. Greenberg), 128-210. Stanford.
Ivanova, V.F.
  1982   *Trudnye voprosy orfografii*. Moskva.
Jespersen, O.
  1966   *Negation in English and other languages*, second edition (orig.
        1917). København.
Keijsper, C.E.
  1985   *Information Structure, With examples from Russian, English and
        Dutch*. Amsterdam.
  forthcoming: "From accent to word order".
Koenitz, B.
  1982   "Zur Thema-Rhema-Gliederung von Sätzen mit Negativpronomina im
        Tschechischen und Deutschen", *Zeitschrift für Slawistik* 5, 27,
        751-759.
Křížková, H.
  1968   "K voprosu o tak nazyvaemoj dvojnoj negacii v slavjanskich jazy-
        kach", *Slavia* 37, 21-39.
Obzor
  1965   *Obzor predloženij po usoveršenstvovaniju russkoj orfografii
        (XVIII-XX vv.)* (ed.: V.V. Vinogradov). Moskva.
Padučeva, E.V.
  1969   "Semantičeskij analiz otricatel'nych predloženij v russkom
        jazyke", *Mašinnyj perevod i prikladnaja lingvistika* 12, 5-35.
Rassudova, O.P.
  1982   *Upotreblenie vidov glagola v sovremennom russkom jazyke, izdanie
        vtoroe, ispravlennoe i dopolnennoe*. Moskva.
Sapir, E.
  1949   "Grading: A Study in Semantics, The Psychology of Grading",
        *Selected Writings of Edward Sapir in Language, Culture, and Per-
        sonality* (ed.: D.G. Mandelbaum), 122-149. Berkeley/Los Angeles.
Savel'eva, L.V.
  1977   "Otricatel'nye konstrukcii v nekotorych prozaičeskich žanrach
        russkogo fol'klora", *Jazyk žanrov russkogo fol'klora*. Petrozavodsk.
Skorobač, A.N.
  1978   "O slitnom i razdel'nom napisanii glagolov s pristavkoj "nedo-" i
        glagolov s pristavkoj "do-" pri naličii otricanija", *Russkij jazyk
        v škole* 5, 96-97.
Starosta, S.
  1978   "The one per sent solution", *Valence, Semantic Case and Grammatical
        Relations* (ed.: W. Abraham), 459-576. Amsterdam.

Tottie, G.
  1980   "Affixal and non-affixal negation in English - Two systems in
              (almost) complementary distribution", *Studia Linguistica* 34, 2,
              101-123.
Verhagen, A.
  1986   *Linguistic Theory and the Function of Word Order in Dutch, A Study
              on Interpretive Aspects of the Order of Adverbials and Noun
              Phrases*. Dordrecht.

NOMINAL ACCENTUATION IN CONTEMPORARY STANDARD RUSSIAN

FREDERIK KORTLANDT

1. It has become customary to derive the accentuation of a word form from inherent accent-generating properties of its constituent morphemes. Though this seems to be a suitable technique in the case of languages with inherent tonal features, such as African languages or Common Slavic, one may wonder if it is equally appropriate for a language like Russian, where accent is a configurational feature. In the words му́ка 'torment' and мука́ 'flour', the stress on the first vowel conditions the absence of stress on the second, and vice versa: there is no opposition with two or zero accents. Thus, stressed and unstressed *u* are not different phonemes because they are not found in one and the same position; phonemic stress is a property of the sequence. It is by no means clear that the descriptive technique which assigns inherent accentual properties to the separate morphemes and eliminates the resulting overspecification by rule should yield an adequate description of the facts, not to mention its explanatory power. As Zaliznjak points out in his recent book on the history of Russian accentuation (1985: 37),

в современном русском языке при одном и том же наборе окончаний могут противопоставляться до семи разных схем ударения, например: ве́ра -- схема *a*, черта́ -- *b*, беда́ -- *d*, губа́ -- *f*, спина́ -- *d'*, нога́ -- *f'* (ср. еще единичное до́ля -- схема *e*). Чтобы отобразить эти различия с помощью маркировок, нужно в идеале ввести семь различных маркировок корня. Если допустить некоторое количество индивидуальных исключений, инвентарь маркировок можно сократить; однако попытка обойтись менее чем четырьмя маркировками уже приводит к непомерно длинным спискам исключений или к иным модификациям техники маркировок, которые в сущности компрометируют саму эту технику

and this is why its theoretical premises should be reconsidered.

2.   The primary function of stress in contemporary standard
Russian is a contrastive one. Since the noun is inflected for
number and case, the stress may or may not differentiate
(1) a stem from other stems,
(2) the plural from the singular,
(3) a plural case form from the other plural case forms,
(4) a singular case form from the other singular case forms,
or any combination of these. The plural case with a distinct
stress is either the nominative, where the stress is retracted,
or the genitive, where it is shifted to the desinence.[1] The singular case with a distinct stress is the accusative, which is in
a few instances identical with the nominative; the stress is
retracted here.[2] As a consequence, one can predict the accentual
paradigm of any Russian noun (except the five words mentioned in
footnote 1) on the basis of the four criteria listed here, without specifying the flexion class of the individual words, and
without assigning accentual properties to the separate case end-
ings.[3]

3.   The large majority of Russian nouns have fixed stress on
the stem. If we regard this as the normal type and mark the
presence and absence of a stress shift according to the four
criteria listed above with the signs - and +, respectively, we
arrive at the following classification.
++++: fixed stress on the stem.
-+++: fixed stress on the desinence.
+-++: e.g., ма́стер, сад, глаз, господи́н, ме́сто, мо́ре.
--++: e.g., вино́, перо́, дно, сук, кислота́, тягота́.
-+-+: e.g., конь, гвоздь, крыльцо́, губа́, ноздря́.
+--+: e.g., волк, во́лос, у́хо, дере́вня, ночь.
---+: 11 nouns, e.g., овца́, семья́, судья́, кольцо́.
-+--: 19 nouns, e.g., гора́, рука́, борода́, у́голь.[4]
-++-: у́гол, у́горь, у́зел.[5]
+++-: заём, наём.
--+-: 10 nouns, e.g., вода́, зьма́, цена́.
----: земля́.
+-+-: госпо́дь, перёд.

Only three of the sixteen logical possibilities are not attested
(++-+, ++--, +---). The accent of a word form can be derived
from the product of the relevant markings: if this is +, the
stress is on the stem; if it is -, the stress is on the ending.

4.   If we want to apply the method advanced here to the adjective, we are faced with the fact that approximately 90 words have
accentual variants. The stress of an adjective may or may not
differentiate
(1) the stem from other stems,
(2) the short plural from the long form,
(3) the feminine from the neuter short singular form,
or a combination of these. The feminine short singular form has
final stress in all mobile types, while the corresponding mas-
culine form is stressed on the stem.[6] If beside + and - we use
the sign o to mark an optional stress shift, we arrive at the
following classification.
+++: e.g., лукáвый, лукáв, лукáва, лукáво, лукáвы.
-++: e.g., смешнóй, смешóн, смешнá, смешнó, смешнЫ́.
+-+: e.g., горЯ́чий, горЯ́ч, горячá, горячó, горячЯ́.
++-: e.g., тóнкий, тóнок, тонкá, тóнко, тóнки.
---: e.g., молодóй, мóлод, молодá, мóлодо, мóлоды.
++o: e.g., влáстный, влáстен, властнá, влáстно, влáстны.
+oo: e.g., пóлный, пóлон, полнá, пóлнó, пóлнЫ́.
+o+: e.g., лёгкий, лёгок, легкá, легкó, лёгкЯ́.
+o-: e.g., сЯ́льный, сЯ́лён, сильнá, сЯ́льно, сЯ́льнЫ́.
-o-: e.g., простóй, прост, простá, прóсто, прóстЫ́.
The accent of the neuter short singular form can be derived
either from the corresponding feminine or from the plural,
whichever is not marked by o.

5.   Pronominal forms are stressed on the ending.[7] In the verb,
the stress may or may not differentiate
(1) a stem from other stems,
(2) the past from the present tense,
(3) the 1st sg. from the other present tense forms,
(4) the fem. sg. from the other past tense forms,

or certain combinations of these.[8] Examples:

++++: ле́зу, ле́зешь, ле́зла, ле́зли.

-+++: блюду́, блюдёшь, блюла́, блюли́.

+-++: ля́гу, ля́жешь, легла́, легли́.

--++: грызу́, грызёшь, гры́зла, гры́зли.

+--+: могу́, мо́жешь, могла́, могли́.

+++-: бу́ду, бу́дешь, была́, бы́ли.

--+-: пойму́, поймёшь, поняла́, по́няли.

++--: приму́, при́мешь, приняла́, при́няли.

6.   The development of the Russian accentual system since Common Slavic times is characterized by a shift from a system where
the accent of a word form can be derived from inherent properties of its constituent morphemes to a system where it is determined by the presence or absence of stress shifts in specific
categories. This development can be viewed as a corollary of the
loss of distinctive tone, which was an inherent feature in Common Slavic times, and the consequent rise of configurational
stress as the only prosodic feature of a Russian word form. A
similar development is attested in Russian word-formation, where
the change is characterized by Zaliznjak as follows (1985: 382):

это, в терминах В.А. Дыбо, "переход от парадигматического акцента к категори-
альному", т.е. переход от системы, где ударение производного слова зависит от
акцентной парадигмы производящего, к системе, где ударение производного определяется только его принадлежностью к некоторой морфологической категории
слов

so that I propose to treat accentuation in flexion and derivation along similar lines. This is only possible if we start from
a theory which takes into account the specific characteristics
of the language described.

University of Leiden

NOTES

[1]   There are five words, belonging to four different accent classes, where the stress is retracted in the genitive plural, viz. дéньги, судия́, сáжень (variant with mobile stress), крýжево, мáсло, cf. Kortlandt 1974: 62.

[2]   There are four words, belonging to two accent classes, where the stress is shifted to the desinence in the nom.-acc. sg., viz. заём, наём, госпóдь, перёд, cf. Kortlandt 1974: 62f.

[3]   The following description does not account for accentual mobility within the stem, cf. class II sub 3-6 of Kortlandt 1974: 62. Here belong six words which take the plural stem formative -∅j-, eight words which take the singular stem formative -in-, and the words знáмя, óзеро, бесёнок, чертёнок. In accordance with the approach of Kortlandt 1974: 60f. I would assume a plural stem formative -∅- before the ending in these four words.

[4]   Only the last word (variant with mobile stress) does not belong to the a-flexion.

[5]   Here belong the numerals вóсемь, дéвять, дéсять, двáдцать, трúдцать and сóрок.

[6]   On the masc. short sg. form cf. Kortlandt 1974: 66.

[7]   Cf. Kortlandt 1974: 66f.

[8]   Cf. Kortlandt 1974: 68f.

REFERENCES

Kortlandt, F.H.H.
   1974   "Russian nominal flexion", *Linguistics* 130, 55-70.
Зализняк, А.А.
   1985   От праславянской акцентуации к русской. Москва: Наука.

THE CASE OF THE TWO CASES:
GENITIVE AND ACCUSATIVE
IN RUSSIAN NEGATIVE CONSTRUCTIONS

ANNIE MEINTEMA

M.V. Lomonosov, author of the first major study of Russian grammar, did not waste many words over case selection in negative constructions. In his *Rossijskaja grammatika* (1755) he simply states:

"Всякий глагол действительный требует винительного падежа сверх именительного: *кто хранит законы, законы сохранят его взаимно.*
Когда же пред ним присовокупляется отрицательная частица *не,* винительный падеж обращается в родительный: *не давай воли языку в пировании*" (Lomonosov 1952 p. 501/502).

In other words: Lomonosov considered the negative accusative inacceptable.

This formulation, however, is in contradiction with real usage: the poetry of A.D. Kantemir (1709-1744) contains many examples of the phenomenon rejected by Lomonosov. In his satires, the number of negative accusatives is even larger than that of negative genitives (Mustajoki 1985 p. 14).

It goes without saying that considerations of form (word stress, rhyme, number of syllables) must have played a part in Kantemir's choice of either grammatical form. It would be erroneous, though, to consider these formal considerations a decisive factor. Firstly, Kantemir was far too scrupulous a philologist to use an incorrect grammatical form; secondly, there are certain examples, both of the accusative and the genitive, in which the choice of the opposite case would have been of no consequence for the compatibility with the rules of syllabic verse, for instance:

... Кто над столом гнется,
Пяля на книгу глаза, больших не добьется
Палат, ни расцвеченна мраморами саду;
Овцу не прибавит он к отцовскому стаду (First satire, vss 11-14)

Уже свечек не кладут, постных дней не знают... (Ibid.,vs. 37).

Когда в гостях, за столом - и мясо противно,
И вина не хочет пить; да то и не дивно (Third satire,vss 175/6).

The most unexpected negative accusative which I have found
in Kantemir's satires is the following:

Бесперечь советует гнева удаляться
И досады забивать, но ищет в прах стерти
Тайно недруга, не даст покой и по смерти (Third satire, vss
                                       182-184).

In my opinion, this example represents a striking illustration of the 'grammatical gap' between Lomonosov and Kantemir -
even if one takes into account that the choice of the genitive
would have brought about a surplus syllable! After all, "Man
macht den Vers nach der Sprache und nicht die Sprache, weil es
die Silbenzahl des Verses erfordert" (Reiter 1986 p. 381).

Apparently, two philologists, contemporaries, both equally
well versed in the Russian language[2], held completely different
views regarding the acceptability of the accusative for the
direct object of negated transitive verbs. The discrepancy between the opinions of the grammarian Lomonosov and the poet
Kantemir started a long period of dispute over this issue. Time
did not bring counsel: there still exists confusion concerning
the object case in negated sentences in Russian. In the present
paper I shall try to elucidate the major viewpoints regarding
the use of the genitive/accusative of· negation. Thereafter I
shall make an attempt to formulate a general rule.

Lomonosov's Jacobinical verdict on the negative accusative
('La mort sans phrase!') was not modified until 1903, when A.I.
Thomson's article *Vinitel'nyj padež prjamogo dopolnenija v
otricatel'nyx predloženijax v russkom jazyke* appeared. In this
article Thomson points out that the negative accusative is far
more frequent than is generally supposed, particularly in the

spoken language. He ascribes its avoidance in the written
language to the prevailing influence of grammatical rules
dictated by school grammars (Thomson 1903 pp. 193 and 207).

Thomson's article not only brought about the end of
genitive supremacy; it is an attempt at an explanation of the
rules underlying the choice of either case. In Thomson's view,
the accusative of negation is connected with concreteness
(*конкретность представления*), the genitive of negation with
abstractness (*абстрактность представления*). The accusative
implies that the action and the object form part of concrete
reality - either objectively, or in the imagination of the
speaker or the subject, e.g.: *Не шей ты мне, матушка, красный*
сарафан (The person addressed is already sewing, or about to
sew, a red sarafan). The genitive implies that the action is
represented as merely possible and the object as not having
been realized, e.g.: *Так как он не нашел подходящей квартиры,*
то он поселился в меблированных комнатах (The appropriate
apartment does not belong to the real world because it was
not found) (Thomson 1903 p. 197).

Thomson claims that negative clauses with the direct object in the genitive do not call attention to the negated action
described, but to the situation brought about by the negated
action (Thomson 1903 p. 211). Thus, *Я не купил шляпу* means 'I
did not carry out a certain action'; the same clause with the
object in the genitive would mean 'I do not have a hat, because
I did not buy one' (for instance, in answer to the question
'Show me your new hat') (Thomson 1903 p. 220).

In 1911, Thomson still holds the same view:

"Ein negiertes Verb beim Genetiv bezeichnet eine abstrakte
Handlung und weist nur auf die Umstände hin, die aus der Ab-
wesenheit der Handlung gefolgert werden - auf einen negativ
bestimmten Zustand. (...) Beim Akkusativ ist der Sinn sozusa-
gen narrativ, beim Genetiv deskriptiv"(Thomson 1911/1912 p.252).

Innovative and enlightening though Thomson's observations
on negative constructions are, they did not result in the formulation of 'eine kurze bestimmte Regel' (Thomson 1911/1912
p. 253). The notions 'narrativity' and 'descriptivity' are ra-

ther elusive; it is hard to grasp why the first example quoted
above should be more 'narrative' than the second, or the
second more 'descriptive' than the first. Besides, the accusative is by no means automatically connected with concreteness,
nor the genitive with abstractness. In order to substantiate
this, I shall give a few examples among which those with the
genitive have, in my opinion, more *конкретность представления*
than those with the accusative:

1.   *"Все дело в том, что они зазнались", брюзжал он про себя*
(...). "они зазнались, они до такой степени чувствуют себя
великими писателями, что перестали даже завидовать друг
другу. Еще завидуют - и то все реже - жены. Жены тоже нашли
свое дело. Мужья уважают друг друга, а жены покупают
мебель. Скоро диваны будут в чехлах, а меня будут укорять
за то, что я не купил себе <u>фетровую шляпу</u>. Классики!"
(Kaverin).

2.   *Кто над столом гнется (...), <u>Овцу</u> не прибавит он к*
отцовскому стаду (Kantemir).

3.   *Раз отказался - <u>другой</u> не дадут* (Proverb).

4.   *Слабость возмущала ее, глупость сердила, <u>ложь</u> она не*
прощала "во веки веков" (Turgenev).

5.   *А Измайлову очень не хотелось уходить, не дослушав <u>спора</u>*
до конца (Akad. Grammatika 1980).

6.   *"Какая, какая причина?" повторила Елена, крепко стиски-*
вая (...) руку Берсенева в своей похолодевшей руке. (...)
"Ну... и что же... вы теперь..." прошептала Елена, невольно
отворачивая голову, как человек, ожидающий удара, но все же
не выпуская <u>схваченной руки</u> Берсенева (Turgenev).

     The first example is not a description of a <u>real</u> situ-
ation, but of a situation which is going to arise if the
subject will not have bought a felt hat: the genitive used
here contradicts Thomson's theory.
     It is hardly possible to corroborate the thesis that
the second, third and fourth example are more 'concrete' or
'narrative' than the fifth and the sixth. The use of the
genitive and the accusative in the examples given above may
be explicable - but not by means of Thomson's theory.
     The connection between the accusative and concreteness

on the one hand, and between the genitive and abstractness on
the other are called into question even by Thomson himself,
when he points out that in negative sentences mass nouns tend
to take the genitive when used in a concrete, and the accusative when used in an abstract sense: "...in *эта примесь не
портит муки* (...) lässt der Akk. *муку* bestimmter den Satz als
abstrakt auffassen" (Thomson 1911/1912 p. 256).

Evidently, the semantic difference between the accusative and the genitive of negation cannot be reduced to 'concreteness' versus 'abstractness'. There must be something
else behind the considerations governing case selection in
negative sentences.

Since Thomson's days, many words of explanation and illustration have been devoted to the issue under consideration. It is beyond the scope of this paper to give an enumeration of the various theories which have been formulated
after the publication of Thomson's articles; for an extensive and up-to-date survey of articles and books on case selection after negated verbs in Russian I refer to Mustajoki
1985.

It is generally observed that the negative accusative
is becoming increasingly prevalent in written Russian since
the middle of the nineteenth century (Comrie and Stone 1978
p. 104; Uglitsky 1956 p. 376) and that most grammars and
textbooks of Russian still suggest that 'normally' the genitive is used with negated verbs (Fuchs 1973 p. 81;
Keil 1971 p. 109; Timberlake 1975 p. 123; Ward 1965 p. 211).
But here, unison comes to an end: there are as many explanations of the genitive/accusative of negation as there are
explainers. An attempt to formulate rules for the use of
either case is like sailing between Scylla and Charybdis.
On the one hand, there is the danger of being too general
and abstract, leaving many cases unexplained or marking
them simply as 'inexplicable uses'. On the other hand,
there is the danger of focusing exclusively on isolated

grammatical, morphological and stylistic forms, which results
in a 'jigsaw puzzle' (Davison 1967 p. 60) instead of the formulation of 'eine kurze, bestimmte Regel'. If, for instance,
the 'reaction' of a gerund clause to the particle of negation
differs from that of a clause in which the direct object is
modified by a predicative instrumental - the first will tend
to take the genitive, the second the accusative - this is because of the difference in function of these cases, not because
of the difference in structure of the clauses.

In the following, I shall first discuss several explanations which have been put forward in order to give a general
rule for the use of the negative genitive/accusative. Thereafter I will compare constructions with a high accusative frequency and constructions with a high genitive frequency.

A theory which bears much resemblance to Thomson's explanation is that of Jakobson:

..."*Я не слыхал этой сонаты* (G) 'ich habe diese Sonate nicht
gehört' - der Nachdruck liegt auf Unbekanntsein der Sonate für
den Sprechenden; *я не слыхал эту сонату* (A) - der Nachdruck
fehlt und der Umstand, dass ich sie nicht gehört habe, wird
infolgedessen zu einer Akzidenz, die die fragliche Sonate aus
dem Sachverhalte der Aussage nicht imstande ist auszuschalten -
die Gegebenheit der Sonate überwiegt: diese Bedeutungschattie-
rung bringt hier der A im Gegensatz zum G"(Jakobson 1967 p. 65).

Pul'kina states that the accusative is possible in colloquial speech and in sentences where the noun denotes a concrete
object or a person (Pul'kina 1974 p. 60). This theory is in
contradiction with usage in belles-lettres; in order to show
this I shall quote three examples from Turgenev, who used a
lot of negative genitives in his work and had ample time and
opportunity to weed his language of colloquialisms:

Мы не можем здесь противиться желанию - не провести параллель
между Шекспиром и Сервантесом.

*Но если бы в это мгновение ты держал в своей руке руку любимой
женщины (...), не* грусть, *Андрей, не* тревогу *возбуждала бы в
тебе природа?*

"Передаю тебе светоч", говорил он ему за два часа до смерти,

"Я держал его, покамест мог, не выпускай и ты сей светоч до
конца" (The speaker has in mind a certain attitude to life,
not a real lamp).

Morison assumes that the genitive is used when the logical stress is on the direct object, and the accusative when
the logical stress is on the verb; according to Morison, in
the case of the negative accusative it may sometimes be best to
regard the verb and object as a whole which is negated, e.g.
Что же стол не накрывают? (Morison 1964 p. 294).

There are examples supporting Morison's theory, e.g.:

Я давно не чувствовала такого внутреннего спокойствия (Turgenev).

Я было так начал одно стихотворение; сознайся: славный пер-
вый стих, а второго никак подобрать не мог (Turgenev).

Вот что: газета "Научная жизнь" готовит против меня статью.
Содержания я еще не знаю (Kaverin).

Сигаретов я не курю.

Я не курю сигареты (The last two examples were elicited from
the spoken language[3]).

In many more instances, however, the material is at vari-
ance. Negated gerund and participle constructions and clauses
where the direct object is a part of the subject's body seldom
have the logical stress on the direct object; nevertheless,
these constructions have a high genitive frequency (Davison
1967 p. 45). To elucidate this I shall give a few examples:

Остроградский курил, не поднимая глаз (Kaverin).

Елена долго не спускала глаз с Берсенева (Turgenev).

Л.С. Желтухин, не кончивший курса технолог (Čexov, describing
a character in a play).

"Дай, барыня, ручку", пролепетала она.
Александра Павловна не дала ей руки, нагнулась и поцеловала
ей в лоб (Turgenev).

In these instances the object, which is in the genitive,
certainly does not have any stress. Besides, it is possible to
regard verb and object as a 'wholly negated whole' here, too.

Diametrically opposed to Morison's theory is Keil's explanation. In his opinion, the difference between the genitive and the accusative of negation is caused by a difference
in the scope of negation: in a negative clause with the direct
object in the genitive, 'das Geschehen' as well as 'das Geschehensziel' are negated; in a negative clause with the direct object in the accusative, only 'das Geschehen' is negated.

Keil's theory conjures up Thomson's spirit, and images
of red sarafans half finished and appropriate rooms never
found: what is realized ('concrete') requires the accusative;
what is not realized ('abstract') requires the genitive.

Keil's rule, like Morison's, is sometimes applicable.
But here again, there are many cases where the theory does not
fit real usage. It does not apply, for instance, to the majority of clauses with a part of the body as a direct object. In
order to elucidate this I can quote Keil:

"...das Geschehensziel wird als nicht vorhanden gekennzeich-
net (i.e. when the direct object is in the genitive, AM), ein
Geschehen findet (wann auch immer) gar nicht statt. D.h.(...)
der Bereich der Negation umfasst zugleich Geschehen und Geschehensziel. Wenn dagegen der Akkusativ erhalten bleibt, so
bedeutet das, dass der Bereich der Negation nur das Geschehen
allein betrifft. Das Geschehensziel ist unverändert präsent,
wird aber vom Geschehen nicht erreicht, weil die dazu nötige
Aktion entweder (beabsichtigt oder unbeabsichtigt) unter-
bleibt oder weil sie unvollkommen ausgeführt wird" (Keil 1971
p.120).

A similar view is held by Schaller, who assumes that
the choice of case for the direct object in negative sentences depends on the "Möglichkeiten des Vorhandenseins eines
Denotates des direkten Objekts" - either "subjektiv" or "ob-
jektiv" (Schaller 1978).

It is hardly possible to use Keil's rule as an explanation for the usage of the genitive/accusative of negation
in the following examples:

*Впрочем, он не выпускал изо рта трубки и имел вид человека
почтенного и незаурядного* (Kaverin).

... но все же не выпуская <u>схваченной руки</u> Берсенева (Turgenev).

In the following examples, the scope of negation is focused rather on 'das Geschehen allein' than on both 'Geschehen' and 'Geschehensziel':

Все мои работы я не публиковал, чтобы не обострять <u>спора</u> (Kaverin).

Грибоедов не мог больше носить в себе <u>своей ненависти, своего отвращения</u> (Lunačarskij).

Философия не устраняла <u>эстетики</u> (Plexanov).

Keil's theory has been criticized on several points by Fuchs, who gives a completely different explanation of the indications for the choice of case:

"Der Genitiv als Objektskasus wird bei Verneinung gewählt, um die Konstituenten Negation + Verb + Objekt zu einer Einheit zu 'integrieren', die insgesamt, als eine 'neue' Informations-(oder 'Relevanz'-)Einheit, auf die Situation und den jeweils erreichten Punkt im Ablauf der Mitteilung zu beziehen ist. Stellt dagegen nur ein Teil der Verbindung ein Element der 'neuen' Information dar, während der Rest schon 'Gegebenes' aufnimmt, oder sollen Teile der Verbindung getrennt eigene 'Informations'einheiten bilden, wird, wie ausserhalb der Verneinung, der Akkusativ gewählt" (Fuchs 1973 pp. 83,84).

In order to illustrate this I shall quote four of her examples:

В окно стук. Встают. Мышлаевский: Не люблю <u>фокусов</u>... Почему не через дверь? (Bulgakov). Every part of the negated clause represents a piece of new information.

(Она купила газету), чтобы завернуть сушки — кулек прорвался в трамвае. Дорогой она, не разворачивая <u>сушки</u>, стала читать газету (Kaverin). The crackers are already 'given'; only the verb contains new information.

Ольга Прохоровна никогда не читала <u>газету</u> "Научная жизнь" и купила номер, чтобы завернуть сушки... (Kaverin).

As this is the first sentence of a chapter, having no connection whatsoever with preceding information, the use of the accusative may seem strange. Fuchs ascribes it to 'erzählerische Raffung':

382

"Bei (fast) streng chronologischer Erzählweise wäre etwa fol-
gendes zu erwarten gewesen: '(O.P. war nach einigen Einkäufen
auf dem Heimweg). In der Strassenbahn riss die Tüte mit *сушки*,
und um diese einzupacken, kaufte sie eine Nummer der Zeitung
Научная жизнь. Diese Zeitung las sie sonst nie...' Statt des-
sen setzt das Kapitel mit einem Satz ein, der den als erfolgt
vorausgesetzten Kauf der Zeitung motiviert; in dem Satz wird
bereits von einem situationsmässigen 'Gegeben'sein der Zeitung
ausgegangen" (Fuchs 1973 p. 87).

*Мы исключили би его из партии, если би он не представил
справку о том, что Черкашин был душевнобольным* (Kaverin).

The information given in the conditional clause is completely
new; the investigation is mentioned for the first time. Fuchs
gives the following explanation for the use of the accusative:

"Das Objekt scheint nicht mitintegriert zu werden, wenn es für
sich so viel Information einführt, dass es nicht gut mit dem
Verb zusammen als eine 'Vorgangseinheit' aufgefasst werden
kann." (In the present example) "wäre Genitiv möglich, wenn das
Objekt nicht die Qualifikation bei sich hätte, die das eigent-
liche 'Überraschungsmoment' enthält. Der gesamte Objektsaus-
druck könnte nur dann im Genitiv stehen (ausgenommen den Fall,
dass das Objekt 'Gegebenes' wiederaufnimmt), wenn diese spezi-
elle Art von *справка* irgendwie gängig wäre, was aber schon
durch den Eigennamen ausgeschlossen scheint" (Fuchs 1973 p.88).

In my opinion, there is much to be said for the explanation given by Fuchs. Still, even Fuchs leaves behind an
amount of 'inexplicable uses' - one of them being an example
which she gives herself:

*Неизвестно было, что кричать. "Вернитесь" или "Я за вами"?
Она не знала его голоса, могла не отозваться, испугаться*
(Fuchs 1973 p. 84).

I consider 'his voice' in the example quoted here already 'given': the subject wants to cry out, he wants to use
his voice. The noun refers directly to the action which is
planned in the first sentence.

Other unexplained examples are two lines from *Князь
Михайло Репнин* by A.K. Tolstoj: Ivan the Terrible is feasting
with his retinue; they sing of former glory,

*Но голос прежней слави царя не веселит,
Подать себе личину он кравчему велит.*

"Да здравствуют тиуны, опричники мои!
Вы ж громче бейте в струны, баяны-соловьи!

Себе личину, други, пусть каждый изберет -
Я первый открываю веселый хоровод!
(...)
И все подъяли кубки. Не поднял лишь один,
Один не поднял кубка, Михайло князь Репнин.
(The czar tries to force Repnin to put on a mask, but he re-
fuses, saying:)
Личины ж не надену я в мой последний час!

Both objects in the genitive - the cup and the mask - contain given information. Nevertheless, the poet did <u>not</u> choose
the accusative, although in both places the accusative instead
of the genitive would not have disturbed the metre. The question
of why the genitive is used here cannot be answered by applying
the explanation proposed by Fuchs.

Most examples quoted above have been elicited from written sources: belles-lettres, newspapers, etc. Timberlake, however, collected his data from a questionnaire, filled up by native informants. On the basis of these data Timberlake finds
that:

"In general, there is an inverse relationship between individuation and the genitive of negation: the more a participant is
individuated, the less likely it is to be in the genitive under
negation, and vice versa" (Timberlake 1975 p. 124). "The reason
why individuation plays a role in the rule of genitive of negation has to do with the function of the genitive. According to
Jakobson, the genitive focuses on the extent to which a participant participates in the event, rather than on the participant itself; it therefore represents a QUANTIFICATION of participation. (...) Individuation is the inverse of quantification:
the more a participant is individuated, the less it can be
quantified, and vice versa" (Timberlake 1975 p. 127).

In my opinion, this is wrong. Not the <u>participant</u> is
quantified, but the <u>participation</u> of the participant.[4] A participant in the genitive may be as much individuated as its
counterpart in the accusative. In order to elucidate this I
shall compare two positive clauses:
- *Дай мне твою книгу.*
- *Дай мне твоей книги.*
The first means: 'Give me your book', the second: 'Give me your

book for a while'. The genitive in the second clause does not
imply that the object is 'less individuated' than that in the
first; the difference in case of the direct object in these
clauses is brought about by a difference in the scope of the
verb - which brings about a difference in the participation
of the object. Thomson ascribes the use of the genitive in
similar clauses to 'Einschränkung der Verbalbedeutung' (Thomson 1911/1912 p.250).

A similar difference is apparent in many negative clauses.
The object in *Я не люблю музыки* is as individuated as that in
Я не люблю музыку; the difference in the choice of the case is
caused by a difference in the participation of the object in
the action. I shall return to this later.

I do not agree that the method applied by Timberlake
should have advantages over the investigation of literary
examples (Timberlake 1975 p. 124). Timberlake's questionnaire
consists of a number of sentences without context. For an explanation of negative genitive/accusative usage, the object
clause itself as well as its 'surroundings' have to be taken
into consideration.

The same objection applies to the experiment carried out
by Mustajoki (Mustajoki 1985 pp. 141-166). Mustajoki's questionnaire is more extensive and the amount of native informants
is larger - but here we have another case where quantity is
not automatically transformed into quality: it is impossible
to solve the Case of the Two Cases by means of examples consisting of isolated sentences - no matter the amount of questions
and persons questioned.

As was indicated above, there is still confusion over the
use of the genitive and accusative of negation; a really satisfying explanation has not yet been given.

It is unquestionable that in some negative constructions
the genitive, in others the accusative is preferred for the object of transitive verbs. However, there is confusion here, too:
Timberlake, for instance, assumes that the accusative is fre-

quent in the case of nouns accompanied by modifiers:

Я газет не читаю, а узнаю новости по телевизору.

Я длинные статьи не читаю. (Timberlake 1975 p. 126).

Restan, on the other hand, points out that the genitive is impossible in *Я не люблю суп,* but can be used if one adds a
qualifying adjective:

Горячий/молочный суп не люблю.

Горячего/молочного супа не люблю (Restan 1960 p. 111).

Davison:"When the object of a negated transitive verb refers to
parts of the body of the subject of the verb, then that object
is in the genitive" (Davison 1967 p. 45). Borras and Christian:
"The accusative will be preferred to the genitive (...) when
the object is a concrete noun denoting a part of the body"
(Borras and Christian 1971 p. 29).

Grammar books - of Russian as well as of other languages - often get maimed by an inclination of the author to provide the readers with fixed, always applicable rules. Even
the authors of the Academy Grammar (1980) have not been able
to avoid this when describing the usage of the genitive and
accusative of negation. They state, for instance, that the genitive is never used when the object is modified by a predicative instrumental, and that the accusative never is used in
constructions with *не иметь* (Ak.Gramm. II 1980 pp. 415-419).
These statements are contradicted by real usage: negative
clauses with a predicative instrumental have a high accusative
frequency, clauses with *не иметь* a high genitive frequency -
but there are counterexamples:

А потому я надеюсь, вы не найдете моего вопроса нескромным
(Turgenev).

Этого чувства нельзя назвать счастьем (Turgenev).

*Теперь мы видим перед собою иностранные книжные лавки. Их
множество, и ни одной нельзя назвать богатою в сравнении с
петербургскими* (Batjuškov).

*Поэтому, мне кажется, нельзя признать последовательным
следующего определения винительного падежа* (Quoted from
Mustajoki).

Не имеет ли он <u>отношение</u> к операции "Горная весна"?
(Quoted from Mustajoki).

What makes a negative construction with a high accusative frequency take the genitive, and vice versa? In order to give an idea of the factors determining this, I shall give a few accusative examples in negative constructions with a high genitive frequency, viz. gerund constructions and clauses where the object is the pronoun *это*.

1.   *(...) и купила номер, чтобы завернуть сушки (...). Дорогой она, не разворачивая <u>сушки</u>, стала читать газету* (Kaverin).

2.   *Я пишу что-то, уже не слушая <u>шепот</u> Сидорова* (Quoted from Mustajoki).

3.   *Если отдельные солдаты допускали ошибки, руководитель, не приостанавливая <u>движение</u> взвода, подавал соответствующие сигналы командирам отделений, которые на ходу устраняли недостатки* (Quoted from Keil).

4.   *Но Суровцев уже понимал, что уйти, не повидав <u>Веру</u>, не в силах* (Quoted from Ak. Gramm. 1980).

5.   *"Расул, достань билеты на таганку?*
Ты можешь все. Пожалуйста, достань?!"
И, обращаясь ко всему аулу,
Я простонал (...):
"Хотите, турпоезд к - Гонолулу,
Пожалуйста! - а <u>это</u> не могу!"   (Gamzatov).

When *это* is the object of an infinitive which is part of a negated finite predicate, there is no smaller genitive frequency. Examples with the accusative:

6.   *"Пусть мне сперва докажут, что на одном пункте земного шара может быть веселее, чем на другом пункте, тогда я поеду". <u>Это</u> ему никто, разумеется, доказать не мог* (Turgenev).

7.   *Однако манкировать старшему... - <u>это</u> я, признаюсь,* dans mon gros bon sens *допустить не могу* (Turgenev).

8.   *В моих руках ты приобрела такой блеск, такую репутацию, - не можешь ты <u>это</u> отрицать!* (Sologub).

In the following I shall give a few examples of 'normal' usage:

9.   *Инсаров уже проходил мимо, не поднимая <u>головы</u>* (Turgenev).

10. *"Барон в этом деле дилетант (...), но в его статье много справедливого и любопытного".*
"Не могу спорить с вами, не зная статьи... (Turgenev).

11. *Шубин произнес всю эту речь в нос (...) и, не дождавшись ответа, продолжал ...* (Turgenev).

12. *Он идет, хотя медленно, не сводя глаз с цели* (Florinskaja, describing a character in Griboedov's *Горе от ума*).

13. *Г-жа Простакова: Да вот, братец, на твои глаза пошлюсь. Митрофанушка, подойди сюда. Мешковат ли этот кафтан?*
Скотинин: Нет.
Простаков: Да и сам уже вижу, матушка, что он узок.
Скотинин: Я и этого не вижу. Кафтанец, брат, сшит изряднехонько (Fonvizin).

14. *Ведь завод останется без специалистов ... Общественность этого не допустит* (Il'f and Petrov).

15. *Вот тут последнее время говорят, что с христианством, или вообще с религией, нужно бороться. Искоренять! Ну, этого я не знаю* (Kaverin).

16. *Так вот как она его любит... Я этого не ожидал* (Turgenev).

17. *Так! Каприз. Каприз? Прежде я этого в ней не замечал* (Turgenev).

It is generally supposed that genitive frequency in negated gerund constructions is caused by 'bookishness' of such clauses. This explanation is unsatisfactory, especially in view of the frequent occurrence of the accusative of negation in gerund constructions: if the genitive were caused by the gerund as such, any possibility of accusative usage would be ruled out.

In negated gerund clauses the choice of case is not indicated by stylistic considerations, but by the function of the clause. In the examples with the direct object in the genitive (9-12), the event described has little substantial value: it only creates a 'décor' for the event depicted in the main clause. In the ninth example, for instance, the gerund clause refers to a mood rather than to an event. *Не поднимая головы* does not refer to the position of Insarov's head, but to the fact that he is in deep thought and does not pay any attention to his surroundings. The use of the word is, so to speak, not literal.

The same tendency is clear in the other examples with
the genitive. In the tenth example the only important information is the fact that the subject is unable to enter into a
discussion; in the preceding text her ignorance of the baron's
article had already been mentioned. *Не дождавшись ответа* implies that Šubin is in a hurry, or too excited to listen to
other people. The words of *не сводя глаз с цели* are used in a
metaphorical sense.

In negated gerund constructions with the accusative, on
the other hand, the event described has as much substantial
value as the event in the main clause: the use of the words
is literal.

Substantial value of the event is especially clear in
the second example, where the gerund clause almost 'pushes
away' the main clause: Sidorov is still whispering, but I do
not listen to it, and despite his whispering I am writing
something. Another highly foregrounded subordinate clause is
given in the fourth example: Surovcev has to see Vera before
anything else. Strictly speaking, the action expressed by the
gerund is more important than the action expressed by the infinitive.

In the first example the crackers are the cause of the
event which is taking place; because of them, Ol'ga P. has to
buy a newspaper. When she starts reading, the crackers are
more important to her than the newspaper, so she takes good
care not to turn them upside down. In the third example the
constant movement of the platoon is as urgent as giving signals to other commanders.

In the same way, it is possible to explain what is behind the genitive and the accusative of negation in two
examples quoted by Ward: *не снимая фуражку* has a literal meaning, for instance: 'It was very cold, so he passed us not
taking off his cap'. *Не скинув фуражки* merely accompanies the
event described in the main clause, for instance:'He was in a

hurry, so he drank a cup of tea without taking off his cap'
(Ward 1965 p. 213).

In negative clauses where the direct object is the pronoun *это*, the accusative is used when the pronoun is wholly
coreferential with what is referred to. In the fifth example,
это is coreferential with the words *достать билеты на таганку*;
in the sixth, with *что на одном пункте земного шара может быть
веселее, чем на другом пункте*; in the seventh, with *манкировать старшему*.

The genitive is used when *это* and the notion to which it
refers are not identical, viz. when the pronoun refers to something broader: 'I do not see *something like that*' (13)... 'Society will not tolerate *a thing like that*'(14)... 'Well, I do
not know if it is *like that*'(15)... 'I did not expect *something
like that*'(16)... 'I never observed *ways like that* in her'(17).

Negative clauses where the direct object is the pronoun
это 'react' to the negative particle in the same way as gerund
constructions: when the words forming the combination 'transitive verb + direct object' are used in a literal sense, i.e.
when the speaker has in mind an action which is perceptibly
existent and which is directed to an exactly defined object,
the accusative is used. When the words are used in a metaphorical, non-definite sense, the genitive is chosen. The difference in the choice of case is brought about by a difference in
the scope of the verb; I would prefer 'Änderung des Verbalbe-
reiches' to 'Einschränkung der Verbalbedeutung'.

The same factor lies at the bottom of the frequent use of
the genitive when the object is a part of the body: such
clauses often do not imply a 'concrete' (in the sense of 'per-
ceptible') action. In order to show this I shall give an
example:

*Все спали или молчали (...), одна Елена не закрывала глаз: она
не сводила их с темной фигуры Инсарова* (Turgenev).

This sentence does not represent a description of a negated action; *не закрывала глаз* here refers to feelings of excitement
and restlessness.

Other examples of the metaphorical use of words which refer to a part of the body were given in the gerund constructions
quoted above.

The non-negated variants of sentences where the direct object refers to a part of the body point, generally speaking, in
the direction of a literal interpretation of the action: *он
поднял голову/закрыл глаза* refer to an action in the literal
sense.

The tendency to use the genitive in constructions with a
metaphorical meaning is also apparent in non-negated clauses;
for instance, *просить чьей-нибудь руки* means 'to propose to
someone'. *Просить чью-нибудь руку* is done by cannibals and chi-
romantists.

There are also examples of accusative usage in expressions
with a metaphorical meaning, for instance:

Чехов не закрывал глаза на отрицательные стороны в сознании (...)
широких масс трудового народа (Saryčev).

А я тогда боялся, как бы он тебе голову не вскружил (Turgenev).

In my opinion, the accusative is used here because the original
literal meaning of these expressions is still strongly felt -
and proverbs and stock expressions tend to be vivid and expressive. Thomson explains such accusatives as follows: "Такие
предложения могут с течением времени получить абстрактное значение в виде поговорок" (Thomson 1903 p. 210).

In order to support the hypothesis on the force behind
genitive/accusative usage I shall give one more example.

As was indicated above, in the clause *Я не люблю суп* only
the accusative is acceptable; when the object is modified, genitive as well as accusative are acceptable.

Here, too, the choice of the case depends on the scope of
the verb. *Я не люблю суп* means: 'I do not like any object which
is soup'. *Я не люблю горячий суп* means: 'I do not like any object which is hot soup', 'I do not like hot soup'. The scope of
the verb includes the object as a whole. *Я не люблю горячего
супа* means: 'I do not like soup which is hot/if it is hot'. The

genitive implies that the speaker does not like the object *суп*, but that this is not always so; the scope of the verb does not include soup which is lukewarm or cold. The scope of *не люблю* is, so to speak, weaker when a genitive is used.

In my opinion, a 'kurze, bestimmte Regel' concerning the choice of case in negative constructions can be formulated as follows:

The <u>accusative</u> is used when a negated verb implies that the action expressed is non-metaphorical, and directed to the object as a part of its whole.

The <u>genitive</u> is used when the scope of a negated verb does not include the object in its whole, either because the connection between the verb and the object is metaphorical, or because the negation is conditional.

Consequently, negations with the accusative often refer to an event which does not take place; the genitive, on the other hand, often refers to a situation which does not exist. Let us compare, for instance, the following examples:

1. <u>*Школу*</u> *она среди года не бросит* (Quoted from Ward).

2. <u>*Школы*</u> *Лена не бросит* (Quoted from Ward).

3. *"К несчастию, без ссор нельзя, а меня все знают, верят мне; вот и позвали меня разобрать одну ссору. Я отправился. (...) По крайней мере недаром хлопотал: уладил его".*
     "И трудно вам было?"
     "Трудно. Один все упрямился. <u>Деньги</u> не хотел отдать" (Turgenev).

4. *"Он не горд?"*
     "Он? Нимало. То есть, если хотите, он горд, только не в том смысле, как вы понимаете. <u>Денег</u> он, например, взаймы ни от кого не возьмет (Turgenev).

The first example implies that the event of leaving school will not take place; the second, that the subject is not a person who is likely to leave school. A similar difference is represented in the third and the fourth examples: the third tells us that the subject did not want to give money on a particular occasion;

the fourth, that the subject is not a person who is likely to
borrow money from anyone.

It is often difficult to notice any semantic difference
between accusative and genitive examples. I do not think,
however, that there are examples of negative clauses
where genitive/accusative usage is really inexplicable.

Rijksuniversiteit Leiden

NOTES

[1] Syllabic versification is a method of composing poetry in fixed lines
of thirteen, eleven, or less (mostly eight) syllables, while the distribution of word stresses is not prescribed, except for the penult. Syllabic
lines are arranged in feminine rhymed couplets.
The larger part of Kantemir's poetry consists of thirteen-syllable lines;
they are divided by a caesura after the seventh syllable. In the first
part of each line, the fourth, fifth or seventh syllable - never the sixth -
must be stressed, in the second part the twelfth.

[2] Although Kantemir was Moldavian by birth and spent the last twelve
years of his life abroad, his mastery of the Russian language is beyond
dispute. Therefore it would be wrong to attribute his frequent preference
for the accusative of negation to a deficient knowledge of Russian.

[3] I wish to record my thanks to Sasha and Lena Lubotsky for providing me
with these examples.

[4] The confusion concerning 'participant' and 'participation' is brought
about by Jakobson, who does not make a clear distinction between these
notions:

"Der G an sich besagt nur, dass der Umfang der Teilnahme des Gegenstandes am
Sachverhalte der Aussage geringer als sein gesamter Umfang ist. In welchem
Masse der Umfang des Gegenstandes beschränkt wird, das bestimmt der sprachli-
che oder der aussersprachliche Kontext" (Jakobson 1967 p. 63).

REFERENCES

Akademija Nauk SSSR
    1980   *Russkaja grammatika* t. II: Sintaksis. Moskva.
Borras, F.M. and R.F. Christian
    1971   *Russian syntax. Aspects of modern Russian syntax and vocabu-
                lary.* Oxford.

Comrie, B. and G. Stone
1978   The Russian language since the Revolution. Oxford.
Davison, R.M.
1967   The use of the genitive in negative constructions.
            Cambridge.
Fuchs, A.
1973   "Zur Wahl des Objektskasus bei Verneinung im Russischen",
            Slawistische Studien zum VII. Int. Slawistenkongress in
            Warschau 1973, München, 81-91.
Jakobson, R.
1967   "Beitrag zur allgemeinen Kasuslehre. Gesamtbedeutungen der
            russischen Kasus", Readings in linguistics II, ed. by
            E.P. Hamp a.o., Chicago and London, 51-90.
Keil, R.-D.
1971   "Zur Wahl des Objektkasus bei verneinten Verben im modernen
            Russisch", Zeitschrift für Slavische Philologie 35, 109-133.
Lomonosov, M.V.
1952   Polnoe sobranie sočinenij. t. VII: Trudy po filologii
            1739-1758 gg., Moskva i Leningrad.
Morison, W.A.
1964   "Logical stress and grammatical form in Russian", The
            Slavonic and East European Review XLII-99, 292-312.
Mustajoki, A.
1985   Padež dopolnenija v russkix otricatel'nyx predloženijax 1:
            izyskanija novyx metodov v izučenii staroj problemy.
            Helsinki.
Pul'kina, I. and E. Zakhava-Nekrasova
1974   Russian. A practical grammar with exercises (Transl. from
            the Russian by V. Korotky). Moscow.
Reiter, N.
1986   "Der Objektgenitiv bei Sachbezeichnungen in serbischen und
            kroatischen Volksliedern", Festschrift für Herbert Bräuer
            zum 65. Geburtstag am 14. April 1986, Köln und Wien, 371-
            -387.
Restan, P.A.
1960   "The objective case in negative clauses in Russian - the
            genitive or the accusative?", Scandoslavica VI, 92-112.
Schaller, H.W.
1978   Das direkte Objekt in verneinten Sätzen des Russischen.
            Frankfurt am Main, Bern, Las Vegas.
Thomson, A.I.
1903   "Vinitel'nyj padež prjamogo dopolnenija v otricatel'nyx
            predloženijax v russkom jazyke", Russkij filologičeskij
            vestnik XLIX, 192-234.
Thomson, A.I.
1911/12   "Beiträge zur Kasuslehre. III. Zur Genetivrektion des
            Verbums im Baltischslavischen", Indogermanische Forschungen
            XXIX, 249-259.
Timberlake, A.
1975   "Hierarchies in the genitive of negation", Slavic and East
            European Journal 19, 123-138.
Uglitsky, Z.
1956   "Accusative and genitive with transitive verbs preceded by
            a negative in contemporary Russian", The Slavonic and East
            European Review XXXIV-83, 377-387.

Ward, D.
    1965   *The Russian language today. System and anomaly.* London.

TOWARDS A PERCEPTUAL ANALYSIS OF RUSSIAN INTONATION*

CECILIA ODÉ

*   This research was supported by the Foundation for Linguistic Research which is funded by the Netherlands Organization for the Advancement of pure research, ZWO.

1. Introduction

1.1 General context

In this article an attempt is made to analyse the intonation of an excerpt of Russian speech using the method of stylization, i.e. an approximation of the original fundamental frequency curve reduced to the simplest possible perceptual form by means of straight lines. The main criterion in this stylization method is perceptual equality between the original utterance and the stylization of that utterance.
This method of analysing intonation, using the Linear Predictive Coding (LPC) analysis-by-resynthesis system, is known as the Dutch School of Intonation, developed at the Institute for Perception Research (IPO) in Eindhoven, the Netherlands, by A. Cohen, R. Collier and J.'t Hart (e.g. 't Hart and Cohen, 1973 and 't Hart and Collier, 1975).

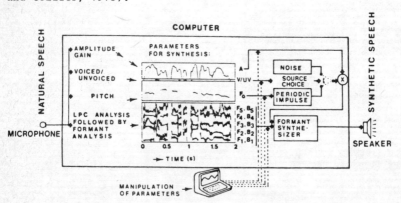

Fig. 1: Diagram of the analysis-by-resynthesis system
(S.G. Nooteboom and A. Cohen, 1984)

A software package called LVS (Leo Vogten System) for speech research on a VAX/11-780 computer with LPA (Laboratory Peripheral Accelerator) input-output facilities contains all the speech processing programmes necessary for my purpose (J. 't Hart et al., 1982). The speech signal is digitized and analysed into thirteen

397

parameters: voiced/unvoiced, amplitude, source frequency, five formants and their bandwidths. The parameters can not only be resynthesised, but also manipulated (see Fig. 1).

Fundamental frequency (Fo) curves, leaving the other parameters intact, are replaced by straight lines and reduced to the smallest number of pitch movements needed for perceptual equivalence with the original Fo curve. In working interactively with the computer, the stylized pitch movements can be made audible and compared with the original Fo curve of the same part of the utterance. If no perceptual differences between stylization and original can be heard while listening analytically, a close-copy stylization is achieved. This type of stylization is introduced by de Pijper and defined as "(...) stylizations, where virtually no perceptual differences appear to exist between stylized pitch contour and original fundamental frequency curve and which are as economical as possible in terms of the number of pitch movements needed" (de Pijper 1983, p.20). Straight lines connect the moments in the Fo curve where pitch switches to another direction (see Fig. 2).

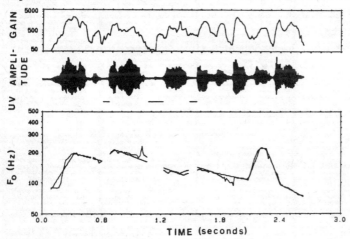

Fig. 2: Gain, amplitude, Fo curve and close-copy stylization of fragment No. 4 'ja repetiroval s Veroj Aleksandrovnoj Davydovoj'

Straight lines can also be drawn step by step, that is in steps of ten milliseconds forward or backward. Any step, stretch or fragment can be made audible and be compared with the original Fo curve of the same part of the utterance.

The acceptability of close-copy stylizations is verifiable by native listeners in perception experiments.

The type of analysis mentioned above differs in many ways from traditional research on Russian intonation. This can be concluded from the literature on the subject, since, to my knowledge, no such analysis has been made of Russian intonation. For the traditional approach see, for example, Bryzgunova (1977). For a survey of the literature on Russian intonation the reader should consult the excellent works of Svetozarova (1982) and Keijsper (1983). Problems of intonation theory will not be discussed here.

The aim of the present analysis of Russian intonation is i) to contribute to the establishment of an inventory of discrete pitch movements in modern spoken Russian; ii) to explore the acceptable free variants and possible combinations of pitch movements; iii) to find the number of reference lines between which pitch moves and to define the approximate distance between those lines in semitones.

Data as to excursion, duration and slope of perceptually relevant pitch movements will be given in terms of their minimum and maximum values (see 2.2), not only in the whole tonic vowel, but in the pre- and posttonic syllables as well if this seems to be relevant for perception (see 4.1 and 4.4).

1.2 Linguistic material and type of speech

The linguistic material or recording is taken from a quasi-spontaneous monologue by the opera director B.A. Pokrovskij. From the original recording of about 40 minutes a selection was made of one longer excerpt with a high diversity in intonation (1min 40s). One phrase and one short excerpt (15s) were added because of some interesting configurations of pitch movements that were missing in the long excerpt but occur frequently in modern spoken Russian.

Though the speaker must have prepared his talk to some
extent, since it is an original recording from Melodija Records,
Pokrovskij improvises freely on his work as an opera director.
This can be concluded from the frequent fluctuations in speech
rate, the hesitations and pauses he makes at syntactically
unexpected moments (i.e. in the middle of a word, or by syllable
lengthening) and his sometimes extreme expressiveness as well as
his idiosyncrasies. Pauses and hesitations that occur in a
syntactically unexpected place or elsewhere within a fragment are
marked in the text (see 1.4).
The long elliptic utterances, the frequent inversion and the
independence of intonation patterns from syntactic structure in
the entire recording justify the decision to call this particular
talk of Pokrovskij quasi-spontaneous. The addition 'quasi' distinguishes between prepared (quasi-spontaneous) and unprepared
(spontaneous) speech; both labels assume that no written materials
are used.

1.3 Parallel text in Russian transliteration and English

The text of the analysed excerpt registered after the
original recording, is given in Russian transliteration and in
English translation. Under the stylized pitch contours (see 2) the
Russian transliteration is printed with a *podstročnik*, a word-to -
word translation, in English under the words with pitch accents.
Punctuation marks have been deliberately omitted.
The excerpt is divided into short stretches. This has been done
for practical and technical reasons of processing the material. A
sentence has been broken off at moments when there was "time
enough" to do so: in pauses, at syntactic and or intonational
boundaries. In this way every stretch of speech (henceforth:
fragment) lasts no longer than three seconds, and can be put on a
Bell & Howell Language Master System card (see 3.1).

RUSSIAN TRANSLITERATION	ENGLISH
1. ja pomnju kak odnaždy	I remember how I once
2. kogda ja stavil operu Rimskogo-Korsakova 'Sadko'	when I was directing Rimskij-Korsakov's opera 'Sadko'
3. s Nikolaem Semënovičem Golovanovym	with Nikolaj Semënovič Golovanov
4. ja repetiroval s Veroj Aleksandrovnoj Davydovoj	I rehearsed with Vera Aleksandrovna Davydova
5. i Georgiem Nëleppom	and Georgij Nelepp
6. scenu Sadka i ego ženy Ljubavy	the scene of Sadko with his wife Ljubava
7. nužno skazat' čto scena nam očen' ponravilas'	I must say that we liked the scene very much
8. scena udalas'	the scene was a success
9. i nam pokazalos' čto my našli	and it seemed to us that we had found
10. kakie-to interesnye vzaimootnošenija	some interesting interactions
11. meždu dejstvujuščimi licami	between the characters
12. kak-to raskrylis' interesno obrazy	their images unfolded in an interesting way
13. v takoj ostryj moment	at such a crucial moment
14. razryva suprugov	of the separation of husband

and wife

15.i kogda scena byla gotova   and when the scene was ready

16.ja pozval na repeticiju   I called for Nikolaj Semënovič
    Nikolaja Semënoviča   to come to the rehearsal

17.on posmotrel   he watched

18.i emu očen' ponravilos'   and he liked it very much

19.on prosto skazal zamečatel'no   he simply said great well done
    molodcy

20.chorošo interesno   nice interesting

21.i davajte ėto repetirovat'   let us rehearse this now
    uže s orkestrom   with the orchestra

22.no vot čto proizošlo   but see what happened

23.kogda my stali repetirovat'   as we started to rehearse
    s orkestrom   with the orchestra

24.ničego ne polučilos'   nothing came of it

25.vse stali nervničat'   everybody got nervous

26.i pervyj konečno stal   and first of all of course
    nervničat' Nikolaj Semënovič   Nikolaj Semënovič got nervous

27.on očen' chotel provesti scenu   he wanted so much to perform
    v tom plane   the scene in the same way

28.v tom ključe v kotorom my eë   in the same key as we had put
    nametili   it in

29.no ničego ne polučalos'   but nothing came of it

30.on ėtogo sdelat' ne mog	he could not do it
31.ėto ne bylo v ego charaktere	he did not have the character for it
32.ėto ne bylo v ego individual'nosti	he did not have the individuality for it
33.togda ja perestavil scenu	then I directed the scene again
34.imeja v vidu emocional'nyj charakter	with an eye to the emotional character
35.tvorčestva Golovanova	of Golovanov's work
36.i togda	and then
37.vsë vstalo na mesto	everything fell into place
38.režissërski možet byt' ėta scena stala menee interesna	from a director's point of view the scene became maybe less interesting
39.no zato ona lučše	but it better
40.točnee sootvetstvovala	closer corresponded to
41.interpretacii Golovanova	Golovanov's interpretation
42.prosto ego charakteru ego temperamentu	simply to his character his temperament
43.ego prirode	to his nature
44.muzikanta i teatral'nogo dejatelja	as a musician and theatre man

45.esli chotite aktёrskomu   if you like to the temperament
   temperamentu dirižёra   of the actor in the director

46.slučajnogo v operach chorošich accidental things never ever
   ničego ne byvaet   happen in good operas

47.i kogda poёt Ol'ga   and when Olga sings

48.eё soprovoždaet orkestr   she is accompanied by the
                          orchestra

49.derevjannymi duchovymi   by the woodwinds
   instrumentami

50.a kogda Lenskij poёt   but when Lenskij sings

51.emu akkompaniruet   he is accompanied

52.strunnaja gruppa   by the strings

53.čto èto nam daёt   what does that tell us

54.kakoj vyvod iz ètogo my   what conclusion must we draw
   dolžny sdelat'   from this

1.4 Notational conventions

The sign # indicates a pause or hesitation within a fragment
(see 1.3). The bold line in the stylized contour indicates the
perceptually relevant pitch movement in and, as we will see,
before the prominent syllable; it can cover more syllables than
just the prominent syllable (see 4.). For that reason a vertical
dash is used to indicate the actual vowel onset in the prominent

syllable.

Note that the bold line does not indicate the acoustic representation (see the discussion in 3.1).

The bold type in capitals in the transliteration of the text under the stylized contours indicates the syllable with a pitch accent. A switch in the direction of a line (that is, in the direction of a pitch movement) does not necessarily announce a following pitch accent.

Where it was unnatural to leave out micro-intonation it was maintained in the stylization. Micro-intonation is a term used for fluctuations in the Fo curve of natural speech that are not intended by the speaker but that are involuntary and caused by a combination of physiological factors.

The text is divided into 54 fragments, No. 1 through No. 54. The number after the full stop in the number of the fragment indicates the pitch accent in the fragment. Thus in fragment No. 21 we have three pitch accents: 21.1, 21.2, 21.3. As mentioned earlier, all punctuation marks have been left out.

All lines should be read without a pause, unless the sign # appears in the text. This sign indicates a pause or hesitation other than at the end of a line. The end of a line indicates a boundary, except for fragment No. 9.

The text under the stylized pitch contours is not the phonetic representation of the actually pronounced text. To indicate the duration of a fragment, the time is given in seconds between brackets at the end of a line. Due to the discrepancy between the duration of a fragment in seconds and the length of the text of that fragment represented in graphemes, the stylized pitch contours do not give an adequate picture of the timing in the original Fo curve. In the "long" fragment No. 4, for instance, the speech rate is high and the name, consisting of forename, father's name and family name, is pronounced in 1.5 s, swallowing many syllables.

2. Text

In this section the stylized pitch contours and the phonetic data of the pitch movements are presented.

405

2.1 Text with stylized pitch contours

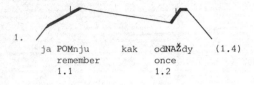

1.
```
ja POMnju      kak    odNAŽdy    (1.4)
   remember           once
   1.1                1.2
```

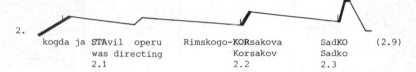

2.
```
kogda ja STAvil  operu   Rimskogo-KORsakova   SadKO   (2.9)
         was directing   Korsakov             Sadko
         2.1             2.2                   2.3
```

3.
```
s NikoLAem    SeMËnovičem    GoloVAnovym   (1.3)
  Nikolaj     Semënovič       Golovanov
  3.1         3.2             3.3
```

4.
```
JA  repeTIroval s Veroj AlekSANdrovnoj      DaVYdovoj  (2.5)
I   rehearsed           Aleksandrovna       Davydova
4.1 4.2                 4.3                  4.4
```

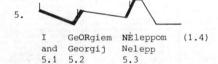

5.
```
I    GeORgiem NÈleppom   (1.4)
and  Georgij  Nelepp
5.1  5.2      5.3
```

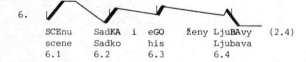

6.
```
SCEnu    SadKA i  eGO   ženy LjuBAvy   (2.4)
scene    Sadko his        Ljubava
6.1      6.2   6.3        6.4
```

406

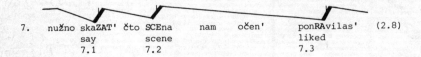

7. nužno skaZAT' čto SCEna   nam   očen'   ponRAvilas'   (2.8)
        say   scene   liked
        7.1   7.2   7.3

8. SCEna   udaLAS'   (1.2)
    scene   was a success
    8.1   8.2

9. i   nam   pokaZAlos'#ČTO   my   našli   (1.8)
               seemed   that
               9.1   9.2

10. kakie-to   inteRESnye   vzaimootnoŠEnija   (2.0)
                   interesting   interactions
                   10.1   10.2

11. meždu   DEJstvujuščimi licami   (1.4)
             acting
             11.1

12. kak-to   rasKRYlis'   interesno   Obrazy   (2.1)
              unfolded   images
              12.1   12.2

407

13.

```
v takoj   Ostryj # moment      (1.7)
          crucial
          13.1
```

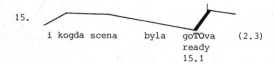

14.

```
razRYva # suprugov (1.4)
separation husband and wife
14.1
```

15.

```
i kogda scena    byla   goTOva    (2.3)
                        ready
                        15.1
```

16.

```
ja    poZVAL    na  repeTIciju  Nikolaja   SeMËnoviča   (2.0)
      called        rehearsal              Semënovič
      16.1           16.2                   16.3
```

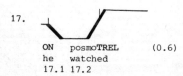

17.

```
ON    posmoTREL     (0.6)
he    watched
17.1  17.2
```

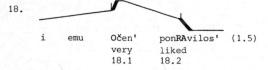

18.

```
i    emu    Očen'    ponRAvilos'  (1.5)
            very     liked
            18.1     18.2
```

408

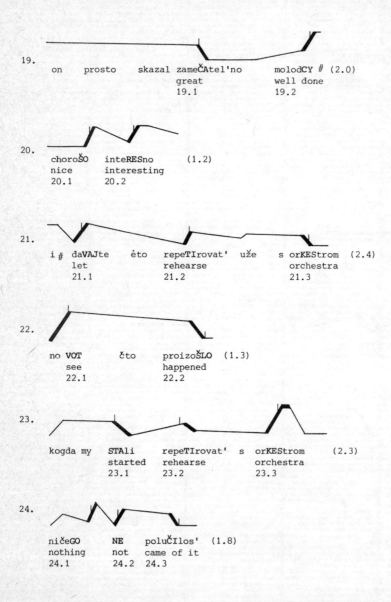

19.

on   prosto   skazal zameČAtel'no   molodCY # (2.0)
                           great   well done
                           19.1   19.2

20.

choroŠO   inteRESno   (1.2)
nice   interesting
20.1   20.2

21.

i # daVAJte   èto   repeTIrovat' uže   s orKEStrom (2.4)
     let   rehearse   orchestra
     21.1   21.2   21.3

22.

no VOT   čto   proizoŠLO (1.3)
   see   happened
   22.1   22.2

23.

kogda my   STAli   repeTIrovat' s orKEStrom   (2.3)
           started   rehearse   orchestra
           23.1   23.2   23.3

24.

ničeGO   NE   poluČIlos' (1.8)
nothing   not   came of it
24.1   24.2 24.3

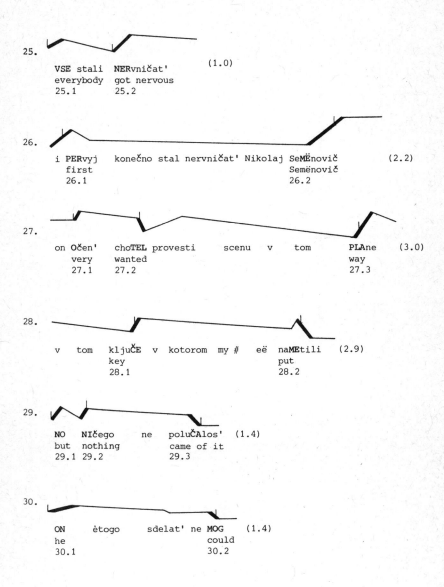

25.

VSE stali NERvničat'   (1.0)
everybody got nervous
25.1   25.2

26.

i PERvyj konečno stal nervničat' Nikolaj SeMĚnovič   (2.2)
first   Semënovič
26.1   26.2

27.

on Očen' choTEL provesti   scenu   v   tom   PLAne   (3.0)
   very   wanted   way
   27.1   27.2   27.3

28.

v   tom   kljuČE v kotorom my #   eë naMEtili   (2.9)
          key   put
          28.1   28.2

29.

NO   NIčego   ne   poluČAlos' (1.4)
but nothing   came of it
29.1 29.2   29.3

30.

ON   ètogo   sdelat' ne MOG   (1.4)
he   could
30.1   30.2

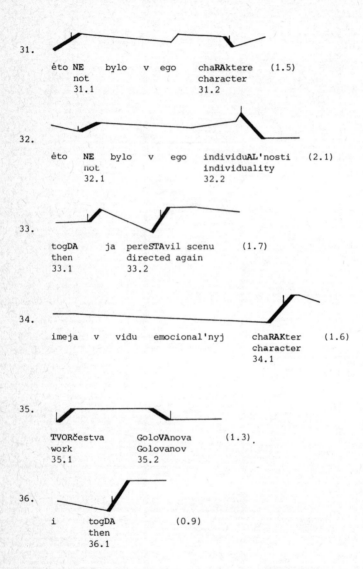

31.

èto **NE** bylo v ego chaRAktere (1.5)
   not   character
   31.1   31.2

32.

èto **NE** bylo v ego individuAL'nosti (2.1)
   not   individuality
   32.1   32.2

33.

togDA ja pereSTAvil scenu (1.7)
then   directed again
33.1   33.2

34.

imeja v vidu emocional'nyj chaRAKter (1.6)
                         character
                         34.1

35.

TVORčestva GoloVAnova (1.3)
work   Golovanov
35.1   35.2

36.

i togDA (0.9)
  then
  36.1

411

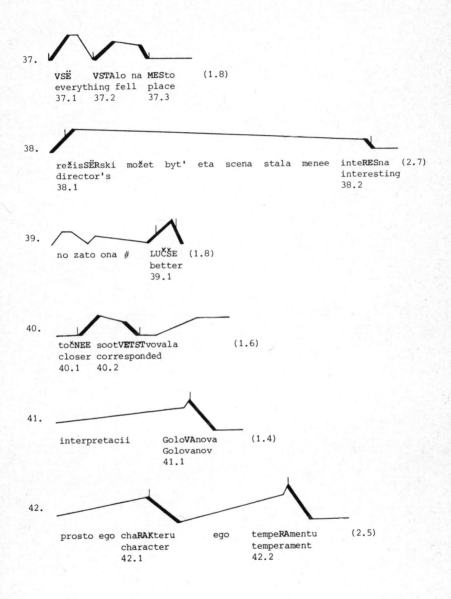

37.
VSË   VSTAlo na MESto   (1.8)
everything fell place
37.1   37.2   37.3

38.
režisSËRski   možet   byt'   eta   scena   stala   menee   inteRESna (2.7)
director's   interesting
38.1   38.2

39.
no zato ona #   LUČŠE (1.8)
                 better
                 39.1

40.
točNEE sootVETSTvovala   (1.6)
closer corresponded
40.1   40.2

41.
interpretacii   GoloVAnova   (1.4)
                 Golovanov
                 41.1

42.
prosto ego chaRAKteru   ego   tempeRAmentu   (2.5)
             character   temperament
             42.1   42.2

412

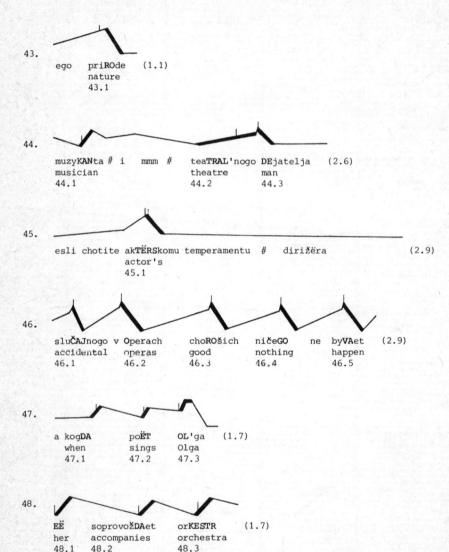

43.

```
ego   priROde   (1.1)
      nature
      43.1
```

44.

```
muzyKANta # i   mmm #    teaTRAL'nogo DEjatelja   (2.6)
musician                 theatre      man
44.1                     44.2         44.3
```

45.

```
esli chotite akTËRSkomu temperamentu #   dirižëra              (2.9)
             actor's
             45.1
```

46.

```
sluČAJnogo v Operach    choROšich   ničeGO    ne  byVAet   (2.9)
accidental   operas     good        nothing       happen
46.1         46.2       46.3        46.4          46.5
```

47.

```
a kogDA       poËT     OL'ga   (1.7)
  when        sings    Olga
  47.1        47.2     47.3
```

48.

```
EË       soprovožDAet    orKESTR   (1.7)
her      accompanies     orchestra
48.1     48.2            48.3
```

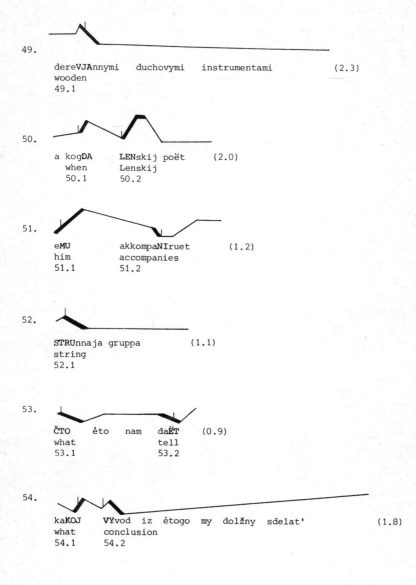

49.

dereVJAnnymi   duchovymi   instrumentami   (2.3)
wooden
49.1

50.

a kogDA   LENskij poët   (2.0)
when   Lenskij
50.1   50.2

51.

eMU   akkompaNIruet   (1.2)
him   accompanies
51.1   51.2

52.

STRUnnaja gruppa   (1.1)
string
52.1

53.

ČTO   èto   nam   daËT   (0.9)
what   tell
53.1   53.2

54.

kaKOJ   VYvod iz ètogo my dolžny sdelat'   (1.8)
what   conclusion
54.1   54.2

2.2 Phonetic data

In the following table the phonetic data are given of only
the *perceptually* relevant pitch movements that are indicated in
the stylized pitch contours (see 2.1) with a *bold* line (see 1.4).
As will be discussed in 3. and 4., the perceptually relevant pitch
movements may include pretonic syllables and virtual movements.
The data consist of duration expressed in milliseconds, excursion
or range in hertz, range in semitones and slope in semitones per
second.
A minus sign before the semitones indicates a fall and no sign a
rise.
Sometimes a pitch movement is followed by a level tone. If this
level stretch is perceptually relevant, it is marked in the table
between brackets.

fragment No.	duration in milli- seconds	range in hertz (Hz)	range in ST = semi- tones	slope in ST per second	group (see 3.1)
1.1	90	178-208	2.7	30.0	I
1.2	110 (80)	147-200 (200)	5.3	48.5	C
2.1	450	96-140	6.5	14.5	I
2.2	90	81-104	4.3	48.1	I
2.3	90	90-217	15.2	169.3	C
3.1	80	114-86	-4.9	-61.0	J
3.2	150	105-84	-3.9	-25.8	J
3.3	200	119-72	-8.7	-43.5	A
4.1	230	86-192	13.9	60.5	I
4.2	120	163-212	4.6	37.9	I
4.3	190	123-142	2.5	13.1	I
4.4	120 (60)	106-217 (217)	12.4	103.4	C

5.1	310	109-71	-7.4	-23.9	J
5.2	130	71-112	7.9	60.7	I
5.3	140	96-227	14.9	106.4	C
6.1	110	156-208	5.0	45.3	I
6.2	180	97-175	10.2	56.8	I
6.3	90	108-131	3.3	37.1	I
6.4	260	123-79	-7.7	-29.5	A
7.1	90	101-138	5.4	60.0	I
7.2	340	104-136	4.6	13.7	I
7.3	90	75-131	9.7	107.3	H
8.1	70	93-114	3.5	50.4	I
8.2	110	71-117	8.6	78.6	H
9.1	50	96-119	3.7	74.4	I
9.2	180	106-80	-4.9	-27.1	I
10.1	220	71-96	5.2	23.7	I
10.2	380	72-116	8.3	21.7	H
11.1	220	91-99	1.5	6.6	I
12.1	110	89-109	3.5	31.9	I
12.2	70	99-109	1.7	23.8	H
13.1	140	78-117	7.0	50.1	H
14.1	70 (200)	84-89 (89)	1.0	14.3	I
15.1	240	101-238	14.8	61.8	E
16.1	120	144-181	4.0	33.0	I
16.2	190	121-188	7.6	40.2	I
16.3	170	138-74	-10.8	-63.5	A

17.1	50	166-93	-10.0	-200.6	J
17.2	140	88-208	14.9	106.4	F
18.1	60	188-263	5.8	96.9	I
18.2	180	135-76	-9.9	-55.3	A
19.1	110	178-96	-10.7	-97.2	J
19.2	200	117-227	11.5	57.4	F
20.1	100	129-208	8.3	82.7	F
20.2	180	126-212	9.0	50.0	E
21.1	100	123-217	9.8	98.3	I
21.2	70	108-142	4.7	67.7	I
21.3	160	98-56	-9.7	-60.6	A
22.1	140 (140)	95-208 (208)	13.6	96.9	I
22.2	300	138-68	-12.3	-40.8	A
23.1	220	158-116	-5.3	-24.3	J
23.2	270	142-112	-4.1	-15.2	J
23.3	160 (80)	86-200 (200)	14.6	91.3	C
24.1	210	90-196	13.5	64.2	I
24.2	110	99-140	6.0	54.5	I
24.3	110	95-69	-5.5	-50.3	A
25.1	100	133-158	3.0	29.8	I
25.2	150	119-172	6.4	42.5	H
26.1	110	121-149	3.6	32.8	I
26.2	210	73-185	16.1	76.7	E
27.1	40	212-238	2.0	50.1	I
27.2	110	212-138	-7.4	-67.6	J
27.3	200	76-188	15.7	78.4	H

28.1	140	108-169	7.8	55.4	I
28.2	170	188-75	-15.9	-93.6	A
29.1	60	163-208	4.2	70.3	I
29.2	60	158-188	3.0	50.2	I
29.3	110	135-82	-8.6	-78.5	A
30.1	100	90-116	4.4	43.9	I
30.2	140	85-54	-7.9	-56.1	A
31.1	200	106-158	6.9	34.6	I
31.2	210	98-84	-2.7	-12.7	D
32.1	130	128-151	2.9	22.0	I
32.2	180	129-64	-12.1	-67.4	A
33.1	50	153-222	6.4	128.9	I
33.2	230	101-222	13.6	59.3	E
34.1	140	82-208	16.1	115.1	E
35.1	110	86-129	7.0	63.8	I
35.2	170	126-81	-7.6	-45.0	A
36.1	240	69-227	20.6	85.9	F
37.1	120	120-200	8.8	73.7	I
37.2	110	83-161	11.5	104.3	I
37.3	100	125-77	-8.4	-83.9	A
38.1	400	128-227	9.9	24.8	I
38.2	230	149-71	-12.8	-55.8	A
39.1	150	208-81	-16.3	-108.8	G
40.1	250	84-138	8.6	34.4	I
40.2	180	138-83	-8.8	-48.9	D

41.1	210	188-74	-16.1	-76.9	B
42.1	180	196-96	-12.4	-68.6	B
42.2	320	185-69	-17.1	-53.4	B
43.1	190	185-84	-13.7	-71.9	B
44.1	170	86-128	6.9	40.5	I
44.2	360	90-121	5.1	14.2	I
44.3	190	121-68	-10.0	-52.5	A
45.1	140	175-91	-11.3	-80.9	B
46.1	150	185-103	-10.1	-67.6	G
46.2	160	192-116	-8.7	-54.5	G
46.3	120	181-112	-8.3	-69.2	G
46.4	130	172-108	-8.1	-62.0	G
46.5	180	163-76	-13.2	-73.4	G
47.1	60	123-166	5.2	86.5	I
47.2	150	135-172	4.2	28.0	I
47.3	70 (60)	175-250 (250)	6.2	88.2	C
48.1	160	106-200	11.0	68.7	I
48.2	150	120-185	7.5	50.0	I
48.3	170	101-178	9.8	57.7	H
49.1	200	185-85	-13.5	-67.3	A
50.1	80	116-156	5.1	64.1	I
50.2	140 (60)	123-270 (270)	13.6	97.2	C
51.1	250	88-204	14.6	58.2	I
51.2	120	149-90	-8.7	-72.7	D

52.1	90	128-104	-3.6	-39.9	A
53.1	150	114-86	-4.9	-32.5	J
53.2	200	99-75	-4.8	-21.8	D
54.1	60	86-112	4.6	76.2	I
54.2	90	80-68	-2.8	-90.0	D

3.   Analysis

3.1 Matching the pitch movements

In the present analysis pitch movements are classified into
ten groups, running from A through J. Every group contains
perceptually similar pitch movements. Phonetic data are given in
2.2. A survey of the stylized pitch movements can be found in 7.
The aim of the survey is to enhance the readability of this
article in such a way that the reader does not have to turn over
the pages to find a certain group.
The classification as such has not been verified in an official
perception experiment. A small group of trained listeners has
accepted my classification. The close-copy stylization of the
whole excerpt, however, has been labelled fully acceptable by a
native audience of about thirty trained listeners. This means that
no perceptually relevant difference was heard between the original
recording and the close-copies. I made the classification by means
of the Bell & Howell Language Master System. A stretch of
maximally three seconds can be recorded on a card with magnetic
tape (see also 1.2). A card does not give any written information
about that stretch, except for its number. Cards can be listened
to in random order by passing them through the Language Master
groove with replay head. For the present analysis all 54 fragments
were recorded on 54 cards.
Actual matching, in order to classify the pitch movements,

could now start by listening to and comparing the cards. Pitch
movements with high resemblance were matched and each group was
listened to repeatedly. If a pitch movement did not really "fit"
into a group after all, it was compared with another group. In
this way, by shuffling and weighing the cards against each other,
ten groups were found to exist.

The task of matching was hampered by a few problems though. By
comparing whole fragments only, one (usually the last) pitch
movement can be classified, but the others might then be disregarded. In order to avoid such a neglect of pitch movements and to
fulfil the matching task properly I recorded the words with pitch
accent on a tape. To make sure that pitch movements preceding or
following another pitch movement within the same fragment were
never left out while matching, both cards and tape recordings were
used for the classification. The pitch movements could now be
compared on the level of the word and on the level of the whole
fragment. Listening from different perspectives is important: for
example, by comparing just words with pitch accents a sawtooth
pattern (see 5.1) or harmonica pattern (see 5.2) cannot be
recognized.

Since declination, the tendency of pitch to gradually float down
during an utterance, is an established feature known in Russian
(Svetozarova, 1982), just as in Dutch and English (Cohen, Collier,
't Hart, 1982), it will not be discussed in this article.

The distance between the reference lines, between which pitch
moves in Pokrovskij's talk, can be found in 2.2.

Group A

To group A belong all falls in tonic syllables with or
without a *zanos* (a rise in the pretonic syllable, a set-up before
the fall, see 4.1) that reach the low reference line and are not
preceded by a rise within the tonic syllable. The pretonic
syllable can be higher than the beginning of the tonic syllable or
on the same level, but it may also contain a gradual rise or a
zanos. The tonic fall can start in the pretonic syllable(s).
Sometimes the tone has reached the low reference line in the
pretonic syllable. In that case the tonic syllable is on the low
reference line, and posttonic syllables continue on that line   In

Pokrovskij we find the following realizations in their *acoustic* representation (note that the bold line here indicates how pitch actually moves in the accented syllable):

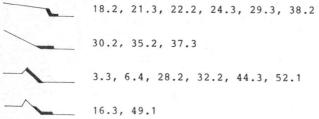

18.2, 21.3, 22.2, 24.3, 29.3, 38.2

30.2, 35.2, 37.3

3.3, 6.4, 28.2, 32.2, 44.3, 52.1

16.3, 49.1

    Group A type accents always announce a major boundary. The group A type of pitch movements can thus be labelled as final falls.
This pitch movement is known in the literature on Russian intonation as Intonation Construction No. 1 (IK-1) in Bryzgunova's classification (1977).
    In three cases, namely in 28.2, 29.3 and 35.2, the fall in the tonic syllable does not really reach the low reference line. Yet perceptually they are too much of an A type to form a separate group. The posttonic syllables continue on the same line, which is not low and which I therefore call the non-low reference line. A fall such as this can very often be observed in spontaneous speech. It has the communicative function of suggesting indefiniteness. A fall to the non-low reference line can easily be confused with a fall in posttonic syllables in group H (see below), which do not but can almost reach the non-low reference line. More examples of both groups are required to eliminate this confusion. For the time being, I suggest that two low reference lines are to be distinguished: low and non-low.

Group B
    Group B consists of another type of fall. It differs from group A in that the tone necessarily falls in the tonic syllable, and thus cannot be level in the tonic syllable on the low reference line as it can be in group A.
Representatives of group B in their acoustic representation (the bold line here indicates the accented syllable) are 41.1, 42.1,

42.2, 43.1 and 45.1:

In the pretonic syllable(s) the tone gradually rises. In 42.2 a *zanos* (see 4.1) is present.

A further important feature of group B is the possible short rise or level high tone preceding the fall in the tonic syllable. This can be observed in 42.2, 43.1 and 45.1. After the rise or level high tone the fall must follow immediately, otherwise the accent can be confused with realizations in group C (see below). The excursion in group B is fairly large and not extremely steep (see 2.2).

The group B type of pitch movements appear as a final fall in 41.1 and 45.1 and occur at a boundary in an enumeration in 42.1, 42.2 and 43.1. As regards the position of a fall, group A type and group B type compete for their choice. What actually makes the speaker decide to use one of the two types is left out of the discussion in this article.

Group B falls show some similarities with IK-2 in the classification of Bryzgunova. As is well known from the literature on Russian intonation, in IK-2 intensity seems to be of some relevancy. In my examples this is just a concomitant feature, since the difference between type B falls and other types of falls can be made audible by changing only Fo.

Group C

Group C represents a pitch movement which is perceptually very easily distinguishable, and known as very Russian.

There are many realizations of the group C type, but they can always be stylized in the same way without any perceptual difference between the stylization and the original Fo. As soon as this stylization was found, all pitch accents of group C could be described in the same terms. In Pokrovskij's talk there are seven of the kind: 1.2, 2.3, 4.4, 5.3, 23.3, 47.3, 50.2. Its main feature is a very steep rise with a large excursion (see 2.2) early in the tonic syllable. Part of the rise can be realized in the pretonic syllable(s). After the rise the tone is high and level and sometimes begins to fall at the end of the tonic

423

syllable. In the posttonic syllable(s) the tone falls steeply and reaches the low reference line and is thus always lower than in the pretonic syllable (the bold line here indicates the accented syllable):

In the present text the group C type is found only at boundaries, but elsewhere in Russian the group C type occurs at a boundary and most frequently as interrogative intonation without question word. In the wh-questions in fragment No. 53 and 54 a group C type does not appear. Pokrovskij does not use many questions at all in his talk. This has probably to do with the fact that the type of speech is a monologue: outside the analysed excerpt Pokrovskij uses the group C type only occasionally as an interrogative intonation in rhetorical questions.

If exactly the group C type of realizations is meant, they correspond to IK-3 in Bryzgunova's classification. This statement cannot be reversed. When Bryzgunova uses the label IK-3 the movement meant is not necessarily a representation of group C, since the label IK-3 as used by Bryzgunova does not correspond to a single type of pitch movement.

Group D

The posttonic syllables are decisive for the description of the configuration of pitch movements in group D. After the fall to the low reference line, on which the tone can continue within the tonic syllable (see also group A), the tone rises and continues in the posttonic syllables on the level reached or rises gradually until the end of the utterance (the bold line here indicates the accented syllable):

The group D type is found in 31.2, 40.2, 51.2, 53.2 and 54.2.
If the posttonic syllables are cut off, the pitch movement within the tonic syllable itself can be classified in group A. Here the posttonic syllables decide that the movement as a whole differs from group A.
The configuration of pitch movements occurs in syntactically

heterogeneous positions. In the present text it is used as a continuation contour in three cases (31.2, 40.2, 51.2) and as a question in two cases (53.2, 54.2).

In the classification of Bryzgunova we find realizations of this type under the name IK-4. As we have seen in group C, we must be very careful in comparing this classification with mine, since Bryzgunova seems to confuse phonetic data with the function and meaning of the seven IK-'s of her system, whereas in my classifi-cation the perceived melodic course is the only criterion.
"The criterion of perceptual discreteness is not always met by Bryzgunova's inventory of contours; some of her IK's are described as being only gradiently different. (...)Examples are some of the nondiscretely different contours (...), which are being differen-tiated because of the different functions they are presumed to have, and some of the "modal realizations" of IK's, which are being classified on the basis of their presumed function instead of their form" (Keijsper 1983, pp.104-106).

An interesting realization of group D is 54.2. The analysis shows a rise and a fall in the tonic syllable, though the whole ut-terance is recognized as a group D type. It was not easy to segment the tonic vowel because of the high speech rate. Isolation of syllables did not make any sense. In trying to manipulate the first accent (54.1) to make the perception of 54.2 easier, the result was another interpretation of the utterance: by changing the pretonic fall in 54.1 into a rise, the word *kakoj* received the only pitch accent, and the word *vyvod* in 54.2 was not perceived as carrying a pitch accent at all. Still, a group D type was recognized. By removing the pitch movement in *vyvod* leaving *kakoj* as it is, we still hear an accent on *vyvod* , so a parameter other than pitch is probably involved here. Moreover, the posttonic syllables were not changed and remain decisive.

Group E

The posttonic syllables are decisive for the description of the pitch movement in group E. (see also group D).

The group E type of pitch movement suggests a continuation. The pitch movement is a full rise in the tonic syllable, followed by one or more posttonic syllables on the high reference line that show declination (the bold line here indicates the accented syllable):

In the present text five movements represent group E: 15.1, 20.2, 26.2, 33.2 and 34.1 (the bold line indicates the accented syllable):

In 26.2 the posttonic stretch continues on the high reference line. However, the posttonic stretch is so short, that perceptually it belongs almost to group F (see below). In 15.1 the entire rise is realized in the pretonic syllable (see 4.1).

In Bryzgunova's classification group E realizations are called IK-6, but the reverse does not hold in my classification (see also the remark in group C).

The group E type competes with some realizations in group H (see for example 27.3 and 48.3), though perceptually there is a difference between the two groups. This problem is discussed in group H.

Group F

If a full and steep rise of the type described in group C and in group E is realized, and the pitch accent happens to be in the last syllable of an utterance or at a boundary, the opposition between the two types is neutralized (the bold line here indicates the accented syllable):

(in 17.2, 19.2, 20.1 and 36.1).

The neutralized group C or group E types are put in group F.
The tonic vowels are longer than in group C and in group E, as is always the case in final vowels. In 2.3 there is no neutralization, because the speaker managed to make a steep and full rise and fall to the low reference line within the tonic syllable and thus it is a realization of the group C type (see above). It would be interesting to find out by which group a native speaker would replace a group F type if he were urged to replace a group F type word by a word with posttonic syllable(s). Sometimes, while

listening to a longer stretch (a whole utterance or a few utterances one after another) it can be guessed by the intonational context what type would probably be used. For instance in 19.2 and 20.1, 20.2 we may assume three pitch accents of the same type in the compliments that are summed up by the speaker. In 36.1 we have a choice between a group C type or a group E type, since both realizations fit into the intonational context. I would like to repeat that I shall not discuss what made the speaker decide to realize a certain pitch movement and what meaning it conveys.

It is questionable whether pitch movements of the type of group H (see below) show neutralization in words with final stress (cf. No. 48.3), since the features of group E and group H have not yet been clearly defined.

Group G

The configuration of pitch movements of the group G type is discussed separately in 5.2 as the harmonica pattern (the bold line here indicates the accented syllable):

There is one utterance in which perceptually the same pitch movement occurs only once, though probably the harmonica is a separate group because of the close succession of the same pitch movement: in 39.1 the speaker "colours" the pitch accent by taking one "fold" of the harmonica, and then, after a pause, he continues the utterance in 40.1 with a neutral pitch accent: 39.1 and 40.1 occur in the same syntactical position.
Note that the group G type of pitch movement in fragment No. 46 is realized in the lexically stressed syllable, whereas in fragment No. 39.1 it is realized after the lexically stressed syllable. Although very interesting in itself, this phenomenon is not discussed in the present article.
Fragment No. 46 is as a whole a group G type:

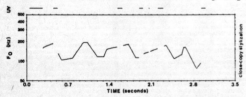

Group H

Group H is probably the most problematic type of all ten groups. As already mentioned, a group H type is sometimes hard to distinguish from a group E or group F type. There are many relevant factors in this respect, for example the posttonic syllables, the intonational context, the acoustic features of the tonic syllable. The realizations of the group H type can also differ from each other. Yet they are perceived as belonging to the same group.

Let us first see where they are found: 7.3, 8.2, 10.2, 12.2, 13.1, 25.2, 27.3 and 48.3. After listening carefully, a more subtle subdivision can be made:

i) a perceptually long tonic vowel: 7.3, 8.2, 10.2, 12.2, 13.1, 27.3;

ii) a higher tone and shorter vowel than in i): 25.2, 48.3.

Since the rises differ from each other in group H, other features that characterize the group H type must be taken into account.

An interesting question is whether group H is indeed a perceptually separate and thus discrete group, or whether it is the same rise of group E but over a smaller range.

A further question is whether a group H type, like the group C and E types, is neutralized if the syllable with pitch accent is the final syllable. To find an answer, a perception experiment must be constructed in which the group E pitch movement is modified into the group H pitch movements and vice versa.

Another problem is the relevancy of posttonic syllables. Is there a significant difference between posttonic syllables that are level, or that continue on the declination line, or that fall but do not reach the non-low reference line? Can anything be said about the type of pitch accent that follows a group H type, or about the length of the following fragment until a boundary or the end of an utterance? In other words, does a group H type convey information about how pitch will continue?

The group H type does not suggest that a conclusion follows soon. The flow of thoughts is unfinished.

Among all the features mentioned, which define(s) a group H type?

Group I

The group I type of pitch movement (henceforth: the neutral
type) is not a main pitch accent before a boundary. Group I
realizations are part of the sawtooth pattern before a main pitch
accent (see 5.1) or occur separately before a main pitch accent.
In the present text the realizations of the group I type are the
most frequent pitch accents: 1.1, 2.1, 2.2, 3.1, 3.2, 4.1, 4.2,
4.3, 5.2, 6.1, 6.2, 6.3, 7.1, 7.2, 8.1, 9.1, 9.2, 10.1, 11.1,
12.1, 14.1, 16.1, 16.2, 18.1, 21.1, 21.2, 22.1, 24.1, 24.2, 25.1,
26.1, 27.1, 28.1, 29.1, 29.2, 30.1, 31.1, 32.1, 33.1, 35.1, 37.1,
37.2, 38.1, 40.1, 44.1, 44.2, 47.1, 47.2, 48.1, 48.2, 50.1, 51.1,
54.1 (a total of 53).
As can be seen in the stylized pitch contours, all type I accents
are perceptual rises; acoustically the tone can be level in the
tonic syllable and sometimes a fall begins within the tonic
syllable (perceptually this is not relevant) (the bold line here
indicates the accented syllable):

The rises are less steep and the excursion is smaller than the
rises in group C, E and F (see 3.2).

The pitch accents 9.1, 11.1 and 14.1 should take a special
place in group I. These are neutral pitch accents in a very long
flow of thoughts. Together with 10.1, 9.1 can be seen as an
extensive sawtooth pattern, whereas 11.1 and 14.1 are neutral
pitch accents after the main pitch accent. Where a group I accent
occurs before a boundary, as in fragments No. 11 and No. 14, the
stretch involved is an "afterthought". In all other cases group I
types, as well as group J types (see below), precede main pitch
accents. So accents in group I itself always occur as "neutral",
non-main pitch accents. In the text a group I type is followed by
the types of group A, C, D, E and H, and preceded by a group J
type or another group I type.

Group J

The description of the group I type holds true for group J.
The only difference between the two groups is the direction of the
pitch movement: in group J the tone falls and is the reverse of

the group I type (the bold line here indicates the accented
syllable):

In the text a group J type is less frequent in our analysis than
the group I type, and it is therefore tempting to make a statement
about this fact. It is too early to say that in modern spoken
Russian a non-main pitch accent is mostly a rise.
Representatives of group J are 3.1, 3.2, 5.1, 17.1, 19.1, 23.1,
23.2, 27.2 and 53.1 (a total of 9).
The group J type always precedes the main pitch accent, so it
always occurs as "neutral", non main pitch accent. The group J
type can be followed by the types of group A, C, D, F, H and I and
can be preceded by the type of group I or by another group J type.

3.2 Combinations found in the text

     Since the group I type and group J type are non-main pitch
accents, and the other groups can be labelled as so-called main
pitch accents, it is interesting to see how the ten groups
combine. The number of groups between brackets indicates how many
pitch accents of the same type occur before the main pitch accent.

```
    (I + (I)) + I + A
            J + J + A
    (I + (I)) + I + C
            J + J + C
            J + I + C
                I + D
                J + D
                I + E
                J + F
        (I) + I + H
                J + H
```


The other groups (B and G) do not occur in combination with

neutral pitch accents or other main pitch accents.

In the table below it can be seen how the ten groups of pitch movement are combined with one another in the text. In the text there are no combinations of main pitch accents within one fragment except for group G where this might even be a rule. Representatives of group B occur only in isolation. All the other main pitch accents are preceded by group I and J types which differ in number and combination.
Note that the ten groups as described in 3.1 are not equivalent. Whereas, for instance, one group is defined by a single pitch movement, we must take more pitch movements into consideration in order to describe the other groups. Thus the ten groups cannot be compared as equal units. Nevertheless, in order to give an impression of the combination of groups in this particular text, they may be represented here on an equal level.
The pitch accents on the x-axis should be read as following the pitch accents on the y-axis within one fragment.

	A	B	C	D	E	F	G	H	I	J
A										
B										
C										
D										
E										
F										
G						x				
H										
I	x		x	x	x			x	x	x
J	x		x	x		x		x	x	x

4. Some further comments on the perception of pitch accents

4.1 The influence of pretonic syllables on the perception of pitch accents

Pitch movements in pretonic syllables affect the perception of pitch accents in a number of ways. I shall only discuss the influence relevant for the present analysis.

The pitch movement in the tonic syllable can be a continuation of a movement in the pretonic syllable. If the excursion of the pitch movement is heard as if it were placed entirely in the tonic syllable, the pretonic and tonic syllables together should be considered as one perceptually relevant unit. Whether this is the case can easily be verified by moving the whole excursion forward in time in such a way that the perceptually relevant pitch movement takes place within the tonic syllable. If there is no perceptual difference with the original, or the difference is not relevant for the recognition of the type of pitch movement, the modification can be accepted. The same holds for cases in which the pitch movement is placed entirely in the pretonic syllable. So we may say that pitch movements which take place either in the pretonic or in the tonic syllable, or in both, and which are sorted out as belonging to one group, are perceptually the same (see Fig. 3).

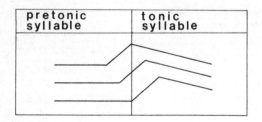

Fig.3: Realizations of rises which are perceptually identical

In Pokrovskij's talk this phenomenon can be found in 15.1 (pitch accent of the group E type, excursion in the tonic syllable is

-2.0 semitones, the excursion in the pretonic is 14.8 semitones) in No. 21.1 (pitch accent in a sawtooth pattern, group I, excursion in the tonic syllable is 4.0 semitones, together with pretonic syllable 9.8 semitones), and in No. 36.1 (pitch accent of the group F type, excursion in the tonic syllable is 14.2 semitones, together with pretonic syllable 20.6 semitones).

If the direction of the pitch movement in the pretonic syllable is different from that in the tonic syllable, the pitch movement in the pretonic syllable makes the pitch movement in the tonic syllable more salient. In Nos. 24.1 and 24.2 we find a fine example (the bold line here indicates the accented syllable):

Within this category the *zanos* (Kuznecova 1960, p.47) takes a special place. A *zanos* is a small and usually steep rise in the pretonic syllable, which provides the possibility of a large excursion of the pitch movement in the following tonic syllable. The latter is mostly a final fall (a group A type) (for example, see No. 6.4), but not necessarily (as in fragment No. 46, all pretonic syllables). A *zanos* occurs within one word (No. 6.4), on a preposition (no examples in my text) or elsewhere over a word boundary (No. 44.3). The occurrence of a *zanos* over a word boundary probably implies that the two words belong to the same prosodic group. More examples are required to verify this suggestion.

A *zanos* is perceptually interpreted as the above-mentioned small and steep rise, even if phonetically the tone in the pretonic syllable is level (the bold line here indicates the accented syllable):

The different realizations of a *zanos* before a prominent fall have been found in group A, B and G.

The pretonic syllables can be relevant for the recognition of certain pitch accents. Whereas in one case the pitch can vary freely in the pretonic syllables, in other cases there are limiting rules for pretonic syllables, as we have seen in the description of the ten groups in 3.1.

433

4.2 The influence of unvoiced stretches on the perception of pitch accents

A study by Collier (1975) has shown that changes in the Fo curve are controlled by the increased or decreased electromyographic (EMG) activity in laryngeal muscles, also during voiceless stretches before voice onset.
The following examples from my text illustrate that voiceless stretches cannot be disregarded.

In unvoiced stretches before the tonic vowel onset, pitch can jump over a considerably larger range than within the tonic vowel itself. There are even cases where such a jump is made from the low to the high reference line, and where the tonic vowel acoustically shows a fall. In these cases the tonic syllable is perceived as rising. A good example is No. 16.2. The unvoiced stretch lasts 180 milliseconds, in which an excursion is made from 121 to 188 hertz (7.6 semitones). After the voice onset, pitch falls in 90 milliseconds from 188 to 149 hertz (-4.0 semitones). Under the influence of the last preceding voiced syllable, which is low, and the unvoiced stretch, in which the jump is made, the tonic syllable is perceived as rising. And thus this pitch accent fits nicely into the sawtooth pattern.

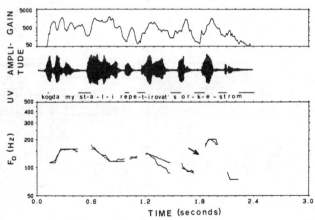

Fig. 4: Fundamental frequency curve and close-copy stylization of fragment No. 23

434

Similar cases appear in Nos. 4.3, 12.1, 21.1 and 21.2: though the
original Fo curve does not show a rise of the neutral type in the
prominent vowel, a regular sawtooth pattern with only rises is
perceived (see also 5.1).

Another example of a virtual rise is No. 23.3 (see Fig. 4).
The large excursion from 86 to 200 hertz (14.6 semitones) is
covered mainly in the unvoiced stretch, whereas the tonic vowel
contains only the last part of the excursion, from 166 to 200
hertz (3.2 semitones).

In view of the phonetic structure of Russian, virtual rises
or falls occur frequently, so I will mention just a few examples:
Nos. 26.2, 33.2 and 48.3.

In the stylized contours the voiced stretches as well as the
unvoiced stretches are rendered in straight lines which are never
interrupted. The lines in the unvoiced stretches are found as
follows. The pitch movement in the last voiced stretch before and
the pitch movement in the first voiced stretch after the unvoiced
stretch are extended in the same direction until they cross: (———
= voiced, ... = unvoiced)

If the phonetic context makes such a stylization impossible (e.g.
a very steep movement, an initial syllable), or a pause is to be
assumed (this can be seen in the intensity curve and the
oscillogram), this is indicated in the text by the sign # (see
1.4).

The perception of unvoiced sounds has many facets as regards
the perception of pitch, depending on phonetic context and
surrounding pitch movements. For the time being, I have mentioned
only the main facts that are relevant for the analysis of
Pokrovskij's talk.

4.3 Initial accents, first words and the perception of
     pitch accents

In the stylized reproduction of Pokrovskij's intonation only
prominent syllables having a pitch accent and pretonic syllables
that are relevant for the perception of a pitch accent type are

marked with a bold line. The first syllables of a fragment and the first words of a phrase or after a syntactic boundary with pitch accent are marked in the same way. There were many other "accents" in these initial positions, but they were not clear enough perceptually to deserve the label pitch accent. However, while listening to the whole speech excerpt, listeners show a tendency to indicate the first syllables/words in a phrase as carrying an accent. This is especially the case when the main pitch accent is many syllables ahead. These cases are listed in the following table (the capitals indicate the stressed syllable):

fragment No.	2: kogDA	15: kogDA	24: NIčego
	7: NUžno	16: JA	31: Ėto
	9: I	18: I	32: Ėto
	10: kaKIe	19: ON	34: iMEja
	11: MEždu	21: I	36: I
	12: KAK-to	23: kogDA	39: NO

As can be seen, these words are mainly conjunctions (5x) and pronouns (10x).

A special case is No. 24: NIčego. The lexical stress is on the last syllable: ničeGO. This syllable has a pitch accent and is also marked as such in the stylized contour. Nevertheless, there is a second accent on the first syllable.

4.4 Posttonic syllables

The grouping of pitch movements presented in 3.1 is in some cases based on the pitch movements in the posttonic syllables. This applies to the following cases.
i) Groups A and D are differentiated in the posttonic syllables. Thus by breaking off a sentence and changing the rise in the posttonic syllables into declination, the group D type changes into group A type (the bold line here indicates the accented syllable):

In this way a question or continuation (group D) becomes a confirmation (group A).
ii) Like groups A and D, groups C and E are differentiated in the

posttonic syllables.

Where in group C and E posttonic syllables are missing because the last syllable contains the final pitch accent, the difference between C and E is neutralized. Such cases of neutralization have been classified in a separate group: group F (see 3.1, group F). As indicated in the discussion of group F, No. 2.3 is an exception.

Note that the difference between groups A and D is not neutralized if the pitch accent is in the last syllable (No. 53.2).

iii) The continuation contours in group H pose a particularly complicated problem. See 3.1 for a description.

Though the present article does not discuss the issue, I would like to point out that a non-prominence lending rise in the last syllable does not exist in modern spoken Russian. Such a rise, which exists in Dutch and English, sounds unacceptable and very non-Russian. Such a rise should not be confused with the rising movement in *posttonic* syllables of group D (see 3.1) and occasionally at the end of the harmonica pattern (see 5.2).

5. Two intonation patterns

This section contains a discussion of two intonation patterns (fixed combinations of always the same configuration of pitch movements) which have been found to exist while matching the pitch movements (see 3.1).

5.1 The sawtooth pattern

The sawtooth pattern consists of one or more pitch accents of the neutral type, i.e. one does not find a main pitch accent in a sawtooth pattern itself, but it is usually followed by a main pitch accent. The prominent syllable in the sawteeth in one sequence either rises or falls. After a rising tooth the tone gradually falls and after a falling tooth the tone gradually rises (the bold line indicates the accented syllable):

In Pokrovskij's talk this pattern is realized in the fragments
Nos. 2, 3, 4, 6, 7, 12, 16, 21, 23, 33, 47, 48 (a total of 12).
In the text some prominent syllables in the sawtooth pattern show
a fall on the acoustical level, whereas the other prominent
syllables in the same sequence acoustically rise (Nos. 4.3, 12.1,
16.2, 21.3). However, on the perceptual level the direction of the
pitch movement in the prominent syllables is always the same in
one sequence, which means that the rise takes place in the
pretonic syllable in some cases. The phenomenon involved here has
been described in 4.1 and 4.2.
The initial accent can be relevant for the recognition of the
number of teeth in one sequence (see 4.3).

The analysis of Pokrovskij, as well as other texts, seems to
indicate that a non-main pitch accent in Russian has the form of a
sawtooth, and not the pointed hat _____ /\ _____
or the terrace pattern ____ /‾‾‾___ _____
which we find in Dutch (Collier and 't Hart, 1981).
While stylizing Pokrovskij's talk, an artificially made pointed
hat or terrace pattern turned out to differ significantly from the
original, and thus had to be rejected. In fragment No. 7 the pitch
accents in the sawtooth pattern have been changed into pointed
hats for experimental purposes. In an audience of native speakers
of Russian (all phoneticians and trained listeners) these pointed
hats were labelled as unacceptable and non-Russian. So we may not
only conclude that a pointed hat is not the neutral type of pitch
accent, but also that it simply does not seem to exist in modern
spoken Russian. A modification from a sawtooth pattern into a
terrace pattern gives the effect of scanned speech and sometimes
it seems as if the speaker wants to sing. So the terrace pattern
also seems to be unacceptable.

The identification of the sawtooth pattern is remarkable in
many respects. To my knowledge, this pattern has not yet been
described in the literature on Russian intonation. Its existence
explains why many of the pitch accents one hears cannot be
classified in any of the seven Intonation Contours (IK-1 - IK-7)
of Bryzgunova (1977), and certainly not in type IK-2 falls and
IK-3 rises (see 3.1). The reason is probably that Bryzgunova
classifies only main pitch accents.

Finally, pitch accents of the neutral types (group I rises and group J falls) in the sawteeth differ perceptually as well as acoustically from rises or falls in any other group, and never occur in Pokrovskij's talk as main pitch accents.

5.2 The harmonica pattern

In 3.1 the harmonica pattern has been described as a separate group (G). The pattern is named by me after its form, though it can be compared to the sawtooth pattern when the latter has only falls in the prominent syllables. The reason for treating the harmonicas separately is as follows.
In the harmonica the movements cover the full range. If two rising pitch accents reach the same maximum in hertz, the last one is always perceived as higher than the preceding accent. This also holds true for the harmonica pattern in sentence No. 46, where the falls are preceded by a *zanos* (see 4.1). For the falls in the harmonica pattern to be perceived as starting from an equally high point, the maxima should occur along the declination line.
An important feature of the harmonica pattern seems to be the close succession of pitch accents, which are all of the same type. At the end of sentence No. 46 the tone rises slightly in the posttonic syllable, as if another similar pitch accent were to follow. The initial syllable of this sentence is high. The falls in the prominent syllables taken in isolation are comparable with the falls in group B.
It is the above-mentioned features, viz. the *zanos*, the prosodic context, the high expressiveness and, presumably, the meaning of the pattern, that justify a separate treatment. More examples of this pattern, which is frequent in modern Russian spontaneous speech, are required for the description of its meaning. Native speakers of Russian, especially linguists and phoneticians, say that this intonation pattern is characteristic of colloquial speech.

6. Conclusions

Perhaps the most important outcome of this article is the stylized representation of the excerpt of Russian quasi-spontaneous speech. It shows that the IPO method of stylizing pitch phenomena of Dutch, British English, American English and German is applicable to Russian as well.
The analysis has made clear a number of issues about Russian intonation, or at least the questions have been highlighted.
I shall confine myself here to a few remarks, since most conclusions that can be drawn are given in the sections above.

It seems appropriate to describe pitch movements in modern spoken Russian as moving between reference lines: high and low. Between those lines a rather broad midfield may be assumed. It does not seem to be relevant to which point in the midfield pitch rises or falls if it does not reach the high or low reference line. The important thing is that the lines are not reached. I therefore suggest that if a middle reference line is used in the stylization model, it must then be seen as a line on which all points in the midfield are summarized, as it were.

As discussed earlier (see 3.1) another reference line seems to exist in Russian spontaneous speech: a non-low reference line. Unfortunately, this line cannot be described in acoustic terms as regards how many semitones the distance between low and non-low should be. Further examples are required. A perception experiment in which the low and non-low reference lines and the lowest points in the midfield are varied can then be set up in order to match the falls to three levels. In such an experiment native subjects have to fulfil the matching task. If these three levels are indeed to be distinguished, more can be said about the existence of "half" movements.

In 5.1 the sawtooth appears as the neutral pitch accent. Again, a perception experiment based on more linguistic materials should prove whether this holds true in all cases.

Another question is whether the group I type is the most frequent non-main pitch accent. Is there any difference between the group I type and J type with respect to their combination with other pitch movements?

441

The table in 3.2 shows that both types combine with the main pitch accents.

The sawtooth pattern also touches upon an important linguistic problem: the fact that the boundaries of prosodic groups and syntactic structures do not necessarily coincide. It is beyond the scope of this article to go into details of this problem, but it should be a subject of serious research.

With my analysis of Pokrovskij's talk several levels of study are involved, viz. perceptually relevant features and acoustically relevant features. The ultimate aim is to represent Russian intonation in terms of perceptually relevant pitch movements expressed in stylized contours.

In my opinion a study of intonational meaning in Russian is impossible without a perceptual analysis of the intonation in the modern spoken language.

7. Ten groups in stylizations: a survey

This section presents a survey of all perceptually relevant pitch movements in the excerpt.
The bold line in the stylized contour indicates the *perceptually* relevant pitch movement (see also 1.4 and 2.1).

441

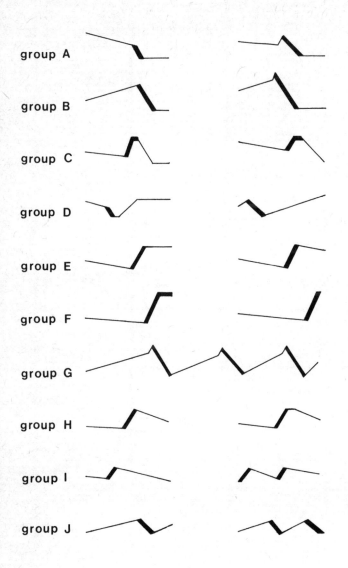

group A

group B

group C

group D

group E

group F

group G

group H

group I

group J

Institute for Perception Research, Eindhoven

REFERENCES

Bryzgunova, E.A.
1977   *Zvuki i intonacija russkoj reči*, Moskva.
Cohen, A., Collier, R., 't Hart, J.
1982   "Declination: Construct or Intrinsic Feature of
            Speech Pitch?", *Phonetica* 39, 254-273.
Collier, R.
1975   "Physiological correlates of intonation patterns",
            J. ACOUST. SOC. AM., Vol. 58, No. 1, 249-255.
Collier, R., 't Hart, J.
1981   *Cursus Nederlandse Intonatie*, Leuven.
't Hart, J., Cohen, A.
1973   "Intonation by rule: a perceptual quest",
            Journal of Phonetics 1, 309-327.
't Hart, J., Collier, R.,
1975   "Integrating different levels of intonation analysis",
            Journal of Phonetics 3, 235-255.
't Hart, J., Nooteboom, S.G., Vogten, L.L.M., Willems, L.F.
1982   "Manipulation of speech sounds", *Philips Technical
            Review* 40, 134-145.
Keijsper, C.E.
1983   "Comparing Dutch and Russian Pitch Contours",
            Russian Linguistics 7, 101-154.
Kuznecova, G.M.
1960   "Melodika prostogo povestvovatel'nogo predloženija
            v sovremennom russkom jazyke", *Učenye zapiski LGU,
            Serija Filologičeskich Nauk,* vyp. 40, 39-71.
Nooteboom, S.G., Cohen, A.,
1984   *Spreken en verstaan*, Assen.
de Pijper, J.R.
1983   *Modelling British English Intonation,* Dordrecht.
Svetozarova, N.D.
1982   *Intonacionnaja sistema russkogo jazyka,* Leningrad.

BLAGODARJA: A REPLY

JAN ODIJK

1.   In the paper *Blagodarja* (Odijk (1984)) I tried to argue that
the difference in Case assignment properties between idiosyncratic
blagodarja and the regular gerund *blagodarja* is not totally arbitrary. To be more precise, given the assumptions made in the paper
mentioned, it follows directly that idiosyncratic *blagodarja* cannot
assign Accusative Case due to properties of Universal Grammar and
the grammar of Russian. The assumptions made do not account for the
fact that idiosyncratic *blagodarja* assigns Dative Case (instead
of Genitive or Instrumental Case). Therefore, I made two suggestions as to how to account for this fact.
     Houtzagers' judgement (see elsewhere in this volume) of this
paper is extremely negative. I hope to show in my reply that this
is not justified, and that his judgement is based on a total mis-
understanding of some of the issues involved.

2.   In section 3.1.1 Houtzagers (henceforth *H*.) observes that
the 'inference' made in section 2 ("We conclude that idiosyncratic *blagodarja* is an adverb") is not valid. However, as is quite
clear from the context, the relevant passage does not contain an
inference at all. Hence, the issue whether the 'inference' is
logically correct is simply irrelevant. The point is not whether
the 'inference' made is correct, but whether the restriction to
the two categories implicitly imposed by me is justified.(See
below, section 6, for a similar issue).
     Is it legitimate to impose this restriction, i.e. are there
other plausible candidates for a categorial characterization of
idiosyncratic *blagodarja*? H. suggests that *V* might be a plausible

candidate. However, I think that this is not a plausible candidate
in the case of idiosyncratic *blagodarja* (although it might be
in other cases, see below). The reason is the following: A
property typical of verbs (but not of prepositions, adverbs, nouns,
adjectives) is that they (in combination with their complements)
define a constituent that requires a subject. This is true of
finite verbs, of infinitives, and also of gerunds (cf. e.g.
Rappaport(1979)). The subject need not be present overtly at
the surface, but there must be a subject at more abstract levels
of representation. This property, so typical of verbs, is not
present at all in idiosyncratic *blagodarja*. This fact would follow
immediately, if we would consider idiosyncratic *blagodarja* not
to be a verb.

3. (*ad 3.1.2*) I agree with H., that my hypothesis is weakened
by the fact that the category Adverb is not really a category
with well-defined properties, and by the fact that, under traditional
assumptions, it incorporates several different kinds of words,
for which it is not clear at all, that they form a natural class.
In fact, one would like to make many, perhaps most, of the words
traditionally called adverbs members of other categories that dó
form a natural class. One might follow e.g. Emonds (1972) and
Jackendoff (1973), who made a part of the adverbs of English
members of the category Preposition, and one might make certain
other adverbs members of the category Adjective. By doing this,
one might either make the category Adverb completely empty, or
delimit its members to a restricted class of words that dó form
a natural class. The crucial property, however, in my hypothesis
with regard to idiosyncratic *blagodarja* is not that it is an
adverb, but that it is [+N] , so that, if one would develop an
interesting theory of adverbs in Russian, it is only required
that the property [+N] remains a property of this word. Whether
that will be the case is unclear in the absence of a theory of
adverbs, but I see no reason to assume that it is unlikely that
this will be so. In short, the unclear status of the category

Adverb certainly weakens my hypothesis somewhat, but it certainly
does not make it untenable for this reason.

4. (*ad 3.1.3*) The simplest system that accounts for the
appearance of the *n*-form can be described in the following way.
First, we list certain classes of words:

-Group A is the class of words that are undoubtedly both
 historically and synchronically 'prepositions' (examples:
 v 'in', *k* 'towards', *na* 'on', etc.
-Group B is the class of words that are undoubtedly both
 historically and synchronically 'adverbs' (e.g. adverbs
 derived from adjectives)
-Group Cl is the class of words for which the choice between
 their being adverbs and prepositions is not obvious and that
 assign Genitive Case (example: *mimo* 'along')
-Group C2 is the class of words for which the choice between
 their being adverbs or prepositions is not obvious and that
 do not assign Genitive Case (example: *podobno* 'like')

For these groups the following properties with regard to the
n-form hold:

-Words from group A invariably require the *n*-form
-Words from group B invariably do not allow the *n*-form
-Words from group Cl invariably require the *n*-form
-Words from group C2 invariably do not allow the *n*-form

If we are to classify idiosyncratic *blagodarja* as being a member
of one of these groups, then it seems most plausible to classify
it as belonging to group C2. The next question that is relevant
is: Can we collapse the groups B and C2 into one group? If this
is possible, then the statement that accounts for the appearance
of the *n*-form can be simplified. Is there any evidence against
doing so? I know of no arguments against it, and H. does not

mention any real ones. In fact, some of the members of group
C2 are formally structured as adverbs are, and semantically
they are also very close to adverbs, e.g. *podobno* 'like' has
the same form as the adverb that can be derived from the
adjective *podobnyj* 'similar'; *soglasno* 'according to' has the
same form as the adverb that can be derived from the adjective
soglasnyj 'like, agreeable'.

There is one slight complication that has to be mentioned.
In substandard Russian certain adverbs seem to allow the *n*-form.
These adverbs, however, assign Genitive Case, and most (if not all)
of them are suppletive comparative forms, which must be listed
separately in the lexicon. All this is probably not accidental.
Their suppletive character might make them easily susceptible
to reanalysis. In particular, they might get assigned to our
group C1, which would account for the appearance of the *n*-form.
So, it seems that this complication does not really affect our
analysis. In fact, it might even turn out to constitute evidence
in favor of it.

Now it might be the case that the analysis given captures
spurious generalizations, or that there are other objections to
it, but H. certainly does not present any real arguments against
it, or against similar analyses. So there do not seem to be
any real objections to using the *n*-test in the way I did.

5.   (*ad 3.2*) H. doubts whether the examples (13)a-é from my
paper contain any real instances of Case Assignment by Nouns.
He suggests that in the examples (b,c,e) Case might be assigned
by "the Verb that is present in D-structure" in these examples,
referring to Chomsky (1981:51). In the passage cited no mention
is made of assignment of Case by Verbs inside Nouns (although it
is mentioned that the *thematic role* of an NP following a Noun
might be assigned by the verbal head (?,JO) of this Noun).
Furthermore, as far as I can see, Chomsky (1981) cannot assume
this, since it would leave him without an account of the distribution of NP in NP's.

Maybe, however, the assumption made is appropriate for
Russian. So let us assume, following H.'s suggestion, that the
Nouns in the relevant examples consist of a Verb plus an affix,
and that the Verb assigns its Case to the NP following the Noun.
This hypothesis runs into severe problems. First, as pointed
out by H. himself, it is unclear how the assignment of Accusative
Case can be blocked in this context in a non ad-hoc way, and it
is unclear why it is blocked here. Second, it is predicted that
in such a context the relevant NP will *always* bear the Case
required by the Verb. Although in most cases the NP indeed bears
the Case required by the Verb, this is *not always* so. There are
well-known examples where the Case appearing on the argument of
a Noun differs from the Case appearing on the argument of a
related Verb, or where specific prepositions accompany the
argument of a Noun, but not the argument of the related Verb.
Third, the relation between the Nouns given in the examples
and the related verbs show the properties of *morphological
relatedness* (in the sense of Chomsky 1970), e.g. neither the
form nor the semantics of the nouns are fully predictable if
the related verbs are given. The approach to Case assignment
sketched would fit in nicely, however, only if the relation
between the verbs and the nouns were a relation of *syntactic
relatedness*.

All these facts are accounted for most naturally by assuming
that the relevant nouns and verbs are two separate items in the
lexicon (that share certain features), and that Case is assigned
in these examples by the Noun. Under these assumptions, the first
objection to H.'s suggestion disappears, since Nouns never assign
Accusative Case; the second objection disappears, since there
may be differences in Case assignment properties between two
different lexical items, even if such items usually share this
property if they are related. And finally, the fact that the
relation between these words shows the properties of *morphological
relatedness* is accounted for directly, since their relation is
described as such. It seems, then, that the cases (b,c,e) really

åre instances of Case assignment by Nouns.

As far as the Genitive Case in the context of Nouns in
Russian is concerned, H. suggests that it might be due to some
general principle comparable to Chomsky's Genitive Rule and/or
his rule of *of*-insertion. The comparison to the Genitive Rule
fails. There is evidence that in English the Genitive Case
(if it is *Case* at all, cf. *the king of England*'s...) is not
assigned by *N*, but in the environment [$_{NP}$ __ ...], cf. the
sentence *John's reading the book* with the structure [$_{NP}$ *NP VP*].
Concerning the rule of *of*-insertion, this is a rule that introduces a preposition, not a Case. As such it is not comparable
to a rule that introduces Genitive *Case* in Russian.
So there is no reason at all to doubt that nouns assign Case
in Russian.

6.   (*ad 3.3*) In section 3.3 H. states that I make a logical
inference that is totally incorrect. The point he wants to make
here totally escapes me. In the relevant passage (section 3. of
my paper) it has not been intended to make a logical inference.
Neither has one been stated here (notice e.g. "we *assume*"). And
in fact, there can be no logical inference here for principled
reasons. In the relevant passage a step is made from facts to
theory, and such steps *cannot* be logical. So pointing out that
an incorrect inference is made in this passage is entirely beside
the point. Furthermore, even if one would take the relevant
passage to represent a logical inference (to do so is incorrect,
as pointed out), then the analogy H. makes between this 'logical
inference' and the one given by him clearly fails. If the relevant
passage is taken to represent a logical inference, then its structure
is of the following form:

        P has property C
        Q has property C
        _____
        P and Q share a property, i.e. C

Furthermore, (and of course, all this clearly does not follow
logically) it is hypothesized that, apart from sharing property
C, P and Q share a property in an abstract system (the grammar
of Russian), i.e. the property 'being specified positively with
regard to the attribute N'.

Given the fact, that the relevant passage does not represent
a logical inference, one might ask, what its status is. It
represents the postulation of an empirical hypothesis suggested
by certain facts. Empirical hypotheses do not follow logically
from facts (if that were the case, we would all be doing logic.
Of course, because of this, empirical hypotheses are not necessarily correct (In fact, for all interesting hypotheses, one can
never know for sure whether they are correct). The plausibility
of a hypothesis can be strengthened by supplying independent
evidence in favor of it. And that is exactly what is done in the
passage immediately following. So the logic of the relevant
passage is simply correct.

There are more points concerning this section that H. does
not seem to have understood. In particular, he seems to conclude
on the basis of my treatment of idiosyncratic *blagodarja*, that
I am forced to consider all 'gerund prepositions' that do not
take *n*-forms adverbs. But that is not the case at all. The
categorial status of each lexical item must be determined
independently. The hypothesis concerning the categorial status
of idiosyncratic *blagodarja* put forward in my paper does not have
any consequences whatsoever for the categorial status of any other
lexical item. In particular, the example given by H. (*sčitaja*)
is most probably of the category Verb. (H. seems to suggest this
himself as well, although he is not very clear about it). It seems
to show the property of verbs mentioned above, i.e. it defines
a constituent that requires a subject. Furthermore, the
complement of this word can be in the Genitive Case if the
negative particle *ne* is present. This suggests that the so called
Genitive of Negation can appear here, which might also be an
indication of the verbal character of this word.

7.   (*ad 3.4*) H. doubts that idiosyncratic *blagodarja* and
the gerund *blagodarja* are synchronically related (i.e. he
doubts the validity of a part of a presupposition of my
question (C)). Of course, the issue whether two forms from a
language are synchronically related or not, is an empirical
issue, which must be determined separately for each pair of
words by supplying evidence. In the case of idiosyncratic
blagodarja and the gerund *blagodarja* the issue seems quite clear:
First, they clearly show formal similarities (same stem:
blagodar', in fact exactly the same form, or, if one assumes
that a comparison must be made between idiosyncratic *blagodarja*
and the verb *blagodarit'*, the form of idiosyncratic *blagodarja*
equals a form from the paradigm of *blagodarit'*). Second,
although the semantic relationship between idiosyncratic
blagodarja and the gerund is not regular, the semantics of these
two words are still very close. In short, I see no reason to
assume that the relation between idiosyncratic *blagodarja* and
the gerund *blagodarja* (or the verb *blagodarit'*) is any different
in nature than e.g. the relation between the noun *bojazn'*
'fear' and the verb *bojat'sja* 'to be afraid of', which are
clearly synchronically related.

    Of course, the assumption that the two *blagodarja*'s are
synchronically related, remains an empirical hypothesis, and
it might be wrong. But it seems to me, that anyone who would
like to suggest that these forms are *not* synchronically related
should have to supply strong empirical evidence in favor of this
position.

    H. states that, even if the two *blagodarja*'s áre synchroni-
cally related, question (C) posed by me remains a strange question.
This is so, he argues, because the type of synchronical relatedness
called *morphological relatedness* allows for arbitrary differences
between related words (at least with regard to certain features).
This type of reasoning totally escapes me. I cannot see how the
fact, that *morphological relatedness* allows for arbitrary
differences between words with regard to certain features makes

it strange, or illegitimate, to investigate whether certain
differences between two specific lexical items are indeed
arbitrary or not.

In the next part H.'summarizes' and evaluates my answers
to the two parts of question (C). Again he clearly totally
misunderstood the issue. Concerning the answer to the synchronical
part of this question, it is claimed by me that the difference
in Case assignment properties between the two *blagodarja*'s is
not fully arbitrary, but follows (partially) from general
properties of Universal Grammar and Russian Grammar, as assumed
by me, and I show how this follows. One might think of this
hypothesis, whatever one likes, and of course (as any empirical
hypothesis) it might be wrong, but it certainly is not an
"empty answer".

Concerning the answer given by me to the historical part
of question C,H. states that "it is not more than a complicated
way of saying what everyone had already guessed". Again H. seems
to misunderstand the whole issue. The answer given to the historical part of question (C) is *not* just a complicated way of
saying what everyone had already guessed, but it is an answer
in which I have stated as precisely as possible, what happened
in the grammar of Russian, shortly after a particular new lexical
item, viz. idiosyncratic *blagodarja* had entered it. A very
specific hypothesis has been given on what it means that
"idiosyncratic *blagodarja* became isolated from the paradigm of
blagodarit' ", as H. puts it.

8.   (*ad 3.5*) Concerning the somewhat more positive contributions made by H. the following remarks can be made. I do not
see how H.'s account of the historical facts is in any way
incompatible with my own assumtions about it. The only new
aspect added is that apparently the Dative Case has been an
option for *blagodarit'* for some time, and that this might give
an account for the question why out of all possibilities that are
available in principle idiosyncratic *blagodarja*'chose' Dative

Case, and not some other Case. This part of H.'s contribution
is fully compatible with my own hypothesis. The other part of
H.'s contribution, i.e. that the choice between the options
available has been made completely on semantic grounds, is not
compatible with my hypothesis (however, not all aspects of
this part are fully clear to me, e.g. what does H. mean when
he uses the notion 'meaning', (cf. "the meaning 'direct
object'"??)), but this hypothesis is at best an alternative
explanation for the relevant facts, and not obviously one that
is to be preferred to mine.

University of Utrecht

BIBLIOGRAPHY

Chomsky, Noam
  1970   "Remarks on nominalizations", in: R.A. Jacobs and P.S. Rosenbaum,
              (eds.), *Readings in English Transformational Grammar,* 184-221.
  1981   *Lectures on Government and Binding.* Dordrecht.
Emonds, J.
  1972   "Evidence that Indirect Object Movement is a Structure Preserving
              Rule", *Foundations of Language* 8, 546-561.
Houtzagers, H.P.
  1986   "On Russian Prepositional *blagodarja*", *Studies in Slavic and
              General Linguistics,* vol. 8, 249-265 (this volume).
Jackendoff, R.
  1973   "The Base Rules for Prepositional Phrases", in: S. Anderson and
              P. Kiparsky, (eds.), *A Festschrift for Morris Halle,* 345-356.
Odijk, J.
  1984   "Blagodarja", *Linguistics in the Netherlands 1984,* 139-145.
Rappaport, G.C.
  1979   *Detachment and Adverbial Participle Clauses in Russian.* Ann Arbor.

ПРИСПОСОБЛЯТЬ(СЯ) ИЛИ ПРИСПОСАБЛИВАТЬ(СЯ)?

АДРИАНА ПОЛС

1. Какую форму Вы бы поставили в следующем предложении вместо точек: приспособляя или приспосабливая?

(1) Лежачих больных он брил в постелях, умело взбивая и ... подушки. (К.А. Федин, Санаторий Арктур, 6, 1936, цит. по БАС, т. 11, с. 134 и 747)

С этим вопросом мы обратились к пяти информантам, носителям русского языка. Один из них колебался и не знал, какую форму выбрать. Он чувствовал разницу между коротким и длинным вариантом, но не мог сформулировать её. Другой информант считал лишь короткий вариант возможным. Два раза была выбрана использованная Фединым длинная форма глагола, а пятый информант считал, что обе формы одинаково возможны.

На первый взгляд кажется, что того же мнения, что и пятый информант, придерживался В.В. Виноградов. Орехова (1978:79) приводит примеры из его труда "Очерки по истории русского литературного языка XVII - XIX вв." (1934), где глаголы приспособляться и приспосабливаться встречаются почти на соседних страницах. На седьмой странице мы читаем:

(2) ...стили русского делового, публицистического и повествовательного языка, несколько приспособляясь к церковно-славянской системе, размещаются по периферии "книжности", "письменности", а чаще остаются в сфере официального делопроизводства и бытового общения (...).

А на девятой странице:

(3) При этом необходимо учесть, что приспосабливаясь к новым условиям применения, киевская традиция церковно-славянского языка сама несколько изменилась, впитав в себя некоторые черты московской традиции (...).

Орехова констатирует: "(...) невозможно "уловить" какие-либо
стилистические цели выбора и предпочтения той или иной вариант-
ной формы". Однако, после перечисления несколько примеров с глаголами осмыслять(ся) и осмысливать(ся), Орехова (1978:79/80)
замечает, что

> Словарь "Грамматическая правильность русской речи" отмечает и стилисти-
> ческие различия в употреблении рассматриваемых вариантов: "Для большин-
> ства глаголов этого типа в современном языке произошло перераспределение
> стилистических функций разных суффиксальных пар несов. вида: в парах,
> где равно возможны оба варианта, формы с суффиксом -а- более разговорны,
> с -ыва- - более книжны".

На стр. 82 она показывает в таблице, каким образом некоторые
глаголы приводятся в словарях. В отношении пары приспособлять-
(ся)/приспосабливать(ся) она дает следующие данные (по типогра-
фическим причинам таблица дается не в горизонтальном, как у
Ореховой, виде, а вертикально):

	приспособлять(ся)		приспосабливать(ся)
Ушаков	1	*	2
БАС	2	*	1
МАС	+	*	+
Ожегов	2	*	1
Горбачевич	2 допустимо		1
Розенталь и др.	2	*	1
Граудина и др.	+		+ чаще в языке газет и журналов

Условные обозначения в таблице

+ форма в словаре приводится; 1 - форма в словарной статье приводится
первой или на нее делается ссылка; 2 - форма в словарной статье приводится второй или со ссылкой на другую вариантную форму (1); * различия между вариантными формами в словаре не указываются; (...) БАС - Словарь современного русского литературного языка. Т. 1-17, М.-Л., 1950-1965. Горбачевич - Трудности словоупотребления и варианты норм русского литературного языка. Словарь-справочник. Под ред. К.С. Горбачевича. Л., 1973;

Граудина и др. - Граудина Л.К., Ицкович В.А., Катлинская Л.М. Грамматическая правильность русской речи. Опыт частотно-стилистического словаря
вариантов. М., 1976. МАС - Словарь русского языка. Т. 1-4, М.,
1957-1961; Ожегов - Ожегов С.И. Словарь русского языка. Изд. 10-е. Под
ред. Н.Ю. Шведовой. М., 1975, Розенталь и др. - Розенталь Д.Э.,
Теленкова М.А. Словарь трудностей русского языка. М., 1976. Ушаков -
Толковый словарь русского языка. Под ред. Ушакова Д.Н. Т. 1-4. М.,
1935-1940.

Данные таблицы в отношении словаря "БАС", вероятно, пере-
путаны: глагол приспособлять(ся) приводится первым, а глагол
приспосабливать(ся) вторым, со ссылкой на короткую вариантную
форму. Это, однако, не значит, что предпочитается короткая форма, напротив. У Горбачевича (1976:63) мы читаем: (см. также:
Горбачевич 1978:160)

Современная речевая практика свидетельствует о том, что в нейтральном
стиле, а также в деловой и научной речи стали более предпочтительными
варианты с корневым а и соответственно передвинутым ударением. Ср.:
(...) приспособля́ть и приспоса́бливать.

Чем оправдывается предпочтение, оказываемое в современном языке
варианту приспосабливать(ся)?

Как я указывала ранее, теория Горбачевича, который рассматривает
исключительно словообразовательные факторы, не может дать
удовлетворительного ответа на этот вопрос (Полс 1983:374-380).
Примеры (2) и (3) взяты из одного и того же научного труда, на-
писанного книжным стилем. Использование глагола приспособляться
во втором примере, а глагола приспосабливаться в третьем, не
может быть мотивировано и стилистическими функциями суффиксов, о
которых говорит Словарь "Грамматическая правильность русской
речи". Но если использование той или иной формы не мотивируется
стилистической разницей между вариантами, то не определяется ли
оно лексической разницей? В настоящей статье мы постараемся дать
ответ на этот вопрос.

2. Действие глагола <u>приспособить(ся)</u> характеризуется тем, что есть кто-/что-то, кто/что делает(ся) пригодным, и есть кто-/что-то, для кого/чего делает(ся) пригодным; при этом важную роль играет фактор "время".

Обозначим течение времени от прошлого к будущему стрелкой слева направо, а действие - пунктиром:

время: ──────────────>
действие: - - - - - - - - -

В случае адаптации более старого к более новому действие происходит параллельно течению времени:

прошлое   ──────────────> будущее
старое, знакомое,   - - - - - - - -> к новому, к незнакомому,
определенное   к неопределенному

В случае адаптации более нового к более старому действие происходит против течения времени:

прошлое   ──────────────> будущее
к старому, к знакомому, <- - - - - - - - новое, незнакомое,
к определенному   неопределенное

Применим эти схемы к примерам (3) и (2):

прошлое   ──────────────> будущее

(3) киевская традиция   - - - -ива- - -> (московская традиция)
     церк.-слав. языка   новые условия применения

(2) церк.-слав. система <- - - -а- - - - стили русского делового,
                                          публицист. и повеств. языка

Вследствие глагольного действия в примере (3) происходит расширение, увеличение возможностей, прибавление чего-либо: киевская традиция языка, впитав в себя черты московской традиции,

несколько изменилась. Киевская традиция приобрела московские
черты и тем самым увеличила возможности своего применения.

Так же, как (более старая) киевская традиция перенимала черты
(более новой) московской традиции, поселенцы в примере (4) пере-
нимают у людей в новой среде навыки, чтобы увеличить возможности
выживания:

(4) Сторванность от родных мест, от привычных условий жизни, постоянная борь-
     ба с окружающей природой часто без необходимых средств производства,
     связь с выходцами из других мест, влияние культуры аборигенов края – все
     это заставляло поселенцев менять привычный уклад жизни, приспосабливать-
     ся, перенимать у соседей трудовые навыки, наиболее отвечающие новым
     условиям.
     (Р.П. Потанина (сост.), Русские свадебные песни Сибири, 1979, с. 3)

Как и переселенцы из этого примера, человек приноравливается к
новым для него обстоятельствам в примере (5). Он по-другому
одевается, питается, живёт. Он перенимает навыки у других людей:

(5) Как медик я поясню эту мысль. У человека, который приспосабливается к
     здешним климатическим условиям, изменяется характер обмена веществ.
     (Статья "Союз трех академий" в журнале "Огонёк", № 39, 1980, с. 14)

В примере (6) к условиям природы адаптируются животные, в примере (7) растения, в примере (8) организмы:

(6) Инстинкт устройства себе жилища-пристанища очень ясно выражен у многих
     животных, птиц, рыб и насекомых. Некоторые пользуются только естественны-
     ми пристанищами, приспосабливаясь к явлениям природы, другие же соору-
     жают специальные жилища для себя, собирая нужный материал, и из него де-
     лают то, что им нужно для обитания.
     (М.Г. Бархина, И.Я. Цагарелли, Мастера советской архитектуры об архитек-
     туре I, М., 1975, с. 423)

(7) Не легко приспосабливаться растениям к суровым условиям природы (в пу-
     стыне).
     (Б.А. Федорович, Лик пустыни, 3-е изд. М., 1954, цит. по БАС, т. 11, с.
     747)

(8) Следовательно, каждый вид организмов приспосабливается к определённой
     величине давления.
     (Russian popular science texts. Medicine, biology, без даты, с. 17)

Пример (9) взят из области искусства:

(9) Искусство средневекового музыканта, <u>приспосабливающего</u> готовые мелодиче-
    ские обороты к содержанию и поэтической структуре того или иного текста,
    Веллес сравнивает с трудом ремесленника (craftsman), работающего по за-
    данным образцам (...).
    (Ю.В. Келдыш, История русской музыки, т. 1, 1983, с. 35)

Музыкант, соединяя готовые мелодические обороты и тексты, соз-
дает таким образом что-то более широкое.
В примере (10) увеличиваются возможности применения Китайской
стенки:

(10) Вся Китайская стенка уже была занята японцами, которые наскоро <u>приспоса-
    бливали</u> ее к обороне.
    (А.П. Степанов, Порт-Артур, II, 4, 1944, цит. по БАС, т. 11, с. 747)

Во всех этих примерах с глаголом <u>приспосабливаться</u> действие происходит параллельно течению времени, от прошлого, знакомого,
более старого к будущему, незнакомому, более новому.
Образ, вызываемый использованием глагола <u>приспосабливать(ся)</u>, -
это приноравливание к новому, обновление, и тем самым увеличение, расширение возможностей. Схематически это можно представить
так:

-ива-

В случае действия по глаголу <u>приспособляться</u> в примере (2), мы
видим движение в противоположную сторону:

-а-

Здесь нет никакого стремления в будущее, никакого расширения,
увеличения возможностей, а, напротив, движение назад, в прошлое,
возвращение к более старым, уже знакомым обстоятельствам, умень-
шение, сужение: (более новые) стили русского делового, публицистического и повествовательного языка не впитывают в себя черты
(более старой) церковно-славянской системы, чтобы лучше ответить
новым условиям, но они, <u>приспособляясь</u>, делаются (опять, как

раньше) более архаичными, книжными. Рассмотрим следующий пример:

(11) Учение приспособляют к понятию ученика.
    (Даль, Толковый словарь, т. 3, 1882, с. 444)

"Учение" - понятие широкое, неопределенное, неограниченное, с
многочисленными возможностями и сторонами. Зато "понятие ученика" - узкое, определенное, ограниченное: что-то может быть свыше
этого понятия. Поэтому, надо считаться с этим ограниченным поня-
тием. То, что является шире (учение), делают пригодным для более
узкого (понятие ученика).
Нечто подобное мы видим в примере (12):

(12) Наука должна приспособляться к делу.
    (Даль, Толковый словарь, т. 3, 1882, с. 444)

"Наука" - понятие широкое, более неопределенное, чем имеющееся,
определенное "дело". Когда наука должна приспособляться к делу,
не все возможности науки могут быть развиты и использованы. Речь
идет об урезывании, сокращении, уменьшении, ограничении много-
сторонней науки, чтобы наука соответствовала делу, наука подчиняется делу. Таким же образом, в примере (13) возможности глаз
ограничиваются темнотой:

(13) Наши глаза мало-помалу стали приспособляться к темноте.
    (Н.А. Морозов, Повести моей жизни, II, 7, 1913, цит. по БАС, т. 11, с.
    749)

В примере (14) осуществление идеалов обусловливается сущест-
вующими экономическими нуждами:

(14) Каждый класс всегда прекрасно, хотя и бессознательно, приспособляет к
    своим экономическим нуждам свои "идеалы".
    (Г.В. Плеханов, К вопросу о развитии монистического взгляда..5, 1895,
    цит. по БАС, т. 11, с. 749)

Приблизительно к тому же периоду, что и этот пример, относится
пример (15), отрывок из "Молоха" Куприна. Инженер Бобров, глав-
ный герой рассказа, упрекает своего собеседника, доктора Гольд-
берга, в том, что тот сейчас говорит об инженерах иначе ("вы
(инженеры) толкаете вперед (...) колесницу прогресса"), чем
раньше. Раньше Голдьберг набрасывался на них: они, мол, своей
техникой испортили общество, безответственным образом ускоряя
"пульс общественной жизни до крайней скорости".
Доктор пытается оправдаться словами:

(15) - Ну да, ну да, голубчик, все это я говорил, - заторопился он не совсем
однако уверенно. - Я и теперь это утверждаю. Но надо же, голубчик, так
сказать, приспособляться. Как же жить-то иначе? Во всякой профессии есть
эти скользкие пунктики. Вот взять хоть нас, например, докторов... Вы ду-
маете, у нас все это так ясно и хорошо, как в книжечке?
(А.И. Куприн, Молох, 5, 1896)

Доктор Гольдберг хочет подбодрить Боброва, который вернулся
домой в удрученном настроении, сомневаясь в пользе своей профессии. Гольдберг считает, что словами: "вы толкаете колесницу
прогресса ..." он сможет помочь своему другу куда лучше, чем
ругая инженеров. Он уменьшает свои притязания и говорит как-то
иначе, чем раньше. Он хочет повлиять на настроение друга.

В примере (16) действие происходит параллельно течению времени,
но тем не менее используется короткий вариант глагола:

(16) Приходил конец всякой старинке и старинным людям. Как хочешь, при-
способляйся по-новому.
(Д.Н. Мамин-Сибиряк, Хлеб, II, 7, 1895, цит. по БАС, т. 11, с. 749)

В примере (16) создается впечатление чего-то положительного,
активного: надо перестроиться на новый лад.

Сравним теперь примеры (17) и (18):

(17) Ласковое сердце Онуши всегда было полно беспокойством за мои неудобства.
Сам он приспосабливался ко всякому случаю.
(А.С. Неверов, Без цветов, 8, ± 1920, цит. по БАС, т. 11, с. 747)

(18) В густой запыленной колонне трудно отличить солдата от офицера. Также на время как будто ослабевает между ними иерархическая разница, и тут-то поневоле знакомишься с русским солдатом, с его метким взглядом на всевозможные явления, – даже на такие сложные, как корпусный маневр, – с его практичностью, с его умением всюду и ко всему приспособляться, с его хлестким образным словом, приправленным крупной солью, которую пропускаешь мимо ушей.
(А. Куприн, Прапорщик армейский, 1897)

В примере (17) об Онуше создается впечатление человека, который устраняет себя, "растворяется" в разных ситуациях: он подвергается, испытывает, всё терпеливо переносит. В примере (18) мы видим русского солдата, способного приспособляться ко всему. Всё указывает на активность: меткий взгляд, практичность, хлесткое образное слово, приправленное крупной солью. Онуша кротко "подвергается" обстоятельствам, русский солдат умело управляет ситуацией.

В примере (19) из Зотушки пытались сделать человека, который может выполнять определенную, существующую работу:

(19) Приспособляли Зотушку к разным занятиям, но из этого ничего не вышло.
(Д.Н. Мамин-Сибиряк, Дикое счастье, 5, 1884, цит. по БАС, т. 11, с. 749)

В следующем примере императрица выступает в разных ролях:

(20) Императрица имела особенный дар приспособлять к обстоятельствам выражение лица своего.
(П.А. Вяземский, Старая записная книжка, 8, 1820-1830, цит. по БАС, т. 11, с. 749)

Императрица делает такое выражение лица, которое лучше всего соответствует определенным обстоятельствам: она остается хозяйкой положения. Приспособленец же маскирует свои взгляды: он как будто скрывается, он не управляет обстоятельствами, а подчиняется им:

(21) Приспособленец, -нца, м. (презр.). Человек, к-рый приспосабливается к обстоятельствам, маскируя свои истинные взгляды.
(С.И. Ожегов, Словарь русского языка, 1973, с. 550)

(22) Приспособленец, нца, м. Беспринципный человек, умеющий <u>приспосабливать</u>, применять к обстоятельствам свои взгляды, вкусы, убеждения.
(БАС, т. 11, 1961, с. 748)

Несмотря на то, что в словаре "БАС" короткая форма приводится первой, тем не менее длинный вариант используется для истолкования других слов:

(23) Озвучивать – (...) <u>Приспосабливать</u> для демонстрации звуковых кинофильмов (помещение).
(БАС, т. 8, 1959, с. 747)

(24) Подлаживаться – (...) 2. <u>Приспосабливаться</u> к кому-, чему-л., согласовываясь в действиях, движениях.
(БАС, т. 10, 1960, с. 422)

С той же целью форма глагола с суффиксом <u>-ива-</u> используется в примере (25):

(25) Глаголы с префиксом под- и суфф. -ива(ть) имеют значение "действием, названным мотивирующим глаголом, сопровождать какое-н. действие, <u>приспосабливаясь</u> к кому-чему-н.": подпевать – "петь, подтягивая, вторя кому-чему-н." .
(Грамматика современного русского литературного языка. Москва, 1970, § 676, с. 284)

В то время, как в словаре "БАС" в таких случаях используется длинный вариант, у Даля мы находим короткий вариант:

(26) Применять – (...) 2. Приноравливать, <u>приспосабливать</u> к чему-либо.
Применяться – 1. <u>Приспосабливаться</u>, приноравливаться.
(БАС, т. 11, 1961, с. 582)

(27) Применять, применить что к чему, сравнивать, прикидывать, прикладывать, прилагать, приноравливать, <u>приспособлять</u>.
(Даль, Толковый словарь, т. 3, 1882, с. 427)

3. Если мы поставим приведенные выше примеры в хронологическом порядке, мы получим следующее соотношение между использованным суффиксом и временем создания произведения:

пример	суффикс	дата
(20)	-а-	1820/30
(11)	-а-	1882
(12)	-а-	1882
(27)	-а-	1882
(19)	-а-	1884
(14)	-а-	1895
(16)	-а-	1895
(15)	-а-	1896
(18)	-а-	1897
(13)	-а-	1913
(17)	-ива-	± 1920
(2)	-а-	1934
(3)	-ива-	1934
(1)	-ива-	1936
(10)	-ива-	1944
(7)	-ива-	1954
(23)	-ива-	1959
(24)	-ива-	1960
(22)	-ива-	1961
(26)	-ива-	1961
(25)	-ива-	1970
(21)	-ива-	1973
(6)	-ива-	1975
(4)	-ива-	1979
(5)	-ива-	1980
(9)	-ива-	1983

Мы видим, что с начала XX века форма с суффиксом -а- постепенно выходит из употребления и заменяется формой с -ива-.

При обсуждении примеров мы уточнили значение глаголов

приспособлять(ся):

приспосабливать(ся):

приспособлять(ся)	приспосабливать(ся)
возвращение к прошлому	обращение, стремление к будущему
отказываться от более широкого диапазона	стремиться к более широкому диапазону
сосредоточивать(ся)	рассеивать(ся)
ограничивать(ся), убавлять(ся), сокращать(ся)	расширять(ся), прибавлять(ся), увеличивать(ся)
подчинять(ся) чему-либо (определенному)	делать(ся) пригодным для чего-либо (неопределенного)
становиться пригодным, превращаясь в кого-/что-то другое, иное	становиться пригодным, вторя, подражая кому-/чему-нибудь другому
качественная перемена	количественная перемена
активно действовать	пассивно подвергаться
проявлять инициативу	подчиняться
кто-/что-то влияет на обстоятельства	обстоятельства влияют на кого-/что-то
создается автономия	автономия исчезает
переход в существующее состояние	переход в новое, неограниченное состояние

4.   Выводы.

В словарях различия между вариантными формами приспособлять(ся) и приспосабливать(ся) не указываются. В современном русском языке прежде всего используется длинный вариант. Предпочтение, которое оказывается форме приспосабливать(ся) в современном русском языке, возможно, обусловлено тем, что глагол уже не употребляется в некоторых из значений, перечисленных в левом столбце. Эти значения передаются сейчас другими глаголами.

Лейденский университет

465

ЛИТЕРАТУРА

BAC
1950–65   *Словарь современного русского литературного языка.* Т. 1–17. Москва–Ленинград.

Горбачевич, К.С.
1976   "Вариантность глаголов с суффиксами вторичной имперфективации '-ыва- (-ива)' и '-а- (-я)'", *Русский язык в школе* (1976), № 3, 62–65.
1978   *Вариантность слова и языковая норма.* Ленинград: Наука.

Даль, В.И.
1880–82   *Толковый словарь живаго великорускаго языка.* Изд. 2-е.

Орехова, Т.П.
1978   "О вариантах форм слова в современной научной речи", *Вопросы русского языкознания*, 77–84, Куйбышев.

Полс, А.
1983   "Употребление вариантов вторично имперфектированных глаголов на -ывать (-ивать) и -ать (-ять)", *Studies in Slavic and General Linguistics 3, Dutch Contributions to the Ninth International Congress of Slavists. Linguistics*, 357–384, Utrecht.

ASPECT AND ITERATION IN RUSSIAN AND CZECH
A Contrastive Study

ANNA STUNOVÁ

1.   INTRODUCTION

1.0. Preliminaries

Although the aspect opposition: perfective vs. imperfective
in Russian and Czech has been defined on the basis of identical
features (see below), the two languages being closely related,
the differences in the usage of aspectual forms are, nevertheless,
not negligible.

In this article, the concrete use of aspectual forms in the
denotation of iterated events will be studied on the basis of
Russian and Czech parallel texts, with a special emphasis on the
differences between the two languages.

1.1. Slavonic aspect and the concept 'internal limit'

In the description of the Slavonic aspect, the concept 'internal limit' plays a very important role. For instance, according to Maslov, the 'real basis' of the Slavonic opposition perfective vs. imperfective is the semantic contrast of achievement
vs. non-achievement of the internal limit of an event (Maslov
1985: 30).

The internal limit of an event, labeled also *terminus* or
'predel', is seen as something which is inherent to the nature
of the event itself. When it is achieved, the event is 'exhausted',
or in other words completed, and a transition to a new state
takes place (Maslov 1978:13). Only terminative verbs which have
achieved this limit, can be perfective.[1]

On a more abstract level, that of general meanings, the Slavonic aspect has been defined in other terms: for the perfective - an event is viewed as an indivisible whole ('celostnost''); for the imperfective - as lacking emphasis on this feature (Maslov 1985: 30).

In contrast to some, mostly older, conceptions of the Slavonic aspect, which consider only one of the features, both notions 'internal limit' and 'indivisible whole' have been definitely included in the recent definition (see *Russkaja Grammatika* 1980: 583). For a survey of various conceptions we refer to the following authors: Vinogradov (1947), Dostál (1954), Maslov (1975, 1977) and Glovinskaja (1982).

1.2. Aspectual differences between Russian and Czech

The content of the aspectual opposition perfective vs. imperfective is not absolutely identical even in such closely related Slavonic languages as Russian and Czech. "Although they show great similarity in general, quite important differences in detail also occur" (Maslov 1985: 31).

On the level of usage of aspectual forms, the major difference between Russian and Czech is the following: in certain instances of usage, a relatively strong predominance of the Russian imperfective has been observed, while in the same speech context, Czech shows a quite high frequency of perfective forms.

This phenomenon takes place e.g. in the following instances: 'iteration', 'gnomic present', 'historical present', 'generalized-factual' meaning of imperfective, 'two-way action'.

An important question arises: are these aspectual differences between Russian and Czech only a matter of detail, as Maslov suggests, or do they have a more systematic character? And, if they are systematic, how must they be accounted for in the description of the aspectual opposition: perfective vs. imperfective?

The way these differences (namely the predominance of Russian imperfective on the one hand, and the quite high frequency of perfective in Czech on the other hand), have been treated in the literature, seems to point to the view that this phenomenon is essentially a matter of the concrete usage of aspectual forms (*usus*).[2]

On the theoretical level, with respect to the system of particular meanings (see below), the following explanations of

the differences between Russian and other Slavonic languages including Czech, have been given.

As to the historical present, e.g., the almost total predominance of the imperfective in Russian has been described as a
matter of neutralization of the aspectual opposition in favour of
the imperfective (Maslov 1974: 119 and 1984: 82, Bondarko 1959:
51). In Russian, this neutralization is considered to have an
obligatory character, while in Czech and other West Slavonic
languages it is said to be facultative.

As to iteration, either the same explanation by neutralization is given (*Russkaja Grammatika* 1979: 772), or it is seen as
a case of 'synonymical concurrence')[3] of the opposition members
in their particular meanings (Maslov 1974: 121 and 1984: 78).
Both in Russian and West Slavonic languages, the imperfective in
the 'unrestrictedly-iterative' meaning concurs with the perfective in the meaning 'vivid exemplification' (or 'particularization'), again in favour of the imperfective. The only difference
is that 'particularization' occurs more often in the West Slavonic languages (see also Bondarko 1971: 216).

'Synonymical concurrence' is regarded as a peripheral phenomenon, or a kind of luxury of the whole aspectual system (Maslov
1984: 82). 'Particularization' is supposed to have an identical
position in all Slavonic languages: it does not change the deno-
tative content of an utterance and it is merely a means of stylistic nuancing (ibid: 81).

In our opinion, however, these explanations of aspectual
differences between Russian and West Slavonic languages, especially Czech, are not sufficient, as they do not fully correspond with
the facts. They even seem to show a certain degree of arbitrariness.

Reference to the usage only, would be rather unilluminating
with respect to the whole aspectual system and the content of the
opposition members; for this reason, this and the theoretical explanation are usually combined.

As to the theoretical explanation, however, it must be remarked that the 'facultative' character of neutralization in
Czech would suggest, in fact, a free choice of aspectual form.
This is often not the case: in certain instances, perfective is
the only possibility.

The Russian system of particular meanings has been thoroughly worked out (see e.g. Bondarko, Bulanin 1967, Bondarko 1971,
Forsyth 1970). However, we perceive in the accounts of aspectual
differences between Russian and West Slavonic languages a certain
tendency to project the Russian system onto other languages. This
projection implies the assumption of identical rules for all
these languages. The views of some authors only, seem to point to
the opposite direction (Petruchina 1978: 57 and 1983: 152, Širokova 1971: 293).

Considering the general tendency in the treatment of the
aspectual differences between Russian and West Slavonic languages,
we advocate an approach which would, on the one hand, take into
account the Russian aspectual system, but which would, on the
other hand, pay more attention to the characteristic properties
of the contrasted languages.

Contrastive studies on aspect should be conducted at the
level of particular meanings, based on concrete instances of usage
of the aspectual forms, and not only at the level of general meanings. This view has been stressed by Maslov (1984: 70, 71).

Only after these partial studies it is possible to acquire
more insight into the character and extent of the aspectual differences between the individual languages. This could lead to a
more nearly optimal characterization of the content of the opposition members in each language on the one hand, and to a better
understanding of the general notion 'Slavonic aspect' on the other
hand.

For this article we have chosen one concrete instance of aspect usage: the iterated event.

1.3. Iteration

An iterated event can be defined, in our view, as a chain of
identical sub-events in which only one verbal form is involved
(for a similar conception see also Timberlake 1982: 315).

In this complex structure, two separate levels have to be
distinguished:
1. the level of the individual sub-event as a part of the chain
   - the micro-level;
2. the level of the whole chain, where the individual sub-event

is not taken into account - the macro-level.
At least one of the two levels is always relevant for the selection of a proper aspectual form.

In the expression of iterated events, delimitation of the
number of individual sub-events is an important factor in the selection of the aspectual form in Russian. As we shall see below,
the situation in Czech is different.

Two groups of cases have to be distinguished in Russian
with respect to aspect selection:
1. the number of sub-events is delimited, either by numerical indication (e.g. 'tri raza'), or approximately ('neskol'ko raz').
2. the number of the individual sub-events is not delimited and
   iteration is expressed, e.g. by adverbials ('často', 'inogda'),
   adjectives ('každyj'), quantified time indication ('po subbo-
   tam'), object in plural, in the verb (habituals), syntactically or by wider context. Often different means of expression
   are combined.
For a detailed survey of means of expression of iterated events
we refer to the following authors: Kučera, Trnka 1975, Širokova
1966, Anikina 1964, Němec 1958.

1.4. Particular meanings and iteration

In the literature on Russian aspect, a number of particular
meanings has been distinguished (as mentioned in section 1.2.).
We shall give here a survey of the particular meanings which have
a special connection with iterated events. The terminology is
borrowed from Maslov and other representatives of the 'Leningrad
school of aspectology'.

1. Summative meaning of perfective ('summarnoe značenie')

(1) Он меня уже два раза убедил[p].

In this and similar cases, an indication of the number of iterated
sub-events is necessarily present. On the macro-level, the individual sub-events are summed to a complex unit of a higher order.
Only expressions indicating delimitation of the number of sub-
events, can have this summing effect and therefore allow the use
of the perfective. As to the micro-level, each sub-event must also
have the properties that allow the use of the perfective: the

internal limit (*terminus*) must have been reached at this level.
With respect to example (1), this essentially means that the
person must have been convinced both times. Otherwise, summing
is impossible and an imperfective has to be used. This would be
an instance of the following type of particular meaning.

2. Restrictedly-iterative meaning of imperfective ('ograničenno-
   kratnoe značenie')

(2) Он меня два раза убеждал[i], но не убедил[p].

In this sentence, the imperfective has a conative nuance: attempts took place without success. However, this nuance is certainly not always present. The proper interpretation depends on
the lexical meaning of the verb and of further context. Instances
of the restrictedly-iterative meaning of the imperfective which
can be interpreted as an iteration of complete, successful events,
are in Russian quite normal. Compare example (2) to the following
one, which is free of any conativity:

(3) Он два раза оборачивался[i]. (Maslov 1984: 79)

3. Unrestrictedly-iterative meaning of imperfective ('neograni-
   čenno-kratnoe značenie')

This type of particular meaning is distinguished from type 2. by
the absence of delimitation of the number of sub-events.

(4) Он меня часто убеждал[i].

This sentence can have two interpretations:
1. attempts have been without success (the same as in (2))
2. every attempt was successful.
In cases like this, the Russian imperfective form itself does
not provide sufficient information for choosing the proper interpretation. A broader context is needed and the lexical meaning of
the verb must be taken into account. The selection of the imperfective aspect here is fully determined by the macro-level, the
aspectual properties of the individual sub-events are not being
considered.

In Russian, the imperfective is the most current form for
the denotation of iterated events, especially in the past tense,
where it is normally the only possibility. The imperfective is

then used irrespective of the message communicated: namely, whether
the attempts were successfull or not. An explicit expression of successful attempts by this verbal form is impossible in the Russian
preterite, when the number of individual sub-events is non-delimit-
ed. Consider the following example:

(5) *Он меня часто убедил[p].

In Czech, however, there is a different situation regarding the
selection of the aspectual form. When the individual attempts
were successful, or in other words, when every individual sub-
event has reached the internal limit, this fact may be explicitly denoted by the perfective form. The combination of the non-de-
limited indication of iteration and the perfective is in Czech
perfectly grammatical, in contrast to Russian:

(6) Často mě přesvědčil[p].

We assume that in this case the micro-level of the iterated event
is decisive for the selection of the perfective, as will be illustrated below.

4. Vivid exemplification ('nagljadno-primernoe značenie') of perfective

(7) Я это понимаю[i], со мной тоже бывает[i] - скажу[p] уверенно и сей-
    час же спохвачусь[p]. (Gor'kij)

In this type of particular meaning, the perfective operates on
the micro-level. This verbal form may be used only if every attempt
was successful. In other words, every individual sub-event must
have reached its internal limit and if isolated, it could be described by the perfective.

However, not all sub-events are denoted by the aspectual form:
one only of the whole chain of individual sub-events is used as a
representative. It is a kind of *pars pro toto* presentation. For the
same phenomenon, the terms 'particularization' or 'singularization'
are also used (e.g. Mazon 1914: 49)

'Vivid exemplification' in Russian has further the following
characteristics:

1. As to the temporal level, the present tense form is most often
   used, even for denoting iterated events in the past. This usage
   of present instead of past has been described by the term 'time

transposition' (Isačenko 1960: 429, 464).

2. The use of perfective in this type of particular meaning is usually not stylistically neutral. It often has an expressive or even an emotional nuance (see also Petruchina 1983: 163).

3. The perfective is bound to special conditions of use. In the majority of cases, it occurs only in certain types of context (e.g. 'kratno-sootnositel'nyj tip konteksta'), where there is a connection with other events. For a detailed survey of the conditions of use and contexts of occurrence see Bondarko (1971: 197 ff.).

4. The perfective in the particular meaning 'vivid exemplification' can almost always be replaced by an imperfective in the 'unrestrictedly-iterative' meaning. This is a case of 'synonymical concurrence' as described by Maslov (1974: 121 and 1984: 78).

As to Czech, the situation is different:

1. A perfective can be used irrespective of the temporal level (see example 6).

2. The Czech perfective is stylistically absolutely neutral, it does not show any colouring at all. For this reason, the term 'vivid exemplification' would be incorrect. Petruchina (1983: 164) proposes to use Maslov's term 'konkretno-tipičeskoe značenie' (concrete typical meaning). In our opinion, this term can be used only in certain cases, when e.g., iteration comes close to the gnomic or historical present. In order to be able to cover all instances of use of the Czech perfective, also in the preterite, the current term 'particularization', being free of any stylistic factors, seems to be presently the most appropriate one.

3. The use of the perfective in Czech for the denotation of iterated events is not bound to such strict conditions as it is in Russian, the frequency of this form is much higher (see also Bondarko 1971: 213, 216).

4. The perfective cannot always be replaced by the imperfective in Czech, in some cases the perfective is the only possibility (see also Petruchina 1983: 165, 166).

5. Potential meaning of perfective ('potencial'noe značenie')

This type of particular meaning is not usually directly associated with iteration. A typical instance of potential meaning is
this: "Ne skažu[p]" (I can't say). However, this meaning has sometimes a connection with iterated events. Consider the following
example:

(7) Иван любой праздник испортит[p].

This sentence can be interpreted as follows: Ivan is a kind of
person, who is apt to spoil every party, given the occasion to
do so. Clearly a modal element is present in this type of meaning.
Compare this to the sentence below, where an imperfective is used
in the unrestrictedly-iterative meaning (as in example 4):

(8) Иван любой праздник портит[i].

The real fact is expressed here, Ivan indeed spoils every party
to which he comes.

2.   MATERIAL

2.1. Texts and method

   We decided to study the problems outlined above in more detail
on the basis of the material of 20th century literary texts of
narrative character - novels and stories. After some preliminary
study we assumed that there was a higher chance of iterated events
occurring here than in other types of texts (e.g. plays).
   The texts used are: 1. Russian originals with their (published) equivalent Czech translations; 2. a Czech original with its
(published) Russian translation. A complete list is given in the
bibliography. The total extent of these texts is almost four
thousand pages, i.e. about two thousand pages per language.
   The original texts have been compared with their translations. All cases of iterated events, either with an explicit indication of iteration, or events which can be interpreted as such
on the basis of context, have been cited. This resulted in a collection of parallel sentences, Russian and Czech.
   We concentrated on the following four verbal forms:
1. perfective preterite; 2. perfective present; 3. imperfective
preterite; 4. imperfective present.

These forms have been counted (see tables) and submitted to a
further analysis with regard to the surrounding context (see below). The verbal forms which have not been included are: the infinitive forms (the infinitive and gerunds) and the analytic imperfective future form occurring very sporadically.

The material has been further ordered in the following way:
the various combinations of the categories Aspect and Tense as
expressed in the verbal form of the original language have been
compared to the corresponding forms in the translation. According to these combinations aspect/tense, the material has been
devided into groups and further analyzed.

2.2. Quantitative data

In this section, the quantitative data of our material will
be presented. Table 1. shows the occurrence of the four selected
verbal forms per language for the entire collection of sentences.

Table 1.
Attested aspectual-temporal forms participating in the expression
of iterated events.

a. Russian

tense aspect	preterite	present	total
perfective	1.3% (13)	9.7% (96)	11% (109)
imperfective	72.4% (717)	16.6% (165)	89% (882)
total	73.7% (730)	26.3% (261)	100% (991)

b. Czech

tense aspect	preterite	present	total
perfective	29.5% (292)	15.3% (152)	44.8% (444)
imperfective	46.1% (457)	9.1% (90)	55.2% (547)
total	75.6% (749)	24.4% (242)	100% (991)

data: Andreev, Èrenburg, Gor'kij, Oleša, Hašek.

The table shows a relatively small difference in tense between the two languages. In Russian, the number of present forms is slightly higher (1.9%). This phenomenon can be explained partly by the 'time transposition' (see section 1.4.) and the use of present tense for denotation of past events in indirect speech after *verba dicendi* in Russian.

As far as aspect is concerned, the differences between the two languages are really striking. Considering the total amounts in column 3, there are 33.8% more imperfectives attested in Russian than in Czech and thus vice-versa, 33.8% more perfectives in Czech.

As to the distribution of aspect over the tenses, the differences are even larger. In the Russian preterite, an almost absolute predominance of the imperfective can be observed, while in the present tense, the amounts of both aspectual forms are more nearly equal.

In Czech, the perfective and the imperfective are current in both tenses. In the present tense, the ratio of these forms is even reversed in comparison with Russian, in other words, the number of perfectives is higher. This can be explained as follows: in the denotation of iterated events which are close to gnomic or historical present, Czech tends to select the perfective. In Russian, the perfective present would often have a future meaning in a similar context, which is not the case in Czech. This is an instance of the interaction of aspect and tense. In Czech, the perfective present seems to have a less close relation with the future meaning than in Russian (see Petruchina 1983: 171). For more details about this phenomenon see Kopečný (1962: 40).

After this presentation of global data we proceed to more detailed information about the various correspondences of verbal forms attested. In the left-hand column, the forms encountered in the original texts are given, in the right-hand columns, the corresponding forms in the translation are presented.

Table 2.
Correspondences of the aspectual-temporal forms.

a. Russian original texts - Czech translation

Russian tense aspect	preterite	present	Czech tense aspect	preterite	present
pf.	100% (5)		pf.	80% (4)	–
ipf.			imp.	–	20% (1)
pf.		100%(45)	pf.	24.5%(11)	71.1%(32)
ipf.			ipf.	2.2%(1)	2.2%(1)
pf.			pf.	39.5%(200)	0.4%(2)
ipf.	100%(506)		ipf.	60.1%(304)	–
pf.			pf.	–	53% (44)
ipf.		100%(83)	ipf.	–	47% (39)

data: Andreev, Èrenburg, Gor'kij, Oleša.

b. Czech original text - Russian translation

Czech tense aspect	preterite	present	Russian tense aspect	preterite	present
pf.	100% (77)		pf.	–	9.1%(7)
ipf.			ipf.	85.7%(66)	5.2%(4)
pf.		100%(74)	pf.	4% (3)	46% (34)
ipf.			ipf.	–	50% (37)
pf.			pf.	3.3%(5)	–
ipf.	100%(152)		ipf.	95.4%(145)	1.3%(2)
pf.			pf.	–	20.4%(10)
ipf.		100%(49)	ipf.	–	79.6%(39)

data: Hašek.

From the table we can read the following facts:

a. The Russian perfective, in the majority of cases, has been translated by means of the perfective in Czech. However, there is a considerable aspect shift in the Czech translation of the Russian imperfective: 39.9% out of the Russian imperfective preterite forms become perfective in Czech. In the present tense, the percentage indicating this aspect shift is even higher: 53% of the Russian imperfectives become perfective in the Czech translation.

b. In the Russian translation of the Czech text, a movement in the opposite direction can be observed. The majority of Czech imperfective forms are translated by the same form in Russian. But this does not apply to the Czech perfective. In the Russian preterite, no corresponding perfective forms have been encountered, the only perfectives are in the present tense (9.1%). In the present tense, 50% of the Czech perfective forms become imperfective in Russian.

The observed aspect shifts in the translations can be schematically represented:

$$R.ipf. \rightarrow C.pf.$$
$$C.pf. \rightarrow R.ipf.$$

Both shifts reflect the same property, namely, the aspectual difference between Russian and Czech in the denotation of iterated events: a strong predominance of the imperfective in Russian and a relatively high frequency of the perfective in Czech (see section 1.2.).

These differences will be treated in more detail in the commentary on the concrete examples in the following section. We shall explore the factors which are the possible causes of the notably higher frequency of the Czech perfective. One such factor could be the relevance of the different levels within iteration, i.e. the micro- and macro-level, for each language. To test this, we shall study the effects of the replacement of a given aspectual form (usually the Czech perfective) by means of the corresponding form of the opposite aspect.[4]

3. DESCRIPTION OF CORRESPONDENCES

In this description we begin with the Russian forms and their
correspondences in Czech, irrespective of the original text or its
translation. The forms will be treated in the following order:
1. perfective preterite; 2. perfective present; 3. imperfective
preterite; 4. imperfective present. In the examples, the original
sentence will be given first and then its translation. The figures
between parentheses indicate numbers of encountered forms per
correspondence, the left-hand part is: Russian original - Czech
translation, the right-hand part: Czech original - Russian translation. At the end of this account longer passages will be dealt
with where various correspondences are combined.

I. Perfective preterite

1. R.pf.pret. - C.pf.pret. (R - C : 5 - 4; C - R : 77 - none)

(1) R. Но раз, другой взглянули^p, улыбнулись^p... (Andreev)
    C. Jednou či dvakrát zvedli^p sklopené oči, usmáli^p se...

The occurrence of the Russian perfective preterite denoting
iterated events is very rare (see table 1). There must be a
special reason for the choice of this form, as in this case, a
delimitation of the number of individual sub-events: 'raz,
drugoj'. This is an example of the 'summative meaning' of the
perfective (see the survey of particular meanings).

Russian perfective preterite occurs also in embedded
clauses. We assume, however, that in some embedded clauses,
the iteration looses its validity. This loss of validity of the
iteration was the reason for not including in the analysis the
few sentences encountered. For the sake of completeness, the
following example is given:

(2) R. Люсьен наспех сочинял^i историю: он забыл^p бумажник дома...
    (Èrenburg)

As we have already mentioned, Russian perfective in the
'summative meaning' can almost always be replaced by imperfective
without special effects. Consider now Czech:

(3) C. Jednou či dvakrát zvedali^i sklopené oči, usmívali^i se...

The first imperfective verb suggests a very slow process. The second one gives the impression of an event presented *in medias res*. We assume that the Czech imperfective here functions on the micro-level, i.e. it refers to one individual sub-event out of the whole chain of iterated events.

2. <u>R.pf.pret. - C.pf.pres.</u> (R - C : 5 - none; C - R : 74 - 3)

(4) C. Já mám, jak se říká[i], vyvinutej pozorovací talent, když už je pozdě a něco se <u>stane</u>[p] nepříjemnýho. (Hašek)

    R. У меня, как говорится[i], очень развит талант к наблюдению, но только когда уже поздно и когда неприятность уже <u>произошла</u>[p].

This is a case when the Czech perfective is used in the 'gnomic present'. The events are presented as a generally valid fact. However, this type of situation can be interpreted as an iterated event.

The Russian perfective preterite fulfills here the 'perfectum function'.[5] The possible motivation for this use can be that the events are not presented in a chronological order. This fact is in Russian stressed by an extra adverb 'uže'.

3. <u>R.pf.pret. - C.ipf.pret.</u> (R - C : 5 - none; C - R : 152 - 5)

(5) C. Stačilo[i] to nejmenší, a důstojník se již <u>loučil</u>[i] se svou posádkou a <u>putoval</u>[i] na černohorské hranice... (Hašek)

    R. Достаточно было пустяка, чтобы офицер <u>распрощался</u>[p] со своим гарнизоном и <u>отправился</u>[p] на черногорскую границу...

The following paraphrase can be given: little was enough and it was already happening. The Czech imperfective adds an extra plasticity to the events and confronts us with them *in medias res*. It is not the actual fact that is stressed here but the possibility of such a fact. This sentence has therefore a modal nuance - in Russian it is expressed by the conjunctive.

4. <u>R.pf.pret. - C.ipf.pres.</u> (R - C : 5 - 1; C - R : 49 - none)

(6) R. (...) чуть что - прощай, (...) и <u>пошел</u>[p] искать где лучше. (Gor'kij)

C. (...) sotva se něco přihodí[p] - sbohem, (...) a <u>jde</u>[i] si
hledat něco lepšího.

This is a similar type of event as the previous one: 'a little is
enough and it is already happening'. The last clause is actually
an addition and falls therefore partly outside the scope of iteration, which makes the use of the Russian perfective possible.

A related usage of the verbs of movement can be seen in the
following example of a non-iterated event. The perfective preterite is used hyperbolically to express an event occurring in the
present or future: 'Pošli!' (Let's go!).

II. <u>Perfective present</u>

1. <u>R.pf.pres. - C.pf.pret.</u> (R - C : 45 - 11; C - R : 77 - 7)

(7) R. Он всю зиму ходил[i] без работы; какая-то работенка пере-
падала[i] - то <u>починит</u>[p] швейную машину, то еще что.
(Ērenburg)

C. Celou zimu chodil[i] bez práce - sem tam sehnal[p] nahodilou
- jednou <u>spravil</u>[p] šicí stroj, po druhé zas něco jiného.

(8) C. A potom ta švanda, když někdy <u>sklouzl</u>[p] a <u>upadl</u>[p] s kali-
chem... (Hašek)

R. Вот смеху бывало[i], когда он, к примеру, <u>поскользнется</u>[p]
и <u>брякнется</u>[p] вместе с чашей...

These two examples are cases of iterated events, which occurred
in the past. In Czech, past tense is consistently used, while in
Russian it is not.

As to aspect, in Russian all introductory verbs are in the
imperfective ('chodil', 'perepadala', 'byvalo'), the latter being
an habitual verb. After this introduction, more events are presented in the perfective, in the sense of 'vivid exemplification'.
This use of the Russian perfective is possible owing to the 'time
transposition', otherwise the imperfective must be used. The exem-
plifying character is stressed in the Russian translation (example 8) by means of an extra expression 'k primeru'.

2.　R.pf.pres. - C.pf.pres. (R - C : 45 - 32; C - R : 74 -34)

(9) R. Я это понимаю^i, со мной тоже бывает^i - скажу^p уверенно
и сейчас же спохвачусь^p. (Gor'kij)

　　C. Dovedu^p to pochopit, stává^i se mi to také (...) řeknu^p
něco jistým tónem a hned se zarazím^p.

This is again a case of 'vivid exemplification' in Russian. As
already mentioned (see section 1.4.), the Russian perfective can
be used in the denotation of iterated events only under certain
conditions. Roughly, these conditions are: 1. 'connection';
2. modality. Sometimes, these two can form one complex.
1. 'Connection' is the most important condition to be met. It is
valid for the majority of cases. It implies that the event(s) expressed by the perfective must have a temporal, causal or any
logical connection with one or more other events. This type of
aspectual context is termed 'kratno-sootnositel'nyj tip konteksta' (see also section 1.4.). A sequence of two connected events
is labeled 'kratno-parnaja konstrukcija' (Bondarko 1971: 204).
It is often the type: "if a, then b". Examples 7, 8 and 9 can be
included under this type.

If the number of events in the series is more than two, it
is a case of the 'kratno-cepnaja konstrukcija' (ibid.: 207). The
following example is given to illustrate this. Note also the
asyndetic character of the construction in Russian. The presence
of the perfective here is already enough to suggest the connection; in Czech an extra conjunction is added.

(10) R. И кругом, как воронье, начальство сторожит^i... Увидит^p,
вырвет^p, в харю тебе даст^p... (Gor'kij)

　　C. A kolem číhají^i úřady jako krkavci, (...) Jakmile jej
uvidí^p, vyrvou^p ti jej, dají^p ti přes hubu...

Regarding replacement of the perfective forms by imperfectives,
in Czech, the imperfectives would clearly indicate a process.
Especially in examples 8 and 10, the presentation would be very
'vivid', so that the hearer is given the impression of witnessing the events himself.
2. We proceed now to the second condition which makes use of the
Russian perfective possible: modality. It is less common than

'connection'. In this case, an explicit connection with another
event is not necessarily present. However, there is an implicit
connection between the event expressed by the perfective, denoting a possibility, and a situation in which the event would actually occur. In the Russian terminology, this phenomenon has been
described as 'potential meaning' (see section 1.4.).

Often, the quality of the subject is stressed, i.e. the type
of person or his/her ability to do something. Consider this example:

(11) R. Она воспитывалась[i] в тепле, ее баловали всем (...) а
сейчас, вот, пойдет[p] семь верст ночью, одна... (Gor'kij)
   C. Vyrostla[p] v teple, hýčkali[i] ji (...), a ted', podívej
se, půjde[p] sedm verst nocí, sama...

Such cases of 'potential meaning' are actually a kind of 'particularization': the Russian perfective operates on the micro-level,
as in Czech.

As to 'connection' and modality in Czech: they might be
present, as in the examples above. But they do not form an absolute condition for the use of the perfective as they do in Russian.
In many instances, the Czech perfective is used when these two
factors are absent.

3.   R.pf.pres. - C.ipf.pret. (R - C : 45 - 1; C - R : 152 - none)

(12) R. Случалось[i], в тяжелые минуты он шепнет[p] про себя, без мо-
литвы... (Andreev)
   C. Někdy se stávalo[i], že tiše a bezděčně šeptal[i] v těžkých
chvílích, aniž se modlil[i]...

This is the only case of this correspondence encountered. The
event took place in the past, which is indicated in the first
part of the sentence by the imperfective preterite 'slučalos''
and 'stávalo se' (it used to happen). The event itself is in Russian exemplified by the perfective and 'time transposition' takes
place. In Czech, there is nothing special about the tense, the
preterite forms 'stávalo se' and 'šeptal' simply denote the occurrence of the events in the past.

As to aspect, the occurrence of the Czech imperfective in

the translation of the Russian perfective, as in this case, is quite exceptional (see table 2a). Perfective would be possible in the following adjusted sentence:

(13) C. (...) že něco (...) zašeptal[p] (...) (that he something whispered)

In any case there must by an object accompanying the verb. But even then, the version with the imperfective is for the native speaker 'more natural'. The verb 'šeptat' is normally intransitive.

4. R.pf.pres.-C.ipf.pres. (R - C : 45 - 1; C - R : 49 - 10)[6]

(14) R. (...) стоит[i] кому-нибудь чихнуть, как его сейчас напоят[p] липовым чаем (...), приготовят[p] горчичники. (Èrenburg)
     C. (...) jak jen někdo kýchne[p], hned do něho lijí[i] lipové thé (...) a obalí[p] ho hořčičnými plackami.

This case can be compared with type I.3 and I.4, where the Russian perfective preterite corresponds with a Czech imperfective preterite and present, respectively. It is the same kind of expression: 'a little is enough and it is already happening'. It seems that Czech, in these expressions, has a certain preference for the imperfective, which evokes a special effect: the situation is presented *in medias res*, the ingressive or terminative phase of the event is being omitted. In fact, the phenomenon *in medias res* can be seen as a kind of process.

The replacement of the imperfective by the perfective in Czech ('nalijí') would have the following effect: all the tea has been poured out (the object is then quantified), with the result that the person is filled up to his ears with all that tea. The synonymous perfective verb 'napojí' (a literary translation), would have a similar effect.

III. Imperfective preterite

1. R.ipf.pret. - C.pf.pret. (R - C : 506 - 200; C - R : 77 - 66)

(15) R. Сыновья выросли[p] шалопаями, ничего не хотели[i] делать и выклянчивали[i] деньги у Фуже... (Èrenburg)

486

C. Jeho synové byli[i] lenoši, nehnuli[p] ani prstem, ale z
Fougera vždy vyždímali[p] peníze...

This is a very common type of correspondence. The Czech perfective could in this case be replaced by an imperfective, but,
in this context, the latter would have a conative nuance: the sons
tried to get the money. Note also the extra adverb 'vždy' (always) in Czech. In about one fifth of the cases when the Czech
perfective is used in iterated events, an extra adverb denoting
iteration is added to it. This fact can lead to the assumption
that the perfective by itself cannot express iteration, as the
imperfective sometimes does.

(16) R. Встречая[i] колющий взгляд маленьких глаз, она робко
двигала[i] бровями. (Gor'kij)

C. A když se setkala[p] s pichlavým pohledem jeho maličkých
očí, plaše škubla[p] obočím.

Replacing the Czech perfective by the imperfective 'škubala'
would have a special effect: a constant movement to and fro.
Every individual event on the micro-level consists then of an
unspecified number of repeated movements. Actually, in this
special case, three levels are involved: the level of the whole
chain (macro-level), the level of one individual sub-event
(micro-level) and the level of one individual movement. We use
the term 'internal iteration' for this phenomenon. The Czech
perfective operates on the micro-level, the imperfective on the
third level of an individual movement within the micro-level.
The macro-level could be in this case expressed only by the imperfective habitual verb 'škubávala'. In Russian, the imperfective operates on the macro-level, the other two levels are not involved. Therefore, the same distinction cannot be made.

(17) R. Он обладал[i] удивительной способностью: за день молодел[i]
или старел[i] лет на двадцать. (Ěrenburg)

C. Měl[i] podivuhodnou schopnost: za den omládl[p] nebo zestárl[p]
o dvacet let.

This is a description of the quality of someone who is able to
get 20 years younger or older within one day. This limit is important for the choice of the perfective in Czech, the process of

getting younger or older, results in the state of being that way
within one day. In this context this interpretation is the only
normal one, due to the quantification or limit. The perfective has
here a resultative nuance. The imperfective in Czech would suggest
that there was a process going on and nothing would be said about
the attained state.

The Russian imperfective in contrast to Czech, does not imply
this progressiveness, but does not exclude resultativity either.
In the denotation of iterated events, the Russian imperfective can
often be combined with typical perfective characteristics, such
as resultativity. This has been described in the literature as
'nesobstvennaja nesoveršennost'' (Maslov 1984: 84).

(18) C. Byl[i] v několika drogériích, a jakmile řekl[P]: "Prosím
láhvičku oleje posvěceného od biskupa", dali[P] se někde
do smíchu a jinde skryli[P] se uděšeni pod pultem. (Hašek)

R. Швейк побывал в нескольких аптекарских магазинах, но
как только произносил[i]: "Будьте любезны, бутылочку елея,
освященного эпископом", всюду или фыркали[i] ему в лицо или
в ужасе прятались[i] под прилавок.

The replacement of the Czech perfectives by imperfectives
would have the following effects: the first one would generate an
ungrammatical clause *'jakmile říkal[i]'. Generally, in this type
of subordinate clause, the perfective is the preferred form. As
to the second verb, 'dali[P] se', the replacement by 'dávali[i] se'
would lead to the following interpretation: at the moment that
Švejk made his request, people would hesitatingly start laughing
in slow motion. This imperfective verb would then denote both ingression and process. As to the third perfective, 'skryli se',
its replacement by the imperfective 'skrývali se' would mean:
people were already hiding before Švejk entered. The temporal and
logical relation with the other events would be broken.

In Russian, the imperfectives in this example do not have
these effects. Replacing them, the other way round, by the perfectives, would generate an ungrammatical sentence.

As to the levels, the Russian imperfective operates here
clearly on the macro-level, while in Czech, the micro-level is
involved.

2. **R.ipf.pret. - C.pf.pres.** (R - C : 506 - 2; C - R : 74 - none)

This is not a typical example of iteration but rather of distributivity. We include it, however, for the sake of completeness, to illustrate this type of correspondence. The Czech perfective can be considered as a case of 'historic present'.

(19) R. Но Иисус молчит, (...) - и один за другим подходили к Иуде смущенные ученики, заговаривали[i] ласково, но отходили[i] быстро и неловко. (Andreev)

C. Ale Ježíš mlčí, (...) zatímco jeden učedník za druhým, plni rozpaků, přistupují k Jidášovi, zdvořile s ním prohodí[p] pár slov, ale pak rychle a jaksi nemotorně poodejdou[p].

3. **R.ipf.pret. - C.ipf.pret.** (R - C : 506 - 304; C - R : 152 - 145)

(20) C. Byl zde také jeden s padoucnicí, ten nám vždy říkal[i], že mu na jednom záchvatu nezáleží[i], tak jich dělal[i] třebas deset za den. Svíjel[i] se v těch křečích, zatínal[i] pěstě, vypuloval[i] oči, (...), bil[i] sebou, vyplazoval[i] jazyk, zkrátka vám řeknu[p], nádherná prvotřídní padoucnice, taková upřímná. (Hašek)

R. Был тут один эпилептик. Тот всегда нам говорил[i], что лишний припадок устроить ничего не стоит[i]. Падал[i] он этак раз десять в день, извивался[i] в корчах, сжимал[i] кулаки, выкатывал[i] глаза под самый лоб, бился[i] о землю, высовывал[i] язык. Короче говоря, это была прекрасная эпилепсия, эпилепсия первый сорт, самая что ни на есть настоящая.

In this example, the events are presented as a process, with a kind of vividness, which makes the hearer imagine himself to be the witness of what is happening. In Czech, passages with a series of imperfectives only, denote usually the situation of a process or development in its totality. Within this total process or development, each event denoted by an imperfective is in itself a process as well. If this idea of a general process or development is lacking, imperfectives are com-

bined with perfectives, which is often the case. In the Russian
passages, a series consisting of imperfectives only, does not
necessarily denote a general process or development; most of the
Russian passages contain only imperfectives.

The replacement of the Czech imperfectives by perfectives in
the example (20) would have the following effect: the idea of a
process would disappear.

(21) R. Приближалась[i] весна, таял[i] снег (...) С каждым днем
грязь настойчивее лезла[i] в глаза (...) Днем капало[i] с
крыш (...) Все чаще на небе являлось[i] солнце. (Gor'kij)

C. Blížilo[i] se jaro, sníh tál[i] (...) Špína každým dnem
bila[i] víc do očí (...) Ve dne kapalo[i] se střech (...)
Na obloze se stále častěji objevovalo[i] slunce.

In this example, a process of approaching spring is being described. Besides the element of progressiveness, an element of growth
can also be observed. This is morphologically expressed by the
comparative and the instrumental case. In our opinion, this is
one of the few cases when the Czech aspect operates on the macro-
level of the iterated event. This is understandable as the notion
of growth clearly applies to this level. Note also that the element of growth disappears when the perfective is used:

(22) C. Na obloze se často objevilo[p] slunce.

4. **R.ipf.pret. - C.ipf.pres.** (R - C : 506 - none; C - R :
49 - none)

There is no attested case of this correspondence in the
material.

IV. **Imperfective present**

1. **R.ipf.pres. - C.pf.pret.** (R - C : 83 - none; C - R : 77 - 4)

(23) C. (...) a potom byl už takovej zvyk, že jakmile bylo slyšet
první kanonádu, že pucflek hned vyházel[p] všechny zábavný
knížky. (Hašek)

R. (...) а потом уже стало[p] правилом: заслышав[p] первую кано-
наду, денщик сразу вышвыривает[i] все книги для чтения.

This is quite a marginal type of correspondence. The events take place in the past, hence the preterite in Czech. The Russian verb is submitted to the 'time transposition'.

The Czech perfective has here a double motivation. A sudden event is being expressed (adverbial 'hned'). The object is quantified (adjective 'všechny'). In such instances, Czech often prefers the perfective. Replacing it by the imperfective 'vyhazoval' would suggest that the person was busy throwing the books out.

2.   R.ipf.pres. - C.pf.pres. (R - C : 83 - 44; C - R : 74 - 37)

(24) C. Já jsem živnostník, když někdo přijde[p], a dá[p] si pivo, tak mu ho natočím[p]. (Hašek)

   R. Я трактирщик. Кто ко мне приходит[i], требует[i] пива, тому и наливаю[i].

Compare the Czech sentence with its modification, where the perfectives have been replaced by imperfectives:

(25) C. (...) Když někdo přichází[i] a dává[i] si pivo, tak mu ho točím[i].

In this sentence, all events are presented as a process, while the Russian imperfectives simply denote iterativity and are neutral with respect to progressiveness. Since the Czech imperfectives express progressiveness, it implies that the events take place synchronically or partially overlap each other. The Czech sentence with imperfectives only, can be interpreted in the following way: while somebody is entering and ordering beer at the same time, the innkeeper is already busy pouring the beer.

(26) R. Галоши у меня тоже неизлечимо разорвались[p], и каждый день я промачиваю[i] себе ноги. (Gorkij)

   C. Moje galoše jsou též nevyléčitelně roztrhané a každého dne si promočím[p] nohy.

The Czech perfective is in this sentence the only possible form. It is a resultative verb, the result being that the person's feet get wet in fact. The Russian imperfective does not contradict this interpretation. The replacement of the Czech perfective would have the following results: if replaced by the bi-aspectual verb 'promáčím', the interpretation would be rather in the direction of the perfective, as in the original sentence. The replacement by the imperfective 'močím' evokes this picture: the person is trying hard to get his feet wet. It is then a deliberate action, which is not what is meant here. The fact that intentionality has some relation to the aspect selection can be demonstrated by the following example (see also Petruchina 1983: 166):

(27) C. Při mytí nádobí pokaždé něco rozbije[P].

'Every time the person washes the dishes, he breaks something'. The action is interpreted as thoroughly unintentional, it just happens because the person is not handy enough. Replacing the perfective by the imperfective 'rozbíjí', would cause an opposite effect: the person deliberately breaks the dishes every time, maybe with great pleasure.

The Russian imperfective is neutral with respect to intentionality.

3. R.ipf.pres. - C.ipf.pret. (R – C : 83 – none; C – R : 152 – 2

(28) C. Vypravovali[i] na četnických stanicích, že když von přišel[P] na inspekci, (...), že tam vůbec inspekci nedělal[i] a jen celej den s vachmistrem z radosti chlastal[i]. (Hašek)

   R. По жандармским отделениям рассказывали[i], что если ротмистр делает[i] ревизию (...) - то уж не инспектирует[i], а на радостях весь день хлещет[i] с вахмистром.

In Czech, preterite is used for all occurrences, while in Russian the fact that the events took place in the past is denoted only by the first verb. All remaining verbs are submitted to the 'time transposition'. Note also that this is an instance of indirect speech and that the Russian present forms occur after a *verbum dicendi* ('rasskazyvali') which can be of influence on the tense selection.

As to aspect, the Czech imperfectives can be replaced by perfectives:

(29) C. (...), že tam vůbec inspekci neudělal[P] a celej den s vachmistrem z radosti prochlastal[P].

In both cases, then, resultativity is stressed. The first perfective puts more stress on the fact that the event never took
place. For the second perfective a modification is needed, the
adverbial 'jen' (only) has to be left out. In the original Czech
sentence, the expression 'celej den' (the whole day) functions as
a time adverbial; in the modified sentence it functions as a
quantified direct object. The perdurative verb 'prochlastal' denotes that the person has been drinking all day long, from the
beginning till the end, doing nothing else.

4. R.ipf.pres. - C.ipf.pres. (R - C : 83 - 39; C - R : 49 - 39)

(30) R. Каждый день приносит[i] новые сюрпризы: (...)

    (Èrenburg)

  C. Každy den přináší[i] nová překvapení: (...)

This is a very regular type of correspondence. However, hardly
any longer passages containing an uninterrupted series of imperfective present forms have been encountered in Czech. In the
majority of cases, both aspects are combined within a passage.
These cases will be treated below.

    The replacement of the Czech imperfective by the perfective
'přinese' would cause no problems.

V. Combinations of correspondences

1. R.ipf.pres. - C.ipf./pf.pres. (R - C : 83 - 39/44)

(31) R. Каждый день приносит[i] новые сюрпризы: то актеры захва-
    тывают[i] театр, то кассиры закрывают[i] окошечко кассы, то
    могильщики отказываются[i] рыть могилы. (Èrenburg)

  C. Každý den přináší[i] nová překvapení: jednou herci obsadí[p]
    divadlo, jindy pokladníci zavírají[i] okénko pokladny,
    nebo hrobníci odmítají[i] kopat hroby.

This passage can be divided into two parts: in the first clause
the fact is mentioned that surprises take place. In the rest of
the passage these surprises are specified in detail. In both
languages, the introductory verb is imperfective. However, as
soon as one specific surprise is being described, the perfective
is used in Czech. The question arises then: why is only the verb

'obsadí' perfective and the other two verbs 'zavírají' and
'odmítají', although specifying, imperfective?

The perfective 'obsadí' is a resultative verb. It is here
obligatory, because the corresponding imperfective 'obsazují'
would have an effect which in this context is unintended. This
imperfective would have a conative nuance, suggesting the following interpretation: although the actors were trying to occupy
the theatre, they did not succeed. The last two Czech verbs
though imperfective, do not suggest conativity or progression
of any kind. The lexical meaning and the entire context plays a
role. Closing a window, for instance, costs less effort than
occupying a theatre. It is not really relevant here to mention
also the actual result of these actions, as in the case of the
theatre occupation.

All Czech imperfectives here may be replaced by perfectives.
However, a 'dry' sort of account of 'pure' facts would then be
obtained. The fact that the events are in a sequential succession, namely that when one event ends, the other one starts, would
be stressed.

2. **R.ipf.pret. - C.ipf./pf.pret.** (R - C : 506 - 304/200)

(32) R. Студент Орлов ухаживал[i] за моей сестрой Верой. Он приез-
жал[i] на дачу на велосипеде. Велосипед стоял[i] над цветни-
ком, прислоненный к борту веранды. Велосипед был рогат.

Студент снимал[i] со щиколоток сверкающие зажимы, нечто
в роде шпор без звона, и бросал[i] их на деревянный стол.
Затем студент снимал[i] фуражку с небесным околышем и
вытирал[i] лоб платком. Лицо у него было коричневое, лоб
белый, голова бритая... Он не говорил[i] со мной ни слова.
(Oleša)

C. Studující Orlov chodil[i] za mou sestrou Věrou. Jezdil[i] k
nám na chatu na kole. Kolo stávalo[i] nad květinovým záho-
nem, opřeno o boční stěnu verandy. Mělo rohy.

Student si vždycky sundal[p] s kotníků blýskavé sponky,
něco jako ostruhy, které nezvoní, a hodil[p] je na dřevěný
stůl. Potom si sundal[p] studentskou čepici světle modře le-
movanou a utřel[p] si čelo kapesníkem. Tvář měl hnědou, čelo

bílé, hlavu vyholenou, měňavou, hrbolatou. <u>Nepromluvil</u>[P]
se mnou slovo.

This passage has the following structure: 1. introduction; 2. spec-
ification. In the introduction is roughly said that the student
used to cycle to visit the speaker's sister. In the second part,
which is indicated by a new paragraph, what happened during each
visit is specified. The behaviour of the student is then described
in detail.

With respect to aspect, the introductory verbs are imperfective in both languages. The Czech verb 'stávalo' is habitual, which
is indicated with the suffix -va-. All the specifying verbs in Russian are imperfective and they denote a regular type of iteration.
In Czech, all the specifying verbs are perfective. An extra adverb indicating iteration ('vždycky') is added. The replacement of
the perfectives by the corresponding imperfectives would cause
the following effects: in this context, the imperfective 'si sundával' instead of the perfective 'si sundal', would denote that
the student was busy taking those things off. It may even suggest
that this was not easy or it took a long time. The third verb,
which denotes a similar action, would have a comparable effect:
the student was busy slowly taking his cap off. The imperfective
'házel' instead of the perfective 'hodil' would indicate 'internal
iteration' - every time the student was busy repeatedly throwing
his cap on the table. In other words, the level of every individual movement, or an act of throwing, would be involved in this
case; it is a level within the micro-level, denoting one individual sub-event. The lexical meaning of the verb plays here
an important role. The imperfective 'utíral si' instead of the
perfective 'utřel si' would have a similar effect as in the case
of the verb 'sundával si'. The perfective 'nepromluvil' can be
replaced by the corresponding imperfective 'nemluvil' without
problems. However, the object 'slovo' would have to be omitted.
All the imperfective verbs, by which the Czech perfectives have
been replaced, denote, in themselves, various kinds of process.

As to the level of the whole passage, these imperfective
verbs combined, indicate a kind of general process, comparable

to examples 20 and 21 of the type III.3. This presentation of
the events has a certain plasticity, giving the hearer the impression of witnessing the events himself.

(33) R. Они часто встречались^i; заходили^i в небольшие кафе на
окраинах; иногда он ее возил^i по мокрым, пустым доро-
гам, гнал^i - сто сорок в час, заражал^i своим беспокойством потом отвозил^i ее и, прощаясь, церемонно целовал^i
руку. (Ērenburg)

C. Stýkali^i se často; chodili^i do malých kaváren na periferii; někdy ji vozil^i po mokrých prázdných silnicích,
jezdil^i rychlostí sto čtyřicet kilometrů za hodinu;
nakazil^P ji svým neklidem; potom ji odvezl^P domů a při
loučení jí obřadně políbil^P ruku.

This passage can be divided roughly into two parts: the first
sentence gives a general introduction; the fact that the two persons often met is indicated. The rest of the passage is a description of the meetings. In Russian, all the verbs are imperfective
- the most usual expression of iterated events.

In Czech, the introductory verb 'stýkali se' is imperfective
as in most passages encountered. We assume that such introductory
imperfectives operate on the macro-level as in Russian. They are
a kind of signal: the following events are iterated. This assumption can be supported by the fact that the introductory verbs
are often habitual and also operate on the macro-level. The imperfective 'stýkali se' could be replaced by the perfective
'setkali se', but the introductory character would disappear;
more context would then be necessary. As to the Czech imperfective
simplex 'chodili', its replacement by the imperfective II. 'za-
cházeli' as in Russian, is not correct. Besides, the ingressive
phase would be unnecessarily stressed. For the replacement of
this imperfective simplex by the perfective 'zašli', an adjust-
ment is needed. Firstly, an extra adverb indicating iteration is
needed (e.g. 'někdy', 'vždy'), secondly, the form indicating
locus has to be changed. In these instances, the Czech perfective
cannot be easily combined with the plural. The plural would indicate distributivity, suggesting that all the cafés had been

visited at the same time. As this is not the intention, singular has to be used. Consider now the adjusted sentence:

(34) C. Někdy zašli[P] do jedné z malých kaváren na periferii (...)

The imperfective verbs 'vozil' and 'jezdil', being undetermined or 'two-way', imply iteration. The determined verbs 'vezl' and 'jel' express only 'one-way'.

It is difficult to replace the Czech perfective 'nakazil' by the imperfective 'nakažoval'; this verb is not much used in general. 'Nakazil' is a resultative verb, the imperfective might have a conative nuance.

The perfective verb 'odvezl' is resultative as well; note also the extra indication of *locus* in Czech 'domů'. The imperfective 'odvážel' would imply that the person was on his way.

The last perfective verb 'políbil' indicates that the person kissed every time, the hand only once. If the interpretation: 'every time several kisses' is intended, in Czech the imperfective has to be used. However, there is a difference in the relevance of the levels of the iterated event. The imperfective in Czech would indicate the 'internal iteration', i.e. this would be valid for the third level: a repetition of movements within the micro-level. The Czech perfective operates at the micro-level. As to the Russian imperfective, it does not explicitely imply nor exclude any of these interpretations, it is neutral with respect to them. As the imperfective in Russian operates at the macro-level of the iterated event, the distinction as in Czech cannot simply be made. The Russian imperfective is ambiguous with respect to the interpretation, Czech has to choose explicitly for one of the two. For Russian, more context is needed for the appropriate interpretation. In this case it is the expression 'ceremonno' and our knowledge of the customs.

Note that the choice of the aspectual form in the Czech text is not arbitrary but that there is a reason for every form and that not every form can always be replaced by its aspectual opposite.

On the level of the whole passage, the aspect fulfills certain 'textual' functions. For instance, the imperfective functions always as an introduction. For the more specific events, which often are a part of the whole, perfectives may be used in Czech (as in the last example: 'nakazil', 'odvezl' and 'políbil'). The reason to use the perfective form is in these cases resultativity for the first two, and one 'unique' movement, which was successful every time, for the third one. Formulated in more general terms, the internal limit (*terminus*) has been reached every time, i.e. at the level of the individual sub-event. This is always the necessary condition for the use of the perfective.

4.   CONCLUSION

The previous discussion of the examples demonstrates that the choice of the aspectual forms denoting iterated events is not arbitrary (see also section 1.2.). While in Russian the imperfective is often the only possible form, the Czech perfective occurs relatively frequently in similar positions.

If the Czech perfective is replaced by its corresponding imperfective, a different picture of the event arises, causing various effects. The event expressed by the (replacing) imperfective contains one of the following characteristics: 1. progressiveness (various kinds); 2. conativity; 3. intentionality or 4. internal iteration. When these effects are not intended, the perfective must be chosen in Czech. On the other hand, the Russian imperfective is not necessarily associated with these phenomena and there is usually no choice between the two aspectual forms.

This clearly points to the relevance of the different levels within the iterated event in each language. While Czech is primarily orientated to the micro-level, for Russian, the macro-level is decisive for the aspect selection (see also Stunová 1983: 13).

To be able to use the perfective in Czech, there must be certain conditions met on this micro-level. The absolute condition is that each individual sub-event must have reached its internal limit (*terminus*).

In the less usual cases that Russian uses the perfective, this condition is also met, but it is in itself not sufficient.

Other conditions must be met as well, the necessary condition
being a 'connection' with other events. For a detailed explanation of this phenomenon we refer to Barentsen (1985: 60 ff.).
Besides, there must be a special reason in Russian to stress the
micro-level, which results in a certain stylistic colouring of
the perfective (i.e. 'vivid exemplification'). In Czech, this
form is usually neutral (see also section 1.4.).

As we could observe, the differences described above can
hardly be seen as a matter of detail. Which place these differences would take in the contrastive description of the Russian
and Czech aspect and in the descriptions of the content of the
opposition members in each language, can be said only after a
number of partial contrastive studies.

University of Amsterdam

NOTES

[1] We use the term 'terminative' in the broadest sense of the word. In the
class of terminative verbs we also include the delimitative and perdurative
verbs, which is not a generally accepted conception.

[2] Consider the following citation from Isačenko (1960: 455): "Različija
meždu russkim i slovackim (češskim) jazykom v otnošenii upotreblenija per-
fektivnogo prezensa v uzual'nom značenii ne javljajutsja principial'nymi:
oba jazyka dopuskajut takoe upotreblenie. Odnako v slovackom i češskom jazykach forma prezensa s/v upotrebljaetsja gorazdo čašče". (The underlining is
mine.)

[3] The terminology is based on: Mathesius: "O konkurenci vidů v českém vyjadřování slovesném", *Slovo a slovesnost* 4 (1938), 15-19.

[4] For this purpose I use my own competence as a native-speaker of Czech.
A number of examples have benefited from the advice of Mrs. A. Grygar-Rechziegel, M.A.

[5] The Russian perfective preterite denotes in the 'perfectum function' a
past event with a present relevance. For a detailed explanation about the
'perfectum function' of the Russian perfective preterite we refer to Barentsen (1985: 62 ff.)

[6] The usual tendency in the Russian translation of the Czech imperfective
is to choose the same form. There are, however, several cases attested,
where the Czech imperfective has been translated by the Russian perfective.
This latter form functions in the meaning 'vivid exemplification'. There
are various reasons for Czech to prefer the imperfective. One of the reasons is that the verbs involved, belong to certain classes of verbs as:
verba sentiendi and *dicendi*. Some verbs of movement without a prefix (as
'jde') are also involved. Consider the following example:

C. Ten vždycky ztratí[p] řeč, když vidí[i] někoho z pánů oficírů.
   (Hašek)

499

R. U nego vsegda, kak tol'ko uvidit[p] kogo-nibud' iz gospod oficerov, jazyk otnimaetsja[i].

Besides, the Russian perfective is a preferred form in such an expression as 'kak tol'ko'.
The presentation of the event *in medias res* is illustrated by the following example:

C. (...) a hlasitě obviňuje[i] ministranta, (...) a hned mu před samou velebnou svátostí napařuje[i] ajnclíčka... (Hašek)
R. (...) gromko obvinjaja[i] ministranta, (...), a potom tut že pered samoj darochranitel'nicej, vkatit[p] ětomu mininstrantu odinočku...

BIBLIOGRAPHY

Anikina, A.B.
1964   "Sočetaemost' glagolov soveršennogo i nesoveršennogo vida s narečijami i drugimi leksičeskimi edinicami, charakterizuju-ščimi sposob. dejstvija", *Naučnye doklady vysšej školy 3*, FN, 165-173.
Barentsen, A.A.
1985   *'Tijd', 'Aspect' en de conjunctie poka* (dissertation). Amsterdam.
Bondarko, A.
1959   "Nastojaščee istoričeskoe v slavjanskich jazykach s točki zrenija glagol'nogo vida", *Slavjanskoe jazykoznanie*, 48-58. Moscow.
1971   *Vid i vremja russkogo glagola*. Moscow.
Bondarko, A., Bulanin, L.
1967   *Russkij glagol*. Leningrad.
Dostál, A.
1954   *Studie o vidovém systému v staroslověnštině*. Prague.
Forsyth, J.
1970   *A Grammar of Aspect*. Cambridge.
Glovinskaja, M.
1982   *Semantičeskie tipy vidovych protivopostavlenij russkogo glagola*. Moscow.
Isačenko, A.
1960   *Grammatičeskij stroj russkogo jazyka v sopostavlenii s slovackim. Morfologija* II. Bratislava.
Kopečný, F.
1962   *Slovesný vid v češtině*. Prague.
Kučera, H., Trnka, K.
1975   *Time in language*. Michigan Slavic Materials 11.
Maslov, J.S.
1974   "Zur Semantik der Perfektivitätsopposition", *Wiener slavistisches Jahrbuch* 20, 107-122.
1975   "Russkij glagol'nyj vid v zarubežnom jazykoznanii poslednich let", *Voprosy russkoj aspektologii. Izvestija gos.ped. in-ta*, t. 146, 28-47. Voronež.
1977   "Russkij glagol'nyj vid v zarubežnom jazykoznanii poslednich let II". *Voprosy russkoj aspektologii II. Učenye zapiski tar-*

500

tuskogo gos. in-ta, vyp. 434, 23-46. Tartu.
1978   "K osnovanijam sopostavitel'noj aspektologii", *Voprosy sopo-stavitel'noj aspektologii*, 4-44. Leningrad.
1984   *Očerki po aspektologii*. Moscow.
Maslov, J.S. (ed.)
1985   *Contrastive Studies in Verbal Aspect. Studies in Descriptive Linguistics* vol. 14. Heidelberg.
Mathesius, V.
1938   "O konkurenci vidů v českém vyjadřování slovesném", *Slovo a slovesnost* 4, 15-19.
Mazon, A.
1914   *Emplois des aspects du verbe russe*. Paris.
Němec, I.
1958   "Iterativnost a vid", *Slovo a slovesnost* XIX, 189-200.
Petruchina, E.V.
1978   "O funkcionirovanii vidovogo protivopostavlenija v russkom jazyke v sopostavlenii s češskim (pri oboznačenii povtorjaju-ščichsja dejstvij)", *Russkij jazyk za rubežom* 1, 57-60.
1983   "Funkcionirovanie prezentnych form glagolov soveršennogo vida v češskom jazyke v sopostavlenii s russkim". Širokova, Grab'e (eds.): *Sopostavitel'noe izučenie grammatiki i leksiki russkogo jazyka s češskim jazykom i drugimi slavjanskimi jazykami*, 152-172. Moscow.
Russkaja Grammatika
1979   (Horálek, K., ed.) Prague Academia.
Russkaja Grammatika
1980   (Švedova, N.J., ed.) Akademija nauk SSSR. Moscow.
Širokova, A.G.
1966   "Sposoby vyraženija mnogokratnosti v češskom jazyke (v sravne-nii s drugimi slavjanskimi jazykami)", *Vestnik Moskovskogo uni-versiteta, Serija fil.* X, 1, 39-58.
1971   "Nekotorye zamečanija o funkcional'nych granicach vida v russ-kom i češskom jazykach". Bernštejn (ed.): *Issledovanija po sla-vjanskomu jazykoznaniju*, 292-298. Moscow.
Stunová, A.
1983   "Het aspect in het Tsjechisch en het Nieuwgrieks (Aspect in Czech and New Greek - a Contrastive Study)" (unpublished M.A. thesis). Amsterdam.
Timberlake, A.
1982   "Invariance and the Syntax of Russian Aspect". Hopper, P.J. (ed.): *Tense-Aspect: between Semantics & Pragmatics*, 305-331. Amsterdam/Philadelphia.
Vinogradov, V.V.
1947   *Russkij jazyk*. Moscow.

TEXTS

A. Russian original text - Czech translation

Andreev, Leonid
1971   *Povesti i rasskazy v dvuch tomach*. T. 2. "Iuda Iskariot. Rasskaz o semi povešennych". Moscow. 131 pp.

Andreev, Leonid
      1979   "Satanův deník. Jidáš Iškariotský. Povídka o sedmi oběšených".
                Prague. 136 pp.
Ěrenburg, Ilja
      1947   *Padenie Pariža.* Moscow. 486 pp.
Erenburg, Ilja
      1950   *Pád Paříže.* Prague. 546 pp.
Gor'kij, Maksim
      1946   "Mat'", *Izbrannye sočinenija.* Moscow. 146 pp.
Gorkij, Maxim
      1951   "Matka". Prague. 315 pp.
Oleša, Jurij
      1974   *Izbrannoe. Zavist'. Rasskazy.* Moscow. 187 pp.
Oleša, Jurij
      1975   *Závist a jiné prózy.* Prague. 173 pp.

B. Czech original text - Russian translation

Hašek, Jaroslav
      1975   *Osudy dobrého vojáka Švejka za světové války.* Prague. 947 pp.
Gašek, Jaroslav
      1958   *Pochoždenija bravogo soldata Švejka.* Kišinev. 747 pp.

THE RISE OF THE NORTH RUSSIAN DIALECT OF COMMON SLAVIC

WILLEM VERMEER

"Dieser Gegensatz zwischen dem slavisch-orientierten
Süden und dem nach der Ostsee gravitierenden Norden
des Ostslaventums kann sehr früh begonnen haben."
(Trubetzkoy 1925:293.)

"Reconstruire le slave commun ne veut pas dire con-
struire un seul système phonétique ou morphologique,
mais plutôt découvrir l'ordre chronologique dans lequel différents systèmes se sont superposés les uns
aux autres." (Trubetzkoy 1922:218.)

1.   *PALATALIZATION AND RETENTION OF VELARS IN NORTH RUSSIAN.*[1]

In the past twenty years much has been written about the North
Russian reflexes of the Proto-Slavic velar consonants *k/*g/*x* in
those positions in which they were (or should have been) subject
to the Second or the Third Proto-Slavic Palatalization. It has become increasingly clear that at an early date North Russian must
have occupied a very special position among the dialects of the
rapidly disintegrating Slavic proto-language. The principal facts
seem to be the following:

A. The oldest and/or most authentic North Russian material
abounds in examples which seem not to have been affected by the
Second Palatalization of velars. The present state of our knowledge
is summarized by Zaliznjak in his recent grammar of the language
of the birchbark documents:

'(...) в новгородско-псковском ареале засвидетельствованы без
эффекта второй палатализации (в берестяных грамотах, топонимах и
современных говорах) праславанские корни: *kěv-, *kěd-, *kěl-

'целый', *kĕl-/*kvĕl- 'дразнить', *kĕp-, *kvĕt- (*kvъt-), *xĕd-, *xĕr-, *gvĕzd-, *gvъrst-. Из общераспространенных корней до полного списка недостает только *kĕn- 'цена'; (...)" (1986:114).

Zaliznjak's description incorporates the results of a great deal of earlier research, in particular by Gluskina (1966) and Stieber (1967:18, 1969), cf. also Zaliznjak's own earlier, and slightly less comprehensive statement (1982:65-66).[2]

B. With respect to the Third (or Progressive) Palatalization matters are complicated (as was to be expected). Proto-Slavic *k* is palatalized more or less to the same extent as elsewhere in East Slavic. Early (pre-1200) birchbark documents offer numerous examples of nouns in -ica (e.g. zadъnica 562, Ipl. vĕvericami 335, Gpl. vĕveričь 105, Asg. gramotiču 424, Asg. dъlžъnicu, Lsg. dъlžъnicĕ, both 449), several attestations of -ъcъ (e.g. Dsg. Stepanъcu 241, otъcъ 9, Dsg. otъčevi 424), and one likely example of -ъce (Isg. celъcem[ъ] 'очельем' 429).[3] As regards *g* the evidence is limited and elusive. Even in the oldest birchbark documents we find forms with palatalization (e.g. Dsg. kъnjazju 527, NApl. userjazi 429).[4] Unfortunately both words are borrowings which do not necessarily reflect local developments. Indeed, it is well-known that forms with *g* corresponding to *z* elsewhere are characteristically Russian, with a noticeable tendency to concentrate in the North, cf., e.g., Shevelov (1964:346) and Ferrell (1970:413-414), with references to earlier literature. As regards *x*, it is well-known that the number of attestations of retained *x* in the key example *vъxъ has been growing steadily since the discovery of the birchbark documents. Less than thirty years ago Vaillant could still write: "des examples allégués de *vx-* en vieux russe sont illusoires" (1958:477). By the time Shevelov wrote his *Prehistory*, the beautiful dative plural vъxemo in birchbark document № 87 had removed all lingering doubt (1964:339). In 1975 Savignac listed eight examples, leaving aside some doubtful modern dialect forms. Now Zaliznjak (1986:116) gives eleven attestations, not counting doubtful cases and the toponym *Вхоѣжъ*, which seems to presuppose the previous existence of a proper name *Vъxovĕdъ. Zaliznjak summarizes:

"(...) материал берестяных грамот заставляет нас признать, что
в древненовгородском по крайней мере для *k третья палатализация
осуществилась (причем в объеме, достаточно близком к тому, что
обнаруживается в других восточнославянских диалектах). Для *g
вопрос остается не вполне ясным; для *x третьей палатализации
не было" (1986:118-119).

C. As is well-known, the most authentic forms of North Russian
do not differentiate between the reflexes of Proto-Slavonic *c and
*č. This is the phenomenon traditionally referred to as "цоканье".
Owing to цоканье, Novgorod scribes copying Church Slavonic texts
had trouble keeping apart the letters ц (c) and ч (č). The pattern
of scribal errors attributable to Novgorod цоканье has recently
been analysed in considerable detail by Živov (1984:263-283). The
results are highly suggestive. It turns out that the scribes were
able to differentiate between the outcome of the Second and that
of the Third Palatalization, at least in the case of the reflexes
of Proto-Slavic *k: the letter ц is correctly differentiated from
ч in those cases in which it is used to denote the reflex of the
outcome of the Second Palatalization (in other words: in those cases
in which the scribes spoke /k/), whereas ц and ч are confused in
those positions in which we expect the outcome of the Third Palatalization (in other words: in those cases in which the scribes
spoke a consonant identical to their reflex of Proto-Slavic *č).
All this evidently corroborates the evidence of the primary sources
investigated by Gluskina and others, or, to quote Živov:

"(...) приведенные данные показывают, что в новгородском диалекте
XI-XII вв. рефлексы II палатализации отличались по своей фонети-
ческой реализации от рефлексов I и III палатализации. Это может
служить дополнительным свидетельством в пользу того, что новгород-
ский диалект не знал II палатализации (но знал, хотя и непоследо-
вательно третью)" (1984:272).

D. It has been known for a long time that the familiar change
of *y into i after velar consonants reached the north a long time
after it had been accomplished in the south. It is natural to connect this with the absence of the effects of the Second Palatalization in the north:

506

"В самом деле, в других диалектах в силу второй палатализации со-
четания *ки, ги, хи* отсутствовали (если не считать иноязычных имен),
что способствовало занятию соответствующих пустых клеток рефлексами
прежних *ки, ги, хи*. В древненовгородском диалекте ситуация была
иной, поскольку сохранялись и прежние *ки, ги, хи*" (Zaliznjak 1986:
119).

2. *THREE AWKWARD ASPECTS OF THE FACTS TO BE EXPLAINED.*

The facts reported in the preceding section are in several
respects awkward. A good explanation will have to express how such
awkward data could be produced by a natural sequence of (linguistic
or extra-linguistic) events.

One thing that is awkward has been mentioned already. I am referring to the different behaviour of the three velars with respect
to the Third Palatalization. Two other problems involve the phonological consequences of the Second and the Third Palatalization and
the position of North Russian in the whole of Slavic.

Speaking in terms of contrastive phonemes, the Second and/or
Third Palatalization (depending on which, if any, was first) introduced a new series of consonants into the system. These newly
produced consonants will be written as follows: /č, dź, ś/ from *k,
*g, and *x respectively (cf. Vaillant 1950:49).

In all Slavic dialects with the exception of North Russian
both palatalizations have yielded an identical outcome. The difference between the two consists merely in the phonological environments in which they operated. As to chronology, it has proved
impossible to separate the two palatalizations (cf. also the overlap in Shevelov's sketch, 1964:351), and since they produce the
same outcome it seems most rational simply to identify them, as
is done, for instance, by Vaillant: "La palatalisation devant ě,
i et la palatalisation après *ĭ* sont un même fait, de même époque,
du moins approximativement, dont le point de départ et identique:
le développement de gutturales mouillées nouvelles" (1950:55). Now
identification seems to be prevented by the North Russian facts.
This is very awkward because it means that the relative chronology
of the two developments has to be determined after all, and it has
also to be explained why two distinct innovations yielded exactly

the same outcome everywhere, with the exception of North Russian,
which behaves as if the Second Palatalization never took place at
all and as if the Third Palatalization only affected *k and maybe
(in part of the cases) *g.

The most immediate reaction to the North Russian facts (a
reaction implicit in much of the literature on the subject) consists in the assumption that the Second Palatalization simply did
not reach the area, which, after all, occupied a marginal position
in the Slavic world. Unfortunately this idea does little more than
restate the facts. In particular it is silent about the problem
as to what it was that prevented the Second Palatalization from
reaching North Russian. This point requires an explanation because
there are no other clear examples of early developments that did
not reach the Novgorod/Pskov area. Throughout the lengthy period
separating, say, the First Palatalization from the loss of the
weak jers, North Russian was wide open to changes coming from the
south. Hence the sudden failure of the Second Palatalization to
reach Novgorod quite definitely requires an explanation.[5]

Thus, there are at least three things about the North Russian
facts which are somewhat awkward and which therefore cry out for
a natural explanation:

A. In North Russian the Third Palatalization seems to have
affected the three different velars to a different extent.

B. It is only in a single Slavic dialect (North Russian) that
we find a difference between the outcome of the Second and that
of the Third Palatalization. At first sight this would seem to
preclude Vaillant's (and others') convenient identification of
the two processes.

C. The idea that the Second Palatalization simply did not
reach Novgorod is unsatisfactory, because in the period involved
the area was open to innovations coming from the south.

3. *THE CHRONOLOGY OF THE MONOPHTHONGIZATION OF DIPHTHONGS.*

In the period when the Slavs were moving towards the Baltic,
the Slavic-speaking area was already vast and it was growing all

the time. This increased the chances for otherwise general innovations to reach different areas in different order, thereby giving
rise to dialectal differentiation. Positing common innovations
that produce dialectal differentiation by hitting different areas
at different moments has become a powerful research tool since
Trubetzkoy (1925:296 and passim) first made a systematic use of
it to explain the rise of several major East Slavic isoglosses.[6]

The difference between North Russian and the remainder of the
Slavic-speaking world receives a natural explanation if we assume
that the monophthongization of diphthongs reached the Novgorod/
Pskov area only after the palatalization had taken place (whereas
elsewhere, as is well-known, monophthongization took place first).
The consequence was that the palatal context necessary for palatalization to take effect (necessary for the new series /ć, dź, ś/ to
arise) was virtually restricted to those cases we associate with
the label "Third Palatalization".

In other words, the North Russian variety of Slavic converted
the velars *k/*g/*x into *ć/*dź/*ś in palatal surroundings exactly
in the same way as more central kinds of Slavic, but owing to the
fact that the diphthongs had not (yet) been monophthongized, the
precise set of palatal surroundings differed from the one we find
elsewhere. Three kinds of palatal contexts have to be looked at:

A. Contexts in which palatalization took place everywhere in
Slavic: these are the cases associated with the label of "Third
Palatalization". Examples: Gsg. *otъka > *otъćа, *stъga > *stъdźа,
Nsg. fem. *vъxa > *vъśa. The velar consonants were retained before
high back vowels (*ъ and *y), e.g. Asg. *otъkъ, Gsg. *stъgy, Asg.
msc. *vъxъ.[7] Presumably palatalization took place also in borrowings which had entered the language since the First Palatalization
had eliminated earlier sequences of velars plus front vowels.

B. Contexts in which palatalization took place everywhere
except in North Russian: these are the cases associated with the
label of "Second Palatalization". Examples: *kělъ > *ćělъ, DLsg.
*nogě > *nodźě, *xěrъ > *śěrъ. In North Russian, palatalization
took place at a stage where in these and similar examples there
was no front vowel which could provide a palatal context: *koilъ,
*nogoi, *xoirъ; when at last the diphthongs were monophthongized,

yielding *kě̃lъ, *nogě̃, *xě̃rъ, it was too late: North Russian had emerged as an identifiable Slavic dialect.

C. Contexts in which palatalization was limited to the North Russian area. These are those cases in which palatalization took place under the influence of an *i* which constituted the second component of a diphthong. In other words: this is a variety of the Third Palatalization which could not operate outside North Russian because it was only there that the diphthongs still persisted in the period when the Second/Third Palatalization took place. This context clearly cannot have accounted for more than a handful of examples, e.g. Gsg. *snoiga > *snoidźa > *sněd́źa, contrasting with retention of the velar elsewhere: *sně̃ga. In those forms in which the velar consonant was followed by a high back vowel (later *ъ, *y) it was retained even in North Russian: Asg. *sně̃gъ.

All in all the new palatal consonants /ć, dź, ś/ must have been considerably less frequent in North Russian than elsewhere.

One might hazard a guess as to why North Russian for a time resisted the monophthongization. It is generally agreed that Baltic and (in particular) Baltic Finnic elements contributed to the rise of North Russian (cf. also Gluskina 1966:482). Now Baltic and (in particular) Baltic Finnic are quite tolerant of the type of rising diphthongs that were completely eliminated in Slavic.[8] The presence of Baltic and Finnic speakers in the Novgorod/Pskov area may have slowed down somewhat the Slavic trend towards monophthongization.

4.   *THE LATER FATE OF THE NEW PALATAL CONSONANTS.*

When the new palatal consonants had arisen and the diphthongs had been monophthongized, North Russian had the same phonological system as other kinds of Slavic. The two varieties of Slavic differed merely with respect to the distribution and the frequency of the new palatal consonants. In North Russian the new consonants were rather infrequent and had a very lopsided distribution:

A. They were limited to stem-final position.

B. In all cases they alternated with plain velars.[9]

C. All three consonants were limited to a mere handful of

stem morphemes; in addition /ć/ occurred in several productive
suffixes.

In other words: /ć/, though quite common, was less frequent
and more unevenly distributed than it was elsewhere in Slavic,
whereas /dź/ and /ś/ were downright marginal. The marginal position
of /dź/ and /ś/ constitutes the motivation for the next thing that
happened. In all cases of alternation the plain velars /g/ and /x/
were restored: Gsg. *snědźa, Nsg. *stьdźa, Nsg. fem *vьśa were replaced with *sněga, *stьga, *vьxa, with the plain velars that were
regular in forms like Asg. *sněgъ, Gsg. *stьgy, Asg. msc. *vьxъ.
This development is responsible for the impression that North Russian differs from related varieties of Slavic in not having carried
through the Third Palatalization in the case of *g and *x. If this
is correct, forms like kъnjazъ and userjazi do not reflect local
North Russian developments, which would have produced *kъnjagъ
(cf. varjagъ, for which a northern origin is plausible) and *use-
rjagi.[10] If the restoration of the plain velars took place in all
relevant cases, it was only in borrowings (e.g. toponyms) that the
palatal consonants /dź/ and /ś/, now even more marginal than before, persisted.

The new consonant /ć/, which was much more firmly entrenched
in the system, was treated in the same way as it was treated in
other varieties of Slavic. In particular it was generalized in
more or less the same cases, e.g. Asg. *otьćь replacing regular
*otьkъ on the basis of the stem form found in Gsg. *otьća. There
is a distinct possibility that Russian dialect forms like otёk and
mesik (Shevelov 1964:346, 1971:311) reflect (if dimly) a variety
of early Russian which deviated in this respect, too.

Afterwards /ć/ merged with /č/, producing цоканье. This change
is usually attributed to the Baltic Finnic substratum/adstratum
which must have been present in the Novgorod area. If /ć/ merged
with /č/, it stands to reason that such instances of /dź/ and /ś/
as had survived the restoration of plain velars in alternating
paradigms merged with /ž/ and /š/. Unfortunately it is inherently
very difficult to find reliable examples of this innovation, because it is only in borrowings that one expects attestations and
because its principal effect consists in concealing the difference

between the palatalizations, so that one cannot know whether North
Russian forms like *Lučesa*, *Seližarovka* or *Ižora* reflect the First
or the Second/Third palatalization.[11]

Alternatively it is not inconceivable that even in borrowings
/dž/ and /ś/ were replaced with /g/ and /x/ prior to the rise of
North Russian цоканье, as a consequence of the massive restoration
of the latter consonants that was going on in alternating paradigms, which must have created the impression that any instance
of /dž/ or /ś/ could be replaced with the corresponding plain (non-
palatal) velar.

5. CONCLUSIONS.

In the preceding sections I have proposed the following chronology in order to account for the facts of North Russian, and in
particular for the awkward characteristics of those facts touched
upon in section *2*:

I. Early developments, up to the rise of /č/, /ž/, and /š/ as
a consequence of the First Palatalization and related innovations
(stages *C1* through *C3* of Kortlandt 1982:184).

II. Second/Third Palatalization. Rise of /ć/, /dž/, and /ś/
in palatal contexts. This development was Common Slavic (Kortlandt's *C4*, l.c.). However, in North Russian it took place in a
different set of environments, because there the diphthongs had
not yet been monophthongized (cf. section *3*). At this stage the
difference between North Russian and other varieties of Slavic was
considerable: North Russian had the new palatal consonants in a
much smaller set of cases and it had diphthongs.

IIIA. Monophthongization of diphthongs. Like the rise of /ć/,
/dž/, and /ś/, this development was Common Slavic. It reduced the
difference between North Russian and related Slavic dialects. The
only remaining difference involved the frequency and the distribution of the new palatal consonants

IIIB. Restoration of /g/ and /x/ in alternating paradigms.
The marginal phonemes /dž/ and /ś/ were replaced with /g/ and /x/
in all cases of alternation, even in cases where other varieties

of Slavic generalized the palatalized consonant. This development
differentiated North Russian from other types of Slavic in two
ways: (1) a small number of stems was generalized in a different
shape, and (2) the functional yield of the new consonants /dž/
and /ś/ was dramatically diminished; indeed, it is possible that
/dž/ and /ś/ were completely eliminated, leaving /ć/ isolated.

    IIIC. Levelling of /k/ and /ć/ in alternating paradigms. In
alternating paradigms which had arisen as a consequence of the
palatalization, either /k/ or /ć/ was generalized along the same
lines along which the same development took place elsewhere.

    IV. The rise of цоканье. The palatal consonants /ć/ and /č/
merged. If any instances of /dž/ and /ś/ were left at this stage,
what one expects is that they merged with /ž/ and /š/.[12] Цоканье
increased again the difference between North Russian and related
varieties of Slavic. To some extent the rise of цоканье can be
regarded as the Novgorod/Pskov counterpart of Kortlandt's "first
simplification of palatals" (1982:185, *C6*).

    The most striking properties of the North Russian consonant
system can be attributed to two otherwise general Common Slavic
innovations which, however, reached the Slavic dialects of the
Novgorod/Pskov area in the reverse order. If this is correct, the
bundle of isoglosses separating North Russian from more southern
varieties of East Slavic continues one of the oldest inner-Slavic
dialect differences to have survived.

University of Leiden

NOTES

[1] I am indebted to my colleague José van Tilburg for drawing my attention to
the subject of the palatalizations in Old Russian, and in particular to Zaliznjak's 1982 article on the subject.
[2] I have not managed to get hold of Gluskina's Russian article on the subject
(1968), a publication which is very often referred to in the literature.
[3] The orthography of the examples has been to some extent normalized. The use
of *č* in examples like *věveričь* and *c* in *celьcemь* is due to the familiar North
Russian confusion of *c* and *č* (*цоканье*). For full information on the examples the
reader is referred to the editions: Arcixovskij & Tixomirov (1953:40-42), Arcixovskij & Borkovskij (1958:34-35), Arcixovskij & Borkovskij (1963:63-64), Arci-

xovskij (1963:23-24), Arcixovskij & Janin (1978:32-33, 35-36, 51), Janin &
Zaliznjak (1986:32). On 424, 429 and 449 Zaliznjak's additional remarks should
be consulted (1986:206-208).
⁴ See the preceding note. On birchbark document no. 527 see Arcixovskij &
Janin (1978:128).
⁵ It goes without saying that the familiar retention of the stop in the Pskov
reflex of Proto-Slavic *-dl- does not count, because it may very well depend on
an earlier (presumably Baltic-inspired) innovation which converted *-dl- into
*-gl-, a sequence in which the stop was retained all over Slavic (cf. Modern
Russian moglá).
⁶ A few arbitrary examples: Andersen (1969:561), Kortlandt (1975:31). I have
tried to show elsewhere (1982) that Rigler's monumental theory of the rise of
the Slovene vowel systems (1963) can be considerably simplified by a consistent
use of Trubetzkoy's principle.
⁷ On this restriction see Belić (1921:26 and passim). The chronological implications of Vaillant's view of the Third Palatalization are conveniently
listed by Kortlandt (1984:212).
⁸ Such instances of monophthongization as have taken place in Baltic and
Baltic Finnic never involve more than a minor part of the available diphthongs.
⁹ There are two types of cases, both rather marginal, in which we do not expect alternation, viz. (1) borrowings, and (2) stems starting in velar + v + a
front vowel which does not reflect an earlier diphthong. On borrowings see the
final paragraphs of section 4. As regards the second type of cases, it is difficult to get reliable data. The stem *kvъt- alternates with *kvĕt- < *kvoit-,
where one does not expect palatalization; the stem *gvъrst- has a fluctuating
root shape; both stems are abundantly attested with initial velars (Zaliznjak
1986:113). There is nothing against assuming that the North Russian treatment
of sequences consisting of velars + v is the same that can be reconstructed for
the remainder of Slavic: they "became k̂v, ĝv, x̂v before front vowels as a result of the second palatalization (Vaillant 1950:55f). The palatalized velars
were the archiphonemes of k, g, x and ć, dź, ś in this position" (Kortlandt
1982:185).
¹⁰ Ferrell (1970:414) draws attention to the fact that an Apl. userjagy is
listed by Sreznevskij (1903:1264).
¹¹ I quote these forms on the authority of Stieber (1967:16).
¹² If this was indeed what happened, it has to be assumed that /dž/ was first
converted into /ž/, as it was everywhere else in East Slavic. What happened
to k̂v, ĝv, x̂v is not quite clear, owing to the character of the evidence (cf.
above, note 9).

REFERENCES

Andersen, Henning
     1969   "Lenition in Common Slavic", *Language* 45, 553-574.
Arcixovskij, Artemij Vladimirovič
     1963   *Novgorodskie gramoty na bereste (Iz raskopok 1958-1961 gg.)*,
               Moskva (Izdatel'stvo Akademii nauk).
Arcixovskij, Artemij Vladimirovič & Viktor Ivanovič Borkovskij
     1958   *Novgorodskie gramoty na bereste (iz raskopok 1953-1954 gg.)*,
               Moskva (Izdatel'stvo Akademii nauk).
     1963   *Novgorodskie gramoty na bereste (Iz raskopok 1956-1957 gg.)*,
               Moskva (Izdatel'stvo Akademii nauk).

Arcixovskij, Artemij Vladimirovič & Valentin Lavrent'evič Janin
1978   *Novgorodskie gramoty na bereste (Iz raskopok 1962-1976 gg.)*,
        Moskva (Nauka).
Arcixovskij, A.V. & M.N. Tixomirov
1953   *Novgorodskie gramoty na bereste (iz raskopok 1951 g.)*, Moskva
        (Izdatel'stvo Akademii nauk).
Belić, Aleksandar
1921   "Najmladja (treća) promena zadnjenepčanih suglasnika k, g i x
        u praslovenskom jeziku", *Južnoslovenski filolog* 2, 18-39.
Birnbaum, Henryk
1978   "Kilka uwag o braku śladów drugiej palatalizacji tylnojęzykowych
        na północno-wschodniej peryferii zwartego słowiańskiego obszaru
        językowego", *Slavia Orientalis* 27/2, 185-189.
Ferrell, James
1970   "*Cokan'e* and the palatalizations of velars in East Slavic", *The
        Slavic and East European Journal* 14, 411-422.
Gluskina, S.M. [= Zofia Głuskina]
1966   "O drugiej palatalizacji spółgłosek tylnojęzykowych w rosyj-
        skich dialektach północno-zachodnich", *Slavia Orientalis* 15,
        475-482.
1968   "O vtoroj palatalizacii zadnejazyčnyx soglasnyx v russkom jazyke
        (na materiale severo-zapadnyx govorov)", *Pskovskie govory* 2 (=
        Trudy vtoroj Pskovskoj dialektologičeskoj konferencii 1964 goda),
        Pskov, 20-43. (Quoted on the basis of Birnbaum 1978:186n. and Za-
        liznjak 1986:218.)
Janin, Valentin Lavrent'evič & Andrej Anatol'evič Zaliznjak
1986   *Novgorodskie gramoty na bereste (iz raskopok 1977-1983 gg.)*,
        Moskva (Nauka).
Kortlandt, F.H.H.
1975   *Slavic accentuation: a study in relative chronology*, Lisse (Peter
        de Ridder).
1982   "Early dialectal diversity in South Slavic I", *Studies in Slavic
        and General Linguistics* 2, 177-192.
1984   "The progressive palatalization of Slavic", *Folia Linguistica
        Historica* 5/2, 211-219.
Rigler, Jakob
1963   "Pregled osnovnih razvojnih etap v slovenskem vokalizmu", *Slav-
        istična revija* 14, 25-78.
Savignac, David
1975   "Common Slavic *vъx- in Northern Old Russian", *International
        Journal of Slavic Linguistics and Poetics* 19/2, 41-52.
Shevelov, George Y.
1964   *A prehistory of Slavic: the historical phonology of Common
        Slavic*, Heidelberg (Carl Winter).
1971   *Teasers and appeasers: essays and studies on themes of Slavic
        philology*, München (Wilhelm Fink).
Sreznevskij, I.I.
1903   *Materialy slovarja drevne-russkago jazyka po pis'mennym panjat-
        nikam 3.*
Stieber, Zdzisław
1967   "Nowe osiągnięcia gramatyki porównawczej języków słowiańskich",
        Rocznik slawistyczny 28, 3-20.
1969   "Druga palatalizacja tylnojęzykowych w świetle atlasu dialektów
        rosyjskich na wschód od Moskwy", *Rocznik slawistyczny* 29, 3-7.

Trubetzkoy, N.
1922   "Essai sur la chronologie de certains faits phonétiques du slave
            commun", *Revue des études slaves* 2, 217-234.
1925   "Einiges über die russische Lautentwicklung und die Auflösung
            der gemeinrussischen Spracheinheit", *Zeitschrift für slavische
            Philologie* 1, 287-319.
Vaillant, André
1950   *Grammaire comparée des langues slaves I: phonétique*, Lyon/Paris
            (IAC).
1958   *Grammaire comparée des langues slaves II: morphologie, deuxième
            partie*, Lyon/Paris (IAC).
Vermeer, Willem
1982   "Raising of *ě and loss of the nasal feature in Slovene", *Zbor-
            nik za filologiju i lingvistiku* 25/1, 97-120.
Zaliznjak, Andrej Anatol'evič
1982   "K istoričeskoj fonetike drevnenovgorodskogo dialekta", *Balto-
            slavjanskie issledovanija 1981*, Moskva (Nauka), 61-80.
1986   "Kommentarii i slovoukazatel' k berestjanym gramotam (iz ras-
            kopok 1951-1983 gg.)", in: Janin & Zaliznjak (1986), 87-306.
Živov, V.
1984   "Pravila i proiznošenie v russkom cerkovnoslavjanskom pravo-
            pisanii XI-XIII veka", *Russian Linguistics* 8/3, 251-293.

STUDIES IN SLAVIC AND GENERAL LINGUISTICS
Edited by A.A. Barentsen, B.M. Groen and R. Sprenger